Sunset
WESTERN
LANDSCAPING
BOOK

Edited by Kathleen Norris Brenzel

SUNSET BOOKS INC. · MENLO PARK, CALIFORNIA

Sunset Books Inc.
Chief Executive Officer: Stephen J. Seabolt
President & Publisher: Susan J. Maruyama
VP, Chief Financial Officer: James E. Mitchell
VP, Manufacturing Director: Lorinda Reichert
Director, Sales & Marketing: Richard A. Smeby
Editorial Director: Bob Doyle
Director of Finance: Lawrence J. Diamond
Production Director: Lory Day
Retail Sales Development Manager: Becky Ellis
Art Director: Vasken Guiragossian

***Sunset Western Landscaping Book* was produced by:**
Editor: Kathleen Norris Brenzel
Managing Editor: Fiona Gilsenan
Art Director, Design and Production Manager: Alice Rogers

Contributing Editors: Scott Atkinson, Jim McCausland, RG Turner Jr,
   Lance Walheim
Senior Editor: Evan Elliot
Contributing Writers: Janice Emily Bowers, Steven R. Lorton,
   Rob Proctor, Pat Welsh, Peter O. Whiteley
Writers: Mia Amato, Sharon Cohoon, Pamela Cornelison, Peter Fish,
   Margaret Learmonth McKinnon, Lauren Bonar Swezey,
   Jennifer M. Wheatley
Editorial Assistants: Tishana Peebles, Joyce Kerr Reeder, Rizza Yap

Production Coordinator: Patricia S. Williams
Copy Editors: Roberta Conlan, Fran Haselsteiner, Marsha Lutch Lloyd,
   Carolyn McGovern
Chief Proofreader and Indexer: Robyn Brode
Computer Production Manager: Brynn Breuner
Computer Production: Phoebe Bixler, Barbara Geisler, Robert Kato,
   Joan Olson
Designer: Elisa Tanaka
Cartography: Reineck & Reineck, San Francisco
Illustrators: Ron Hildebrand, Lois Lovejoy, Rik Olson, Mimi Osborn,
   Mark Pechenik, Reineck & Reineck, Wendy Smith-Griswold
Photography Editor: Ann Leyhe
Principal Photographers: Philip Harvey, Saxon Holt, Charles Mann,
   Rob Proctor, Chad Slattery, Michael Thompson
Photo Stylists: Anthony Albertus, Joanne Masaoka Van Atta

Cover photograph: Charles Mann, New Mexico garden
Title page photograph: Kathlene Persoff, Rosa banksiae, *California*
Masthead photograph: Laurie Dickson, Colorado garden
Endpapers photograph, hardcover edition: Saxon Holt, Miscanthus
   sinensis *'Gracillimus'*

Foreword

The idea for this book's regional format was born in the window seat of a San Francisco-bound jet, high above the Rocky Mountains. Noon, on a bright April day. I'd just completed the last leg of a wide swing around the West, talking with home gardeners and garden professionals, and visiting gardens and nurseries on behalf of the 40th anniversary edition of the *Sunset Western Garden Book*. Now, four weeks and countless cities after this adventure had begun, I settled back in my seat aloft to reflect on the places I'd visited. Outside the window, knife-edged peaks slipped silently by, their flanks covered with snow that sparkled like glazed sugar. Velvety conifers and leafless aspens poked up from the shadows in the gullies between them. Denver, which I'd left minutes before, was but a few sparkles on a vast brown plain disappearing into the horizon behind the left wing.

As I marveled at the contrast between mountains and plain, the thought hit me: no single garden book has ever shown garden design ideas for folks living down there among those coniferous mountains and on that dry, windy plain, as well as in the West's countless other distinct microclimates. (The *Western Garden Book* is an exception, but its thrust is plants and practical gardening, not design ideas.) Instead, we garden makers were turning to glossy garden books from England and the East Coast that promised endless green lawns and picture-perfect delphiniums.

But these mountains and plains, as well as deserts to the south and beaches to the west, bore no resemblance to each other, let alone to England. My travels around the West in such a condensed period of time simply magnified the differences. In Seattle, the wet streets glistened below leaden-gray skies, but blooming daffodils promised spring. In Southern California's beach towns, warm breezes rustled the palm fronds and firecracker-red blossoms unfurled on the coral trees. In Phoenix, my feet kicked up ochre dust as I traipsed through nurseries ablaze with scarlet bougainvillea, hot pink zinnias, and golden marigolds —a startling cacaphony of flower colors against an endless blue sky. And in Denver, rain, snow, and sun slugged it out for command of the skies while—in greenhouses—the first tender, green shoots of the season to come poked timidly above pot rims.

Everywhere I went, gardeners asked me questions. But their questions and concerns were firmly grounded in their own back yards, not in "general gardening." They wanted region-specific answers. In the desert, they wanted to know how to deal with caliche (hardpan soil) or what to plant around swimming pools. In the Northwest, they asked for names of plants that would grow well along the windy coast, and for ways to keep birch bark from cracking in winter sun. In California, where wildfires had ravaged many gardens in Oakland, Malibu, and Santa Barbara just months before, they asked how to landscape for fire.

Indeed, the magnificent diversity of weather and terrain in the West presents us with unique challenges and opportunities that gardeners elsewhere don't face. It determines the shape and style of our gardens, the plants we can grow in them, and the way we use them. And it triggers our gardening seasons: while Denver gardeners are preparing to set out the first of their one-season plantings, desert gardeners are getting ready to pack it in for the summer and head for the shade of a ramada.

But I noticed something else during my travels. Western garden styles are changing. We are redefining the garden—its shape, its purpose, the way we use it. Our gardens are extensions of our houses. We furnish them, and accessorize them, and design them to fit our fantasies. We give them a sense of place, taking our design cues from the natural terrain around us and from our climate. We plant them with natives or with plants that are well adapted to the area, and define them with structures such as ramadas or outdoor kitchens that reflect an ability to live outdoors year-around. Even our garden art and furnishings often hint at the heritage of the region.

We're creating gardens that make sense for western conditions. We've entered the age of the Northwest garden, the Southwest garden, the California garden, the Rocky Mountain garden — landscaping styles that are distinctly different from each other, as well as those in England and the rest of America.

This book highlights those differences. But it also addresses the problems and opportunities that affect garden design in the West. And it recognizes that the greatest gardens are perfect marriages between plants, structures, and settings.

For design ideas, we turned to landscape professionals—architects and designers who create gardens in the West for a living. You can copy their designs or take inspiration from them. Our heartfelt thanks go to those many landscape professionals, garden suppliers, and experts in such related fields as climatology, soils, and wildfires—listed in the back of the book—for enthusiastically sharing with us their expertise, sources, materials, or plans.

Kathleen N. Brenzel

Kathleen N. Brenzel
Editor

THE WESTERN DIFFERENCE

In the late 1930s, western landscape architect Thomas "Tommy" Church and his contemporaries began engineering a profound break from centuries of landscaping traditions. Instead of working in the style of the grand manor houses—or what has been called the "lawn, border, and foundation planting bungalow style"—they began designing gardens that were more flexible, more human oriented and more usable. They believed that carefully crafted gardens were for every house, not just for great estates. They treated their gardens as outdoor rooms, as extensions of indoor living spaces that flowed beyond the house foundations to the property lines. They took into account all possible perspectives on a garden, even the views up through trees. And they pioneered the extensive use of paving throughout the garden and low maintenance planting—a boon for today's busy families.

Camellia

This new breed of garden designers focused on function more than style, believing that gardens should accommodate their owners' lifestyles. "Landscaping," Church wrote in his 1955 book *Gardens Are for People,* "is logical, down-to-earth, and aimed at making your plot of ground produce exactly what you want and need from it."

Today this emphasis on outdoor living is pervasive in the West, and taken very much for granted. It has come to define the western garden. For contemporary garden designers, it is the overriding theme of any plan. Other elements also play a part, however, in shaping today's western gardens, among them:

TOPOGRAPHY. The West is a land of superlatives. It contains the country's highest mountain (Mt. McKinley, Alaska, elevation 20,320 feet), lowest desert (Death Valley, 282 feet below sea level), deepest lake (Crater Lake, Oregon 1,932 feet), and virtually all the country's mountain peaks higher than 10,000 feet. This restless landscape provides scenic backdrops for many gardens. Increasingly, landscape professionals—working with the natural topography and using natural materials—recreate nature's refreshing randomness in the garden.

CLIMATE. As the map at right shows, North America is divided into two distinct garden provinces: the arid West, and the much wetter East. Water is the West's most precious resource. Less rain falls in a year in Los Angeles than in a day in parts of the East. As a result, there are practical reasons for growing plants well-adapted to the aridity.

LIFESTYLE. Where winters are long and cold, outdoor amenities may be limited to patios, trellises, and gazebos. But in the West's mild climates, where we can barbecue a turkey outdoors on Thanksgiving day or gather camellia blooms for Christmas bouquets, a garden is furnished to accommodate a variety of outdoor activities. It might have a spa or hot tub for long, slow soaks on starlit nights; an adobe oven, a state-of-the-art grill, or a fully operational kitchen complete with wet bar, cooktops, and refrigerator for outdoor dining and entertaining; a cozy fireplace or fire pit to take the chill out of evening air; or even a TV built into a patio wall for watching football games.

PLANTS. The low-elevation West is one of the world's finest gardening climates. Within this huge piece of territory—roughly a ragged L extending from Bellingham, Washington to San Diego to Albuquerque—winters are mild enough to grow a special array of pleasing and productive trees, shrubs, ground covers, and vines that can't be grown where it snows and freezes all winter every winter. Established lowlanders take some of these "privilege plants" for granted, but newcomers delight in being able to grow such cherished plants as rhododendrons and azaleas in the Pacific Northwest; bougainvillea, camellia, citrus, jacaranda, oleander, and olive in California and—along the mildest Southern California coast—fragrant stephanotis, plumeria, and pikake (Arabian jasmine). Add to these a palette of beautiful native plants, and the planting possibilities are endless.

THE ENVIRONMENT. There's a movement among many of today's landscape professionals to preserve what remains of the natural world and to design gardens that express respect for the natural order. Many landscape designers are recreating natural-looking plant communities in their gardens, whether aspen groves or dry chaparral, or incorporating into their plans such existing features as desert washes or rocky outcrops.

Says San Francisco landscape designer Chris Jacobson, we can "celebrate the beauty of our native surroundings rather than mow, overwater, and poison them. We can translate our garden desires into terms that make sense for our climates."

Not all of us are lucky enough to live on the edge of wild land—to have as our backdrop mountains or deserts or crashing surf or aspen groves. But we can acknowledge the climate and the land in which we live through appropriate choices in plants and structures and through thoughtful gardening practices.

How to use this book

The *Sunset Western Landscaping Book* is a companion to the *Sunset Western Garden Book*. To find out more about plants mentioned throughout these pages—where they grow best, their growth habits, and how to care for them —turn to the encyclopedia section of the *Sunset Western Garden Book*. Plants are listed by genus and species first, then by common name, if any. Zone numbers that follow the plant names tell you which regions the plants grow in; if you're not sure which zone you live in, find your location on a climate map in the *Sunset Western Garden Book*, and read the corresponding zone descriptions.

The numbers on this map show the average inches of rain each indicated city receives between May 1 and October 31. Note the difference in rainfall between the arid West and the regions to the east of the 100th meridian.

CONTENTS

PLANNING YOUR GARDEN

When you want to create a beautiful and functional place for outdoor relaxation, the reality of your bare or overgrown yard may seem utterly daunting. So before you turn your first shovelful of soil, close your eyes and picture your dream garden. Does it have spacious patios for parties and a place for children to play? Or is it serene and secluded, with roses and a wisteria-covered gazebo for quiet contemplation? Is it wild, with native shrubs and rambling vines, or tailored, with a white picket fence around a square lawn? Make a list of the features the garden should contain and include your favorite plants. On the following pages you'll discover how to plan space for your activities, how to choose the right plants, and how to work with your soils and microclimates. Then you can match garden styles to your house and region, and you'll be on your way to making your dream garden a reality.

PLANNING WITH A PURPOSE

When designing or renovating a home landscape, think first about the range of activities you wish to enjoy in it. Do you frequently entertain outside with dinners and special events? Do you pursue activities such as swimming or tennis? Or do you find enjoyment in simply relaxing in a quiet outdoor retreat? Be realistic about the space required for each purpose you identify and about your site's potential. Most sports are difficult on a steeply sloping lot, for example. You will also want to be considerate of your neighbors. Raising llamas may not be appropriate (or legal) in a residential setting, for example, and few neighbors would appreciate a noisy skateboard ramp next door.

Personal goals

Your family's needs will also dictate other aspects of your design. If children or elderly or disabled persons use the garden, you may value safety and ease of movement. Secure fences are a safeguard against the potential dangers of swimming pools, driveways, and roads. Similarly, graded paths and ramps, night lighting, and stable deck and stair railings make a garden accessible.

To make the garden more comfortable, you may slightly modify the climate. In southwestern gardens, for example, trees or shade structures offer respite from the heat. In coastal areas, walls or dense plantings buffer strong winds. In mild climates, sun pockets collect warmth and overheads provide cover on rainy days.

Gardening goals

Like most gardeners, you probably have both aesthetic and practical aims in mind. You may wish to beautify your property with colorful flower borders and beds. You might want to provide space for growing fruits, vegetables, or herbs for use in the kitchen, or for particular collections such as roses or rock garden plants. Beauty and functionality can also be incorporated into the garden structures you choose; well-designed decks, pathways, and patios will ultimately increase the value of your home. Similarly, some structures can serve dual purposes, such as benches that reveal hidden storage beneath.

Finally, consider how much upkeep you're willing to take on. To reduce the amount of time and effort your garden will require, avoid high-maintenance features such as lawns, sheared hedges, or trees that drop autumn litter. And you may want to install an automatic irrigation system that not only saves time but also delivers water most efficiently.

As illustrated at right, a garden can be designed to incorporate its occupant's various goals. This garden plan will appear in various stages later in the chapter, as you follow the process of landscaping from start to finish.

A WELL-DESIGNED LANDSCAPE

G

NORTH ▶

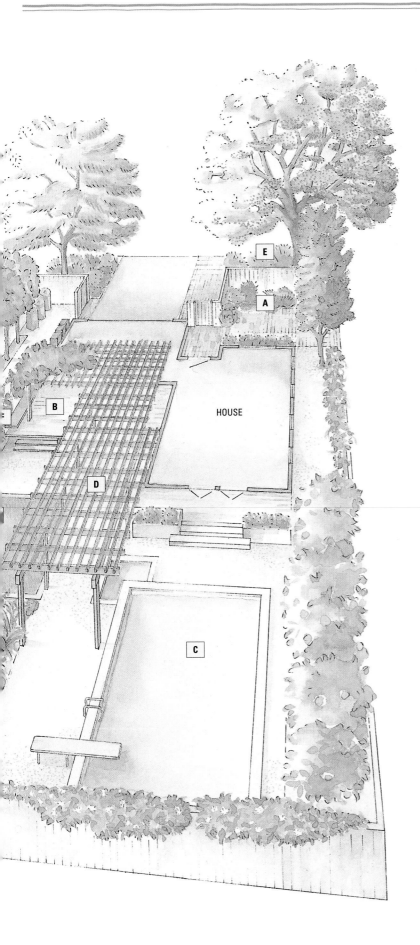

HOUSE

LANDSCAPING GOALS

A. Create privacy. The walled patio is really an extension of the living room. It creates an enclosed space and conceals the front yard from passers-by. The fountain masks traffic noise.

B. Invite entertaining. A broad deck wraps around the family and dining rooms to offer plenty of outdoor space for dinner, parties, or simple relaxation in view of, but removed from, the swimming pool.

C. Provide recreation. The swimming pool is a great way to cool off on hot summer days. (Solar water-heating panels on the roof could extend the season of use in the West.) A trellis shelters the spa.

D. Modify the climate. Clothed with vines, this arbor shades southern exposures from the summer sun, while allowing the low winter sun in to warm the interior. Around the pool, screen plantings filter the strong summer winds.

E. Beautify the property. Lush plantings between the sidewalk and patio wall create an attractive view from the street, soften the lines of the house and wall, and add color.

F. Grow a kitchen garden. Raised beds along the south side of the rear yard offer an ideal spot for raising herbs and vegetables, and are convenient to both the kitchen and the garden work area next to the garage.

G. Attract wildlife. Plantings, native and otherwise, and a birdbath lure birds and butterflies. The deck supplies a secluded place for viewing.

H. Reduce water use. A small lawn saves more water than a large one would; other features that lower consumption are an irrigation system, grouping plants with similar water needs, and liberal mulch throughout the garden.

A WELL-PLANNED GARDEN

A. Relaxation and enjoyment of nature are found in this courtyard garden, a relatively small site with a sizable koi-filled pool at center stage. (In southwestern gardens, a water feature such as this helps cool the air.) Garden walls of varying heights are festooned with climbing roses, adding to the sense of privacy and filling the air with fragrance. Low-maintenance plantings grow between pavings, softening the look of the patio but reducing the amount of foot traffic it will tolerate. The bench is positioned in the ideal spot for an observer to view the peaceful pool.

B. Low maintenance results from the simple plantings in this Northwest garden. Ground cover replaces a labor-intensive lawn or perennial bed that might more typically be found lining the pathway. The terrace offers space for entertaining or simple contemplation, yet is roomy enough even for large parties. The neighbor's house is close, but a vine-covered arbor offers seclusion. Vines and other plantings help soften the solid lines of the brick wall.

MEETS A VARIETY OF NEEDS

C. Beautiful and easy to care for, this front entrance lowers maintenance needs by replacing traditional features such as a front lawn and flowers with slow-growing grasses and ground covers. Contrasting hues painted on the house compensate for any lack of color. Camellias shade the windows, cooling the indoors. An assortment of containers and figurines adds interest and a casual look to the steps.

D. Recreation is the key in this desert garden. A large swimming pool cools the hot air and provides relief from the relentless summer sun. And when temperatures drop in the evening, an outdoor fireplace keeps the patio warm. Cacti and other native plantings require little irrigation. The naturalistic placement of rocks recalls the surrounding landscape.

E. Edible and ornamental plants are blended in this coastal garden, which mixes and matches vegetables, herbs, and flowers. Frequently harvested low-growing perennials and herbs are planted in front; taller vegetables and flowers are still accessible in the center, and the tallest flowers are in the back.

COLD-AIR POCKETS

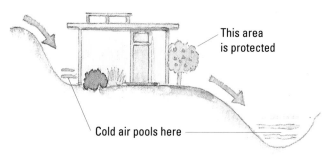

This area is protected

Cold air pools here

Cold air flows downhill like water, and "puddles" in basins. It can be dammed by a barrier such as a house, wall, or fence. So if you build a sunken patio or planting area, you may find yourself shivering, even when higher or more protected surroundings are balmy.

AIR FLOW

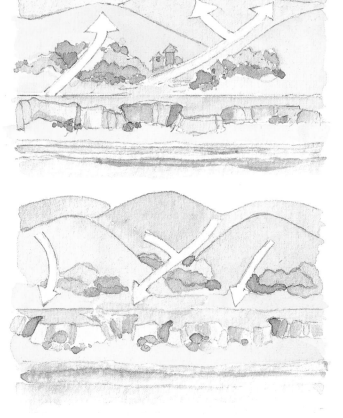

During the growing season, air tends to flow from the ocean onto the land during the day (top) and from the land back to the sea in the evening (bottom). Prevailing breezes are intensified in canyons and in narrow passages that lie parallel to the wind. Winds can also speed up as they pass between two houses, creating a wind tunnel.

THE EFFECT OF

In planning a landscape, it's important to consider the weather and climate in both your region and your garden. The path and angle of the sun, the seasons of the year, and the wind patterns around your property all affect your opportunities for outdoor living, your choice and placement of plants, and the overall design of your landscape.

A tender palm freezes in one garden, while its twin thrives in a garden just down the street. A ground cover blooms heavily in the sun, but grows thin and sparse a few feet away in the shade. It's microclimate that is responsible. Most gardens have several microclimates—areas that are a little warmer or cooler, wetter or drier, more or less windy than others. Microclimates are created by a combination of factors, including sun angle, wind direction, and the exposure and topography of your site.

Air temperature and movement

Because warm air rises and cold air sinks, cool air tends to pool in low places and to back up behind obstacles such as hedges and houses, creating frost pockets. Slopes are the last features in a landscape to freeze, because cold air constantly drains off them, mixing with nearby warmer air as it flows. Flat areas, by contrast, cool off quickly as heat radiates upward, especially during nights when the air is still and skies are clear. Any overhead protection reduces this loss of heat.

If you check your garden on a morning when the temperature is around 32°F, you'll see where frost has collected. Keep tender plantings away from these areas or provide the plants with extra frost protection (see pages 302–303).

During the daytime, air is drawn inland from the cool ocean. At night, as the land cools off faster than the ocean, air flow is reversed. This movement of air means that most seashore gardens lie in the path of winds. For those who live at the base of canyons, the effects can be even more pronounced, leading to wind tunnels and strong breezes.

Other influences

Keep in mind, too, that structures and materials influence microclimates on your property. The presence of water—a swimming pool, pond, or water feature—can slightly cool the air. Certain hardscape materials reflect sun and heat better than others. Light-colored masonry paving and walls spread sun and heat and they can be uncomfortably bright; wood surfaces are a little cooler. On the other hand, dark masonry materials retain heat even after dark. And plants and buildings can filter or block wind.

MICROCLIMATES

Sun and shade

In summer, the morning sun rises in the northeast, arcs high across the southern sky, and sets in the evening to the northwest. This long passage means extra hours of daylight—by the time of the summer solstice in June, approximately 16 hours in Seattle and 14⅓ hours in San Diego. By contrast, the winter sun rises in the southeast, passes low across the southern sky, and sets to the southwest. Days are much shorter at winter solstice in December, approximately 8½ hours in Seattle and 10 hours in San Diego.

That shifting sun angle means longer shadows in winter when the sun is low in the sky—leaving a greater part of the garden in shade during the dormant season and more of it in the sun when plants are growing. The pattern of sun and shade also varies depending on the time of day; at noon, when the sun is highest, there is little shade to be found.

SUN ANGLES

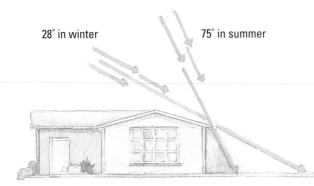

28° in winter   75° in summer

In winter, the sun crosses the sky at a lower angle than it does in summer. The effects can be pronounced, especially on north-facing exposures. The illustration above shows how the ground is shaded by the house at noon in summer and winter.

Exposure

Slopes that drop to the south or southwest get more heat during the day than those that drop to the north or northeast. Similarly, walls that run east and west reflect extra heat and sunlight onto plants on their south sides. Walls that run north and south reflect extra heat to plants growing on their west sides, but cooler micro-climates are created on their east sides. Sunny locations are best for heat-loving plants, but the soil is also affected, drying out faster and requiring extra irrigation.

SUMMER AND WINTER SHADOWS

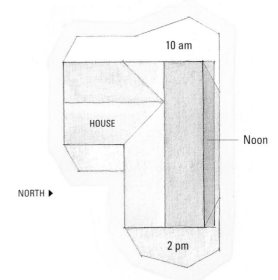

10 am

HOUSE

Noon

NORTH ▶

2 pm

In summer, only those areas immediately beside the house are shaded. Note how features of the house, such as the roof, affect the shadows below.

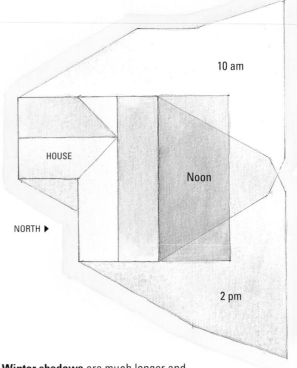

10 am

HOUSE

Noon

NORTH ▶

2 pm

Winter shadows are much longer and can shift dramatically within the space of a few hours. Compare the shadow cast at noon to that cast at 2 pm.

SEASONS

	MOUNTAIN ZONES 1-3

The best gardens mirror the seasons. Old blooms pass, new ones magically take their place. The plant palette never fades, just evolves. When flowers are gone, foliage sets the garden alight with dazzling fall shades of red, plum, orange, and gold. Then the fiery berries of shrubs and trees take over, followed by winter's striking silhouettes and colored bark.

Good gardeners make sure that their gardens have some interest every day of the year. Some feature year-round flower color—from the earliest camellia blossoms to the latest fall roses. Others fill the air with ever-changing fragrances, starting with earliest spring hyacinths and lilacs and lasting through the winter with the crisp scent of cedar and pine. Still other gardens are eclectic, filled with blooms for cutting in spring, fragrance in summer, fiery leaves in fall, and fascinating peeling, striped, colored, or checked bark patterns in winter. In any garden, you can put all these things together—and give your garden its own personality in the process. The secret is knowing what to plant and when to plant it.

Find the column for your region, then use it as a design tool to help you choose plants for interest to cover each season. Planting and bloom times for a sampling of favorite landscape plants are listed by month. These are guidelines only; include your own favorites in your four-season plan. The *Sunset Western Garden Book* provides further details on the regional adaptability of plants.

Chart key

ANNUALS: Cool-season annuals bloom in winter and early spring. Warm-season annuals bloom in late spring, summer, and early fall.

PERENNIALS: Most perennials flower once a year for weeks or even months, then die back in winter, only to grow back from the roots or woody top growth the following spring. Regular deadheading can extend their period of bloom.

BULBS: This term refers to plants that grow from bulbs, corms, tubers, and rhizomes. Fall-planted bulbs flower in spring, spring-planted bulbs bloom in summer.

TURF GRASSES: Most are available as either sod or seed. Their period of dormancy varies from one region to another (see pages 206–207).

BARE-ROOT PLANTS: These are typically deciduous plants (roses, vines, trees, shrubs, and even some perennials) that go dormant in winter and are sold then with no soil around their roots. They're inexpensive, easy to transport or buy through the mail, and adapt easily to most garden soils.

BEDDING PLANTS: These may be annual or perennial flowering plants used for massing in flower beds. They are typically sold in small pots or packs.

Month	MOUNTAIN ZONES 1-3
January	Plant seeds of cool-season annuals indoors. Knock snow off trees and shrubs to keep branches from breaking.
February	COLDEST TIME OF THE YEAR.
March	Plant bare-root roses, shrubs, trees, and vines as soon as they are available.
April	Continue planting bare roots. Plant flowering perennials and permanent landscape plants such as container-grown shrubs and trees. **In bloom:** early-spring bulbs.
May	Plant lawns and perennials. At end of month, plant heat-loving annuals like marigold and petunia. **In bloom:** cool-season annuals, spring bulbs, spring-flowering shrubs.
June	Plant annuals (bachelor's button, calendula, lobelia, pansy, sweet alyssum, verbena, viola), perennials and summer bulbs. Sow native grasses.
July	**In bloom:** cool-season annuals, some warm-season annuals, alpines, perennials.
August	Plant seeds of annuals and perennials, including wildflowers.
September	Plant spring bulbs, lawns (seed or sod), trees, shrubs, vines, ground covers, and flowering perennials. **Fall color:** aspen and birch; crabapples are ripening.
October	Early in the month continue to sow wildflower seeds over rock gardens and hillsides. Cut back perennials. **Fall color:** aspen, larch, and maple.
November	Prepare for winter. Protect young trees from bright winter sun with wraps (see page 323).
December	

PACIFIC NORTHWEST ZONES 4-7	NORTHERN CALIFORNIA ZONES 7-9, 14-17	SOUTHERN CALIFORNIA ZONES 18-24	SOUTHWEST DESERTS ZONES 10-13
Plant cool-season annuals and bare-root plants.	Plant cool-season annuals and bare-root plants. **In bloom:** cool-season annuals such as cyclamen, Iceland poppy, and primrose.	Plant cool-season annuals, bare-root plants, and flowering shrubs. **In bloom:** evergreen pear and camellia.	Plant cool-season annuals and bare-root plants.
In bloom: witch hazel and pussy willow; crocus are starting to emerge.	Sow seeds of warm-season annuals indoors, and plant bulbs. **In bloom:** azalea, camellia, and daffodil.	Plant summer-blooming bulbs. **In bloom:** azalea, coral trees, daffodil, flowering plum, freesia, ranunculus, Iceland poppy, and cool-season annuals.	Plant desert marigold, evening primrose, penstemon, and salvia. **In bloom:** cool-season annuals.
Plant flowering shrubs and trees from containers. **In bloom:** camellia, evergreen clematis, daffodil, plum, and quince.	Plant citrus, perennials, and summer annuals. **In bloom:** ceanothus, daffodil, flowering cherry, fremontodendron, poppy, and fall-planted annuals.	Plant citrus and summer annuals. **In bloom:** ceanothus, fremontodendron, and other natives.	Plant warm-season annuals, bulbs (zones 12–13), and citrus. **In bloom:** bougainvillea, desert marigold, and old saguaro.
Plant summer annuals, perennials, lawns (seed), and trees. **In bloom:** flowering cherry and western dogwood; it's tulip time in Skagit Valley.	Plant summer-to-fall perennials, tender shrubs and vines, citrus. **In bloom:** tulip, wisteria, and annuals.	Plant tender vines (bougainvillea) and tropicals (hibiscus). **In bloom:** ceanothus, iris, roses, and annuals such as stock and snapdragon.	Plant lawns (zones 11–13), perennials, and tender vines (zone 13). **In bloom:** desert willow, mesquite, palo verde, and desert marigold.
Plant summer annuals, bulbs, perennials, and fuchsias. **In bloom:** eastern dogwood, iris, lilac, rhododendron, and wisteria.	Plant warm-season annuals and lawns from seed. **In bloom:** iris, lavender, penstemon, rhododendron, roses, and many other perennials.	Plant warm-season annuals, lawns from sod, and perennials. **In bloom:** bougainvillea, jacaranda, and roses.	Plant summer bulbs, tender ornamentals (in zone 10), and warm-season annuals. In zones 12 and 13, plant hybrid Bermuda grass as soon as nighttime minimum temperature rises above 65°F.
Plant summer annuals. It's rose festival time in Portland.	Plant large container arrangements. **In bloom:** clematis, lavatera, and Shasta daisy.	Plant gardenia, hibiscus, and plumeria. **In bloom:** crape myrtle (inland), daylily, cape honeysuckle, fuchsia, hibiscus, Matilija poppy, and plumbago.	Plant palms. **In bloom:** caesalpinia.
In bloom: hollyhock, lily, and Shasta daisy. False spiraea and *Aster frikartii* blooms are starting.	**In bloom:** warm-season annuals and crape myrtle (inland); hydrangea and lily.	**In bloom:** crape myrtle (inland), ivy geranium (coast), bougainvillea, and hibiscus.	HOTTEST TIME OF THE YEAR.
In bloom: dahlia, native goldenrod, oriental lily. Time to cut down iris.	**In bloom:** dahlia, fuchsia, purple coneflower, and tuberous begonia.		
Plant crocus, daffodil, hyacinth, native iris, and tulip. **In bloom:** dahlia and chrysanthemum. **Fall color:** vines and maple.	**In bloom:** chrysanthemum, dahlia, delphinium, and salvia.	**In bloom:** plumeria (coast), chorisia, and salvia.	Plant freesia, harlequin flower, and cool-season annuals.
Plant ground covers such as cotoneaster, heather, kinnikinnick, and vinca. **Fall color:** ash, ginkgo, maple, oak, and 'Shirotae' cherry tree.	Plant spring bulbs, perennials, ornamental trees, shrubs, vines, and cool-season annuals. **Fall color:** crape myrtle (inland), birch, liquidambar, persimmon, and pistache.	Plant spring bulbs, trees, shrubs, vines, perennials, and annuals. Overseed warm-season grasses with ryegrass. **In bloom:** chrysanthemum and late salvia.	Plant trees, shrubs, vines, perennials, annuals, and spring-blooming bulbs such as daffodil, Dutch iris, and tulip. Sow wildflower seeds.
Plant trees and shrubs that bear fall berries.	Continue fall planting. **In bloom:** cosmos, gloriosa daisy, and Mexican bush sage.	**In bloom:** early camellia, primroses, and roses.	Overseed warm-season lawns (zones 12–13).
Winter fruit color: cotoneaster, holly, and pyracantha.	**Winter fruit color:** toyon and pyracantha. **In bloom:** early camellia, winter annuals.	**In bloom:** Sasanqua camellia and roses.	**Winter fruit:** navel oranges.

PROBLEM SOILS

The colored areas on this map indicate regions where more than 25 percent of the land has certain soil characteristics, described in the legend below. In the regions colored cream on the map, less than 25 percent of the land shares these problematic characteristics.

Very acid soil (pH 5.6 and lower)
Acid soil with salt
Acid soil with hardpan
Acid soil with salt and hardpan
Very alkaline soil (pH 8.4 and higher)
Alkaline soil with salt
Alkaline soil with hardpan
Alkaline soil with salt and hardpan
Hardpan (within 20 inches of soil surface)
Salty soil

SOILS OF THE WEST

More than any other factor, your garden's soil will determine which plants you can grow—and whether they'll thrive. Although you can modify the climate in your garden only slightly, you can do almost anything with soil.

Before you can alter your native soil, however, you should know something about it. Garden soils are usually characterized by their texture, described as sandy, silt, or clay. Sandy soil has relatively large particles, drains fast, and usually doesn't hold nutrients well. Silt has intermediate-size particles. Clay has tiny particles that hold nutrients and water well, but not air; when clay dries, it gets as hard as brick (which is why the California missions were built with it). The perfect garden soil is loam—a light, crumbly mixture of approximately equal parts of sand, silt, and clay, with at least 4 percent organic matter by weight (which can translate to 25 percent by volume). Organic matter does a good job of holding water, nutrients, and air, and is loose enough for roots to penetrate easily. Most gardens don't start out with loam, but there are ways you can develop it (see pages 316–317).

But soil texture isn't the whole story. The map at left, prepared with help from USDA's Natural Resources Conservation Service (NRCS), shows the regions where more than 25 percent of the land is likely to have problems with soil chemistry (including excess acidity, salinity, or alkalinity) or with structure (hardpan close to the surface). For more information about your region's soil type, contact your local NRCS office.

Soil pH

Another measure of soil is pH, measured on an acid-to-alkaline scale of 0 to 14. Every plant has a preferred pH (the same as the soil in the plant's native range), but most plants are adaptable enough to grow well in anything from pH 5.5 to 7.5. Soils with a pH measurement above 8 or below 5 restrict plant growth, because it becomes difficult for plants to absorb nutrients.

In arid parts of the West, soils tend to be alkaline—that is, with a pH measurement above 7. Alkaline soils are high in calcium carbonate (lime) and other minerals such as sodium. Some native plants, including palo verde and many desert wildflowers, prefer this type of soil. Where there's abundant rain and snow, as in western Washington, soils tend to be more acid, with a pH below 6. Native azaleas and rhododendrons grow well in acid soils, which tend to contain plenty of organic matter.

Every region has its surprises, however. Southern California has sulfurous pockets of soil where pH plummets to around 3 and nothing grows. But the soils surrounding these pockets are alkaline, in the pH 7 to 8 range.

You can amend soils to alter their pH—for example, make them more alkaline with lime or more acid with peat or acid fertilizer. If you live in an area with naturally acid or alkaline soil, it will probably be necessary to repeat the amendment periodically.

Salinity

Salinity is the amount of soluble salt in the soil. It's calibrated in millimhos, which measure electrical conductivity. Too much salt (above 4 millimhos for most plants) interferes with plants' ability to take up water, causing leaf burn and decline. Plants native to regions with high salinity, such as the desert and the seashore, often thrive in salty soils. But if levels cross 16 millimhos, as they do regularly in Las Vegas, for example, even salt-tolerant plants have trouble.

Soluble salt measurements aren't the same as sodium readings—sodium (which, in practical terms, can be equated with alkalinity) isn't necessarily soluble. As a result, treatments for sodium and soluble salt problems are different.

Hardpan

Hardpan, called caliche by desert gardeners, is an impermeable layer of earth that can be up to several yards thick. It usually forms in regions that get just enough rain to dissolve minerals and carry them a few inches below the surface, but not enough to leach them out all together. After decades of this process, these minerals cement the soil together into a pan layer.

The closer hardpan is to the surface, the more trouble it causes. It prevents plant roots from reaching nutrients and deep water, leading to stunted, dwarfed growth. Areas that have hardpan within 20 inches of the soil surface are shown on the map.

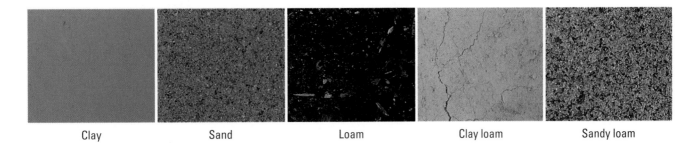

Clay   Sand   Loam   Clay loam   Sandy loam

UNDERSTANDING YOUR SITE

Before tackling the design of your garden, you need to understand the opportunities and problems presented by your property, then find a way to balance those features with your goals for the garden. The preceding pages on microclimates, soil, and seasons will help you identify many of the natural conditions on your site. You will also need to evaluate any man-made features in your garden and any plantings that have been introduced, especially trees and shrubs. Sketching out these features on paper gives you a base plan, a working document for the design stage.

You'll save yourself hours of measuring if you can find any of the following: a deed map that gives actual dimensions and the orientation of your property; a topographical plan, with contour lines showing the exact shape of your site; or architectural plans that depict the site plan with the location of all buildings. If none of these are available, you will need to measure your property yourself and transfer the dimensions to the base plan, preferably on graph paper, using a scale of ¼ inch for 1 foot.

Later, slipping this base plan under a sheet of tracing paper, you can sketch designs to your heart's content. This gives you a chance to try out a variety of ideas before laying out everything on site—or worse, installing a structure or plantings and finding they don't suit the space, the property's microclimates, or your needs.

Starting to plan

Next, identify those aspects of the garden that you wish to keep, as well as those you want to change. If you have just moved into your home, don't pick up your shovel and start digging just yet. Try to live with a new property for a full year; you will get to know your garden through the seasons and can experiment with various plants. A design you make with a thorough knowledge of your garden will fit the land better. But don't be afraid to be ruthless; there is no need to design your garden around an existing feature, living or nonliving, just because it is there.

If you are landscaping just one problem area of your garden, consider the impact the upgrade will have on the rest of the site. Suppose you wish to plant a row of trees to add privacy to your front yard. Would this create too much shade? Keep in mind the garden as a whole, both for the present and the future.

SHOW THE FOLLOWING ON YOUR BASE PLAN:

Compass directions, which will help you identify exposures and patterns of sun and shade.

Boundaries and dimensions of the lot and the outlines of the house and other structures.

Location of all windows and doors on your house; note the height of their sills above the exterior grade.

Eaves, overhangs, downspouts, and drains.

Existing paved areas; their condition and usefulness.

Existing steps or ramps; their condition and usefulness.

Location of easements and setback boundaries.

Existing plants: sizes, shapes, and general health of all plants, especially trees.

Topography: high and low points, slope gradients.

Soil conditions: areas that have been raised or filled; soil texture, fertility, and pH.

Direction of prevailing winds throughout the year.

A BASE PLAN

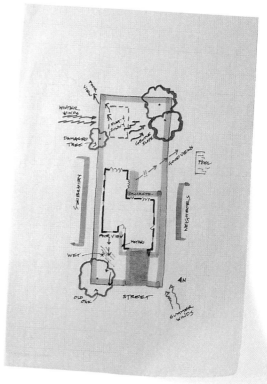

ANALYZING YOUR GARDEN

Here are some of the problems and opportunities presented by this site. Compare each with the illustrations on pages 12–13 and 38–41 to see how the final design deals with them.

A. **The front view** from the living room is of noisy street traffic, passersby, and parked cars.

B. **Damp pockets of soil** can limit plant choices.

C–D. **Warm air blows** in summer from the southwest **(C)**; winter winds blow from the north **(D)**.

E. **Concrete terraces** reflect excessive heat into the home; they are too small for entertaining.

F. **Neighbors' homes** are very close to the property line, thus limiting privacy.

G. **Gently sloping land** and existing trees could be incorporated into the garden design.

H. **Open, sunny areas** in the rear and on the south side yard offer space for a swimming pool or for sun-loving plantings.

I–J. **Rear views** from the patio are pleasant in one direction **(I)** but unpleasant in another **(J)**.

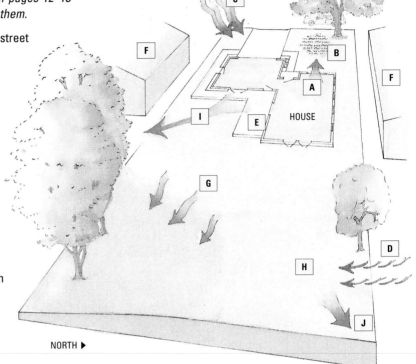

NORTH ▶

Other Considerations

Local zoning or other laws may restrict or prohibit your planned construction. Consult the following documents, agencies, or individuals before proceeding with your design and note any relevant restrictions on your base plan.

YOUR PROPERTY DEED:

Exact location of property lines.

Easements or rights-of-way.

Building restrictions.

Tree removal restrictions.

YOUR LOCAL BUILDING OR PLANNING DEPARTMENT:

Setback requirements.

Height limitations for fences, buildings, or other structures.

Lot coverage guidelines.

Safety codes for pools and spas.

Requirements for firewalls between adjacent buildings.

Open burning restrictions for firepits.

Building codes for all construction.

Tree or historic preservation ordinances.

Building permits for fences, retaining walls above 30 inches in height, other garden structures, and electrical or plumbing work.

YOUR LOCAL UTILITY COMPANY:

Location and depth of underground utility lines.

Building or planting limitations under power lines.

YOUR WATER COMPANY:

Restrictions on water use for irrigation, pools, and water features.

Limitations on the size of lawns.

YOUR NEIGHBORS:

Their views into your property (and your view into theirs) and your mutual need for privacy and quiet, sunlight and air flow.

Their concerns about existing trees and other plants, structures, and shared walks or driveways.

Homeowners' association restrictions.

WESTERN GARDEN STYLES

Now that you have thoroughly evaluated your site, you can turn your attention to matters of style. The West's moderate climates allow enormous flexibility in garden design. Influences from the Mediterranean, the Orient, and the tropics have inspired western gardeners for years. From these influences have emerged styles that are unique to the West and that help to distinguish gardens of this region from the rest of North America.

Although mixing and matching elements from different garden styles can be effective, if you want your garden to have a distinct character and to look well planned, you'll need a clear and unifying theme.

The style you choose guides many decisions affecting your garden's design: the kinds of plants and how they are combined; the structures you incorporate

Striking plants and bold colors are well suited to desert settings.

into the landscape; and the materials you choose for fences, gates, walls, and walks.

Select a garden style that is both compatible with the architecture of your house and appropriate to your climate. Some types of architecture strongly suggest a particular style of garden. For example, a formal garden would suit a large Georgian home but would look out of place around a simple Craftsman bungalow. Other styles are more accommodating: a modern or contemporary house can be equally attractive surrounded by a garden designed in a tropical, oriental, or Mediterranean style.

Sometimes the building's materials will have the strongest influence on the choice of a garden style. A house constructed of natural stone or brick, for example, may call out for a rustic, naturalistic, or artistic landscape rather than a precise formal garden.

A. Mediterranean gardens in the West usually spring from the Italian, Spanish, or Mission architecture of the house, which often features stucco walls and tile roofs. Paving or gravel takes the place of lawns. Evergreen trees and shrubs, occasionally sheared, form green enclosing walls, while fragrance is provided by citrus, lavender, rosemary, and roses. Terracotta pots contain colorful annuals and herbs. The bright colors of flowers and painted structures stand up to the intense light of California and the Southwest.

B. Tropical gardens are lush, green, and at their best—outside of Hawaii—in coastal climates from San Diego to Santa Barbara and around the San Francisco Bay Area, where winters are frost-free and summers are mild. Dense plantings suggest tropical jungles; vines might scramble up palm trees and orchids or bromeliads might dangle from tree trunks. A pond or fountain is typically featured somewhere in the garden. This style is equally at home around contemporary or Victorian houses.

C. Oriental gardens tend to symbolize nature. A single tree represents a forest, a patch of gravel suggests a riverbank, a swath of raked sand mimics water. Best suited for the misty Northwest, these gardens depend on shaped trees and shrubs, both evergreen and deciduous. Green dominates, with floral displays limited to a few flowering cherries, camellias, or azaleas in spring; maples provide fall color. Structures are built of natural materials such as bamboo, stone, and wood.

D. Formal gardens relate strongly to the architecture of the house, usually Georgian, Mediterranean, French, or Victorian. Harmony and balance in the architecture are reflected in the symmetry of the plantings. The precise placement of evergreen trees and shrubs, for example, provides a strong pattern in the landscape, emphasizing an axial arrrangement with obvious focal points. Sheared hedges line walks or outline beds that contain herbaceous plantings for restrained seasonal color.

E. Artistic gardens may be whimsical or they may treat the garden as pure art or as an abstraction of the natural world. Strong forms and bold colors can alternate with soft textures and quiet corners. Floral colors may influence the colors of structural elements, or vice versa. Some artistic gardens are mostly hardscape (paving and structural elements), while others are full of unusual plants and garden art.

F. Avant garde design relies on spare man-made forms as well as nature's own to achieve drama. The hardscape elements may dominate, and even provide most of the garden's color. Carefully selected plants tend to be chosen and placed for sculptural effect, or a single plant may be massed to create a block of color, as in the garden at right, where large groupings of salvia and lavender have been placed to increase the visual impact of their blossoms in flower. Patterns of light and shadow are also integral to the garden's design.

G. Rustic gardens suit many different architectural styles, including the adobe pueblos of the Southwest, the Craftsman cottages of the early 1900s, and updated versions of the mountain cabin. The overall mood of the garden is informal and casual, with rampant, and usually colorful, plantings. A rustic garden need not solely feature native plants, but its naturalized plantings appear to drift in random arrangements amidst untrimmed shrubbery and rough grasses.

H. Naturalistic gardens imitate the authentic look of their region without holding to a strict standard of native planting. Exotic (non-native) plants are included if they blend with the native flora in a way that reflects the casualness of the wild. Colorful plantings may predominate, and the flowering season is likely to be extended by means of irrigation. Natural materials such as stone, adobe, and wood are the best choices for structures and surfaces. In the Northwest garden at right, autumn leaves are left unraked, punctuating the pathway and understory with color.

I–K. Native gardens give primary importance to the cultivation of plants native to the region, usually to the exclusion of exotic species. On properties adjoining natural areas, the garden can merge with the native plants beyond, making the garden seem larger. Such gardens may also provide an opportunity to return natives to an area from which they were eliminated by development. There are few restrictions on planting compositions, which can vary from the entirely natural and seemingly unplanned **(I, J)** to more orderly arrangements **(K)** or even striking and dramatic designs. The key to planning a successful native garden is to understand the cultural needs of the native plants and to group them accordingly. Shown here, from top to bottom, are native gardens in Colorado, Arizona, and California.

Bubble Diagrams

To experiment with various arrangements of space in your garden, try the designer's trick of using simple "bubble diagrams." These quick studies can be drawn on tracing paper over the base plan you have made of your property (page 22). Each bubble (actually a rough circle, square, or oval) should represent a particular activity or garden space that you hope to incorporate into the design, and each should be approximately the size and shape needed. Make the bubbles different colors to distinguish them from each other (use green for planting areas, blue for a pool, and brown for decks and patios).

Let the bubbles overlap where activity spaces will merge with each other. Where spaces need to be separated, draw a line to suggest a screen or barrier. Simple cross-hatching can designate areas that need overhead protection from the sun. Show steps as sets of parallel lines and roughly indicate entrances to the house or front yard.

Sketch several versions, considering with each one the microclimates, potential views, and existing features identified on your base plan. Note how well the placement of activities in each diagram takes advantage of the warm spots and shady areas in your garden. Look for smooth transitions from one space to the next and address practical issues by including spaces for work, storage, and service areas.

After you have done several diagrams, lay them out and compare the different arrangement of spaces, then settle on the one that will form the basis for your final design.

DESIGNING YOUR GARDEN

N ow that you've identified the basic features and found a garden style you like, you are ready to put your creativity to work. The first step is site planning—creating and arranging the activity spaces in your garden. Study carefully how all these spaces relate to the rooms inside your home and try to locate the outdoor activity spaces near their indoor counterparts. For example, if young children are a part of the family, place their outdoor play space near a room in the house where you spend a lot of time, so that you can keep an eye on them. Organize vegetable and herb gardens near the kitchen, if possible, to make it easy to bring the harvest to the table. Decide whether some areas of the garden should serve multiple functions—whether a sheltered walkway could also house a composting area, for example.

Look at the entire garden and lay out spaces that will flow logically and easily from one to the other. Plan a circulation path that won't require walking through a work area or past the trash cans to get from a sitting area to the swimming pool. Settle on an arrangement of planted areas that will permit grouping plants according to their irrigation needs. As you sketch, you'll begin to make general decisions about the plants and structures you'll need and where they should go. Even if you don't use bubble planning (left) to help you mock up some designs, refer frequently to your base plan to remind you of site features and conditions.

Odd-shaped lots

Don't be concerned if your lot is not the simple rectangle shown in the previous pages. Not all of the urban and suburban West is laid out on a grid pattern with rectangular lots. Many properties, because of topography or the street pattern, have an irregular shape or are carved out of uneven terrain. The cul-de-sac subdivision, for example, results in pie-shaped lots with minimal street frontage and plenty of private space, while in some older communities, deep and narrow lots are often common. And, of course, sloping lots present a different set of challenges from those on flat ground. Whatever the size and shape of your lot, the tips and techniques described here will help you make the most of it.

Before getting carried away with the excitement of creating a whole new garden, now is a good time to consider the time, effort, and financial implications of your decisions. Like many homeowners, you may want to approach the landscaping process in stages. If so, identify features you'd like to have right away and those that can be added as time and money allow.

THREE GARDEN SHAPES

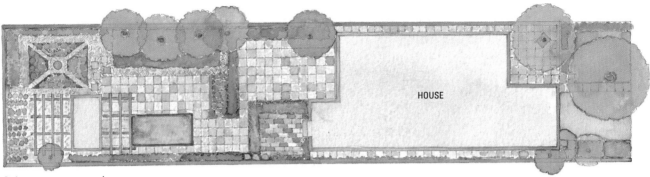

A. Long, narrow garden

A. Avoid the feel of a bowling alley in a long space by dividing it into smaller units, each for a different function. Staggering the spaces disguises the linear character of the lot. Here a hedge separates a large dining terrace from a secluded bedroom retreat and from the swimming pool. The pool terrace merges into a graveled herb garden. Behind the pool house is a small vegetable patch with a work area under the arbor.

B. Don't be discouraged by a small lot; make it seem larger by concealing the property line with dense shrubbery, emphasizing long diagonal lines, and hiding parts of the garden from view. Here the focal point at the end of the angled deck is a bench that looks toward a curved bench beyond the pond, not visible from the main deck. A tall, angled hedge screens a functional vegetable garden and the fences support berries and vines, making use of every possible gardening space.

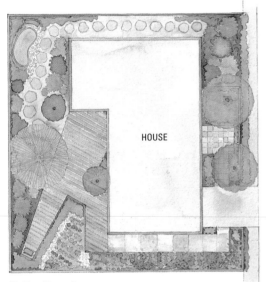

B. Small garden

C. Opportunities abound in odd-shaped lots such as this corner cul-de-sac, where there is plenty of room for a series of different garden areas. Terracing the gentle slope of the fenced side yard creates a generous vegetable, herb, and cutting garden within easy reach of the kitchen. A continuous patio area that unites all parts of the garden widens at the rear to provide ample space for entertaining. A small, circular lawn nestles into one corner. A secluded terrace and shade-loving plants fill the narrow side yard.

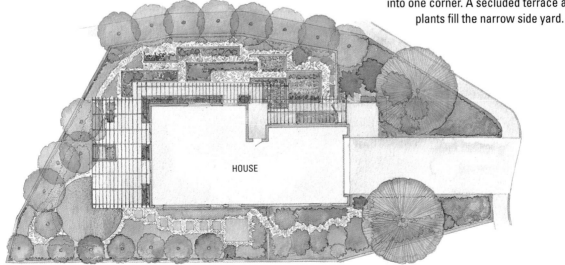

C. Irregular garden

THE LANGUAGE OF LANDSCAPE DESIGN

Whatever landscape style you choose, your plan will be most successful if you observe some simple principles of design, which in turn requires that you become familiar with the terms used by landscape professionals. Some of these terms are used throughout the broad field of design. Focal point, symmetry, and asymmetry, for example, are used by architects, interior designers, and graphic artists alike. Other terms, such as berm and borrowed scenery, are specific to landscape architecture. As you go through this book, you'll see these terms used to describe the features of various gardens. And as you follow the process of creating a successful garden, you'll have an easier time communicating with professionals if you use their lingo.

A focal point is an object like this tree to which the eye is drawn by its placement in the garden. In formal gardens the focal point is usually at the end of an axis. In less formal gardens a focal point may appear anywhere in the garden, but its distinctiveness will attract attention and encourage movement toward it.

Borrowed scenery is a concept adapted from Japanese gardens where views beyond the borders of the garden are incorporated into the design to make the garden seem larger. Here the distant trees, hills, and cityscape are obviously not part of the property, but it feels roomier because of the view.

A. The texture of plants and other elements is enhanced by the play of light and shadow on their surfaces. Textures may be fine or coarse, delicate or bold. Here, a coarse-textured hosta and lacy-textured ferns stand out against the bold texture of the boulder.

B. An axis is the centerline of a view or walk; in this formal garden it runs from the bird bath to the bench. Elements often align on either side of the axis. In a less formal garden, the axis may be a visual line between two significant elements.

C. Berms and swales are landscape features, usually man-made, that let you make changes in grade for privacy, for wind control, to deflect runoff, or simply for beauty. A berm is a low mound; a swale is a depression.

D. An accent draws attention to itself by contrasting boldly with its surroundings, as this strap-leafed *Phormium* stands out from its neighbors. Accents add variety and depth to a composition or emphasize a particular spot in the landscape.

E. Symmetry exists when matching elements are balanced on either side of a central axis, most commonly seen in formal gardens like this one. Asymmetry occurs when those elements are different; this may be found in both formal and informal gardens.

DESIGN BASICS

Experienced landscape professionals work with several basic design principles; after years of practice, they have absorbed these guidelines so completely that they apply them automatically when designing a garden. Design principles apply at all levels of landscaping, from the most elaborately constructed feature to the simplest of planting compositions.

You can learn a lot by studying gardens that you visit or see in magazines, as well as from those illustrated here and throughout this book. Note the application of the principles explained here and keep them in mind as you flesh out your landscape plan.

In well-designed gardens no one plant, structure, or feature stands out too much, but rather all the parts work together to establish a sense of *unity*. Note how plants or construction materials are used with *repetition* or placed for dramatic *emphasis*. All the elements should be in *proportion* to the rest of the garden and in *scale* with the size of the house, the property, and the people who live there. Also, note how *harmony* is achieved by balancing *simplicity* (in form, texture, and color) and *variety* (in materials and plants).

A. Simplicity reigns here with a serpentine hedge of fine-textured *Westringia fruticosa* drawing a distinct line between the rough lawn of the garden and the native oak woodland. The hedge is of sufficient scale to keep people from wandering into the natural garden, where the oaks have been pruned up to reveal the simple repetition of their trunks.

B. Repetition and emphasis are featured in this voluptuous border. The bold form of a variegated century plant is repeated in the distance as a unifying element that ties together a border of diverse plants; the distant specimen, however, is raised up in an urn to add more variety to the garden. Each century plant, by its texture and dramatic coloring, gives emphasis to its spot in the border, adding depth to the planting.

C. Harmony is established among diverse elements in this Northwest garden nook. The plants grow well together in shade and coolness, and their different textures create variety and add depth. A simple gravel path unifies the garden. The hostas opposite the chair and further along the path add emphasis and invite movement throughout the garden.

D. Unity of design is the essence of this garden. The form and materials are simple (stone, wood, and evergreen shrubs), establishing a quiet harmony. Variety is provided by the bold shapes of the boulders, all the same type of rock but of different shapes; the rock is repeated in the crushed-stone surfacing. Fine-textured grasses call attention to the top of the broad steps, which connect the distinct spaces of the upper and lower garden. The distant view is brought in to the scheme as borrowed scenery.

DESIGN TRICKS

In addition to basic design principles, professionals have an array of tricks at their disposal—techniques that help overcome typical challenges or simply make the garden more attractive and livable for occupants and visitors alike.

Some of these ideas are very basic, such as understanding the dimensions of the human body in designing the height and size of structures in the garden. For example, the best ratio for stair risers and treads is based on dimensions that are the most comfortable for people to climb (see page 398). Similarly, pathways are the most comfortable when they are more than 4 feet wide, and built-in seating for decks or benches should be 16 or 17 inches deep.

Other techniques involve altering the perception of space by manipulating

Gardens are for people. Keep the garden comfortable by designing stairs and furniture that reflect human measurements and proportions.

materials, colors, and textures; by taking advantage of changes in the garden's elevation; or by placing elements to mask the size and shape of a space.

Bring your garden design to life by incorporating some of these tricks. They can be particularly helpful if you are renovating or upgrading an existing landscape or if there is a particular area of your garden with which you have never been especially pleased.

As you develop your ideas, refer to your bubble plan and the basic design principles to make sure you haven't forgotten your original intentions amid the flurry of other considerations. There will be plenty of opportunity to add whimsy and interest to the garden as you choose plants, structures, and accessories to complete your garden's design.

A. Make the garden appear larger. Judiciously placed, a mirror is a simple way to create the impression of a larger space. The mirror in this garden reflects the stems of the bamboo, suggesting another planting beyond the wall in a further "room" of the garden. The bold foliage in the lower righthand corner seems to advance toward the viewer, increasing the feeling of depth, especially when seen against the reflected bamboo clump.

B. Create a series of spaces. In this garden, the clever division of a small space into four smaller "rooms" begins with the paved terrace at the lower right and includes the shady nook in the rear. Angled hedges and walls disguise the relatively tight borders of the property; steps suggest distinct spaces. Pots of flowering plants offer opportunities to change color arrangements and can be moved to make way for more activity space when needed.

C. Emphasize diagonal lines. In a small or narrow garden, diagonal lines disguise the actual shape and dimension of the garden. Here, walks, walls, and beds intersect at angles to the perimeter to mask the garden's tiny size; the sitting area seems more distant when placed at the opposite corner of the property. Diverse paving materials not only add variety to the ground plane but further emphasize the different spaces within the garden.

D. Conceal parts of the garden. Even the smallest garden can be made to feel larger by hiding a portion of it from full view. Add mystery and expectation by not revealing the whole garden at once; let windows and portals lead your visitors to discover new spaces beyond. Here, arched openings lead to several rooms in progression around the corner of the house. Each entices with just a suggestion of what's waiting to be seen.

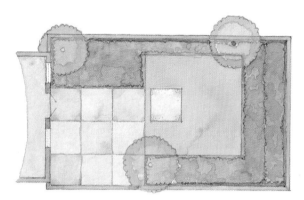

A. Square plan

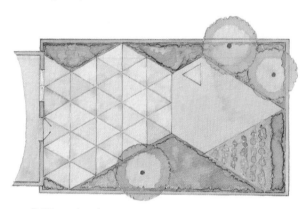

B. Triangular plan

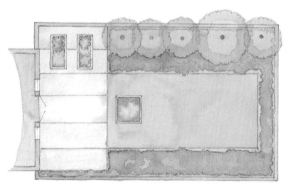

C. Rectangular plan

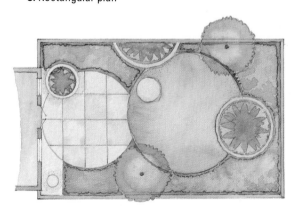

D. Circular plan

THE TOOLS OF

When your experiments with bubble diagrams have resulted in a rough sketch, lay a clean sheet of tracing paper on top of it. On this sheet, begin drawing in the various elements of the final design—hard-surfaced areas, enclosing walls or hedges, arbors or trees for shelter, gardening spaces, and perhaps pools, hot tubs, potting tables, compost piles, or dog runs. This schematic drawing will be rough at first, but it will take shape as you continue.

Designing with shapes

At this point, keep in mind two tricks of the landscape designer: first, work with clear, simple shapes, and second, relate those shapes to the lines of your house. A design that is made up of familiar shapes such as squares, rectangles, triangles, and circles is easier to understand than one filled with abstract lines. Repeating a familiar shape brings simplicity and order to the design, unifying beds, borders, paving, walls, arbors, and other features. To add interest, vary the sizes of the shapes you work with, and allow them to overlap or interlock. But don't use too many little shapes, or you will end up with a very busy design.

ONE GARDEN, FOUR WAYS

A–D. These simple plans were created for the same basic lot using one of four different geometric shapes (square, triangle, rectangle, or circle) to guide the design. Each design presents a similar arrangement of paved terrace, small lawn area, and planting beds with a mix of ground covers, shrubs, and trees. But the repetition of a different geometric shape gives each design a distinct character.

To follow this approach in your own garden, select a shape that appeals to you. If you choose a square, rectangle, or triangle, use that shape as a grid module; you can form modules with convenient dimensions such as 3 by 3 feet or 3 by 6 feet, or you can use different sizes for various elements. No grid is needed for circular elements; simply use circles of different diameters, allowing some to overlap and others to stand alone. Whatever shape you use, play with the alignment and position of elements in a symmetrical or asymmetrical arrangement. Eventually you will settle on one that pleases you.

SUCCESSFUL DESIGN

Working with grids

After playing with simple geometric patterns, you may feel that a little more variety is necessary: a curving line may be needed to connect two rectangular spaces, or a diagonal line to emphasize the longest dimension in a small garden. As you become more adventurous in your design, you will find it easier to work with a grid module (a square or rectangle of 4, 5, or 6 feet) repeated over and over, like the squares on a checkerboard or the bricks in a wall. Fit the garden's structures and plantings to the dimensions of that module, allowing some elements to intersect or interlock with each other, while letting others split a module in half. The dimension of one or two modules can form the radius for a curved line.

The grid system speeds the decision-making process as you determine the dimensions of decks, pathways, and planting beds. It also allows you to quickly calculate quantities for paving, decking, or soil amendments, and simplifies do-it-yourself installation by letting you pave, pour, or plow only one module at a time.

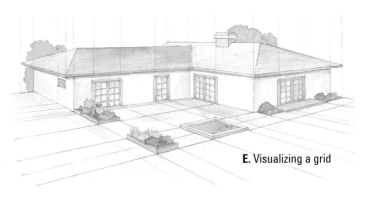

E. Visualizing a grid

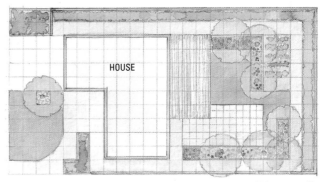

F. Large trellis

VISUALIZING A GRID

E. Connect the garden to the architecture of your house with gridlines that run out to the garden from major features of the house. Here, lines marking the doorways, windows, and corners of wings have been drawn on the plan of the garden. Elements such as flower beds, paved terraces, and pools can then be placed within this irregular grid pattern.

THREE PLANS FOR A RECTANGULAR LOT

F–H. The three gardens at right use the same simple 5-by-5-foot grid to show very different design solutions for a rectangular property. Garden **F** incorporates a large overhead trellis or arbor to shade a portion of the paved terrace, while an L-shaped fence and planting bed screen a vegetable garden, compost area, and work area from view. Garden **G** allows more space for a sweeping lawn, backed up by a curving line of trees to enclose the garden; a round pond echoes the curve of the lawn. Garden **H** places a bold, circular lawn just off center, almost surrounded by a paved surface of varying width.

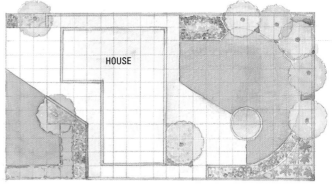

G. Spacious lawn

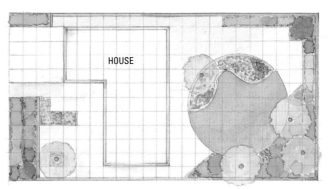

H. Circular lawn

ENCLOSING THE OUTDOOR ROOM

Focus next on creating structure in your garden, defining spaces with horizontal and vertical planes. Just as the rooms in your home have walls and ceilings to give them form and function, so should the spaces in your garden be designed with enclosing fences, walls, or hedges, and ceilings of tree canopies, arbors, or fabric awnings.

Walls and fences

Walls and fences serve several functions in a garden. They can modify the climate by shading areas that are too warm or reducing the chilling effects of strong winds. They can collect the sun's rays to warm a cozy spot or direct cooling breezes to moderate the temperature. A well-placed fence or wall can screen unsightly views while framing those you wish to enjoy; it can also enhance the feeling of privacy by blocking a neighbor's view into your garden. Low walls, perhaps with a built-in bench, define but don't confine a garden space. Both green and nonliving walls add beauty and expand the gardening space on a small lot by supporting "vertical gardens" of climbers or espaliers.

Ceilings and canopies

Though it may seem odd to consider ceilings or roofs in the out-of-doors, both create comfortable and functional spaces in the garden. While a swimming pool or vegetable garden needs only the sky for a cover, other activities in the garden will benefit from more intimate overheads. Sitting and dining areas need overhanging tree branches, arbors, or vines on taut wires to protect from excessive sunlight. When rain interrupts an otherwise perfect day, a solid roof over the dining terrace allows you to remain outside. A partial or retractable cover is ideal where the climate can change measurably in one day or through the seasons. Carefully placed, a tree or overhead structure can also screen out a tall building nearby or block views from your neighbor's second-story windows into your private garden. An overhead can also support a collection of hanging potted plants, thereby increasing gardening space.

Plants or structures?

Structures such as walls, fences, and overheads are generally more expensive than hedges, shrub borders, or vines for trellises, but you should balance the additional cost against how quickly you want the garden to take shape. Plants usually take several years to achieve as much screening and enclosure as a fence, and trees may take ten years or more to provide the shade created by an arbor built in a weekend. If neither money nor time is an object, space may be. Hedges, shrub borders, and trees take up more room than does a 6-inch-thick fence.

CANOPIES AND BARRIERS

NORTH ▶

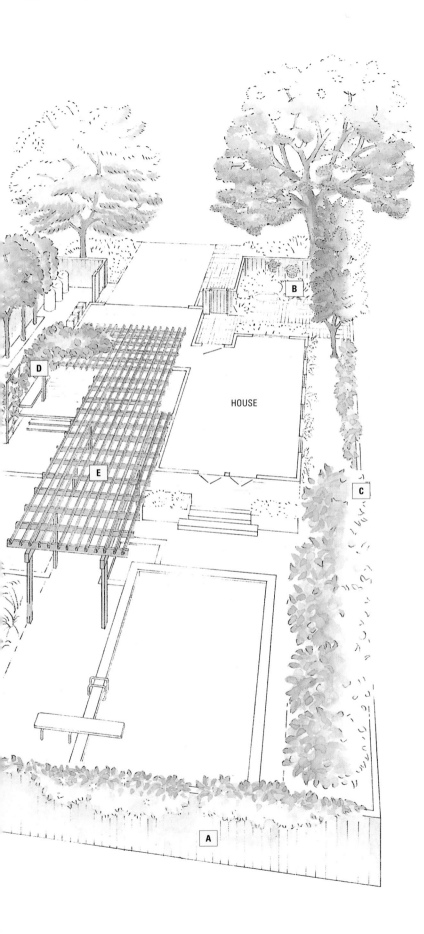

HOUSE

CHOOSING ENCLOSURES

A. A fence around the rear and side yards defines the garden's boundaries, while supporting vertical gardening (vines, espaliers, or hanging pots). Maintaining the same fence design throughout unifies the garden with a common backdrop. Choose a material that suits your home's architecture.

B. Extending the fence into the front yard creates a small, private sitting area adjacent to the living room. Use the inside wall for a collection of interesting wall sculptures or hanging baskets filled with colorful annuals. The large native oak provides a generous but open canopy overhead.

C. Hedges and trellises on the property line are generally not subject to zoning restrictions. Here a simple wire trellis for vines is extended above the maximum fence height to increase privacy and the sense of enclosure. The citrus trees form a tall, unsheared hedge for the same purpose.

D. The lattice screen along the south side of the main deck provides seclusion from the neighbors as well as a support for flowering vines. Its open structure allows cooling breezes to flow through.

E. The overhead arbor covering the deck protects people and plants from the heat of the midday sun. The wooden crosspieces of the arbor run from east to west to provide maximum shading.

F. Existing deciduous trees create a shady roof over this tiny "wild garden" retreat. Bare branches allow warming sunlight through in winter, encouraging year-round use.

CHOOSING SURFACES

A. The main deck, raised above grade, offers a generous and firm surface for outdoor entertaining. Suitable for furniture of all kinds, it serves well for games, parties, cooking, and simple relaxation.

B. The tiny deck in the "wild garden" marks a quiet retreat, with just enough space for two or three chairs within view of the pool and main deck. Its rough wood suits the rustic corner.

C. The flat lawn of dwarf tall fescue offers a soft surface for relaxation in the sun, playing youngsters, or a cavorting dog. It also serves as a low foreground to both the rose garden and the "wild garden."

D. The pavement of the pool deck has solid footing for swimmers and an easy surface to keep clean. It is broad enough for sunbathing without seeming to dominate the rear of the yard.

E. The paved side yard offers a generous surface for moving equipment in and out of the rear yard. It also provides a smooth surface easy to keep clean around the compost pile and the potting table.

F. The graveled side yard allows passage to and from the front courtyard and the rear yard, while permitting the informal planting of ferns and other shade-loving plants, as well as the vines that screen the bedroom windows.

G. The front paving of brick presents a gracious entrance walk and extends into the private courtyard. This hard surface is safe in all weather conditions, and the small pavers make the walk and courtyard appear bigger than they are.

PLANTINGS AND PAVINGS

NORTH ▶

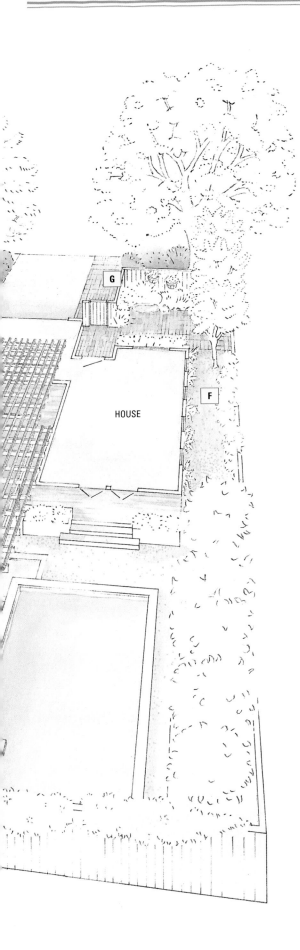

FLOORING THE OUTDOOR ROOM

Just as indoor floors serve many purposes, those in the garden also meet different needs. The most obvious is as a surface for walking, playing, or placing furniture. Garden floors can also modify the climate: a large concrete slab will reflect the sun's heat into windows and under arbors, while dark pavement such as asphalt will collect heat during the day, then release it at night. In contrast, a lush ground cover will reduce the air temperature by several degrees. Garden floors can be decorative as well as functional, providing an unbroken carpet of green foliage or an elaborate planting of brightly colored flowering plants. They also play a protective role, covering the soil and preventing erosion from exposure to the rain and wind, as well as controlling the runoff of excess water.

Flooring materials

Outdoor floors can be much more varied in character than those indoors. They can be permeable or paved to make them impervious to water. Areas where traffic is heavy require a firm surface; paving units of concrete slabs or brick, block, or stone can be laid on either sand or mortar. Wood is a serviceable flooring material, particularly when raised above ground level as a deck. Softer, more permeable floorings able to handle fairly heavy traffic include gravel and crushed stone in varying grades and organic mulches of redwood bark or sawn tree rounds.

Living surfaces

Where a sports or play area calls for a soft but sturdy, cushionlike floor, a lawn of turf grass is about the only solution; these grasses will tolerate the often intense activity of children and athletes. To keep a well-used lawn in top condition, you'll need to schedule regular maintenance. This is probably the most time-consuming of all gardening tasks. Although a few other living ground covers will tolerate a small amount of foot traffic, most will not take any more than occasional wear.

The turf grasses most commonly used in lawns originated in regions with steady moisture, either in northern Europe or the subtropics. Most respond poorly to the arid climates of the West without tremendous amounts of water, often a limited resource. Give serious thought to the purpose of the lawn you are considering; if it is not to be used as an activity surface, investigate other ground covers or hard surfacings that will conserve water better than common turf grasses.

FROM PLAN

Before drawing up your final plan, you may wish to consult a landscape professional to assist with some element of the design or its implementation. Although many homeowners prefer to tackle the entire design and construction of their garden themselves, others rely on various professionals to help with some of the steps along the way.

The role of landscape architect

Creating a garden can call for the addition of patios, decks, dining areas, play yards, shade structures, drainage systems, and perhaps a pool or spa. Designing such structures and relating them to a coherent plan for your outdoor environment is where a *landscape architect* comes in.

In addition to determining the most effective use of paving, planting, and lighting, landscape architects are licensed to design exterior structures, solve site problems such as ungainly slopes and poor drainage, and give advice on siting a house and locating service lines, entries, driveways, and parking areas. A landscape architect is familiar with landscape and building materials and services, and can suggest cost-saving options.

For individual services or for simple consultation, landscape architects usually work at an hourly rate. More commonly, however, a landscape architect provides a complete package, from conceptual plans to construction drawings and supervision of an installation; fees will depend upon the complexity of the project, its length, and the degree of supervision required.

Other professionals

Landscape architects are not the only professionals involved in the creation of fine gardens. The terms *landscape designer* and *garden designer* apply to professionals who may be self-taught or may have the same academic credentials as landscape architects, but may lack a state license. The focus of their work is more likely to be residential gardens, and if you are not in need of a complex deck construction or high retaining wall, they may well serve your needs. Their fees may be lower than those of a landscape architect. A landscape designer usually works in conjunction with a licensed *landscape contractor,* an important professional, especially when major construction—beyond the limits of do-it-yourself projects—is involved. A licensed contractor is trained in methods of earthmoving, construction, and planting.

TO REALITY

You may work directly with a contractor, or your landscape architect or designer may select and supervise the contractor. In either scenario, the contractor will submit a bid, either as a lump sum or as a figure based on the estimated time and materials. The latter approach allows more modifications during construction.

Finally, there are professionals who work primarily with plants. *Horticulturists* are trained in the selection and care of garden plants; many have some design training as well. If you are merely looking for plants to complete a design, you can work with a horticulturist. *Arborists* are trained in the care of trees and other woody plants; although not usually able to prepare a design for your garden, they can guide you in the handling of existing trees on your site, identifying healthy ones and those needing pruning, shaping, or removal. Local nurseries may also offer design services and may have talented designers on their staffs; but beware of free design services, as the designer may be obligated to work only with plants and other materials offered by the nursery employer.

Finding the right professional

Begin by identifying the professional services you need. Be realistic in assessing the amount of work you want to do yourself. Collect names from friends and neighbors—even if it means knocking on doors when you spot a good design. Then call each of the designers or contractors whose work you like to set up an interview either at your home (there may be an hourly fee for this) or at their offices (often free). Inquire about the nature of their work, their workload, and their fees. Most important, ask for references—other residential clients whose gardens may give you an idea of the range and quality of the designer's work or the caliber of the contractor's construction. Above all, you must feel a rapport between yourself and the professional; you will be working closely on the design and installation of your garden and need someone with whom you feel comfortable.

When the designer of your choice makes the first visit to your site, use the time wisely. Prepare in advance a list of wishes, needs, and problems that must be dealt with in the design, making sure everyone in the household has had a chance to participate in this step. Give serious consideration to your budget and your time schedule. When a design is complete, meet with the contractor and the designer to make certain that the contractor understands the design and is comfortable working with the materials proposed.

To protect yourself from any surprises, be sure to request a contract from any professionals you hire. This legal agreement should spell out the services to be provided, the schedule to be followed, and the fees to be charged.

Computer-aided Design

Of the several dozen landscape CD-ROMs and software programs currently on the market, most are for Windows-compatible computers and are similar in format: you must first electronically render your site by means of the program's computer-aided drafting tools, then you must experiment with the placement of structures, plants, and accessories.

Some programs allow you to work from a scanned image of your property; others require you to position shapes to create an electronic design. Some programs can manipulate elements, such as slopes, or provide a three-dimensional view of the design.

Once the plan is accurate and to scale, you can start to place various elements in the digital landscape. Although

many programs offer choices such as perennials and annuals, trees and lawns, and even special effects such as lighting, shade patterns, growth rates, or seasonal changes, none offer extensive databases of plants. Some allow you to print out your final plans to show to a landscape or nursery professional.

Landscape programs can be fun to play with, but they can't give you good design advice. The best electronic garden design tool may be a plant encyclopedia (such as the Sunset Western Garden CD-ROM, *inset) that helps you select plants for your garden based on specific search criteria, such as flower color, bloom time, growing conditions, or regional adaptability.*

THE DESIGN MOCK-UP

Whether you have completed the design of your garden yourself or have in hand a professionally rendered landscape plan, the next step is to translate the design to your property. If you are having difficulty visualizing the finished garden or can't quite decide on the specifics of certain elements, you may wish to mock up the design on your property. Seeing an approximation of the layout on site in the form of stakes, strings, and markings will help you to determine the exact dimensions necessary for some features, such as decks, terraces, and walks. Even if you feel your paper plan is final, be prepared to make some adjustments as you lay out the design on site until the arrangement of spaces and elements feels just right.

There are a variety of methods for staking out your design. Choose the one that works best for your situation; the choice will be likely to depend on which features predominate—straight

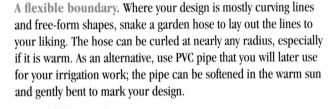

A flexible boundary. Where your design is mostly curving lines and free-form shapes, snake a garden hose to lay out the lines to your liking. The hose can be curled at nearly any radius, especially if it is warm. As an alternative, use PVC pipe that you will later use for your irrigation work; the pipe can be softened in the warm sun and gently bent to mark your design.

Colored powder. Limestone or gypsum, common soil amendments, can be used to lay out free-form designs such as the outlines of beds and borders. Powdered chalk of various colors is useful if you have overlapping elements. Measure corner or end points, then dribble a line of powder along the outlines. To make changes, simply turn the powder into the soil and start again.

lines or curving lines, geometric forms or free forms. Use materials that you have on hand or that can be found at your local hardware store or garden center, such as bamboo or wooden stakes, kite string, clothesline or garden hose, powdered gypsum, lime, or even flour.

Live with your design layout for a few days before making any final decisions or beginning construction. Walk through or sit in your "mock garden" several times to be sure that it provides you with the spaces you need, circulation paths that are comfortable, and garden areas that suit your interests and the time you have to spend maintaining them. When you are ready to begin construction, mock-up techniques will also come in handy. Staking is often used to mark an area of concrete to be poured; colored powder can show the true boundaries of planting areas in borders and beds, and a hose snaked along a pathway can help guide the placement of pavers or bricks.

Strings and stakes. For straight or gently curved lines, mark each corner with a short stake and connect them with strings to outline paving areas, deck construction, pathways, hedges, and planting beds; use taller stakes to mark fences and walls. Then test how they affect traffic circulation through the garden and whether they block any important access points or views.

A mock garden. Tall stakes can stand in for trees or elements like fountains, sculpture, or posts for overhead construction. Large pieces of cardboard on the ground can indicate paving or decks; cardboard can represent fences and walls. Note any shadows cast by your planned vertical barriers. The neighbors may stare, but you will get a much better sense of how your design is shaping up.

A

B

REAL-LIFE DESIGN

Visiting Eric and Mary Holdeman's garden in Puyallup, Washington, is like stepping into a forest meadow. Towering fir, spruce, and cedar trees surround the garden, making it private and shady. Across the lower portion of the lawn, a perennial bed sends up blooms throughout the seasons. Tidy vegetable beds hug the house just outside the back door. Colorful shrubs clamber up a trellis near the front door.

None of this was in place when the Holdemans moved into their house. "This was my first true attempt at building a garden from scratch," says Eric Holdeman. "All top soil (if any) was gone, and we had lots of rocks."

Before starting the project, Eric drew a rough diagram of the site, then paid a local nursery $150 for a customized list of plants and combinations that worked well in the Northwest. "That [plan] gave me a starting point," he says. "A little professional help goes a long way." Then the Holdemans set a few basic goals: to build brick-on-sand walkways, to plant trees and a perennial bed, and to continue with square-foot gardening (growing vegetables in small spaces).

Bare dirt to shady retreat

Eric, Mary, and their two children devoted the first year to installing the garden's "bones"—the brick paths, rock walls along the hill in the back, and areas of grassy lawn. These projects consumed the family's first summer in Puyallup. "For the kids, 'How I Spent My Summer Vacation' was more like 'How I Helped Dad with the Yard,'" notes Eric. "This was our Disneyland."

The next year, the Holdemans planted perennials, a vegetable garden near the house, and more trees. Then came the refinements: a rockery, an arbor, and stairs next to the rock wall, low-voltage lighting, a garden bench, and a sundial.

Even now, the garden continues to evolve. "I spend a lot of time just looking around the garden from different angles," Eric says. "Figuring out what to tackle next is both a challenge and a joy."

The initial work cost several thousand dollars, including bricks for the walkways, stones for the rock wall, and plants. The Holdemans' best advice to those who want to begin from scratch? "Don't be afraid to make mistakes. If a plant is not working in one place, dig it out and move it."

Eric lays bricks on the side-yard path.

Mary cuts the bricks with a brick saw.

E

A. South side yard, before. Viewed from the back of the house, the porch steps lead to an empty side yard filled with possibilities. The proximity of the side yard to the kitchen calls for easy access to vegetable beds. Some color is needed to brighten the area beyond the porch.

B. South side yard, after. Seen from the front, the side yard is now filled with plants that are surrounded with mulch. Concrete stepping-stones provide a temporary walkway, meeting up with the brick path that leads to the back of the house.

C. Backyard, before. By the end of the first year, this is what the walks and back flower border looked like. First, the Holdemans installed a brick-on-sand walkway. The rock retaining wall at the base of the sloping backyard required almost 10 tons of rocks to complete. A lawn was installed on the yard for temporary cover before the Holdemans determined what plants would grow best in the garden. Spring-blooming bulbs were the only plants put in the ground at this point.

D–E. Backyard, after. Ferns, bulbs, evergreen shrubs, and perennials combine in a long, narrow border above the rock retaining wall, where they offer a succession of blooms throughout the year. Beyond the back lawn, shrubs and more perennials create a shady woodland garden beneath tall trees. Where side yard meets backyard a sun dial, one of the later additions in the yard, rises from surrounding leafy carpet bugle (*Ajuga reptans*).

*A gardener's work is never done. Eric Holdeman knew he wanted this second side yard to contain a lot of plants, but it took time to figure out what was likely to thrive in the shade. Rather than leave the yard unplanted (**F**), he continued the brick path from backyard to front (**G**) and planted a temporary lawn (**H**). The following year, he uprooted large patches of grass to plant flowers and ground covers, continuing until the plants fully replaced the lawn (**I**).*

GARDENS OF THE WEST

The West sets the stage for our gardens. Its mountains and deserts, seasides and valleys have long supplied the backdrops for our plantings. Lately, however, we've begun turning to these western lands—rather than places east of the Continental Divide—for design inspiration. From Seattle to San Diego and Tucson to Denver, regional garden styles are emerging, as western gardenmakers recognize the futility of growing tropicals where conifers and deciduous trees reign, or of carpeting the desert with lawn.

No longer jarringly assertive, today's regional gardens echo or blend into the surroundings and reflect their region's heritage, be it Spanish, Asian, or Native American. Whether they mimic plant communities that grow on nearby hills, along earthquake faults, or in tidal pools edging the Pacific, the gardens pictured on the following pages are supremely adapted to the land and the climate that nurtures them. They touch the land lightly.

THE PACIFIC NORTHWEST

The natural power of the Northwest molds and guides the Northwest garden. Up here, nature doesn't serve us, we serve nature.

—Robert Chittock, Seattle

The Northwest that I love is vast and mighty—a wildly diverse stretch of land that includes Washington, Oregon, Idaho, Montana, British Columbia, and Alaska. Grandeur defines it. Jagged mountains nudge wild coastlines; narrow, wooded valleys turn broad and pastoral as they approach the sea. Around Puget Sound, tidal flats give way to sand dunes covered with wispy grasses or cliffs cloaked with myriad ferns and conifers. East of the Cascades, vast stretches of rocky desert are dotted with sage and sprinkled with wildflowers.

Clearly, dramatic terrain dominates this region. It dazzles the eyes and sparks the mind. But when it comes to gardening and landscaping, three other elements have conspired to produce a distinct garden style: the climate, the plants, and the people.

Two climates influence Northwest landscaping: moist and mild west of the Cascade Range, dry and harsh on the east side. On both sides of the Cascades you'll find gardeners who tinker with nature, imitating the landscape on the other side. In Portland, Seattle, Victoria, and Vancouver, gardeners treasure their sages, alliums, and sedums, and turn sunny slopes into quick-draining micro-deserts. In Spokane and Boise, many gardeners won't do without shade beds, fern collections, moss, and rock.

Nearly any kind of plant can flourish in the gentle climate west of the mountains. Native plants admired around the world thrive in our wetlands, forests, meadows, and high alpine country. Conifers such as cedar and Sitka spruce carpet the land. Beneath them, thick scrambles of devil's club, huckleberry, salal, or rhododendron are shaded here and there by stands of alder or vine maple.

Perhaps because forests cloak much of the Northwest, gardeners here seem unafraid of big plants. Drive through any neighborhood and you'll find enormous trees such as Douglas firs and bigleaf maples dwarfing houses. Dense, mixed plantings grow among these trees; vines scramble up their trunks and thrive in the shade of their great canopies.

Northwest gardeners have a special relationship with green—whether lime green, emerald green, or blue-green. Often, especially in cold weather, some of our greens take on a coppery or purplish blush. Put a collection of greens against one of our gray winter skies or next to a wet cobalt blue or charcoal-colored rock and the effect is striking.

In spring, our rhododendrons bloom gloriously. In fall, the hills are aflame with gold from maples and birches. And in winter, deciduous trees etch the leaden sky with black lines. Brilliant berries sparkle with dew, bark glistens, and witch hazel graces us with a sprinkling of sweetly fragrant

yellow flowers. Strangely, it's in my winter garden—among the conifers and naked shrubs and winter fruits bright with raindrops—that I often feel closest to nature.

Two cultures, English and Japanese, also influence Northwest garden style. Walk through urban Portland, Seattle, or Vancouver in summer and there's no denying the British presence. Hedges form leafy backdrops for tall lilies and colorful perennials. Roses climb walls, and summer annuals spill from pots in devil-may-care combinations.

The Japanese influence reveals itself in our use of wood and stones, in our careful choices of texture and color, in the way we use pines and other conifers, and in the way we prune broad-leafed evergreens to better see their structure.

What other elements make the Northwest style? I can't say whether it's a weathered cedar fence, a dwarf rhododendron sprawling over a rock, a palette of greens meandering down a slope, or a mass of camellia blooms on a shrub framed by a pair of powerful fir trunks. But when I'm in a true Northwest garden, I know it—as surely as I know the smell of rain.

—*Steven R. Lorton, Seattle*

THE DELL
Rhododendrons abound

The grand dames of the Northwest landscape take center stage in this enchanting garden near Bellevue, Washington. The woodland garden on the eastern shore of Lake Washington is the perfect setting for rhododendrons of all kinds. In spring, lightly ruffled blossoms in colors ranging from creamy white to yellow and red bring alive the softly textured background of green foliage.

Owners Ned and Jean Brockenbrough created the garden to show their rhododendrons and azaleas to best advantage. They consider it a work in progress, and for good reason. Ned hybridizes and produces many varieties of rhododendrons each year, and he's always eager to try out his ready supply of seedlings. If a plant doesn't perform well in a new setting, there's always an understudy waiting in the wings.

Ned's test garden is behind the house; the lake-facing front yard is the showplace. There the Brockenbroughs blend rhododendrons with dogwoods, ferns, and deciduous azaleas, whose framework of branches adds winter interest between evergreen plants.

Ned trims bottom branches from some of the rhododendrons so he can grow anemones, dwarf kinnikinnick, and maidenhair ferns beneath them.

ABOVE Blooming mounds of white rhododendrons (including *R. yakushimanum* and *R. mucronatum* 'Sekidera') flank the steps and terrace.

ABOVE RIGHT The test garden blooms in a carnival of color. 'Unique' rhododendron, native western red cedar, and native hemlock border the greenhouse.

RIGHT Rhododendrons 'Pink Pearl' and 'Beauty of Littleworth' with pink dogwood brighten the garden in spring behind low-growing azaleas. Sword ferns and lily-of-the-valley grow among boulders.

Acer palmatum 'Dissectum'

AFLAME IN AUTUMN
Japanese maples are living sculptures

Each fall, when the Japanese maples in this waterfront garden near Gig Harbor, Washington, turn red, orange, yellow, and plum, they create brilliant backdrops for the owners' permanent collection of garden art. More than 25 sculptures—of wood, metal, glass, ceramic, stone, and even neon—rise among boulders or atop mossy knolls. The maples themselves are carefully positioned to show off their shapely branches.

Setting off both maples and art are ground covers such as *Ajuga reptans* 'Purpurea', silvery woolly thyme, and bright chartreuse Scotch moss. All add soft textures between rivers of smooth stone.

Nature helped determine the garden's design. Severe storms one winter devastated what had been a traditional landscape of lawns and shrubs. Torrential rains brought water, rocks, and soil cascading through the property from the slopes behind it.

Surveying the damage, the owners decided to use the pattern laid down by the storm as the starting point for a new landscape plan. Additional rock was trucked in, and carefully controlled ground covers replaced lawns.

Today, the maples are placed and pruned so they'll show to best advantage. They thrive in filtered sunlight in the shadow of towering Douglas firs and cedars that form the boundaries of the garden.

ABOVE Red Japanese maple flames like a bonfire in the light shade of Douglas firs.

LEFT The venerable Japanese maple 'Beni Shidare' and the smaller 'Crimson Queen' share a moss-carpeted knoll.

TAPESTRY OF GREENS
For a plant collector

In many "eclectic" gardens, a seemingly artful mix of plants often devolves into a jumble. But in his Portland garden, Dan Heims has created a blend of colors and textures that keeps its shape year after year.

How does Heims orchestrate his plantings so well? He masses plants of roughly the same size. On the perimeter of the site, for example, flowers and big-leafed perennials conceal a roadside drainage ditch. Japanese maples screen out the traffic. Inside this miniforest, hostas and other shade lovers carpet the forest floor while clematis and roses clamber along deck rails and up trellises. During the warm months, a red banana plant rises above it all.

To keep his garden in balance, Heims doesn't put "bully" plants—aggressive growers—beside "wimpy" plants. He also keeps his options open. "Every garden is an unending story," he says. "You just keep adding chapters."

BELOW LEFT Shrubs and trees of different heights create leafy privacy screens that block the outside world. The fine, ferny foliage of Japanese maples contrasts with bold hosta leaves.

LEFT Foliage in various shades of green and red creates a rich tapestry. In the foreground, hostas spread their oval leaves among ferns and annuals. In the background, rare purple *Cordyline indivisa* fans out its grasslike leaves.

ABOVE Like a clearing in the woods, the gently curving lawn is ringed with tall Japanese maples and an understory of hostas in various colors and leaf markings. The foliage of the trees has a "cathedral window" look, especially when sunlight shines through it.

A "WILD" BEACH
On Puget Sound

View gardens are tough to design: they have to complement the surrounding scenery without blocking or overpowering it. To make those principles work in a garden on the south end of Puget Sound's Maury Island, designer Tim Holtschlag looked to nature. Taking a cue from the low vegetation that covers seaside dunes, he mixed and matched dozens of grasses, perennials, and shrubs to get the tapestry of texture and color you see here.

Owners Pat and Bob Morgan couldn't be more pleased. Beyond the garden's all-season appeal, it meets their low-maintenance mandate. There's almost no watering, weeding, or fertilizing to do, and no lawn to mow.

FACING PAGE A weather-bleached wooden boardwalk zigzags from house toward beach through mounds of cotoneaster, yellow cinquefoil, 'Silver Brocade' dusty miller, Russian sage, and Siberian iris.

LEFT Ornamental grasses, mounding shrubs, and rock mulch visually tie this garden to its surroundings.

BELOW Tucked behind a windmill palm, leatherleaf sedge, and bursts of blue oat grass, a small pool adds interest. Beyond, the contrasting leaves and colors of cinquefoil, Siberian iris, *Artemisia* 'Powis Castle', butterfly bush, and Spanish broom texture the landscape.

BELOW LEFT Misty lavender Russian sage tones down cinquefoil's bold yellow blooms.

Most of the plants Holtschlag chose are naturally drought-tolerant, so they need help from overhead sprinklers only in the driest weather. For weed control, Holtschlag laid landscape fabric between plants, hiding it under a layer of gravel and rock. The rock also acts as a water-conserving natural mulch.

Plants get a dose of slow-release fertilizer at planting time and an occasional scattering of fertilizer after that. The garden's only serious maintenance comes during spring and fall prunings, and when perennials are divided every few years.

A Cottage Garden
With Northwest flavor

The beauty of this cottage garden in Seaview, Washington, is its casual elegance, profusion of blooms, and rich, continuous color. Well-placed furnishings and garden art complement the effect.

Designed to yield cutting flowers for indoor and patio arrangements, the garden includes a good showing of perennials, bulbs, and grasses. Foxglove, lupine, monkshood, and old-fashioned roses bloom among shrubs that provide abundant foliage texture.

Every month brings brightly colored blooms, starting in January with early flowering bulbs, continuing through spring and summer with foxgloves and roses, and closing the year with asters and feverfew.

Owner Dale Brous attributes her garden's success to "good bones"—a solid design structure that keeps complementary plants in steady bloom. Now that this structure is set, Brous lets nature reseed plants for her. "If it looks reasonable, I leave it," she says. "If not, I pull it out and move it." Regular maintenance keeps Brous's garden neat in winter and tidy in spring.

Other keys to success include overplanting to discourage weeds, and mixing plant heights for visual interest.

FACING PAGE Shasta daisies, foxgloves, Russell lupines, and an old-fashioned apothecary rose *(Rosa gallica* 'Officinalis') demonstrate the wisdom of mixed-height planting.

LEFT Window boxes overflowing with violas and pots bursting with scented geraniums and petunias brighten this back porch. A decorative birdhouse and catnip-filled urn make whimsical porch-fellows.

BELOW A bent-twig love seat backed by lilac bushes, a lady fern *(Athyrium filix-femina)*, and a lattice-supported climbing red rose create a cozy garden setting. A miniature rose, potted geranium, and monkshood add bright accents of pink and purplish red.

YEAR-ROUND SPLENDOR
In the Pacific Northwest

With a bit of luck and a lot of planning, a garden should look as pleasing in winter as it does in summer. Bark, foliage, conifers, the sculptural forms of leafless trees, and frost-browned grasses—all, if

used well, can spice a winter landscape. Yet it's rare to find all these elements harmonizing in a single garden as they do in this one in Woodinville, Washington, belonging to landscape designer Terry Welch.

Handsome plantings stand out against rich backgrounds: swaths of lawn and water, stands of dark green western hemlock, a screen of alders that's rich green in summer, tawny and bare in winter. Broad-leafed evergreens are ever present.

Upon this canvas Welch put bold strokes of color, grouping several plants of the same species for visual impact. For its brilliant white bark, *Betula jacquemontii* grows in groves. Along the pond in winter, waves of gold and crimson are produced by yellowtwig and redtwig dogwoods. Near the pond in spring, rhododendrons and azaleas erupt in their own brilliant yellows and reds.

ABOVE All leafed out in spring and summer, dogwoods, junipers, and birches stand out against blue water and tall Douglas firs. Come winter, they supply beautiful colors and textures.

ABOVE RIGHT A sheltered bell and weathered fences give this section of the garden a Japanese look.

FAR RIGHT Weeping copper beeches *(Fagus sylvatica* 'Purpurea Pendula') and Japanese maples are living sculptures in a wide bed before tall Douglas firs. Blue-flowered *Lithodora diffusa* grows in front.

RIGHT Mossy vine maple branches arch over longleaf *Mahonia nervosa* and three kinds of ferns (deer, sword, and lady) in a garden corner that mimics a Northwest rain forest.

ABOVE Yellow flowers of Exbury azaleas light the path in spring beside *Pinus contorta*.

RIGHT Bright deciduous azaleas flame like fire against the serene backdrop of a mirror-smooth pond and a Japanese-style pavilion.

BELOW Low-growing rhododendrons, crowned with spring blooms, edge a small pond and some smooth, bluish boulders.

GARDEN ROOMS
Offer quiet corners

Azalea

When Bill Overholt describes his garden in Seattle, "cool and calming" are the first words out of his mouth. White flowers and furnishings accent an oasis of green, designed by landscape architect Robert Chittock. "I need to arrive home, shut the gate behind me, and enter a restful world," Overholt says.

For his summer whites, Overholt turns to flowering perennials. Billowy masses of white geraniums fill the sunny spots; white impatiens form icy sheets in shady areas. In spring, white azaleas bloom in cool dollops and snowy mounds. The flowers, the furniture, and the dense green background of boxwood and clipped holly create a cool, pristine look even on the sultriest days.

Manicured hedges create distinct garden "rooms," with plants of various heights giving them the lushness of a forest. Tree branches dip from above while plantings atop boxes and pedestals reach from below.

INSET A potted Japanese maple crowns multilevel plantings of white impatiens, hosta, and a small-leafed ivy *(Hedera helix* 'Hahn's Self Branching'). Clipped Wilson holly trees and a wisteria-covered trellis add two more tiers of vertical accents.

RIGHT Trimmed Japanese boxwood hedges, an Italianate birdbath, and formal garden furniture refine this shady sitting area, which was once an ordinary patio.

ABOVE Passing clouds play across the mirrored surface of a glass gazing ball. Sun-loving plants such as marigolds and marguerites surround spiky New Zealand flax.

RIGHT In fall, ivies and euonymus are enlivened by bright chrysanthemums. Beyond the flagpole, Mount Rainier hovers above the horizon.

A PLACE IN THE SUN
Bringing a rooftop down to earth

On his deck overlooking Seattle's Pike Place Market, John Fikkan has orchestrated an ever-changing show of blossom and foliage, color and texture that underlines the dramatic skyline beyond. In this tiny space (just 8 feet wide by 10 feet long), he has artfully arranged plantings in containers to give the deck the depth of an in-ground garden.

In summer, a New Zealand flax *(Phormium tenax)* anchors the composition. To this foundation Fikkan adds fillers chosen for their ease of care and long bloom periods—geraniums, impatiens, lobelia, marguerites, marigolds, petunias, zinnias, and dwarf sunflowers come out in full force.

Come fall and winter, Fikkan uses flowering cabbage and kale, chrysanthemums, and sometimes small conifers—dressed up at holiday time. When spring arrives, cyclamen, primroses, and bulbs take center stage, accented by forsythia and other spring-blooming shrubs.

BORROWING NATURE
Natives and friends

Northwest natives pair with exotics in this woodland garden in Shoreline, Washington. The property is home to native plants such as kinnikinnick, Oregon grape, and mountain hemlock, as well as imports such as Chinese witch hazel, Armenian oak, and Mediterranean cyclamen.

Depending solely on Northwest natives throughout the year would make a garden drab indeed, says owner Mareen Kruckeberg, who designed the garden and tends it with her husband, Arthur, an expert in Northwest native plants.

Most of the exotic plants are grown from seed—including one oak that Mareen started from an acorn. Seeds come from countries with climates similar to that of the Northwest.

The Kruckebergs select plants that blend well based on texture, color, form, and growing requirements. Whether native or exotic, the occupants of this world-in-a-garden get along beautifully. Planted in softly curving borders that edge the lawn, they mingle in the dappled shade of tall trees.

ABOVE Western columbines *(Aquilegia formosa)* bring lacy foliage, a fairylike quality, and hummingbirds to this Northwest garden.

RIGHT Northwest natives and old-world exotics encircle a teak bench to create a quiet garden room. Camellia 'J. C. Williams', Chinese witch hazel *(Hamamelis mollis),* and rhododendron blooms add soft color in the background. All told, the garden encompasses the elements of a mature forested landscape, complete with understory, midstory, and canopy.

INSET, LEFT Fringe-cups, another native, send up urn-shaped flowers on tall stems.

INSET, RIGHT False lily-of-the-valley *(Maianthemum dilatatum)* makes an attractive woodland ground cover. White spring flowers give way to red summer berries.

CALIFORNIA

*I like gardens that connect their owners with the
real world of earth, weather, seasons, and change.*
—Chris Jacobson, San Francisco

Throughout the history of gardening, regional styles of landscaping have arisen from a sense of place—from the land and its climate and from the people and the plants that inhabit it. But how can one capture the essence of these factors in a state as vast and varied as California? The name alone stirs a host of conflicting images: snow-topped mountains and endless beaches; wilderness and movie sets; desert scrub and redwood groves; a splash of California poppies in a neglected vacant lot.

California's 800-mile length spans some 10 degrees of latitude, with the largest number of microclimates of any state. Scores of native plants are adapted to its various zones. As for the people—of all states in the union, California is the most culturally diverse. Could anyone boil down the contrasts and contradictions of such a place and create for it a definable landscape style?

Hardly. Nevertheless, 200 years ago it almost happened.

California's first gardeners were Franciscan friars who brought with them from their homeland in southern Spain a Mediterranean garden style with Moorish influences—the fountain-centered patio, axial paths, and water-saving methods of irrigation. They imported plants, such as the citrus tree, date palm, pepper tree, and olive, all well adapted to the California climate. Even today, gardens that hark back to these elements tie us to California's history, giving us a satisfying sense of place.

By the mid-20th century, when I came to California, the state's Spanish landscape had been largely erased by an influx of new residents who hailed from climates with more rainfall and who brought with them the plants of their homelands. Imported water was plentiful and inexpensive, so gardeners used it with abandon. The result was bewildering. In one city block I discovered English, Italian, Moorish, and Japanese gardens rubbing elbows with a Hawaiian jungle. Lawns were immense. West Los Angeles seemed like a gigantic stage set. I was a transplant, too. I loved lush meadows, woods, and running streams, but instinct told me this place cried out for a different approach. Only when I climbed the fire road into the chaparral did I sense reality.

Now as we enter the new millennium, gardeners are searching for ways to live in harmony with the land. A series of tragedies—droughts, fires, earthquakes—combined with water restrictions have made us reconsider priorities and learn to appreciate our state for what much of it really is—a very dry place. It's not all desert, however. Only the areas east of the mountains are truly deserts. The earliest explorers traveling on foot through Southern California's coastal valleys described a verdant land. They marveled at large groves of oaks, wild roses growing in profusion, green meadows of native bunchgrass, and vast fields of lupine and other wildflowers still blooming in July.

Today's savvy gardeners use plants adapted to dry summers and winter rains to re-create pieces of this lush landscape. Cultural diversity continues to produce an invigorating mix of garden designs, but all are now unified by a common aim: to save our resources. Some gardeners still design English-style borders or even jungles, but with drought-tolerant plants. Others raise organic vegetables irrigated with drip systems in raised beds. I know a garden where native plants use the surrounding hills as a backdrop, and many where native plants are combined with others from similar climates around the world.

Lawns are shrinking or disappearing altogether, replaced by flowers. Patios are expanding to provide more space for the outdoor lifestyle that's synonymous with California. Softly spilling fountains attract birds and provide a water element so necessary to the human psyche— and they also mask urban noise. Disasters that at first seemed to be unmitigated tragedies have prompted a greater awareness of California's power and spirit. Today's gardeners are recapturing the romance that's native to this state.

—Pat Welsh, Del Mar, California

CALIFORNIA CASUAL
Water soothes the soul

California's early mission courtyards inspired the design of this multilevel garden in Saratoga. Like its predecessors, this peaceful retreat adapts well to the dry but ocean-tempered climate. Native and Mediterranean plants mingle in rock-edged raised beds. There is no lawn. Water is used judiciously—just enough to calm the soul. It animates the garden with trickling sounds as it spills from a fountain into a shallow, rock-lined "rill" (sunken irrigation ditch). From there it rushes into a pond that

was formerly an in-ground spa.

Broad paths of permeable paving—flagstone and decomposed granite—replaced an old concrete patio. The concrete was recycled to form walls for the raised beds. A cap of flagstone and a veneer of stacked rocks mask the concrete to finish the raised beds.

To blend new flora with established plantings—holly-leaf cherries, maytens, and oleanders—San Francisco garden designer Chris Jacobson chose a palette of drought-tolerant plants: daylilies, rosemary, fortnight lilies, lavender, ornamental grasses, succulents, and verbena. Lush ferns thrive in shady pockets. In summer, golden angel's trumpet flowers fill the air with fragrance. To save water, all plants are irrigated with a drip system.

ABOVE Framed by a blue-stained gate, a rock-edged raised bed borders a meandering path of decomposed granite.

RIGHT Spa-turned-pond nestles in a private pocket of the garden. Small rocks, flagstone, and boulders add textural interest and blend with the muted tones of the lavender and grasses.

FAR LEFT Bog in a pot: tall, sculptural horsetails thrust from an antique terracotta pot at the edge of the pond.

LEFT Water cascades from an overturned pot, then flows to a sunken pond and recirculates through a filter hidden behind shrubbery.

FAR LEFT, BELOW Sturdy but delicate-looking native giant chain ferns highlight border plantings that include Japanese maple, mondo grass, and *Pennisetum setaceum* 'Rubrum'.

NEAR LEFT, BELOW Garden paths flow around a raised bed planted with feathery mayten trees, squat mugho pines, silvery lamb's ears, and spiky fortnight lilies.

BELOW Fragrant angel's trumpet adds color to a raised bed. The flagstone cap on the wall serves as a garden bench.

MEDITERRANEAN LIVING
In an urban Eden

Mediterranean gardens often have two personalities. The side presented to the public is reserved and restrained. But the private side—hidden behind walls and seen only by family and friends—is rich, sensual, and luxurious. The garden designed for this Spanish Mission house in North Hollywood, by landscape architect Jerry Williams, exhibits this attractive double nature.

The front garden, seen by motorists and pedestrians, is pleasant but deliberately low-key. Plants are soft and subtle in tone, durable in disposition, and Mediterranean in origin—lavender, olive, rosemary, sea lavender, and society garlic. Blue-greens and silver-grays predominate. Flowers are few. Watering and maintenance are minimal.

But step inside the garden at the rear of the property, and you step into another world. Plants are boldly textured, brightly colored, and tropical in flavor. Foliage tones shift toward emeralds and limes. Rich fragrances perfume the air and the burble of running water soothes the spirit.

Such dual-personality gardening makes perfect sense in an urban environment, says Williams. Save the splash—and the high maintenance—for the private areas you really use.

ABOVE RIGHT What the world sees is low-maintenance Mediterranean. A soothing palette of silvers, blues, and grays complements this Spanish-style house on a small city lot.

RIGHT High walls protect this backyard oasis from public view. King and queen palms add texture; flowers such as angel's trumpet add fragrance and color. Concrete triangles lead to a pond, where a small stone cherub sits in the shade of Australian tree ferns *(Cyathea cooperi)*.

ALL SHOOK UP
Inspired by geology

Slips and folds of land along earthquake faults inspired this garden in El Cerrito. "California has a folded and faulted landscape," explains owner and designer Jana Olson Drobinsky. "As two tectonic plates collide, rocks are tipped up and the earth wrinkles. I wanted my garden to be a joke on California geology, so I created California geology in miniature."

The central focus of Olson Drobinsky's garden is a large raised bed surrounded by a quirky mix of "found" objects, all precisely arranged to appear twisted and distorted as if pushed from the depths. In one corner of the raised bed, bricks, pipes, and bottles mimic a newly formed rock outcropping. Small- and medium-scale plants such as *Sedum oreganum* and *Sesleria caerulea* spill from cracks and crevices.

In another section, an artful jumble of peach-colored concrete, pale bricks, rocks, and flagstone houses a well-established collection of spreading and tumbling plants. Yellow yarrow, orange monkey flower, orange geum, and mat-forming *Scleranthus biflorus* and *S. iniflorus* grow in and around the outcrop.

The lower garden is devoted to a red fescue meadow surrounded by a "chaparral" landscape planted with English lavender, Santa Cruz Island buckwheat, sunflowers, tufted hair grass, and *Verbena bonariensis*. Steel manhole covers from a supplier of recycled materials serve as pavers.

Olson Drobinsky started with a blank slate, developing the garden from bare soil. Since the yard had a steep slope, a retaining wall was needed to level the

Achillea

upper tier for a vegetable garden. "I had lots of leftover materials from landscaping jobs, so I decided to do something completely different," she says. She even used champagne bottles for their color and shape. "Now I refer to my raised bed as coming from the Hedonizoic Era."

ABOVE Champagne bottles, clay sewer pipes, and bricks in two colors re-create a faultline landscape.

LEFT "Outcrop" is made of bricks and concrete. Ground covers, perennials, and succulents fill the cracks.

ABOVE Old manhole covers make unusual stepping-stones across a "pond" of creeping red fescue. Their patterned surfaces provide texture and traction.

INSET *Sedum oreganum, Sempervivum arachnoideum,* and *Sesleria caerulea* thrive amid ridges of pipes, bricks, and bottles.

RIGHT Inspired by waving grass, this pink-and-purple fence bends and twists behind English lavender and *Verbena bonariensis*.

THE TROPICS
California-style

Warm summer days are especially sweet in a garden such as this one. Its lush appearance belies a surprising hardiness—many of the trees and shrubs that are now mature survived a killing freeze shortly after they were planted.

Bougainvillea

Gerry and Gus Panos of Hillsborough wanted a garden reminiscent of climates they love to visit—the Caribbean, Hawaii, Greece, and Mexico. So landscape designer Michael Postl chose plants that would lend a tropical flavor but still survive Northern California winters.

Specimen plants trucked in from Southern California include agaves, aloes, bougainvillea, cycads, golden goddess and timber bamboo, honey bush, jacaranda, and a variety of palms. Most of the plants require little irrigation. The palms get by with rainfall alone; the jacaranda and cycads are somewhat thirstier.

INSET A Mediterranean fan palm beside the pool creates a striking double effect.

RIGHT Blazing bougainvillea adorns the patio—but this vigorous climber must be kept in check. Easier to care for are the agaves and palms that grace carefully selected spots around the edge of the seating area.

Mimulus aurantiacus

A MEADOW RETREAT
Keeping the city at bay

The pungent perfume of sage, the frequent flashes of birds' wings, the snooze-inducing drone of buzzing insects: this site has all the elements of a chaparral-covered hillside. But, all sensory evidence to the contrary, this rustic garden is right in the heart of urban Los Angeles.

The creator of this illusion is movie director Scott Goldstein. A New York transplant, he fell in love at first sight with the nearby Santa Monica Mountains. So when the corner lot next to his property came up for sale, he bought it, walled it in, and created his own "wilderness" as a buffer between his home and the surrounding city. Having rescued some indigenous oaks and pines from the developers' bulldozers, he planted native perennials and wildflowers beneath each tree, then set down a serpentine path of decomposed granite.

Goldstein says that the simulated wildness of his garden is nearly as good as the real thing. The red-tailed hawk that has taken to hovering over the property in search of ground squirrels seems to agree.

FACING PAGE A mission-inspired fountain in one corner of the garden attracts hummingbirds and other wildlife. The massive boulder under an oak makes an attractive perch for human visitors, as do hickory benches and gazebos scattered throughout the property.

LEFT Late afternoon sun lights up a sea of fragrant sages below a coast live oak. Beyond the rustic hickory gazebo that divides the garden into distinct sections lies a "fantasy meadow" of local sedges and blue grama grass sown yearly with annual wildflowers.

BELOW Sages and lupines form a floral island under a rescued oak. Paths resemble hiking trails in wild chaparral country. Near the gate, the dead stump of a toyon provides a pillar for native clematis and morning glory vines.

EARTHLY SEASCAPE
Taking cues from the deep

Oceanside gardens present practical problems. Plants in them must withstand salt spray and prevailing winds; soil erosion must be curbed to keep landscapes from toppling into the sea. But the aesthetic challenges these sites offer can be even more daunting. What garden could compete with the Pacific?

Wisely, this Newport Beach garden doesn't challenge the scenery; it complements it. Landscape architect and scuba diver Lisa Gimmy has created a property filled with "sea shapes." New Zealand flax resembles kelp, the flower stalks of pride of Madeira take the place of coral branches, and the rosette forms of agaves mimic sea anemones. Even the twin terraces, which follow the outline of the shore, look as if they've been carved by the ocean rather than shaped by man. The colors in the garden—buff terrace stone and melaleuca bark, muted blue-green foliage—echo the natural hues of the shoreline. The total effect is landscaping so at home in its setting that it looks like an underwater garden revealed at low tide.

ABOVE The cozy sandstone terrace provides an ideal site to observe a spectacular view. Pavers are dry-set so that water can reach the soil; woolly thyme grows between them.

INSET Prostrate ceanothus spills over terrace walls like sea spray. In this setting, agaves and aloes look positively aquatic.

RIGHT The red-edged blades of New Zealand flax brighten a sea of pride of Madeira.

INTO THE WOODS
Touching the land lightly

For some lucky westerners—especially those living on or near wild land—nature provides the perfect landscaping. Using existing trees and shrubs as part of the design helps a garden blend seamlessly into the surrounding landscape.

This property, nestled on a hillside above California's Napa Valley, proves how respectful a new garden can be. Landscape architect Jack Chandler started his work well

before house construction began. The area beneath the native oaks and madrones was roped off to protect root zones from damage by heavy equipment. From there, the garden's design called for leaving nature's best features intact. Moss-covered boulders and orange-red madrone bark provide color and texture. The muscular trunks of the native trees provide strong sculptural elements.

To preserve a natural environment, Chandler added gravel walkways. Fallen yellow leaves add color to the forest floor. A few plants were added. Two olive trees frame the doorway in the classic Tuscan style. Boston ivy clings to walls. Rhododendrons contribute spring color.

Germander fills some of the shaded areas. Nothing is planted near the native trees; their roots are easily damaged, and the trees themselves suffer when they receive water intended for new plantings.

ABOVE Moss-covered boulders and native oaks and madrones give this Tuscan-style house a settled, mellow look. The house's soft coral color blends with the surroundings rather than overpowering them.

LEFT View through the arched entryway frames the garden and its comfortable transition to the natural landscape beyond.

COASTAL CHAPARRAL
Blurring the boundaries

No line of demarcation separates this Laguna Beach garden from the wild country around it. The two landscapes blend seamlessly, and that's exactly what owners Gary and Betsy Jenkins wanted. It was the site—above a triangular sweep of chaparral that plunges sharply to the beach—that first attracted them, so they sought a garden that would celebrate its surroundings.

Landscape designer Jeff Powers, a native plant enthusiast, understood their vision. To soften the angular edges of the Jenkinses' starkly modern house, he planted low-care natives such as toyon and artemisia near the foundation. For the transitional area farther from the house, he chose drought-tolerant plants in the blue-green to gray-leafed range to reflect the tones of chaparral. To further blur the line between civilization and wilderness, he minimized hardscaping and used deliberately rough materials such as broken slate.

Though everything in this garden was carefully planned, the human imprint seems slight, as if nature could regain the upper hand at any time. In other words, say the Jenkinses, it's perfect.

ABOVE The plunging slope below the property provides a breathtaking view of the Pacific. But the harsh winds that sweep up this grade are rough on plants. Tough ones, like *Hesperaloe parviflora*, *Romneya coulteri*, and *Leonotis leonurus*, are best for this exposure.

LEFT The arched surface of the slate patio seems to vanish into the brush—especially when viewed from indoors. The trail of switch-backs does the same.

FACING PAGE, TOP A path of broken gray slate links the garden with wild chaparral.

FACING PAGE, BOTTOM A wall of live oaks and silvery *Artemisia arborescens* creates a privacy screen for the site's unsheltered patio. Matlike dymondia fills the gaps between stone slabs; red-flowered *Rosa mutabilis* adds a splash of color.

BORN OF FOG
In a North Coast clearing

Viewed through a veil of coastal fog, this garden in Philo recalls a dreamy scene by Claude Monet. And for owner Virginia Macedo Mitchell, the garden is a dream come true, for it echoes the meadow-and-water gardens found outside her home city, Rio de Janeiro.

In this landscape, orchard, herb garden, ornamental garden, and water meet. Big beds of golden coreopsis and purple coneflower share softly rolling slopes with nut, cherry, olive, pear, and plum trees. Lush grasses and foliage fringe the pond and mimic lowland meadows and bogs. The world above reflects in the pond's still water, spreading shimmery color between the lily pads.

The garden was a goat paddock in a small forest clearing before landscape designers Christopher and Stephanie Tebbutt transformed it. They took their design cues from the natural landforms; the pond was dug at the garden's lowest point.

ABOVE Dark pink flowers of fountainlike fairy wand cloak the pond's banks. Water lilies and tiny yellow water poppies (*Hydrocleys nymphoides*) adorn its surface.

RIGHT Weeping willows, rushes, and water lilies create an Impressionist composition. Giant coast redwoods in the background and poplar-style Chilean willow trees add vertical accents.

LEFT Near the pond, *Phormium tenax*, low-growing *P. colensoi*, and 'Stella d'Oro' daylilies front a background of bamboo and eucalyptus.

THE SOUTHWEST

*What's unique about the Sonoran Desert is
its abundance of native plants, including
trees and large succulents. In desert
gardens, plants should complement such
natives in color, texture, and scale.*

—Carol Shuler, Phoenix

Gardeners newly arrived in the desert sometimes grieve for the plants they can no longer grow, or can grow only with a maximum of effort—apple, camellia, clematis, dahlia, lily, pear. As one failure follows another (gardenias refuse to bloom, zucchinis collapse and die), they may well wonder what sort of place they have come to, what sort of garden it is possible to have.

A wonderful garden, is the answer—but only if they are willing to adapt to the desert instead of fighting it.

Gardening in the Southwest is an act of courage. Temperatures fluctuate widely, rain is unpredictable, and even the briefest storms are ferocious. In the hottest summers, the mercury rises to 110 degrees or more, and leaves of fig and jasmine scorch in the heat. In the coldest winters, when the thermometer drops below 18 degrees, passion flower and bougainvillea vines freeze to the ground, sometimes never to emerge again. Across the desert, annual rainfall varies from a few inches to nine or ten. Winter storms often bring gentle, soaking rains, but summer thunderstorms can rip fronds from palm trees and hammer cornstalks down to the ground.

Gardens that survive climatic hazards could well succumb to the depredations of hungry desert animals. Doves make quick work of broadcast seed. Curve-billed thrashers uproot tender seedlings. Any number of birds peck at ripening tomatoes, figs, grapes, and peaches. Cottontail rabbits nibble anything within reach, not excluding the thorniest rose bushes or the bark of young trees. Even a gardener's prize cactus isn't safe: undeterred by spines and needles, beetle grubs and jackrabbits munch on the succulent stems, and wood rats eat the flowers.

Despite these and other difficulties, desert gardeners are as avid as gardeners anywhere else, perhaps more so. One could argue, after all, that gardens are all the more essential in the desert. Anyone who has driven across the Southwest knows its vast and empty spaces, those wide valleys bordered by smooth blue mountains that are in fact not smooth or blue but brown and rough and uncompromisingly wild. As highway bridges cross one dry streambed after another, even a casual visitor realizes that here the word "river" recalls the past or awaits the future—some other month or year when rain falls in abundance, turning sandy washes into running streams.

It is possible to learn to love this landscape—many of us have, and we would choose to live no place else on earth. But even lovers' eyes become starved for something green and moist. Thus the need for gardens.

Thus the designs for our gardens, too. Where rain is scarce and reservoirs easily overtaxed, gardeners must be water-conscious. More and more, desert gardeners forgo large lawns and big, leafy hedges that demand more in water than they return in pleasure. Instead of looking to Illinois or Oregon for inspiration, desert-adapted gardeners find their model in the desert itself, where native trees and shrubs survive on rainfall alone.

The variety of native plants available in nurseries should hearten gardeners who want to diversify the home landscape. Using natives alone, anyone can create an oasis garden, a butterfly garden, a hummingbird garden, a wildflower garden, a night-flowering garden, even a vegetable garden. Native trees such as desert willow, ironwood, mesquite, and palo verde offer shade in summer and densely flowered canopies in spring. Red- or pink-flowering shrubs such as salvia, chuparosa, fairy duster, and ocotillo draw hummingbirds into the garden. Evening primrose, angel's trumpet, and yucca open their large, white blossoms at night, attracting hawk moths as their pollinators. Native Americans gardened in the desert for millennia  before Anglo-Americans arrived, and the crops they developed—unique kinds of beans, melons, and squash—are delicious and more easily grown than many commercial varieties. In short, there is no need to grieve for the plants that cannot be grown; it's better to rejoice in the abundance of those that can.

—*Janice Emily Bowers, Tucson*

OPEN TO THE DESERT

Like an outpost in the wilderness, this Rancho Mirage, California, garden gives respite from the sun, yet is open to the untamed desert at its edge.

Within the garden, order prevails. Furnishings of cast cement are bold and blocky, planting beds are geometric, and saguaros are planted in lines. But designer Steve Chase preserved the desert aesthetic with colors and textures that blend with the region's sand, stone, and flora.

Farther from the house, a more casual plan applies. Pebble and rock paths lead from manicured areas to the wild-looking landscape beyond.

Though gardening in this wild slice of desert poses unique challenges, it offers rare rewards. Among them are unsurpassed views of the Santa Rosa Mountains, bats sipping nectar from cactus blossoms at dusk, and parched land that bursts into spring green following winter rains.

LEFT Craggy peaks create a majestic backdrop for an outdoor "room" off the living room.

FACING PAGE Softly aglow at dusk, this gazebo contrasts boldly with the landscape beyond. The pyramid of glass blocks creates a focal point at the end of a water channel.

RIGHT Stately saguaros and chollas grow among boulders, mimicking the desert beyond.

RIGHT Pebble and rock paths, flanked by palo verde and cacti, lead from the patio to the wildlike plantings farther from the house. Come spring, the palo verde glows with golden blooms.

BELOW Magenta verbena illuminates the spring garden against a sculptural background of a cactus and boulders.

BELOW RIGHT Contained by poured aggregate paving, cacti grow in a neat row with a rock mulch covering the ground between.

FACING PAGE Like surfacing bubbles, barrel cacti, interspersed with ocotillo in this formal courtyard planting, shape views from inside the house and out.

LIVING AL FRESCO
In the Sonoran Desert

The desert flows effortlessly into this garden in Tucson—through walls designed to pass each other without touching. That's the way the owners wanted it. When they first moved here, they were mesmerized by the stark beauty of the Sonoran Desert, and wanted their garden to preserve the character of its setting.

Landscape designer Paul Serra took advantage of the sloping site by designing three distinct levels. On the top level, the one closest to the house, an outdoor kitchen has everything the owners need to cook complete meals. Flagstone steps lead down to the midlevel pool, which is edged with boulders to give it the look of a natural pond. On the lowest level the desert takes over.

Throughout the garden, *bancos* (bench walls) provide seating for party guests and for quiet contemplation. In one area, the *bancos* are grouped around a firepit that provides a source of warmth on chilly evenings.

ABOVE Palo verde and desert spoon usher in the wild landscape.

LEFT Boulders and desert plants—euphorbia, justicia, verbena, lantana, cycads, and blue *Salvia clevelandii*—give the pool the look of a desert oasis.

Parthenocissus

GLORIOUS GRASSES
Replace a thirsty lawn

O rnamental grasses are clearly the stars of this Santa Fe garden. They contribute alluring textures and colors to a landscape already rich with artful plant combinations.

Designers Tina Rousselot and David Lovro responded to the area's restrictions on garden water by replacing an ever-thirsty lawn and perennial garden with hardy grasses, drought-tolerant plants, and rivers of adobe-colored gravel. Shades of green and silver and accents of red and blue were chosen to complement each other. Beds were heavily mulched with shredded pine bark and outfitted with a drip system.

Rousselot, an experienced oil painter, treated the landscape as a canvas and the plants as a palette. Tapering paths and curving flower beds seem to converge on the horizon, giving the illusion of depth and distance. Plantings of grasses, blue spiraea, lamb's ears, sedum, and yucca on either side of the path create a sense of movement as they blend in garden beds.

ABOVE Raven grass and a border of dwarf fountain grass encircle *Sedum telephium* 'Autumn Joy' and orange-red yarrow blooms. Posts and *vigas* (roof logs) of the portal at right support Virginia creeper and wisteria.

LEFT Lime-colored *Miscanthus sinensis* (left), dark red Japanese blood grass, lavender blue spiraea (right), and magenta-red cosmos frame the gravel path. Borders of silver lamb's ears, artemisia, and 'Rosy Glow' sedum (foreground) unify planting beds.

TAMING NATURE
Along a desert wash

Native plants and subdued colors give this Scottsdale, Arizona, property the look of untamed desert, but in fact it's a carefully cultivated garden. Designer John Suarez planned it to blend with its surroundings.

The garden visually flows from inside the house to the desert. Chocolate flagstone paves interior and exterior floors and paths. Adobe walls snake along the patio, embracing prickly pear, saguaro, barrel cactus, and pots of red geranium in their gentle curves. Pyracantha, the only exotic landscape plant here, spills over the wall, bright with cloud-white flowers in spring. A small ramada shelters a patio dining area and fireplace.

Beyond the wall, native plantings meander along a wash of river rock placed at the garden's lowest point. Small outcroppings of desert plants and well-worn boulders echo the textures and contours of house and patio walls.

ABOVE Potted geraniums splash the patio with bright color. Assorted cacti in the planting pocket are surrounded with a mulch of gold decomposed granite.

INSET, RIGHT The desert sun sparks a ghostly glow in spines of teddy-bear cholla (*Opuntia bigelovii*).

FAR RIGHT Young saguaros rise above boulders beside a wash of river rock. The tallest saguaro was already there when the garden was installed.

EASY ENCHANTMENT
Water wise in Santa Fe

When Santa Fe residents were called upon to cut their water use by 25 percent, Ann Mehaffy redesigned her garden to suit the region's persistent drought. She reduced her full-size vegetable garden to a small corner of the yard, created meandering pathways using crushed Santa Fe brown gravel, and planted unthirsty perennials and trees. Planting areas were mulched with straw, and new soaker hoses replaced the old drip system.

The new design has been so successful that Mehaffy has cut her residential water use by 50 percent. And except for occasionally deadheading spent blooms or moving an errant volunteer or two, her garden is maintenance-free. She also had some fun with the design by incorporating whimsical touches such as a brilliant red gate in a wall of terracotta, an umbrella whose pole appears to float above the ground, and a metal handprint that waves through the windowed door of the vegetable garden.

ABOVE A tranquil "streambed" of gravel meanders around a sitting area toward the red gate. In the foreground flower bed, Shasta daisies, Jupiter's beard, and frothy stipa grass rise behind cosmos, blue spiraea, *Erysimum* 'Bowles Mauve', and Russian sage. A graceful 'Santa Rosa' plum tree grows just behind.

FACING PAGE Pink saponaria blooms (foreground, left), ribbon grass *(Phalaris arundinacea),* red spikes of knotweed, lemon yellow toadflax blooms, and clumps of blue fescue create lively colors and rich textures in the garden. The coyote fence (poles, background) adds to the garden's regional charm.

SOUTHWESTERN COLORS
Paint a geometric theme

I t's a modest little garden," says landscape architect Steve Martino. "But everything in it is very studied and refined. I took all of the things I like and put them into one garden."

The colorful sculptures and walls were inspired by the famous Mexican architect Luis Barragán, the sunken garden by ancient ruins in the Southwest, and the water channel by those used in Moorish architecture.

Martino also wanted to give owner Jay Hawkinson something unexpected. "Jay is an art director and likes offbeat things and colorful geometric forms, like spheres, cubes, and triangles," says Martino. So he used a geometry theme.

The garden is bordered by the walls of a housing development. Martino hid these walls by adding new ones inside them. A low lavender-mauve wall provides extra seating. A narrow channel carries water from a fountain to a pond. A shade structure made of brightly colored fabric shelters the patio.

The garden contains few plants, but each one was placed where its form shows to best advantage. Some of Martino's favorites are *Bauhinia congesta,* brittlebush, Parry's penstemon, prickly pear cactus, quail bush, and *Verbena gooddingii.*

Verbena

ABOVE RIGHT A blue pyramid commands attention in this Phoenix garden.

RIGHT A half-circle pool connects to a water channel that cuts between two walls. The stone ball carries the geometric theme.

FACING PAGE The orange wall provides a vivid foil for agave, verbena, ocotillo, and other desert vegetation beyond.

THE ROCKY MOUNTAINS

A garden is the foreground for a natural landscape. But it should have living spaces, too, and sufficient enclosure. Plants needn't be native to the region, but they should blend with the background.

—Chris Moritz, Bigfork, Montana

The gardens of the Rocky Mountain region are as varied as the land around them. Foothills rise sharply from the plains. Range after range of mountains ripple from east to west, from the desert Southwest to well past the Canadian border. Raging rivers cut through them; placid lakes shimmer among them.

Wherever people garden in this region of contrasts, success is dictated by their understanding of the land—whether plains, foothills, or high mountains. Native plants offer clues. Grasses dominate the semi-arid plains, giving way to mountain forests of spruce, pine, and aspen. Moist upland meadows support a vast array of wildflowers. As peaks rise ever higher, wind and cold make life difficult for trees; they relinquish the slopes to alpine plants of great beauty—columbine, penstemon, and tiny coral bells.

No single garden style predominates. Rocky Mountain gardens draw upon many influences, just as the people here reflect a diversity of backgrounds. There are charming cottage gardens and grand borders; water gardens that reflect the midday sun and woodland gardens that create a refuge from it; rock gardens that showcase tiny alpine jewels amid native stone. At the foot of the Rockies and in high mountain valleys, a history of farming, ranching, mining camps, and ski chalets manifests itself in a rough-hewn garden style. In the foothills, some gardens mimic the grandeur of nature—complete with aspen groves, boulders, and man-made trout streams. In other areas, gardeners reproduce the Victorian architecture that marked the gold- and silver-mining boomtowns.

Rocky Mountain gardeners get the best results when they duplicate the natural habitat of the plants they wish to grow. Conditions are affected not only by elevation, topography, and moisture, but also by exposure and by the trees, walls, and paving that create the garden's microclimates.

Chances for success also increase when plants are either native to the area or come from a similar climate (Turkey or Central Asia, for example). Some plants are so adaptable that they find homes in many different gardens. Herbaceous perennials and bulbs are stars here, because in winter they go dormant and stay insulated beneath protective layers of soil—and, with any luck, snow—when temperatures plunge below zero.

Newcomers to the Rocky Mountain region often complain about the difficulties of gardening here. But just as they learn to equip their cars with snow tires and antifreeze, or to heat and cool their homes efficiently, they learn to work with the conditions in their gardens. It takes time to understand our sizzling days that can turn into bone-chilling nights; winds that intensify as they roar through mountain passes or across the plains; thunderclouds that boil up and threaten to drop hail at almost any time; unpredictable rainfall and unexpected frosts at both ends of the growing season; and growing seasons that are all too short. Even winter snows can't be counted on, either for a profitable ski season or for an insulating blanket that might protect our buried roses.

After a while, despite the obstacles, gardeners begin to see opportunities and advantages. Abundant sunshine promotes strong growth and encourages rapid flowering, even at high elevations. Low humidity keeps pests in check. And our palette of plants is vast and varied.

In each garden, the elements of ever-changing sky, rippling water, natural materials, and our cultural heritage may play a part. Whatever you make it, a Rocky Mountain garden becomes a part of the land—infinitely varied, exciting, and beautiful.

—*Rob Proctor, Denver*

RANCH DRESSING
High-country humor

When Laurie and John McBride bought a ranch near Snowmass, Colorado, their friends and family wondered if this city couple had lost their marbles. But Lost Marbles Ranch is flourishing. A backdrop of deep blue mountains, green pastures, and ever-changing sky sets the stage for a garden of drama and whimsy.

To frame vistas and mark entrances, Laurie's father, John Mack, built charming arbors from branches he gathered. A scarecrow called Camilla guards the produce, aided in the war against visiting deer and elk by family dogs and geese. Groves of quaking aspen highlight the garden but are carefully placed so as not to screen the view from favorite seating areas.

Laurie's love of watercolor painting prompted her initial interest in gardening. She soon began to express her artistry with plants and now favors easy-care perennials like bellflowers, columbine, ox-eye daisies, pansies, poppies, and shrub roses, all of which thrive in the cool temperatures under sunny skies.

ABOVE Columbine glow beneath sheltering aspen groves. Stone patios extend from the house for dining and entertaining.

LEFT An arbor of gathered branches bridges a tiny stream where geese forage among ox-eye daisies.

RIGHT Laurie fenced one of her flower borders with iron headboards salvaged from the barn. "A proper bed deserves a proper headboard," she explains.

ABOVE Pinks, lavender, and herbs thrive with young fruit trees against a wall that offers an enticing view through antique glass. Family pets have the run of the place.

RIGHT Daisies and columbine self-sow beneath quaking aspen.

Aquilegia caerulea

ABOVE A stone wall encircling the vegetable and cutting garden holds heat, an important consideration in a high-altitude setting with a short growing season.

RIGHT A curtain of blue mountains sets off patio plantings of Iceland poppies, geraniums, and double petunias.

INSET A selected palette of gold, white, blue, and pink benefits from a splash of red-orange Asiatic lilies.

CLASSIC BORDERS
Backed by conifers

A framework of curving flower borders defines Bea Taplin's garden, enhancing the lovely site—on a gentle slope in Cherry Hills Village, Colorado—without dominating it. "Taking advantage of the vistas has been my priority," explains Taplin.

Terraces of native stone provide structure and an easy transition between the classic clapboard house and a flax-filled field below. Pine and blue spruce stamp the garden as a Colorado original and enhance the vibrant colonies of stalwart perennials. Pink, yellow, and blue flowers show Taplin's preference for pastels, but dashes of scarlet and orange enliven the mix. The white blossoms of Asiatic lilies, baby's breath, and daisies sparkle amid pale yellow yarrow, royal blue delphinium, and brassy daylilies and ligularia. The emerald lawn—a playground for children and pets—further sets off the colorful borders.

Shrub roses and lilacs screen a vegetable garden from the main garden. Taplin's granddaughter tends her own small plot there, alongside rows of vegetables and flowers for cutting. "I love bouquets in the house," says Taplin, "but the real pleasure is in growing the flowers for them."

ABOVE An inspired combination of Asiatic lilies, baby's breath, and yarrow sparkles in the sylvan setting.

LEFT Contrasting shapes and textures create an air of casual elegance, with spikes of golden ligularia and mullein, blue delphinium, and ethereal pink checkerbloom lining the walk to the pool.

PAINTING WITH PLANTS
In a cabin garden

On the western slope of the Rocky Mountains, just a stone's throw from the Roaring Fork River, Angela and Jeremy Foster have created a high-altitude garden that beautifully reconciles Old World influences and New World realities.

The Fosters, originally from England, cultivate some of the flowers they grew in their homeland, but their landscape owes its chief impact to the rich hues of jewel-toned blooms rather than the soft-toned English ideal. "I look to mountain meadows for inspiration," says Angela. "I love the soft spring flowers, like columbines, but then the meadows here glow with magenta, yellow, and blue." She approaches color as her favorite painter, Henri Matisse, would—balancing bright hues with liberal strokes of blue. "I can't paint," says Angela, "but I feel like I can in my garden."

The lushness of the summer garden belies the harsh winters faced by the Fosters at this nearly 7,000-foot elevation. They rely on a blanket of snow to insulate their plants against freezing temperatures.

ABOVE A venerable apple tree arches over part of the south-facing garden where lavender, lilies, and roses perfume the air.

RIGHT Rustic bowers give the garden surrounding a century-old log cabin an authentic country charm. Native columbine blend easily with European perennials like delphinium, Maltese cross, veronica, and yellow globeflower.

INSET A unique bird feeder holds the foreground; blue spruce complete the scene.

STREETSIDE GARDEN
A plantswoman's paradise

Heads turn as people pass Lauren Springer's yard in Windsor, Colorado. She has turned a drab corner lot surrounding a 1920s Craftsman bungalow into a traffic-stopping garden.

Billowing perennials on the quarter-acre lot suggest a

spontaneous cottage garden, but all the plants (including bulbs and shrubs) are well chosen to work together. Springer calls her efforts "Darwinian" gardening—weeding out plants that can't stand up to harsh conditions. Take her "hellstrips," for example. These sun-baked patches between the sidewalk and the street are hostile to lawns or thirsty flowers. So Springer killed the existing lawn and filled the strips with resilient natives, especially penstemon, as well as exotics that can take the heat, scarce rainfall, periodic hail, and cold winters.

More protected areas close to the house support a broad range of shrubs, perennials, bulbs, and dependable annuals in the deeply worked, compost-enriched loam. Irrigation is minimized to encourage plants to delve deeply for moisture and withstand the rigors of the climate.

ABOVE Hardy perennials and bearded iris thrive in close company.

RIGHT Resilient natives like *Eriogonum umbellatum*, 'Pink Beauty' fleabane, and *Penstemon barbatus* 'Elfin Pink' complement 'Helen Elizabeth' Oriental poppy and the deep maroon leaves of self-sowing red orach (*Atriplex hortensis* 'Rubra').

INSET A profusion of plants replaced a dull and thirsty lawn.

WAVES OF COLOR
In a city grove

F ew gardeners can boast a home-grown forest, but that is what Norma and Wayne Hazen set out to create, over 30 years ago, when they planted their first saplings on a square, 1-acre lot in Wheat Ridge, Colorado. Blue spruce, pine, and oak now make a handsome backdrop for the flowers the Hazens cherish.

Garden designer Tom Peace works with the Hazens to ensure an ever-changing panorama of blooms in the borders as well as in containers on the terraces and lawn. The show starts with early spring daffodils and tulips and concludes with autumn crocus and asters. In between, blooms come in waves of campanulas, daylilies, iris, pinks, and salvias, complemented by columbine, liatris, penstemon, and native poppy mallow.

Throughout the property, the transition from flowers to forest is made seamless by the integration of shrubs, dwarf conifers, and clumps of aspen. Lichen-covered stones add drama. Changes of level and the border's curving shape make the garden look much larger than it is.

RIGHT Containers of flowering maple, purple heart, succulent blue senecio, and bronze-leafed fuchsia typify the fabulous foliage throughout the garden.

ABOVE Perennial beds disappear into the trees. Blue spruce and pine enhance the brilliance of yellow yarrow, magenta dianthus, chartreuse lady's mantle, purple *Salvia nemorosa* 'May Night', and silver lamb's ears.

RIGHT Creamy white *Aruncus dioicus* floats above waves of purple *Geranium platypetalum*, scarlet geum, yellow *Lysimachia punctata*, and deep pink prunella.

Rudbeckia hirta
'Marmalade'

COUNTRY IN THE CITY
A garden writer's laboratory

B reaking with the tradition of the manicured city lawn, Rob Proctor set out to create an environmentally friendly garden surrounding his Denver home. "The neighbors were horrified one summer when I moved in and let the front lawn die. One of them kept sneaking over at night to water it," says Proctor. But now they come by nearly every day to see what's in bloom.

Proctor, a garden writer, uses his 1-acre property as a giant laboratory in which to grow more than 2,000 species of perennials and bulbs. "The challenge," he says, "is to make an experiment look like a garden." With Denver's annual precipitation a scant 13 inches, it makes sense to group plants by their sun and moisture requirements. About half the garden, devoted to native and adaptable plants, receives little or no supplemental irrigation. The remainder, featuring relatively traditional border perennials and annuals, receives more according to need.

ABOVE RIGHT Golden hop twists among purple coneflowers in a freestyle arrangement.

RIGHT A strict "no-bare-earth policy" creates a rich tapestry of colors and textures, including the spikes of *Verbascum bombyciferum*, purple gayfeather, and sunflowers.

FAR RIGHT Proctor's passion for lilies, such as Asiatic hybrid 'Ariadne', sparks the summer show. The bulbs enjoy the dense plantings of companion plants—tall *Cephalaria alpina, Digitalis lutea*, golden hop, lamb's ears, and dainty tunic flower—that shade the soil and keep their roots cool.

LANDSCAPING WITH STRUCTURES

Structures give your garden its shape and dimension. By paying attention to the materials you use to build them, you can enrich your outdoor space with subtle texture and color.

Garden structures also play strong architectural roles. Fences and trellises can create separate "rooms," while low, wide walls provide seating as well. Gazebos, arbors, and overheads add shelter, privacy, and support for plants. Spas, outdoor kitchens, and patios can re-create the ambience and convenience of an indoor room for enjoyment outdoors.

Structures are the costliest part of the garden, so plan them with care and learn your local building codes before you start. The design should blend well with the architecture of your house and its setting. Finally, choose the most durable and suitable materials you can afford to ensure that your structures are long-lasting as well as pleasing.

ARBORS AND TRELLISES

Think of a sturdy frame for vines. Then imagine sun-dappled shade and filtered breezes rustling the leaves. Maybe there's a swing, a picnic table, a spa, or a fireplace. An arbor or trellis can add a leafy roof and walls to this garden "room."

An arbor or trellis launches your garden into another dimension—the vertical—while doubling as an accent, shelter, or privacy screen. These structures can support plants, tie together garden areas, define zones of use, direct foot traffic, and mask a plain or unsightly feature such as a garage or tool shed.

Although the distinction between arbors and trellises is not hard and fast, arbors tend to be major structures, whereas trellises are more delicate. Arbors can be partially attached to a house wall or roof, or built freestanding, colonnade-style. The frame of most arbors is similar in construction to many overheads

The bold lines of this arbor play off the shape of the nearby pool, wrapping two sides with a leafy colonnade and creating a hammock frame. Built-up joinery evokes a handcrafted look.

and some gazebos, but arbors are generally less enclosed. When deciduous leaves drop in winter, an arbor allows the sun to shine through and warm the interior, a basic but ingenious means of seasonal climate modification.

The stark lines of walls and fences can be softened by colorful climbers—when fastened to a wall or fence, a trellis makes an ideal plant support. Trellises may also be freestanding or mounted to an arbor or deck to serve as a windbreak or privacy screen.

You can make your own trellis or buy a commercial model at a garden center or through a mail-order supplier. Some types are made of wooden strips or lattice, others of natural vines or more sturdy wrought iron. Whatever the material, the trellis must be strong enough to support the weight of mature plants and durable enough to stand up to the rigors of your climate.

A. **Gently arching** above a passageway, this arbor links house to garden and frames an inviting glimpse of private spaces. The curved shape is echoed by a symmetrical wall fountain. Sturdy stucco columns atop brick-and-plaster knee walls support the roofing members.

B. **A simple, rustic overhead** combines sturdy 6-by-6 posts with spare roof framing. Vines snake up the posts and out across plain, galvanized pipes. A raised, casual tub fountain provides soothing sounds of water.

C. **The curving features** and sinuous lines of this arbor and bench swing create a sense of movement. The lumber was cut from 8-by-8 and 12-by-12 redwood beams salvaged from a demolished barn.

A BASIC ARBOR

Beams bridge posts; local codes specify sizes and spans

Lattice screen adds privacy and shade; doubles as a trellis

Piers of cast concrete are embedded in poured concrete footings

A. **The thick growth** of a trumpet vine forms a shady garden roof above this Mediterranean garden niche. Statuesque concrete pillars and a built-in bench are dressed with decorative tile. A formal pattern of brick covers the floor beneath.

B. **Natural vines** woven together create this rustic trellis, which bridges the gravel path and highlights a gentle curve. The structure is built from two stick frames with overarching branches. Make one yourself or look for a prefabricated version.

Designing an arbor

The key to arbor construction is to think of a crisscross or stacking principle, with each new layer placed perpendicular to the one below it. Keep in mind that, although you build an overhead from the ground up, you should design it from the top down. First choose the kind of roof you want. That decision will influence the size and spacing of the support members below.

Whether freestanding or attached to a building, the structure is held up by a series of posts or columns. These support horizontal beams, which in turn support rafters. In a house-attached overhead a ledger takes the place of a beam and the rafters are laid directly on the ledger. The rafters can be left uncovered or covered with lath, lattice, poles, or grape stakes.

Rafters sit atop beams and are spaced for plant support or shade. Orientation determines the extent of shade cast below

Posts are 4-by-4 lumber or larger; post-to-beam connections may need bracing. Metal anchors secure posts to piers or to a concrete slab

Concrete footings extend below the frost line, supporting posts and the weight of arbor and plants

In most cases arbors are built from standard dimension lumber. To increase the life of an arbor, use only pressure-treated or naturally decay-resistant materials such as redwood or cedar heartwood. Open arbors don't collect much rain or snow, so they need only support the weight of the materials themselves, plus the weight of any plants growing on them. For added strength, brace the structure where the posts meet the beams.

As you plan, check with your local building department to find out about the regulations affecting the size, design, and construction of your project. In most communities, you'll have to meet building codes and obtain a building permit before you begin work. For do-it-yourself details, see Overheads, pages 374–375.

Shopping for a Trellis

An easy and attractive way to support twining and vining plants is with handcrafted trellises, available from garden retailers and mail-order suppliers. Some sources carry an impressive array of trellises, ranging from hand-forged metal to woven willow, that can serve as decorative elements as well as plant supports. Woven wooden or vine trellises bring a casual touch to the garden, while the architectural wooden and metal ones generally look more formal.

These trellises are extremely simple to use. Most come ready to install: just push the posts into soil next to a wall or in a planter box, plant a vine nearby, and wrap the stems around the supports. A few need minor assembly, and some wooden ones with "feet" must be anchored to a wall.

For the creative do-it-yourselfer, hardware stores and home centers also stock lath, lattice, galvanized wire, plastic clothesline, copper plumbing pipe, and assorted fasteners that can be fashioned into a trellis. Simply mount redwood strips, copper pipe, or prefabricated lattice panels to fence posts or a wall. Use lag screws or galvanized nails for fastening to wood and expanding anchors for stucco or masonry. Whenever possible, leave some room between trellis and wall.

Both of the trellises shown here are simply constructed. At top, four arched, prefabricated trellises were lined up, anchored in concrete, and fastened to the walls with barbed nails. The trellises were joined with overhead 2 by 2s. The trellis at right is entirely prefabricated.

DECKS

A deck sets the stage for outdoor activity and expands the total living space of a house. A properly planned deck forms a focal point in the landscape, redefines grade, and provides new views of the garden and its surroundings. Built to accommodate seating, tables, or a spa, a deck can function as an outdoor room.

Decks can abut the house or tuck into a remote corner of the garden. The classic attached deck is typically accessed from the house through French or sliding doors from a living room, kitchen, or master bedroom—or all three. So when planning your deck, keep in mind interior traffic patterns as well as outdoor ones.

Why build a deck rather than a patio? Your site or the style of your house can be determining factors. A deck can bridge bumps and slopes or "float" over swampy low spots that might sink a brick patio. Decking lumber is resilient underfoot, and it doesn't store heat the way masonry can, making a deck cooler in hot areas.

A low-level deck can link house and garden at flower height, offering a new perspective on garden beds. Such a deck makes a good replacement for an existing concrete slab—you can often use the slab as a base for the deck. A low-level wraparound deck links interior spaces with a series of boardwalks or landings. You can follow your home's shape or play off it with angular extensions or soft curves.

If you're faced with a hilly, poorly drained site, try cantilevering a deck over the steep slope, or settle on a step-down, multiplatform arrangement.

Detached decks form quiet retreats, whether tucked behind lush plantings or elevated to catch afternoon sun or shade. The route to such a deck can be direct or circuitous. You can enhance the feeling of a hideaway with the addition of an overhead, fountain, spa, or hot tub.

Design options include decking patterns (see page 371) and railing styles.

The ultimate feel of a deck is determined by the details, and safety is the only limit.

Redwood and cedar heartwood are still top choices for western decks, but take a look at pressure-treated lumber, too—newer types are smooth, not perforated, making them more attractive. Other options include recycled or man-made products (see pages 384–385).

Coat any deck periodically with a wood preservative or stain (see pages 368–369) to prevent water absorption and reduce the swelling and contracting that lead to cracking, splintering, and warping.

A. Transition zones on this deck are signaled by changes in decking pattern. Built-in benches, planters, and steps are integral to the design. An open overhead repeats the angular geometry beneath.

B. This pondside deck with attached "boat dock" sets the stage for summertime ease. The rayed decking pattern emphasizes the fluid curves of the waterline. To gain the effect of water flowing under the deck, pressure-treated posts are set on concrete piers and footings, then decking is extended a foot or two over the water.

C. The warm, rich tones of redwood heartwood are elegantly showcased here. Overlapping angles and changes in decking direction signal steps, highlight benches and planters, and turn a potentially plain deck into an architectural statement.

D. Crisp redwood decking, formed by alternating 2-by-6 and 2-by-4 boards, both accents and bridges a rectangular pool. These strong, simple decking lines are echoed in the fence and trellis.

Deck-building guidelines

Lumber grades vary greatly in appearance and price. One cost-saving trick is to determine the least expensive lumber for decking and trim that's acceptable to you (see pages 366–367). Whatever the species and grade of visible wood, it makes sense to use pressure-treated lumber for the substructure. It stands up to weather and in-ground conditions, and is less expensive, too.

A deck can be freestanding or, as shown here, attached to the house with a horizontal ledger. Concrete footings secure precast piers or poured tubular pads, which in turn support vertical wooden posts. One or more horizontal beams span the posts; smaller joists bridge ledger and beams. The decking itself, typically 2-by-4 or 2-by-6 lumber, is nailed or screwed to the joists. The design shown, while standard, is but one of many options.

Overheads, benches, railings, and steps are often integral to a deck's framing. While it may be feasible to add these extras later, it's simplest to design and build the whole structure at once. While you're planning, think about whether you'll need to install plumbing pipes for running water or wiring for electrical outlets and outdoor light fixtures. And if you need extra storage space or planters, build them into the deck as permanent features.

One advantage of building a deck as a do-it-yourself project is that much of the engineering work has probably been done for you. Standard span tables (listing safe working spans by dimension for each of the common lumber species) are widely available—most lumberyards have them. Remember that these are minimum guidelines; for firmer footing, choose beefier members or reduce the spacing between them.

Posts taller than 3 feet may require bracing, especially in areas prone to earthquakes or high winds. Elevated decks must be surrounded with railings for safety, with slats no more than 4 to 6 inches apart (again, check local code). Fascia boards, skirts, and other trim details can dress up the basic structure.

A low-level deck is the simplest kind to build, but a simple raised deck like the one shown at right can also be constructed by a homeowner. Generally, decks that are cantilevered out from an upper story or over water or a promontory must be designed by a qualified structural engineer and installed by a professional. Decks on steep hillsides or unstable soil, or those more than a story high should receive the same professional attention.

A BASIC DECK

Decking boards are nailed or screwed perpendicular to joists; they are typically 2-by-4 or 2-by-6 lumber

Storage bin can be concealed under built-in bench

Railings (maximum openings specified by local code)

Fascia (trim)

Rim joist secures joist ends

Planters on deck require adequate drainage; deck must support weight of soil and plants

Doors to deck lead from dining or living room, kitchen, or bedrooms. French or sliding doors are best choices

Electrical lighting and outlets may be 120 volt or 12 volt and may require permit to install

Ledger secures deck to house framing. Flashing guards against moisture

Beams bridge posts; they may be single timbers or twin 2-by members that "sandwich" posts as shown

Joists are typically spaced 16 or 24 inches center-to-center, and secured to ledger with joist hangers

Posts are secured to piers with post anchors. Minimum post sizes and spacings are set by local codes

Poured concrete footings extend below the frost line

Piers are made of precast concrete and embedded in poured footings

A. This elegant deck features curved rails that were formed by bending and laminating together thin layers of redwood.

B. Steel railings with taut cable barriers, common in commercial construction, here furnish a residential deck with safety, open views, and contemporary style.

C. Stepping up and over the dunes, this pavilion features curved seats and railings that echo the ocean waves. Gaps are left to allow gusting winds to blow through.

FENCES AND GATES

Fences and outdoor screens can transform a garden into a secure, attractive retreat from the outside world. When well designed, they filter the sun's glare, turn a biting wind into a pleasant breeze, and mute the cacophony of street traffic, noisy neighbors, and barking dogs. As partitions, they divide the yard into separate areas for recreation, relaxation, gardening, and storage. Fences serve many of the same purposes as walls, but are generally less formal in appearance, easier to construct, and, when you calculate labor costs, less expensive.

Most fences are built partly or entirely of wood. The versatility of wood as a fencing material is reflected in the wide variety of its forms—split rails, grape stakes, dimension lumber, poles, and manufactured wood products such as plywood and tempered hardboard. Though the design possibilities are endless, wooden fences fall into one of three basic types: post-and-rail, picket, and solid board. The one you choose may depend on the function the fence is to serve; a board fence may be the best choice for a full privacy screen, for example. Fences can also be designed to "edit" views with the inclusion of louvers, slats, lattice, or see-through trellises that provide some glimpse beyond.

Alternative materials beyond boards, slats, and timbers include vinyl, galvanized wire, plastic mesh, or ornamental iron. Vinyl fences are readily available, easy to maintain, and simple to install. If you don't like the look of wire or mesh fencing, plant annual vines such as morning glories or nasturtiums for quick cover, or install plantings for permanent cover (see pages 202–203).

Whatever your choice of fencing, coordinate the fence with the style and materials of your house. A picket fence that would be too dainty for a contemporary stone and glass house might look fine

Spare post-and-rail zigzags mark boundaries. Poppies and roses dress up the fence with scarlet blooms.

with a colonial brick or clapboard structure. Louvered or board fences, however, can complement a variety of western house styles.

Most communities have regulations restricting fence height. In many places the maximum allowable height is 42 inches for front yard fences and 6 feet for backyard fences. Tall fences are also more difficult to build and require more materials. An alternative way to gain more height is to train a plant to clothe the top of a fence.

Normally a boundary fence is commonly owned and maintained by both neighbors. Make every effort to come to a friendly agreement with your neighbor on the location, design, and construction of the fence. (One option is a "good-neighbor" fence with crosspieces mounted in alternating directions.) If you can't come to an agreement, you can circumvent the problem by building the fence entirely on your land, just a few inches inside your boundary.

Choosing a gate

Place a gate for access, to frame a view, or to make a design statement in tandem with the fence. You may want to build the gate in a style and material that match the fence, but you can also choose a contrasting material or design, such as a wooden or wrought-iron gate within flanking brick pilasters. A low picket gate or one made of airy lath invites people in with its open, friendly appearance; a high, solid gate guards the privacy and safety of those within.

The minimum width for a gate is usually 3 feet, but an extra foot creates a more gracious feeling. If you anticipate moving gardening or other equipment through the gate, make the opening wider. For an extra-wide space, consider a two-part gate or even a gate on rollers designed for a driveway.

A. Oriental motifs of house and garden are echoed in this weathered board fence. Vertical louvered-top insets in alternating sections combine with open "windows," and the pagoda roofs match the house roof tiles. Branches of horizontally trained weeping Atlas cedar (*Cedrus atlantica* 'Glauca Pendula') cascade down the fence. An edging of rubble provides contrast.

B. Combining materials adds interest to a fence. Here, the fence also echoes both the house and paving materials. Rounded plaster pilasters match the house wall and provide solid support to fence sections of lashed, unpeeled logs. Carefree, single-color drifts of poppies and Jupiter's beard (*Centranthus ruber*), along with a single, snaking vine, complete the casual look.

C. A visual barrier need not be solid; this one creates a garden focal point while allowing an observer to see through to the landscape beyond. Six-by-six posts are tied together with horizontal rails; the uprights are alternating lengths of lattice lashed to the rails. Each upright rests on an accompanying stone pad—a novel way to add interest and fend off ground rot.

Building a fence

Most wooden fences have three parts: vertical posts, horizontal rails or stringers, and siding. Posts are usually 4-by-4 timbers; rails are usually 2 by 4s. Fence siding can range from rough grape stakes to ready-cut pickets, from finished boards to plywood panels. Posts should be made of pressure-treated or decay-resistant redwood or cedar heartwood. Redwood can be left to weather naturally, but fir or pine should be painted or stained.

If your fence will be on or near the boundary line between your property and your neighbor's, make certain you have the property line clearly established. If there's any doubt, call in a surveyor to review it.

Few lots are perfectly smooth, flat, and obstruction-free. If your fence line runs up a hill, build the fence so that it follows the contours of the land, or construct stepped panels that will maintain horizontal lines (see pages 372–373).

Building a gate

A basic gate consists of a rectangular frame of 2 by 4s with a diagonal 2-by-4 brace running from the bottom corner of the hinge side to the top corner of the latch side. Siding fastened to the frame completes the gate.

Choose strong hinges and latches. It's better to select hardware that's too hefty than too flimsy. Plan to attach both hinges and latches with long galvanized screws that won't pull out, and be sure to use galvanized hardware.

A. Color galore. This striking metal gate is dressed with verdigris flourishes and topped off with a cross-hatched trellis.

B. The rounded profiles and lathe-turned posts of this board-faced gate soften the angular plantings that surround it.

C. Boards below and open latticework above dress up a traditional gate.

D. Open, graceful grillwork fills this curved frame; above it is a leafy trellis.

A CLASSIC GATE

Latch secures gate to post

Pickets may have decorative tops

Rails are 2-by-4 lumber

Swing clearance between fence and posts is usually ½ inch

Footing is poured concrete, typically ⅓ the post depth

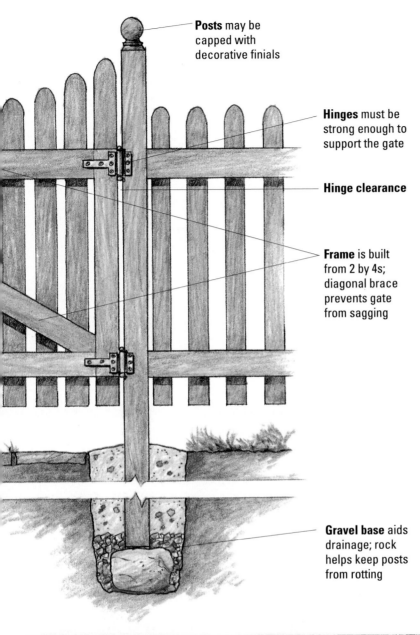

Posts may be capped with decorative finials

Hinges must be strong enough to support the gate

Hinge clearance

Frame is built from 2 by 4s; diagonal brace prevents gate from sagging

Gravel base aids drainage; rock helps keep posts from rotting

Fence Details

E. Clean pickets gain appeal from this custom design; the options are endless.

F. Architectural quality is furnished by alternating-width boards atop a kickboard, bamboo horizontals, and detailed posts.

G–H. Finishing touches. A driftwood fence houses a thriving spillage of succulents (**G**). Gate handles get a lot of use, so this "fish" (**H**) attracts notice.

FIREPLACES

Congregating around a toasty fire adds comfort and intimacy to garden gatherings. After sundown, flickering firelight enhances the surroundings. As a practical bonus, the warmth of a fire allows westerners to enjoy outdoor entertainment even when days and evenings are cool.

Although the site for an outdoor fire need be little more than a hole in the ground, the most attractive fireplaces are designed to complement the landscaping and the architecture of the houses they accompany. In the proper location, a fireplace can add wind protection and privacy to a patio. Some fireplaces are attached to the main house or outbuildings; others stand alone.

Outdoor fireplaces contain all the basic elements of indoor ones: a center firebox, with a back wall that reflects the radiant energy of the fire outward, and a chimney, which improves the draw and lifts any smoke above roof height. According to most building codes, a chimney must rise 2 feet above any structure within 10 feet of it, so chimney height becomes more important when the fireplace is close to the house.

In the dry West, common sense dictates that you take extra care with fireplaces. Chimneys should include a spark arrester—a screen that prevents large embers from escaping.

You can build an outdoor fireplace with a prefabricated metal firebox (often called a zero clearance fireplace) or with masonry (usually concrete blocks) and firebrick. The metal units use prefabricated double- or triple-wall chimney sections, so that the shell surrounding them can be made of wood, if it suits the design. Masonry fireplaces use prefabricated chimney sections or more traditional terracotta or brick flue interiors. An optional natural gas line can help get fires off to a fast start.

Before adding an outdoor fireplace, check with your local building department. A freestanding fireplace is considered a separate structure that requires a building permit. It must meet codes for both chimney height and setback. You may wish to apply for a variance on side-yard setbacks so that your fireplace can sit closer to the property line.

If you want your outdoor entertainment area to include more than a fireplace, you can integrate different types of equipment—gas cooktops, ovens, barbecues, and refrigerators—in your design. Don't forget to plan comfortable seating and to set aside a convenient spot nearby for firewood.

A. Fire and water. This tall, graceful fireplace marks one wall of an outdoor "room" (other boundaries are the overhead arbor and the adjacent house). Details on the fireplace echo both house and patio; the arbor ties the large chimney to the earth.

A

B. Spiral sculpture. Beneath the dark desert sky, a low, curving wall unfurls around this upward-spiraling fireplace. Low benches with broad cushions surround the step-down central area. The stucco on the walls and fireplace is a deep terracotta color.

C. Freestanding and graphic, this stucco fireplace rises from a long hearth faced with slate tiles that match the surface of the poolside patio. The firebox and wood-storage area are identical in shape. A broad chimney and large pots add impressive scale.

GAZEBOS AND RAMADAS

An enclosed garden structure is a refuge away from household bustle, a place to sit quietly or to host a party on a warm evening. It provides shade during the day and shelter during cool evenings, yet is open to breezes, the scent of flowers, and—if near a pool or fountain—the sight or sound of water.

When most of us say we're going to sit outside, we walk out our back door directly onto a patio or deck. But putting a structure away from the house changes how you perceive and use the outdoor space. To find the best site for the structure, walk around your property, glancing back at the house. Look for a vantage point that provides long, diagonal views across the garden and avoids unsightly areas. Consider which exposure you want—if your main deck or patio is in full sun, you may prefer to find a shady corner, for example. Then start to think about the design of the structure itself.

Western gazebos

Reminiscent of country bandstands in small-town parks, gazebos can be romantic garden hideaways. The traditional gazebo is a freestanding version of an overhead, with either six or eight sides and sloping rafters joined in a central hub at the roof peak. Often the hexagonal or octagonal sides are partially enclosed with lath, lattice, or even metal grillwork. Climbing vines may adorn it.

In the West, gazebos often differ from the old-fashioned Victorian-style version. Construction can either be substantial, with hefty corner columns and stacked beams, or light, with little more than four posts connected by pairs of 2 by 6s. The design may be enhanced by features such as path lighting or downlights, built-in benches or swings, window boxes, fountains, or spas.

A

The ramada idea

Traditional ramadas are simple structures, often rustic, that originally provided shelter from the sun during harvest time. Derived from the Spanish word *ramaje* (which means arbor), they were built of mesquite or cottonwood poles and ocotillo stems, and were open on at least three sides to take advantage of breezes.

Though Southwest in origin, the ramada idea translates well to many other regions and climates. Modern versions are permanent structures, which may be freestanding or attached to houses. Roofs can be solid or partially open. Materials vary according to the design of the house and garden. If you're using wood in a hot climate, it should be thick enough to withstand the sun of many summers; thin wood such as lath tends to dry out and crack.

Canvas or split bamboo shades offer protection from wind and low-angled sun. A fan increases air circulation and cools the structure. For evening use, some lighting—either electric or perhaps just lanterns or luminarias—is essential.

Add a table and chairs to turn a ramada into an outdoor dining room; or add a low perimeter wall for extra seating.

A. This formal six-sided gazebo looks at home in its lush, green setting. Open, airy framing forms a seating area beneath a randomly patterned shingled roof.

B. Desert shelter is provided by a ramada that is open to the landscape and to cooling breezes. Plaster walls, one with an open window, join a peeled turned post and log roof rafters to define the room.

C. Atop a raised platform, a simple frame becomes a Japanese "engawa" overlooking a large, serene pond.

D. An updated gazebo design combines a four-post structure with a six-sided, stepped roof and a built-in knee wall.

AN ELEGANT GAZEBO

Hub is eight-sided, secures rafters

Roofing may be siding, shakes, or shingles

Post bracing here is mainly decorative

Rafters run from posts to hub, supporting the roofing members

Posts are 4 by 4 or larger lumber

Knee walls are formed from prefabricated lattice panels

Concrete slab forms the floor and supports ground-level gazebo. Other options include wooden deck framing, piers, and concrete footings

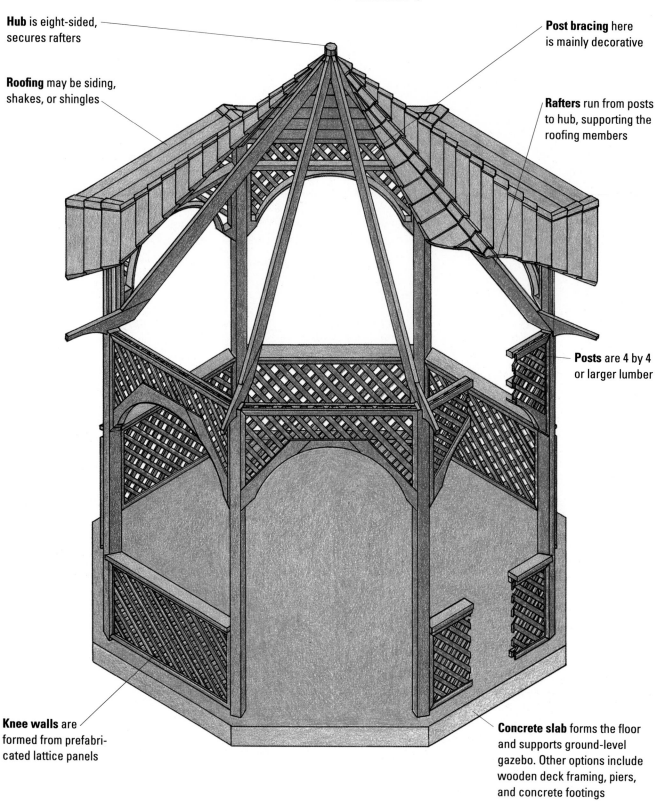

Planning an overhead

Although there are many designs for gazebos and ramadas, most are constructed from the same basic building components. They all need to have a foundation, posts or walls, beams, rafters, and some type of roofing material. The standard components of a traditional gazebo are shown at left; instructions for building a simple overhead structure are given on pages 374–375.

With few exceptions, support for an overhead comes from a simple post-and-beam frame that can be easily built by a do-it-yourselfer. As with most outdoor structures, this frame should be built from sturdy, decay-resistant lumber. A more traditional (and elaborate) six- or eight-hubbed roof is a bit trickier to lay out and assemble. Framing connections, which often determine the overall style of the overhead, can be made most easily by means of the many prefabricated metal connectors now available.

Remember that if the roof is solid, it must be pitched to allow water to run off. To permit easy clearance and avoid a closed-in feeling, make the overhead at least 8 feet high.

No matter who builds and designs it, the one person sure to get involved in your project is the local building inspector. The inspector can help you determine footing dimensions and the sizes of the posts and roof components you'll need to use. If the structure is far from your house, it's a good idea to run electrical lines for lighting the area; once again, the building inspector will get involved. Also check on local setback and height requirements.

Ready-made Gazebos

If building an entire gazebo from scratch appears a bit overwhelming, look into building one from a kit. Several companies manufacture traditional gazebos in kit form, complete except for the foundation. You construct the gazebo atop a concrete slab, deck, or foundation of piers or crushed stone. For most types, assembly takes a weekend or two and requires only basic tools and skills and the assistance of a helper.

Even though a kit costs less than a custom gazebo, it's still a major investment, so be sure you know what you're getting. Connections should be made with galvanized or brass hardware, and machining should be carefully done so that assembly is relatively easy. Details, such as railings or bracing, are worthy of close scrutiny. Read the assembly directions beforehand to see if they're easy to follow.

Find out whether the gazebo is made from redwood or cedar heartwood or from less expensive softwood or pressure-treated lumber. Can the wood be finished naturally or must it be painted? If the latter, is it available preprimed?

Also, make sure you know what's included in the price of the kit. Who pays for delivery? Are flooring and floor framing included? What about benches, screens, and steps? Many kits allow you to choose between open railings or lattice panels and other finishing details.

Tropical retreat. This large outdoor pavilion calls to mind another era, blending shade and shelter and providing enticing glimpses of the outdoors. Interior details include classic lattice walls, arched roof rafters, and a cool slab of painted concrete.

KITCHENS

Family cookouts and entertaining are often centered around the barbecue. But although its familiar kettle shape may still sit outside, you can go a step further—bringing the comfort and convenience of an indoor kitchen to a poolside or patio.

The layout of your outdoor kitchen and your choice of cooking elements will depend on your favorite cooking technique, whether you prefer grilling, stir-frying, or griddle cooking. More sophisticated masonry units incorporate built-in smokers, commercial-quality woks, or pizza ovens that accompany the traditional grill. So-called ultimate grills feature high-technology components like high-output side burners, smoke injectors, and infrared heating elements.

Facilities around the barbecue may include preparation and serving areas, storage cabinets, a vent hood, an under-the-counter refrigerator, a sink with garbage disposal, a dishwasher, a wet bar, and a place to eat. L- or U-shaped layouts allow for buffet counters and dining peninsulas with ample storage shelves and cupboards beneath. Built-in entertainment centers with TV or audio/intercom systems are other possible additions.

Maintaining and cleaning outdoor cooking facilities can be a challenge. Use protective grill covers and rugged materials such as concrete and tile so that you can clean the kitchen area simply by hosing it down. (Place watertight electrical outlets out of the way of routine cleanup.)

The built-in pizza oven is the focal point of this kitchen. But other amenities are readily at hand, including a gas-fired barbecue, a mini-refrigerator, and a small sink. Lights built into the overhead trellis enable cooks to monitor their progress.

Most outdoor kitchens are at least partially sheltered by a simple overhead or housed in a gazebo. Depending on the site's exposure and microclimate, you may need to add screens, trellises, or even heavy-duty sliding doors to help screen wind and hot sun or provide temporary enclosure during winter months.

Electricity and plumbing

Install lighting much as you would for an indoor kitchen. Effective downlighting illuminates preparation areas; more diffuse fixtures, perhaps dimmer-controlled, can create the ambience desired for a dinner party. Decorative minilights or other accents add a background glow and provide safety when other lights are off.

You must route water supply pipes, drainpipes, and electrical cable or conduit to the kitchen—beneath the concrete slab if the site is detached or, if it's next to the house, by means of an exterior wall or overhead. In cold climates, pipes should be insulated or equipped with valves at low points to facilitate drainage in winter. Drainpipes must slope toward the main drain, which may be difficult depending on the existing drainage layout.

Outdoor electrical outlets, light fixtures, and switches must be protected by watertight boxes; all outdoor outlets must also be protected by a ground fault circuit interrupter (GFCI), which shuts off power to the circuit in case of an electrical short.

If you're planning an extensive kitchen addition outside, it's best to consult a landscape architect or contractor familiar with such additions.

A. Outfitted for serious cooking, this kitchen houses tile-covered counters, a spacious sink, built-in barbecue, mini-refrigerator, and weathertight electrical boxes—all sheltered by a tile roof. The step-down allows guests to lounge at bar height. A central drain aids cleanup.

B. A majestic arbor shelters this outdoor gas barbecue and sink area. The pavings, columns, and counters were made of "cast" stone—actually poured concrete—and the beams and rafters are 60-year-old, remilled Douglas fir.

PATHS

Although it's true that the shortest distance between two points is a straight line, garden walkways often work best when this idea is ignored.

In fact, a path is most interesting when it provides a series of experiences along the way. It can alternately reveal and conceal special plantings, a piece of sculpture, a small bench, or a valley view. On a small lot, space expands when you obscure the pathway's end or use "forced perspective," gradually diminishing the width of the path to make it appear longer.

Tailor your choice of materials to the task at hand. Major access walks should be made of brick, pavers, concrete, unglazed tile, or uniform stone slabs for easy traffic flow and an even, nonskid surface. Leave space between pavers for low-growing ground covers.

On the other hand, a rustic path of gravel or bark chips can meander through the garden, its serpentine form leading you around each bend until the path ahead disappears, its uneven texture and natural colors blending into the surroundings.

Adobe blocks, rough cobbles, wood rounds, and other casual stepping-stones also make appealing paths, especially when embedded in a less expensive, contrasting filler material, such as river rock or wood chips.

Another choice is lumber—redwood or cedar decking atop a pressure-treated base, or pressure-treated timbers or railroad ties laid side by side.

Well-defined, broad edgings of brick, boards, timbers, or concrete arranged at right angles set a formal tone, which can be further emphasized with a low edging of clipped boxwood.

Unless you've chosen a highly porous material like gravel, plan to pitch the path slightly to one side for drainage, or build it with a slight crown in the center. Runoff needs about ¼ inch of slope per foot.

A

At night, shielded path lights (see pages 276–277) provide plenty of illumination but little glare. Their low-voltage wires can be snaked through garden plantings, adjacent to planting beds, or along edgings.

How wide should your path be? It depends on how you'll use it. If it will wind discreetly through a garden and serve only as a walking surface, 2 feet is adequate. To allow room for lawn mowers and wheelbarrows, make it 3 feet wide. For two people to walk abreast, as in an entry path, it should be 5 feet wide.

Finally, if your terrain is a little too steep for comfortable walking, plan for one or more broadly spaced steps.

A. An exuberant garden filled with a profusion of plants calls for a path with originality. This one features rocks and recycled fencing set in gravel at a variety of angles. The design allows a natural rise in level at the far end.

B. Crushed gravel creates a flowing "stream" and suits a variety of edgings. To one side of this path is a formal hedge border, while the other side is flanked by a mortared-stone raised bed brimming with vegetables and herbs.

C. Around the bend of a path can be a small treasure waiting to be discovered. This one is marked by a bench and blurred with encroaching plants. Earthy common brick is set in a basket-weave pattern atop a sand bed, allowing other plantings to creep between the cracks.

D. Wide and deep, concrete stepping-stones are softened by interplanting with scented ground cover (gravel or rounded pebbles are other filler options). Stepping "zones" should be spaced no further than a comfortable stride apart.

PATIOS

Many people think of a patio as a simple rectangle off the back door. If you have a small, flat lot, perhaps that's your best design option. But with even a little more space, you can expand a patio in almost any direction.

Why not consider a series of interrelated patios connected by steps, or a detached, protected patio in the corner of your lot? A neglected side yard off a small, dark bedroom may be the spot for a private, screened sitting area. Or an existing driveway could be converted: concrete turf blocks soften a drive's appearance yet allow for traffic; planted areas between flagstones and pavers achieve the same effect. Enclosed by a gate and accented with plantings, the area could turn into an entry courtyard.

Basic paving options for patio floors include masonry

Classic patio materials combine in this entry courtyard floor. Seeded-aggregate concrete alternates with bands of brick; the same brick also edges borders and raised beds.

units, poured concrete, and loose materials such as gravel and wood chips. Your choice depends mainly on whether you would prefer a formal or an informal patio. Brick, trimmed stone, and cobblestones look formal if set in mortar in a symmetrical pattern. Adobe or tile impart a Spanish or Mediterranean flavor. Irregular flagstones or mossy bricks laid in sand achieve a softer, cottage-garden look, as do spaced concrete pavers.

Poured concrete tends to give a commercial rather than a residential feel to a garden. Seeded-aggregate, textured, or stamped concrete are more user-friendly. Leave plant pockets in a freshly poured slab, or shape curved forms and fill them with concrete. The resulting pads—with plant spaces in between—can be smoothed, textured, and finished to resemble natural stone or "seeded" with another texture (see pages 382–383).

For economy and a comfortable, casual look, consider such loose materials as pea gravel, river rock, or wood chips. These filler materials both accent and expand your patio borders. They'll help improve surface drainage, too. For a closer look at these choices, see pages 376–377.

When combined, masonry and low-level wooden decking complement one another and allow great flexibility for your patio in shape, texture, and finished height. Although masonry surfaces must rest on solid ground, decks can span sloping, bumpy, or poorly draining areas nearby.

Whether you lay it, hammer it, set it, or pour it in place, a patio almost always requires an edging. Repeat the edging material elsewhere—on paths, for example, to visually link elements in the landscape. Edgings can also connect different areas of a garden: a brick-edged patio, for example, may taper off to a brick path that leads to a lawn, again edged with brick.

A. This patio "oasis" combines earthy materials with a naturalistic garden pond to bring moisture to a dry landscape. The paving is a mosaic of small river rock and larger fieldstones set in concrete; flagstones mark the pond's edges.

B. Smooth concrete needn't look cold. This patio floor is laid with butted concrete pavers finished to resemble Mexican tile —a fitting companion material to the adobe wall beyond. An almost identical look can be gained by coloring and stamping cast concrete.

C. Tightly fitted bluestone units provide the flooring surface for this formal patio, which serves both as a perch for viewing the garden beyond and as a foreground for a concrete-edged garden pond.

Patio-building pointers

Most patios are constructed either as a poured concrete slab or atop a bed of clean, packed sand.

A concrete slab suits heavy-use areas and formal designs. The slab should be at least 4 inches thick and underlaid with 2 to 8 inches of gravel. Wooden forms define the slab's shape. A thinner concrete pad, typically 3 inches thick, can serve as a base for masonry units such as ceramic tile or flagstones set in mortar.

For casual brick, paver, and cobblestone patios and walks, use a sand bed. A layer of gravel provides drainage and stability; damp sand is then carefully leveled—or "screeded"—on top. Paving units, either spaced or tightly butted, are prevented by edgings from shifting .

In general, patios laid in sand are good do-it-yourself projects. Concrete work is more demanding because there's little room for error; the trick is to pace your formwork and to limit the "pour" to small sections at a time.

If you're thinking of adding an overhead to your patio, you'll find building instructions on pages 374–375. Posts can straddle the paving area atop concrete piers and footings, or be affixed directly to the patio surface with post anchors.

A. This lattice lanai made from painted redwood adds a classical look to this veranda, while filtering bright sunlight. Overheads such as this link the patio to the house architecture.

B. "Pocket patio." This circular, paver-lined patio is set off from the garden by a slight raise of level and a simple roof. The freestanding overhead was fashioned from sturdy posts, a framework of beams, and prefabricated lattice panels.

C. Rigid square paving blocks are visually softened by spacing them atop a level bed of soil; the cracks leave space for ground covers, hardy herbs, or grasses.

D. A smattering of yellow handmade tiles brings a blast of color to one corner of a rustic brick patio.

Renovating Concrete

If you have a deteriorating patio or driveway, you can either demolish it and build anew or, in some cases, install a replacement surface. Asphalt is usually best removed, but an existing concrete slab, unless heavily damaged, can serve admirably as a base for brick, pavers, tile, or stone. Another possibility is to construct a low-level deck over the slab. Or you can break up damaged areas of concrete and let casual plantings grow in the resulting gaps.

Professional solutions include the treatment of concrete with one of three methods: bonding, staining, or top-coating. In bonding, a mix of colored cement and a binder is sprayed over the entire surface. Then cracks are blended into a network of faux grout lines created by stenciled patterns or by a special tape that's later removed. The cost, depending on the complexity of the design, ranges from one-quarter to one-third that of total replacement.

Several companies also offer chemical stains in a variety of colors that can be applied directly to the surface of an existing slab to give it a camouflaging patina. Contractors will often score a cracked concrete slab into shapes and apply different colors of stain to them to draw the eye away from the cracks.

A top coating that completely covers a cracked concrete surface can make a dramatic change. One innovative covering is made of ground-up bits of colored recycled rubber bonded together with a clear epoxy. Other contractors specialize in adding aggregate top coats or floating on a new colored mix, which can then be stamped or textured.

PLAY YARDS

Kids love the outdoors and need a place to expend their energy. Yet young children (and some older ones) have little sense of danger, so play areas must be both fun and safe. The first decision to make when planning a play yard is where to place it. Preschoolers feel safer—and can be more easily watched—if the play area is close to the house. You may prefer to corral older, noisier children within view, but farther away.

Also take into account sun, wind, and shade. Hot sun increases the risk of sunburn and can make metal slides or bars, as well as concrete walks, burning hot, so install slide surfaces facing north. If your property is in the path of strong winds, locate the play yard inside a windbreak of fencing or dense trees. Dappled shade is ideal. If you have no spreading foliage, position the play yard on the north side of your house, construct a simple canopy of lath or canvas, or plan a play structure that includes a shaded portion.

Many public playgrounds feature metal play structures rather than timber, because wood may eventually rot and break. Still, wood is a warmer and friendlier material—and a good-quality wooden structure will last as long as your children will be using it at home.

Some timbers used in play structures are pressure-treated with a chemical preservative, especially if they'll be buried underground. Though the Environmental Protection Agency considers these chemicals safe in regulated amounts, check the kind of preservative used before purchasing or building a play structure, and consider alternatives, such as rot-resistant cedar or redwood.

Perhaps you'll want a play structure scaled beyond your youngster's present abilities. Some structures allow you to add or change components as your child grows. Many mail-order companies offer structures that you can assemble yourself. Before you buy, try to view an assembled structure and talk with the owners to evaluate its safety and design. Look through the instructions beforehand to be sure you can carry out the assembly.

Allow at least 6 feet of space around all sides of swings, slides, and climbing structures for a fall zone, then cushion it well. A 3-inch layer of wood chips is one choice; increase the depth to 6 inches under a swing. Shredded bark holds up well, even in windy areas or on slopes. Use ¼- to 1-inch particles of Douglas or white fir bark. Sand provides another safe landing for falls. For children, the more sand, the better—even a depth of 12 inches is not too much. Building a low wall around a play yard will help to contain loose materials, keeping the cushion thick and reducing the cost of replenishing.

Turf grass also makes a functional play surface. (But avoid mixtures that contain clover, as its flowers attract bees.) Keep grass about 2 inches high for maximum cushioning.

Most children, starting as early as they can manage, fall in love with wheels. For tricycle wheels, plan a smooth concrete path at least 24 inches wide, preferably as wide as 4 feet. Gravel paths are frustrating for kids on vehicles—or for very young walkers.

Along boundaries the need for fencing is obvious. Also securely fence the play area from the driveway, as well as the pool, a spa, or any other body of water. You may need to fence off sharp or heavy tools, garden supplies, and garbage cans, too.

A. Gangplanks, turrets, and ramparts, all coated in electric colors, ensure plenty of fun. Forgiving wood chips and ground cover link the structure with the garden.

B. Is it an ark, a gingerbread house, or a sand castle? This beachside playhouse provides a fun-filled setting for all sorts of heroic play.

C. Stained pine presents a quiet facade, but this structure packs playhouse, ladder, observation deck, slide, swing, and storage bins into one dynamic design.

PONDS AND FOUNTAINS

It doesn't take much water to soothe the soul—even the smallest pond can have a cooling effect on a garden. The size of your pond will be restricted by the space available, but its shape and style are only limited by your imagination. If you wish to start small, consider the portable decorative pools available at garden centers and statuary stores, or create your own tub version (see page 291).

Large traditional ponds of brick, concrete, fitted stone, or tile can blend as easily into contemporary gardens as formal ones. They present the opportunity to introduce color and texture to the garden with aquatic plants like water lilies and floating hyacinths. A raised pond with brick walls provides a classic home for goldfish and koi.

Water features fall into one of three categories: spray fountains, waterfalls, and spill fountains. Spray fountains are most suitable for formal ponds and are made versatile by assorted heads that shoot water in massive columns or lacy mists. Waterfalls send a cascade toward the pond from a simple outlet pipe. Spill or wall fountains flow from the outlet into a pool or series of tiered pans or shelves. They're good choices for smaller gardens and can even stand alone, independent of ponds (see pages 288–289).

Placing the pond

The obvious spot for a pond is where everyone can enjoy it. But because children find ponds irresistible, the safest locations are in fenced backyards. Check with your local building department about any requirements for fencing with self-latching gates, as well as setbacks from property lines, electrical circuits for pumps and lights, and pond depth. Generally, ponds less than 24 inches deep do not need a building permit.

Spray fountains add life to any pond; they are available with jets, pumps, and accessories.

If you are planning to add plants or fish to your pond, first consider the climate in your garden. The pond must be protected from wind and situated away from deciduous trees that shed a steady supply of leaves and twigs into the water. Proper drainage is also important: *don't* choose a low-lying (or "bottom") area that will constantly overflow in wet weather. And remember that the backyard needn't be the only place for a pond. The addition of moving water to a front patio or entryway both cools the air and blocks the noise of passing traffic.

Often it's the border that harmonizes the pond with the surrounding landscape. The choices are many: a grass lawn; an adjoining bog garden or rock garden (often piled against a partially raised pond or used at one end of a sloping site); native stones and boulders; flagstones laid in mortar; a wide concrete lip (especially useful as a mowing strip if grass adjoins the area); brick laid in sand or mortar; redwood or other rot-resistant wood laid as rounds or upright columns; terracotta tiles; or railroad ties.

You can find flexible pond liners at home and garden centers or through mail-order catalogs. Although PVC plastic is the standard material, it becomes brittle with exposure to the sun. More UV-resistant—but twice the price—are industrial-grade PVC and butyl-rubber liners. Some pool builders prefer EPDM, a roofing material, available in 10- to 40-foot-wide rolls. Most liners can be cut and solvent-welded to fit odd-shaped water features.

Another option is a preformed fiberglass pool shell. A number of shapes and sizes are available, but many are too shallow to accommodate fish. Although these cost more than PVC-lined pools, they can be expected to last longer—up to 20 years.

A. Look to the landscape for guidance on edgings, shape, and scale. Boulders and plants interspersed around an edging of irregular flagstone help this pond blend into its surroundings.

B. Tucked into a corner of a redwood deck, this angular tub garden is fed by a built-in spill fountain. A mossy ground cover and surrounding planters piled high with impatiens and lobelia add lushness.

C. Contemporary masonry is featured in this edging of interlocking pavers that match the patio floor. A compact pond mirrors a colorful border filled with foxgloves, lilies, poppies, and roses.

A SIMPLE POND

Outlet is 120 volts and powers pump

Plant shelf

Sand bed, 2 inches thick, cushions liner

Submersible pump circulates water to waterfall or fountain jet

Prefilter helps keep pump free of debris

Flexible liner follows shape of hole; tucks under flagstone edgings

Depth of 24 inches is best for plants and fish

Building a pond

Garden ponds range from complicated formal reflecting pools and deep, plant-filled koi ponds with sophisticated pumps and filters to simple ornamental styles with just a couple of water plants and a few goldfish. A do-it-yourselfer can easily build a pond such as the one shown above—much of the work lies in excavating the hole and adding a sand bed for cushioning. Complete step-by-step instructions are given on pages 400–401.

The sound and sight of water tumbling down a small stream and over a waterfall can add to the pleasure of a pond. To create a stream, mound up soil collected during the pond excavation, then form a waterway in the mound and cover it with a length of liner material. Stack broad, flat rocks like steps, overlapping and slanting down from one level to the next.

A submersible pump will circulate water from the pond to the head of the waterfall or stream. You can find a variety of pump sizes at home and garden centers or through mail-order pond suppliers. (The volume of water and the height of its lift determine the size of the pump required.) A built-in flow-reducing valve on the pump's outlet side will reduce the flow of water in the falls. Most pumps come with a small strainer on the intake side, but this can easily become clogged with debris. It's best to add a large prefilter, available from the same sources.

To power the waterfall or fountain pump, or any adjacent lighting, you'll need a 120-volt outdoor outlet with a ground fault circuit interrupter (GFCI) near the pond. You must get an electrical permit before installing a new outdoor outlet.

KOI

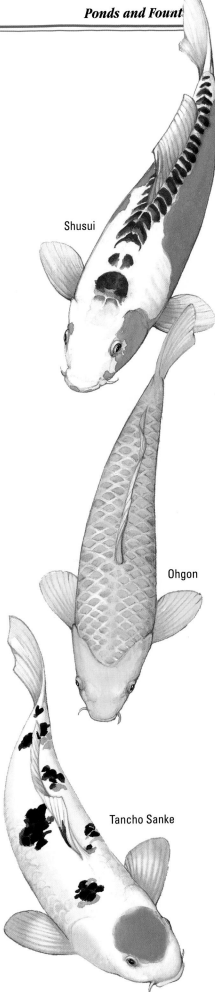

Shusui

Ohgon

Tancho Sanke

oi are carp, not goldfish. In fact, they
are bigger than goldfish (even up to 3
feet in length), and the magnificence of
their hues and patterns is captured in colorful names such as
"living jewels,"
"flower carp," and
"brocade carp." Koi
are also known as
"samurai," or war-
rior fish, thanks to
their deserved repu-
tation as determined
swimmers able to
negotiate rapids and
ascend waterfalls.
Whatever name you
use, koi bring beau-
ty to garden ponds.
They can become
family pets, follow-
ing owners around
the pond, taking
food from outstretched fingers, even allowing themselves to be petted. Koi outlive
almost any other kind of pet and can well
outlive their owners.

Prize koi command great prices. If
you're a beginner, it's best to start with
inexpensive fish, then move to more
expensive choices as your expertise
evolves. A koi club or helpful dealer can
start you off on the right track.

*These colorful koi are just youngsters;
in coming years they could grow up to
several feet in length.*

It is crucial to have a pond of adequate
depth for koi. A koi pond should be no
shallower than 18 inches and ideally
between 24 and 36 inches, or deeper. It
must also be large
enough so the fish
have room to swim
around; 1,000 gal-
lons is the minimum
requirement. That
translates to a pool
roughly 10 feet long
by 8 feet wide, and
20 inches deep.

A koi pond will
need to have alter-
nating depths: shal-
low areas where the
fish can feed and
you can watch them,
and deeper areas
for the koi to go
when surface water
heats up or starts to freeze—or to escape
a raccoon or other predator. Don't use
rough stone below the water line; fish can
be injured by rubbing against the edges.

The addition of koi to a pond calls for
some extra equipment, generally a pump
for aeration and a filtering system—either
biological, mechanical, or both—to
remove potentially harmful impurities such
as ammonia from the water.

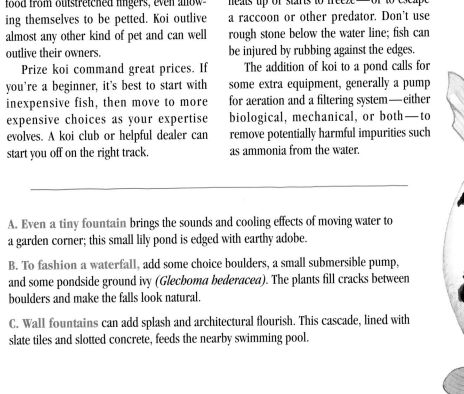

A. Even a tiny fountain brings the sounds and cooling effects of moving water to
a garden corner; this small lily pond is edged with earthy adobe.

B. To fashion a waterfall, add some choice boulders, a small submersible pump,
and some pondside ground ivy *(Glechoma hederacea)*. The plants fill cracks between
boulders and make the falls look natural.

C. Wall fountains can add splash and architectural flourish. This cascade, lined with
slate tiles and slotted concrete, feeds the nearby swimming pool.

POOLS

In recent years, swimming pools have been slimmed to fit home landscapes rather than overpowering them. High operating costs and increased maintenance, coupled with smaller lots and smaller families, mean that most homeowners need to tailor a pool's size and design to their needs. So before you fall in love with a pool design, ask yourself a few questions.

Are you lap swimmers, or do you like to just soak in the pool? How much available space do you have? Don't rule out a pool because you think you don't have room; some can be shoehorned into tight sites and constructed on even limited budgets.

The architectural maxim "form follows function" definitely applies to pools. Children need a wide, shallow area; lap swimmers require a long, straight section. Unless it will be used for diving, a pool need not be deeper than 4 to 5 feet. For lap swimming, one long axis, preferably 40 feet, will suffice; the width can be as little as 7 or 8 feet.

As with garden ponds, you'll need to study the sunlight patterns in your garden, at least through the swimming season. And if winds regularly blow onto your property, look for the most protected spot or install plantings or other barriers to block the winds. A pool can be installed on a hillside if you use retaining walls, but installation is much simpler and less costly on level ground.

Because of its size, you may not be able to make your pool completely private. In general, however, the more secluded it is from neighbors and passersby, the more comfortable you'll be. And although the pool needn't be immediately adjacent to your house, there should be clear access from the pool to a changing room and bathroom. You'll also want it convenient to reach—and well lit—in the evening.

Plan for a paved area or deck surrounding or adjoining the pool. As a general rule, the poolside area should be at least equal to the area of the pool itself, and should drain away from the pool. Install a nonskid surface that keeps as cool as possible and one that won't reflect light. It's best to isolate lawns and planting beds from the pool; otherwise, swimmers will drag plants and soil into the pool with each entry.

With the addition of boulders, flagstones, bridges, and other freeform edgings, naturalistic pools and adjacent spas can double as garden ponds. Two other intriguing options are the vanishing-edge pool, where the pool merges with a surrounding view; and the "wade-in beach" pool, which helps swimmers, especially children, to enter the water gradually.

A. Lap pools contain plenty of room for serious aquatic workouts. This one fits a cramped side-yard space. It serves as architectural garden pond and spill fountain, too.

A

B. Tucked into a thriving Southwest landscape, this compact shape shows that a pool needn't dominate the property. The effect is more like a natural desert pond than a traditional backyard pool.

C. "Vanishing-edge" pools are designed to merge with a surrounding view. This pool appears to spill right into the rose garden that lies just beyond.

Pool Safety

For pool owners with children—or with young visitors or neighbors—accidents remain a constant threat. That's why all swimming pools require protective barriers.

Although height requirements vary, most communities insist that properties with pools have a fence that completely encloses the yard (or the fence might surround three sides of the garden and connect to the house). The fence should have self-closing gates with self-latching mechanisms that are beyond the reach of young children.

Another fence, at least 5 feet tall, should enclose the pool or separate it from the house. If it has vertical bars, they should be no more than 4 inches apart, and the fence should have no horizontal pieces that could provide toeholds for climbing. The pool should be clearly visible from the house; panels of safety glass, clear acrylic, or see-through mesh can enhance the view.

All gates to the pool should be child-resistant, self-closing, and self-locking. Areas immediately outside the pool fence should not have chairs or other objects that can be easily moved or climbed.

Doors and windows that lead from the house to the pool can be made more secure with additional locking mechanisms installed at least 5 feet above the floor. Options for sliding glass doors include locks for the top of the moving panel and its frame, automatic sliding door closers, or removable bars that mount to the frame.

A properly installed and approved safety cover is also critical. The safest types either have tracks mounted to the decking or fastening devices set in the pool deck (this type is especially good for odd-shaped pools). Never allow swimming in a partially covered pool; completely remove the cover before entering the pool.

Pool equipment includes the pump, heater, and filter. You'll need to provide a concrete slab to support them, ideally hidden from sight and sound by screen, shrubs, or a lushly planted trellis. Place the slab between 25 and 50 feet from the pool; any closer and the noise may be overwhelming; any farther away and you'll need larger equipment to pump water the extra distance.

Before building a swimming pool, look into the legal requirements set forth in deed restrictions, zoning laws, and building, health, and safety codes. Also familiarize yourself with the building codes that apply to associated structures such as decks, fences, and overheads.

Constructing a pool

Pools can be built above ground or completely or partially in-ground. Fully in-ground pools are accessible from patio areas and fit best into most landscapes, but both above-ground and partially in-ground pools can be integrated into your garden's design.

A

For the structure, concrete (usually sprayed as gunite or shotcrete and reinforced with steel) combines workability, strength, permanence, and flexibility of design. Interior finishes include paint, plaster, and tile, in ascending order of cost. To keep the price down, save tile for details—edgings, step markers, and around the water line.

Vinyl-lined pools are usually much less expensive than concrete, because the liner is prefabricated and because the pool can be installed in as little as a few days. The liner generally rests on a bed of sand and is supported by walls made of aluminum, steel, plaster, concrete block, or wood. These walls can extend above grade, making them especially economical for sloping sites. Vinyl is not as durable as concrete, but leaks can be repaired.

Fiberglass pools consist of a one-piece rigid fiberglass shell supported by beds of sand. These pools are also fairly quick to install, but the choices of pool shapes and sizes are limited.

Some homeowners choose to start out with above-ground pools, such as the familiar vinyl-lined pool or "found objects" such as vats and tanks. Since no excavation is required, an above-ground pool can be easy to install and certainly costs less than an in-ground type. These installations, whether temporary or permanent, are most successfully integrated into a garden's design when recessed at least partially below grade and built with a surrounding deck or raised platform.

Renovating a Pool

Too often, swimming pools follow familiar dictates of pool design, with white plastered walls and precast coping (edging), a band of blue tile, and a surround of gray concrete. But updating such a pool doesn't require you to spend a fortune.

The most common repair for older pools is replastering, which repairs minor cracks, hides stains, or changes the pool's color. Replastering does not necessarily disturb the tile, coping, or surrounding deck, and it brings the most dramatic change for the least amount of money. Dark-colored plaster lends the appearance of a deep lagoon and may even provide a source of solar heating for the water.

You can also choose to install new tile in the pool. Confined to the water line, just below a line of decking, new tiles can add subtle color accents or more lively contrasts.

New coping or a deck surround can dramatically improve the look of an old pool. Flagstone, boulders, and planting pockets break up hard-edged geometry, making the setting more natural. Replacing gray concrete decking around the pool with terracotta tiles or warm-toned wood can blend the pool with an updated house style or naturalistic landscaping.

Surrounding a pool with a new selection of plants can transform its appearance and help merge the pool with the landscape. The addition of a spa or waterfall is another way to give a pool new appeal.

When renovating an older pool, you may need to rework plumbing, gas, or electrical lines, which can considerably increase the cost of the project.

A. Natural stone edgings and lush border plantings blend spa with pool and pool with landscape. A fluid shape is key to making the pool blend in with its surroundings. The small waterfall tumbles out of a mortared-stone retaining wall.

Spas and Hot Tubs

Whether the focal point of a garden or a private retreat, a spa or hot tub has understandable appeal: an invigorating bath alfresco, enlivened by jets of water, in a vessel large enough to accommodate both social and solitary soaks.

Spas also double as decorative water features. Waterfalls, fountain jets, formal tile or natural stone borders, and exit streams that meander to a swimming pool all link the spa with its surroundings.

What are the differences between spas and hot tubs? Primarily materials and form, not function. Both massage bathers with a froth of hot, bubbling water. The support equipment for spas and hot tubs is virtually identical. But hot tubs are made of wood—in fact, they tend to resemble large, usually straight-sided barrels. Contemporary spas depart from the rustic simplicity of hot tubs, running the gamut of design choices from boxy portable models to installations of pool-size proportions.

Spas fall into two general categories—portable and in-ground. The portable, or self-contained, spa is more like a home appliance: it doesn't have to be permanently installed and comes as a complete unit, ready to be plugged into a 120-volt outlet (or wired to a 240-volt circuit). Its support equipment, or "skid pack"— and every other necessity except water—is part of the package. A "skirt," typically made of redwood, surrounds the shell.

In-ground types can be set into a hole dug into the ground or into an above-grade surface such as a deck. Shopping for an in-ground spa means choosing between a factory-molded shell and a more expensive, longer-lasting shell made of concrete.

Today, when the concrete shell is used for a new spa, in many cases it adjoins a new swimming pool, and the two will share the same site and support equipment. Concrete spas can be custom designed so that they have attractive, sculptural lines.

A spa can double as a water feature. This built-in, naturalistic spa resembles a garden pond perched atop a mountain—with a view of distant chaparral-covered hills.

A finish of colorful plaster or gleaming tile can enhance the spa's appearance.

Though less costly than a concrete spa, the plastic in-ground type is more expensive than most portables, but it is likely to last longer. The majority of in-ground spas are made of acrylic reinforced with fiberglass or of high-impact thermoplastics. The technique used to manufacture spas makes possible nearly any shape and depth, along with contoured, built-in seats.

An offshoot of the spa industry is called the "swim spa"—an elongated version of an in-ground spa in which swirling white water is propelled by two or more strong hydrojets. Without moving forward an inch, a swimmer can cover miles by swimming against this raging current.

Hot tubs

One of the most common statements of tub lovers is that the wood surrounding their soak feels good to touch. They also like its pleasant, musty aroma.

Whether made of redwood, cedar, teak, or another wood, hot tubs boast a classic beauty. With a greater gallonage than most spas, tubs also give a deep soak.

Hot tubs may have a natural appearance, but they require careful maintenance and diligent upkeep. Excessive chlorine or bromine will attack the wood; too little will allow harmful bacteria to lodge in the wood's porous surface. And if a hot tub is drained and then allowed to dry out for more than two days, leaks can develop as the wooden staves shrink.

A. Designed to fit the patio, this architectural wall fountain-cum-spa masks noise and brings the cooling effects of falling water. Such combination spas are especially useful for small-space lots or urban gardens.

B. A spa with flagstone steps and edgings sits just steps above the nearby swimming pool, lending privacy to those taking a soak. Bathers can enjoy soothing views of pool, garden, and nearby hills.

A SPA SURROUND

Overhead screens sun, weather, and wind

Privacy screen

Skirt hides the spa's support system. Built-up perimeter doubles as bench seating

Wooden decking provides insulation and absorbs moisture. Space decking boards for best drainage

Downlights increase safety at night

Spa logistics

A number of practical considerations enter into your choice of a spa site. You're probably already familiar with sun and wind patterns in your yard, but now is a good time to take a careful look. Try to anticipate when you're likely to use the spa or tub; then find one or more sites where sun, shade, and wind will be to your liking at that time of the day.

If the spa or tub will be the hub of social gatherings or if you plan to use it at night before retiring, you'll want to install it near or on a patio or deck attached to the house. On the other hand, consider a site away from the house—perhaps an odd, unused corner of your lot—if you want seclusion.

You'll feel more comfortable in a spa or tub if it is well hidden from passersby. Build an arbor or a gazebo around the spa, or screen it with live plantings or an arrangement of fences and walls.

Regardless of where the spa or tub is located with respect to the house, you'll need to provide a way of getting there that's comfortable, even for bare feet. A paved walk from the house would be ideal, with masonry or wood paving around the spa or tub itself.

Local laws regard a spa or tub as an "attractive nuisance," just as they do a swimming pool. Spas and tubs must have secure covers to keep unsupervised children out of the water. Consult local zoning ordinances to find out what covers, fencing requirements, setback limits, and other equipment might be required.

Because a portable spa is self-contained, it's easy to install, requiring nothing more than a concrete slab or sturdy deck underneath. You may choose to surround your spa with benches, screens, or other amenities to create an integrated outdoor environment. Some spa dealers sell these components in kit form.

A

Many portable spas run on 120 volts; the electrical outlet you use must be part of a 20-amp circuit that doesn't service any other heavy-draw appliances. Nearly all portables are now wired with ground fault circuit interrupters (GFCIs); if not, your outlet or its circuit must have such protection added. Some designs allow you to run the equipment on 240 volts, accomplished by adding a new circuit and hardwiring the spa directly to it. Although the spa will no longer be as portable, the result of the additional voltage is that the spa will heat up much more quickly.

Although in-ground spas are rigid, they're not self-supporting; they must be set in sand that is, in turn, held in place by stable earth or rigid retaining walls. Above-grade in-ground spas must be surrounded by retaining walls to contain the supporting sand. Hot tubs are simpler to install above grade, though they must be built so that air circulates around their sides and base; this retards the decay to which wood is prone. Often a deck or skirt surround is added at or just below the edge of the tub for lounging. Custom-built concrete spas are usually included as adjuncts to swimming pools and are built at the same time as the pool.

Spa or hot tub siting is also, to some extent, governed by plumbing and the spa's support equipment, which must stand a short distance away. Heaters, pumps, and filters are compact, but they require connections to electrical and gas lines. The expense of running these lines may also limit your choice of location. If you're using solar heating panels, you'll need to find a place for them, usually on the roof; this may dictate a site near the house.

Many spas come with built-in, low-voltage lights. But be sure to light steps, deck edges, and other potentially hazardous places.

A. An in-ground acrylic model is installed flush with the surrounding deck. The wooden edging follows the spa's circular shape. Recessed spas such as this must be supported below with special framing or footings.

B. Reminiscent of classic water features, this elegantly shaped spa doubles as a reflecting pond. It is surrounded by ashlar stone pavings. Twin arbors provide shade and visual symmetry.

STEPS

In addition to their obvious practical function—as transitions between different levels or from one garden feature to another—steps can be accents that set the mood for an entire landscaping scheme.

Most dramatic are wide, deep steps that lead the eye to a garden focal point. A set of stairs can also double as a retaining wall, a base for planters, or additional garden seating space.

Materials influence step styles. Poured concrete and masonry block usually present a formal, substantial look. Unglazed tiles, concrete pavers, and adobe have a similar effect. Natural materials such as stone and wood add an informal touch and fit into less structured gardens. Such informal steps also have a simpler construction (see pages 398–399).

Spanish-style stairs combine unglazed paver tiles on treads and painted accents on risers.

decision about width. Simple utility steps can be as narrow as 2 feet, but 4 feet is the usual recommended width for outdoor steps. To allow two people to walk side by side, steps should be at least 5 feet wide.

Ideally, the depth of the tread plus twice the riser height should equal 25 to 27 inches. For both safety and ease of walking, the ideal dimensions are a 6-inch riser with a 15-inch tread. Though riser and tread dimensions can vary, their relationship remains the same. Risers should be no lower than 4 inches and no higher than 8 inches. Treads should never be smaller than 11 inches. And all the risers and treads in any one flight of steps should be uniform in size.

To design your steps, work out your plan in detail on graph paper. Try different combinations of risers and treads, widths, and configurations to achieve the necessary change of level.

Matching the building material used in a patio or for garden walls helps unite a garden's overall landscaping. On the other hand, contrasting materials draw attention to the steps and the areas of the garden they serve. Combining materials can create a transition between unlike surfaces. For example, you can link a brick patio to a concrete walk with steps made of concrete treads (horizontals) and brick risers (verticals).

Regardless of the material you use, put safety first: treads should give safe footing in wet weather. And steps should be adequately lit at night with unobtrusive, nonglare path lights or fixtures built into risers or adjacent step walls.

Scale is another important consideration. Principal entries require steps that are inviting and that allow several people to climb them at one time. Service yard steps, on the other hand, can be scaled down to fit their more limited use.

Your garden layout and the steps' function will influence your

Soften the edges of a series of steps, and help walkers find them without difficulty, by placing containers or open beds along their borders. You can even add planting pockets within a wide series of tiers as long as the greenery won't impede smooth travel.

If your slope is too steep for even 8-inch risers, remember that steps needn't attack a slope head-on: sometimes the most appealing solution is an L- or even a U-shaped series of multiple flights. Break the runs with a wide landing between, using the transition to house a reading nook, a rose bed, or a wall fountain.

Rarely will the steps fit exactly into a slope as it is. You may need to cut and fill the slope to accommodate the steps. If you have questions about your site, if your steps will touch a public access area such as a sidewalk, or be connected to a building, you should contact your local building department.

A. An oriental garden features rough-hewn stepping-stones that bridge a garden stream and wind gently up the grade behind. Extra-thick stones create casual step risers.

B. Wide landings of seeded-aggregate concrete are softened by blue star creeper, saxifrage, sweet alyssum, and other low plants that grow in 3½-inch-wide pockets at the base of each riser.

C. Mortared brick steps have a formal look, but these are softened by a curved layout and adobe edgings that serve as shelves for containers and the plants that spill over from the hillside.

D. Pea gravel is captured between risers made from broken pieces of an old concrete patio. A retaining wall and river rocks flank the loosely filled treads.

WALLS

Walls define space, provide privacy and security, edit views, screen out wind and noise, and hold the earth at bay. They bring an unmatched sense of permanence to a garden; in fact, some of the world's oldest structures are walls. Once you've determined a wall's function, you can choose its location, height, width, and degree of visual permeability. You'll also need to select materials that coordinate with the style and design of your house and existing garden structures.

Among the typical materials for garden walls are masonry units or blocks, uncut stone, and poured concrete. The easiest materials to use yourself are masonry units: brick, concrete block, or adobe—all uniform units with modular proportions that you assemble piece by piece. You can choose a decorative pattern for laying the courses, incorporate a solid or open-work face, vary the thickness, and employ combinations of materials. Glass-block sections let light pass through, as do upper edgings of lath, lattice, and trellises.

In the hands of a sensitive mason, stone forms walls that seem to be integral to certain landscapes. Stone that is prominent in your region will look the most natural in your garden. However, poured concrete offers more design possibilities because surface texture and shape are established by wooden forms. Most of the work goes into constructing and stabilizing these forms; the actual "pour," for better or worse, is accomplished quickly. (Consult a contractor for any poured concrete wall more than a few feet high.)

Before beginning any wall, ask your local building department about regulations that specify how high and how close to your property line you can build, what kind of foundation you'll need, and whether or not the wall requires steel reinforcement. Many municipalities require a building permit for any masonry wall more than 3 feet high. Some, especially in areas of seismic activity, may require that the wall be approved by an engineer.

Retaining walls

A gentle slope may be tamed with a single low retaining wall or a series of garden steps that hold the surface soil in place. A long, steep slope divided into terraces by two or three substantial walls provides attractive landscaping opportunities.

Retaining walls act like dams. Clay soil, when saturated, brings tons of pressure to bear on them. If you live in a seismic area, your wall must also withstand potential shock loads. And it must rest on cut or undisturbed ground, never on landfill. Hire a professional contractor if extensive grading is required.

Engineering aside, you can build a retaining wall from any of the materials discussed above. Wood is another easy option for retaining walls, whether various-size boards or railroad ties or wood timbers set vertically or horizontally.

On a low, stable slope, you can lay uncut stones or chunks of broken concrete without mortar or footings. Fill the crevices with colorful plantings.

New systems for building concrete retaining walls don't require you to mix a single bag of concrete. These walls are built with precast modules that stack or lock together via lips, pins, or friction. They are ideal for 3- or 4-foot retaining walls (see pages 396–397).

Where engineering is critical, poured concrete may be the only solution. But the labor required can make a concrete wall a costly project. You can make concrete more interesting by using rough form boards to texture the finish or by applying a surface veneer.

A. Tightly crafted, this cut-stone wall features raked joints so that mortar is unobtrusive. The result is dramatic and contemporary.

B. Oozing extruded joints in this brick wall take their cue from rustic adobe styling. The staggered top line is reminiscent of an overgrown ruin; an outdoor window makes the wall less domineering.

C. Flawlessly fitted ashlar stone presents an artistic front while serving as a sturdy retaining wall for the planting beds behind.

D. Exterior plaster veneer softens the plain, strict look of a concrete block core. This curved wall evokes scenes of Southwest adobes and steps up to a bold, eye-catching entry gate.

E. This pleated wall stands like sculpture in a Southwest garden. Colors such as this can be painted over the plaster or worked into the coating.

Wall-building basics

Regardless of the type of wall you plan to raise, you will have to support it with a solid foundation, or footing. Poured concrete is about the best footing you can provide because it can be smoothed and leveled better than other materials. Usually, footings are twice the width of the wall and at least as deep as the wall is wide. But consult local codes for exceptions.

For very low walls (no more than 12 inches high) or for low raised beds, you can lay the base of the wall directly on tamped soil or in a leveled trench.

In most cases, a freestanding wall more than 2 or 3 feet high should have some kind of reinforcement to tie portions of the wall together and prevent it from collapsing. Steel reinforcing bars, laid with the mortar along the length of a wall, provide horizontal stiffening. Placed upright (for example, between double rows of brick or within the hollow cores of concrete blocks), reinforcing adds vertical strength that can keep a wall from toppling due to its own weight.

Special steel ties of various patterns are made for reinforcing unit masonry and attaching veneers to substructures. An example is shown on the facing page.

Vertical columns of masonry, called pilasters, can be tied into a wall to provide additional vertical support. Many building departments require that they be used at least every 12 feet. Also consider placing pilasters on either side of an entrance gate and at the ends of freestanding walls. When you're building the foundation of your wall, the footing will have to be twice the width of the pilasters.

A. This dry stone retaining wall presents pleasing textures and contains ample pockets for plants within its nooks and crannies.

B. Cast concrete retains the stamp of its vertical form boards, but still provides softly colored edgings for yuccas and ornamental grasses growing through a "riverbed" of flagstone rubble.

A BRICK WALL

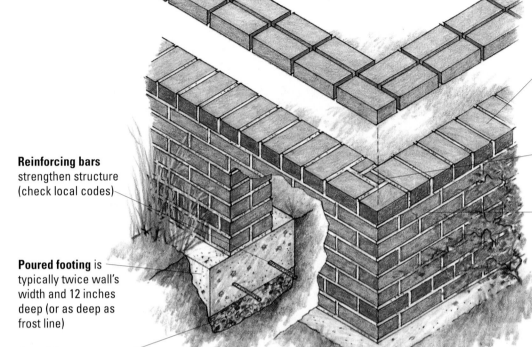

Header course (every fifth, sixth, or seventh course) spans front to back, helps lock the wall together

Corners overlap with ¾- and ¼- inch "closure" bricks

Common-bond wall has staggered joints from course to course. Double-thickness ("double wythe") wall is much stronger than a single row of bricks

Reinforcing bars strengthen structure (check local codes)

Poured footing is typically twice wall's width and 12 inches deep (or as deep as frost line)

Gravel base ensures good drainage

A CONCRETE BLOCK WALL

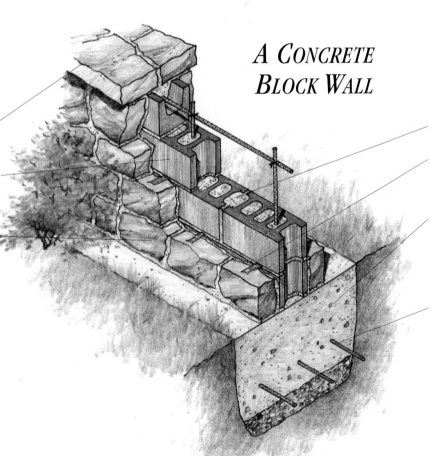

Bond-beam block adds strength at top

Concrete block core is set with ⅜-inch mortar joints

Stone veneer set in mortar covers block core

Grout

Wall ties help connect veneer to block core

Poured footing is typically twice wall's width and 12 inches deep (or as deep as frost line)

Reinforcing bars strengthen structure (check local codes)

LANDSCAPING WITH PLANTS

Plants soften outdoor structures, but they also play other roles. Trees, vines, and tall shrubs provide shade, privacy, and protection from wind. Perennials brighten beds and borders. Ground covers blanket the soil. Some plants attract wildlife; others prevent erosion, produce flowers for bouquets, or perfume the air.

At its best, a garden puts plants where their unique qualities are shown to advantage and their heights, colors, and textures play off one another. Silvery foliage defines borders in moonlight. Wispy grasses shiver in the slightest breeze and capture the golden light of a late afternoon sun in their feathery seedheads. Palms create drama near swimming pools as their distinctive shapes are mirrored in still water.

Simply allow plants to play the roles they were born to play—then stand back and watch them flourish.

TREES

W hether they are palms rustling near California's beaches or aspens shivering on the mountain slopes of Colorado, trees help define the general character of a landscape. In a garden setting, trees serve so many purposes—both aesthetic and practical—that few gardeners would consider doing without them. Trees offer cooling shade, provide shelter, and establish perspective. Trees can frame special vistas and block out unattractive views. They can also make dramatic statements, enhance the garden with sculptural effects, or form the dominant focal point of a landscape.

Although trees may be the most expensive individual plants to buy, they can be relied on to give permanence to any landscape. Not surprisingly they are particularly valued in new

Trees dominate this simple, Japanese-inspired stream garden. The graceful form and delicate texture of the Japanese maples offer year-long visual interest; during the growing season, their feathery leaves cast dappled shade on the azaleas and other moisture-loving plants below. The contrast of dark evergreen trees provides a beautiful backdrop.

housing developments. Often overlooked is the role trees play in a house's energy conservation. For example, a tree-shaded house will require less air conditioning in summer than an exposed one. And if deciduous trees, which lose their leaves in winter, are planted around the south side of a house, the warmth of winter sunshine will be able to penetrate to the interior of the house, helping to reduce heating and lighting costs.

Your choice of trees will be determined largely by their purpose in the landscape. To block the sun, for example, select only trees that develop sizable canopies. If you need a screen, look for trees that produce branches on their lower trunks, or combine trees that have bare lower trunks with shrubs or walls. For a focal point, choose a tree that displays flowers or fruits, or one with attractive foliage, bark, or a striking bare silhouette in winter.

Tree characteristics

Trees usually live for decades, if not centuries. Each year new growth springs from a framework of last year's branches to form a gradually enlarging structure. Tree silhouettes vary greatly from one species to another (see above right), and a tree's ultimate shape may not be obvious in young nursery specimens.

Though the range of shapes is enormous, all trees are classified as either *deciduous* or *evergreen*. Most *deciduous* types produce new leaves in spring and retain them throughout the summer. In the fall, leaf color may change from green to warm autumnal tones, and the trees then drop their foliage for the winter, revealing bare limbs. *Broad-leafed evergreens,* such as many magnolias, have wide leaves similar to many deciduous trees, but these cover the plant year-round. (Older leaves may drop, however.) *Needle-leafed evergreens* include trees with needlelike foliage—firs, spruces, and pines, for example—and those whose leaves are actually tiny scales, such as cypresses and junipers. Because they keep their foliage in winter, conifers retain their appearance throughout the year, though their colors may change slightly during cold months.

TREE SILHOUETTES

Columnar Narrowly oval Cone shaped Globular Horizontally spreading Weeping

Selecting trees

To avoid disappointment, choose plants that will flourish in your garden's conditions. What are your summers like? Are they hot, cool, dry, or humid? Does your region experience summer drought? If trees are not perfectly suited to your environment, consider placing them where the conditions can be moderated, such as in irrigable or sheltered positions near the house. Young trees can easily succumb to frost, so buy only those plants that can survive the lowest temperatures normally found in your area. In mild-winter regions, select trees that don't need winter chill to set flowers or fruits the following season. Although a tree that does need chilling may grow and produce foliage in mild climates, it may never bloom.

Take into account the ultimate height and growth rate of a tree *before* you buy it. A desire for shade or privacy may tempt you to purchase a fast-growing plant, but a tree that soon overpowers its space will prove a poor choice, forcing you to prune heavily, remove the tree, or live with your mistake.

Trees known to have aggressive root systems or those that drop masses of leaves or fruits should be planted in a background location, not near pools or patios. Likewise, avoid siting trees with brittle wood in wind- or storm-swept areas; instead, use them as specimen trees in protected locations and position them away from a house or roadway. Some trees are susceptible to

pests or diseases prevalent in particular regions. The European white birch *(Betula pendula),* for example, succumbs to a borer in the East but thrives in most western states. For diseases that affect trees in the West, see Regional Problems and Solutions, pages 318–321.

Depending on the species of tree, foliage color can vary from greens and pale yellows to almost-black reds. The bark of many trees also features striking patterns and hues. And, of course, numerous trees provide spectacular color with their spring or summer blooms or their late-season berries.

In addition to the visual appeal of trees, many westerners live in climates perfect for decorative and delicious fruit- and nut-bearing trees, including avocado, citrus, fig, macadamia, and pistachio.

PLANTING TREES

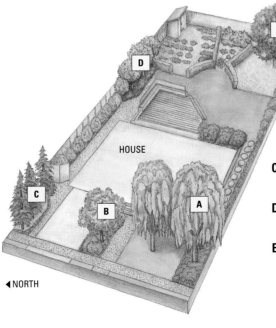

HOUSE

◄ NORTH

A. Mature deciduous trees lend an established look, and shade the front of the house in summer.

B. Fruit tree in bloom adds color to the front walk.

C. Needle-leafed evergreens screen the driveway year-round.

D. Citrus trees thrive in the heat of south- and west-facing walls.

E. Broad-leafed evergreen offers privacy and shade without excessive leaf litter.

THE IDEAL PATIO TREE

Height is under 40 feet when tree reaches maturity.

Species is free of pests and diseases, particularly any that could quickly destroy or disfigure a small tree.

Canopy is tall enough to walk under and wide enough for at least two people to sit under.

Roots won't lift up paving, form sprouts, or invade lawns or nearby planting beds.

Litter is minimal, as leaves, fruits, flowers, and seedpods fall only once a year and are easily cleared up.

SMALL PATIO TREES

A good tree for patios and decks is well mannered. Its roots remain under the ground, rather than prying up paving or invading nearby flower beds. In addition, it does not produce pollen to plague allergy sufferers or drop leaves or messy fruits. Even when fully grown, a patio tree should not be too tall, yet its canopy must be high and wide enough to cast overhead shade.

Small deciduous trees work well, as long as you don't mind sweeping up their autumn leaves. Consider a graceful Japanese maple or a crape myrtle, which, with its multiple trunks, brings dappled shade and a touch of elegance to a patio. In mild-winter areas, broad-leafed evergreens such as citrus provide fine, deep shade year-round, along with their tasty fruits. Needle-leafed evergreens, however, are not recommended as patio or shade trees; their rangy growth habits require frequent pruning, they often

drop spiky needles, and the shade cast beneath their boughs is extremely dense.

In general, the best patio trees are small and relatively slow growing; for quick effect, purchase an older tree. For example, a crape myrtle in a 24-inch box can be 9 or 10 feet tall. It is likely to be about four years older and twice the size of the same species in a 5-gallon nursery can. Although few retail nurseries stock trees larger than those in 15-gallon cans, you can often find larger trees through wholesale suppliers. A landscape architect, contractor, or garden designer will also be able to help with such a purchase, as well as provide necessary planting assistance.

October, when temperatures are cool and rains are on the way, is the best month to plant most ornamental trees. Wait until spring before planting any tree that is just barely cold-hardy.

Acer palmatum

Great Choices for Patios

FOR ALL AREAS:

Cercis canadensis 'Forest Pansy'
EASTERN REDBUD

Fraxinus angustifolia 'Raywood'
RAYWOOD ASH

**Prunus blireiana,
P. cerasifera 'Purple Pony'**
FLOWERING PLUM

Pyrus calleryana 'Cleveland Select'
ORNAMENTAL PEAR

Sophora japonica 'Regent'
JAPANESE PAGODA TREE

FOR COOLER AREAS:

Acer palmatum
JAPANESE MAPLE

Amelanchier canadensis
SERVICEBERRY

FOR HOTTER AREAS:

Celtis sinensis
CHINESE HACKBERRY

Lagerstroemia indica
CRAPE MYRTLE

Olea europaea 'Swan Hill'
FRUITLESS OLIVE

Caring for Landscape Trees

Forming a strong trunk. *A young tree develops a strong trunk faster if its lower branches are removed gradually. At first, allow the branches on the trunk to acquire thickness. As the tree matures, shorten the lower branches so that growth will be directed upward to increase the tree's height. Eventually, you may remove all the lower branches.*

Preserving the roots. *Healthy roots are vital to a tree's well-being. If you install paving underneath an established tree, avoid solid materials such as poured concrete—they will totally prevent air and water from reaching the roots. Instead, leave as much open soil as possible around the trunk, and select a paving design that allows water to penetrate. Set bricks or paving stones in sand, rather than cement, or use loose materials.*

Any major soil removal around a tree (for construction of a retaining wall, for example) will take with it some of the roots that sustain and anchor the tree. Try to preserve the existing grade beneath the tree by making elevation changes beyond the branch spread. Seek professional advice for soil-level changes over 2 feet deep.

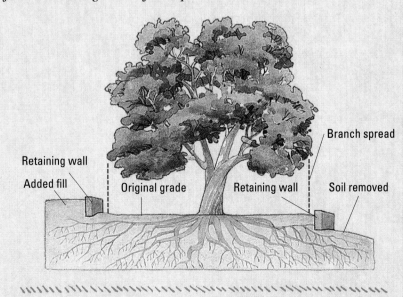

Retaining wall
Added fill
Original grade
Retaining wall
Branch spread
Soil removed

falling limb from tearing bark on the trunk. Then cut through the branch from the upper side. Avoid using pruning paints or tree sealant to seal the wound; these products have no effect on a tree's ability to resist infection.

If pruning alone won't open up views, consider having any offending trees removed. Keep some trees on the edges of your outlook, however, as these are the ones that frame the view.

Windowing. Some trees that are close to a house or patio grow so densely that they block views of the surrounding landscape. 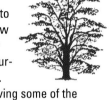 By selectively removing some of the lateral branches (below), you can open up the tree, creating fully framed views—or windows—of whatever lies beyond. When you window a tree on one side, balance it with some pruning on the opposite side, even if both sides are not obstructing the view.

FRAMING VIEWS

Trees are so valuable to any landscape that they should be incorporated into a view— or used to enhance it—whenever possible. They are wonderful for establishing a sense of perspective for distant vistas, such as a body of water or mountains, creating closeness and intimacy within a grand panorama. And city lights become magical and animated when seen through leafy, rustling branches at night.

Occasionally, however, trees interrupt key parts of a view and require selective pruning. As with any tree surgery, pruning to perfect a view must be carried out without endangering the health of the tree. Depending on how you wish to frame the view, several techniques will accomplish this: windowing, thinning, skirting up, or crown reduction. If you are not an experienced pruner, don't attempt to prune large trees. Hire a professional arborist who knows how to do the job properly. In many states, arborists must be licensed, and carry their own insurance; you can find an arborist by checking in the Yellow Pages under Trees, by asking for recommendations from friends, or by contacting the American Society of Arborists.

If you are skillful enough to remove a good-size tree limb, look for its branch collar—a raised lip or wrinkle at the junction of the trunk and limb. Make a preliminary cut on the underside of the branch just beyond the collar to prevent the

This spacious oceanside view is enhanced by a windowed pine. The tree's open structure, combined with the pattern of its trunks and branches, increases the depth of the view. The horizontal layers of the lower branches echo the line of the horizon.

Thinning. Selectively thinning the branches of a midrange tree can open up views, and gives a tree better resistance to the wind. Do not prune the main limbs, but clear out bunches of foliage and the smaller branches that grow between them (left). Remove weak limbs and vertical water sprouts first, and any branches that are rubbing or crossing each other. Then you will have a better view of the overall branch shape and can prune selectively along the main limbs. As you work toward the ends of each main limb, prune less vigorously in order to leave a natural-looking, broad, and bushy top.

Skirting up. Removing some of the lower limbs (also known as limbing up) of a midrange tree can reveal a view without ruining the lines of the tree (right). As a rule of thumb, don't skirt up more than half of the tree's height, less if possible. If the tree is top-heavy, thin it so that it doesn't look like a lollipop.

Crown reduction. To lower a tree's canopy, use a technique called crown reduction (not shown), which reduces the size of the tree while retaining its natural growth lines. Prune the tallest branches as far down to the trunk as possible, but near small side branches that point in the same upward direction. If there are no such branches, track the tall limb down to one of its own upward-pointing, robust secondary branches. Cut just above this branch.

Why Not Top?

Topping—reducing the height of a mature tree by sawing back its top limbs—is the quickest way to ruin a tree's appearance forever. It does not reduce the height of a tree for long, either. Unlike a bushy hedge that soon sprouts new growth after being sheared severely, an older tree does not grow back in a natural-looking way when trunk leaders or top branches are pruned to stubs. Instead, the tree sends out scores of weak shoots from the cutoff points; often these shoots are taller, coarser, and denser than the natural top. A topped evergreen, for example, may develop patchy tufts of needles along its trunk, which may block a view and make the tree look rangy.

Some topped trees might eventually regain their beauty, but the recovery can take decades. A good professional arborist will not top a tree, but will try other techniques to scale it back.

Gardening with shade

Trees in the garden naturally result in shady areas. And as trees grow, the amount of shade they cast increases—sometimes beyond the limits that many plants can tolerate. When selecting plants, keep in mind that all shade is not created equal. Though most trees cast the dappled light usually referred to as light, or partial, shade, some tree canopies are so dense that they allow no light to penetrate. Planting to create shade—and landscaping in the presence of shade—calls for a little extra diligence in the planning stages. Choices of colorful plants for shade are more limited than those for the sun. But you can create interesting effects by combining plants for foliage texture and color.

A. In spring, wild phlox and the foamy white flowers of *Tiarella* blanket the ground beneath a stand of native pink azaleas. The leggy branches of the shrubs add a light touch to a landscape heavily shaded by dense trees.

B. The cool water of a mossy birdbath is framed by the white plumes of *Astilbe arendsii* 'Avalanche' and the airy fronds of wood fern *(Dryopteris),* two perennial plants that thrive in deep shade. At the rear, reedy eulalia grass *(Miscanthus sinensis)* suggests a pondside setting.

C. Striking forms dominate this woodland-edge border, where shade-lovers are drawn from many plant families. A globe artichoke dominates the center, its silvery leaves providing the perfect foil for the soft yellow *Lysimachia* and deep purple columbines. A red-stemmed Japanese maple lights up the background.

Plantings beneath trees need not be confined to ground covers. Here a profusion of shade-loving plants flourishes in the dappled light beneath a dogwood and a golden locust. Both trees burst into white bloom in early summer; the foliage plants below feature soft hues that prevail throughout the growing season.

A Shade Garden

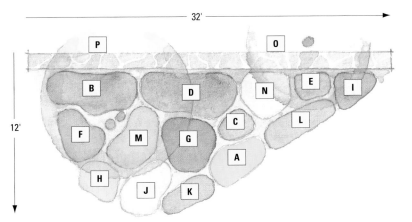

The Plants

PERENNIALS

A. Alchemilla mollis
LADY'S-MANTLE **(2)**

B. Anemone hybrida 'Honorine Jobert'
JAPANESE ANEMONE **(5)**

C. Arrhenatherum elatius bulbosum 'Variegatum'
BULBOUS OATGRASS **(1)**

D. Berberis thunbergii 'Atropurpurea'
RED-LEAF JAPANESE BARBERRY **(2)**

E. Digitalis purpurea
COMMON FOXGLOVE **(4)**

F. Helleborus argutifolius
CORSICAN HELLEBORE **(3)**

G. Helleborus orientalis
LENTEN ROSE **(3)**

H. Hosta 'Chinese Sunrise' (4)

I. Hosta sieboldiana 'Elegans' (1)

J. Lamium maculatum 'White Nancy'
DEAD NETTLE **(3)**

K. Liriope muscari
BIG BLUE LILY TURF **(3)**

L. Liriope muscari 'Variegata'
BIG STRIPED LILY TURF **(4)**

M. Thalictrum aquilegifolium
MEADOW RUE **(3)**

N. Thalictrum rochebrunianum 'Lavender Mist'
MEADOW RUE **(3)**

TREES

O. Cornus rutgersensis 'Aurora'
STELLAR DOGWOOD **(1)**

P. Robinia pseudoacacia 'Frisia'
GOLDEN LOCUST **(1)**

Chinese fountain palm
(Livistona chinensis)
Strongly drooping, dark green leaf tips resemble a fountain. Remains trunkless for years; develops a broad head and ultimate height of 15 ft. Makes a fine patio palm if sheltered from the wind and hot afternoon sun. Hardy to 22°F.

Mediterranean fan palm
(Chamaerops humilis)
Blue-green or silvery green leaves make this desert palm outstanding. Clumps if not pruned. Can survive temperatures as low as 6°F, yet also endures baking sun and drought. Grows slowly to 20 ft. Leaf stems carry sharp spines.

King palm
(Archontophoenix cunninghamiana)
A regal palm, much used in landscaping. Eight- to ten-foot dark green leaves; purple flowers. Fast growing to 20 to 40 ft.; up to 60 ft. in mildest climates. Takes some frost when established. Grows best out of wind; needs abundant water. Not suited to desert gardens.

PALMS

Nothing says Southern California like palms. Yet while many of its palms are exotics from the tropics of South America, Asia, and the South Seas, only a few grow wild in shaded canyons near Palm Springs. Others, such as the Canary Island date palm, come from Mediterranean climates similar to those found in California, and look quite at home along city streets as far north as San Francisco and Redding.

These graceful trees are magnificent landscape plants if you choose the right ones. The ten at right (shown at age 15 to 20 years) are well-tested choices for home gardens.

Palms are especially effective near swimming pools because they do not drop leaves. Fronds, whether fanlike or feathery, reflect beautifully in the water; the curved trunks of a mature Senegal date palm create a tropical island setting.

When carefully placed, palms produce dramatic effects in the garden. Night lighting in particular shows off their stateliness and spectacular leaves. You can backlight them, shine spotlights up on them from below, or direct lights to silhouette them against a pale wall.

Young palms, especially slow-growers such as the Mediterranean fan palm, make good shrubs, staying low for five to ten years (you can move them when they get too tall). Shade-lovers, such as bamboo palm or lady palm, thrive under trees, laths, and overhangs.

To add to the lushness of a group of palms, cover the trunks with climbing philodendrons or other vines. If you live in coastal Southern California where winters are mild, mount orchids such as cattleya high on their trunks.

If you have space, groves of palms of various sizes and leaf patterns give the effect of a verdant tropical jungle. Here, the stiff fronds of a slow-growing Mediterranean fan palm present a vivid contrast to the drooping foliage behind.

King palm

PALMS FOR HOME GARDENS

Chinese fountain palm

Mediterranean fan palm

Paradise palm
(Howea forsterana)
The classic, almost inde-structible, hotel lobby palm. Dark green leaves require occasional trimming. Grows slowly to 20 to 30 ft. Wind tolerant. Best in frost-free areas; needs abundant water and partial shade on the coast, full shade inland.

Queen palm
(Syagrus romanzoffianum)
Lush, plumelike leaves, 10 to 15 ft. long. Grows quickly to 30 to 50 ft. tall. Shelter from driving winds; needs abun-dant water and regular fertil-izer. Suffers in 25°F frost, but may occasionally survive freezing spells.

Lady palm
(Rhapis)
Dense palm; multiple stems bear dark green, glossy leaves. Makes good screen but grows slowly. Requires little pruning. *R. excelsa* grows to 5 to 12 ft., *R. humilis* to 18 ft. Prefers rich, moist soil and protection from harsh sun and drying winds. Hardy to 22°F.

Windmill palm
(Trachycarpus fortunei)
Stiff, upright shape; hairy brown trunk. Can reach 30 ft. in warm-winter areas; will be shorter in other regions. Looks best in groups of three or more. In desert, prefers afternoon shade. Fronds get shabby in wind and must be trimmed. Hardy to 10°F.

Bamboo palm
(Chamaedorea)
Clumping, bamboolike growth gives an oriental look to *C. costaricana, C. erumpens,* and *C. seifrizii.* All grow slow-ly, *C. erumpens* to 5 ft., the other two to 10 ft. Frost ten-der; needs ample water and a shady spot.

Mexican blue palm
(Brahea armata)
Pretty desert palm with silvery blue leaves. Mature plants produce striking white blossom stalks. Heat and wind tolerant. Thrives with regular watering. Hardy to 18°F. Slow growing (about 6 in. a year); may reach 40 ft. Prune old leaves and flower stalks each year, but beware of spiny leaf bases.

Pigmy date palm
(Phoenix roebelenii)
Soft, feathery leaves; stem grows slowly to 6 ft. Wind resistant but tender, and suffers below 28°F. In warm regions, prospers outdoors with some shade and mod-erate watering.

Paradise palm   Queen palm   Lady palm   Windmill palm   Bamboo palm   Mexican blue palm   Pigmy date palm

SHRUBS

I f you try to visualize your property without shrubs, you'll quickly grasp the importance of these plants in landscape design. Without them, there would be no hedges to keep children and pets safely in bounds, no lilacs or roses to gather for bouquets. House lines would be stark and angular without the softening effect of feathery evergreens or bushy hydrangeas.

Just as a large sofa or bulky upholstered chair can help fill a room, shrubs can add weight and substance to a landscape. They become permanent fix-

*Northwestern favorites, azaleas and rhododendrons transform
a simple staircase into a hidden entryway.*

tures, altering traffic flow and framing views. Planted near a wall, they create attractive backdrops; set close together, they form a living fence. For example, clipped boxwood, just a few feet high, helps to define a formal garden, while a staggered row of loose, flowery oleander *(Nerium oleander)* works well as a privacy screen. And a hedge of thorny, dense shrubs, such as barberry and natal plum *(Carissa macrocarpa),* makes an effective barrier against unwelcome intruders.

Judiciously placed, a single flowering shrub can punctuate

the landscape as a focal point; short or dwarf shrubs, when grouped together, can add heft and structure to a flower border or create a smooth transition from tree canopy to ground level.

Like trees, shrubs are either deciduous or evergreen. They grow in a variety of rounded, tapered, or fountainlike shapes. With their showy flowers, fruits, or autumn foliage, shrubs offer seasonal appeal. Some, however, have decorative foliage throughout the growing season. Others, such as daphnes, lilacs, and viburnums, are primarily valued for their fragrance.

With hundreds of shrubs available, one key to successful landscaping is to select bushes that suit your garden's site—its soil conditions, available sunlight, and water resources. Certain favorites such as azaleas and rhododendrons, for example, thrive in the semishade of overhead trees and acid soil that is both moisture-retentive and fast draining. Rosebushes, on the other hand, prefer bright light and a slightly alkaline soil.

To ensure low maintenance, choose shrubs with similar cultural requirements, and remember that for shrubs to look their best they must be given adequate space to grow into their natural shapes. A small smoke tree *(Cotinus coggygria)* purchased in a gallon container will ultimately fill an area 6 to 8 feet wide, but it will lose much of its billowy charm if restricted to less space. Plant annual or perennial flowers to add color around newly planted shrubs until they fill out.

Pruning needs

In general, shrubs require regular pruning to keep their shape, to reduce diseases and pest problems, and to produce plentiful blooms. Consider the amount of seasonal work you are willing to do before making your final selections. Most flowering shrubs are pruned after their blossoms fade; for example, a May-flowering lilac should be pruned in June. Other deciduous shrubs bring forth long stems each year from the base and benefit from an early-spring removal of some older stems. Most evergreens, however, can be pruned at any time of year; exceptions are bloomers such as camellias.

As for young or recently installed shrubs, correct pruning at the proper time of year will lead to bushier plants with more flowers—which may or may not be the look you desire. For more advice on pruning and caring for shrubs, consult a gardening professional or the *Sunset Western Garden Book.*

Leptospermum scoparium 'Pink Pearl' (*left*),
Hibiscus rosa-sinensis 'Brilliant' (*right*)

Shrubs as Trees

Some of the best flowering shrubs are medium- to large-size plants that have been trained to a treelike form with a single, upright trunk. These are known as standards. Others are multitrunked shrubs, such as the oleander above, that have been pruned up to form a treelike canopy.

Certain shrub standards, such as azalea, flower in spring; others, such as hibiscus and the Paraguay nightshade, bloom for most of the growing season. For an accent near a front door, color on a deck, or a focal point at the bend of a path, consider a rosebush, gardenia, or lantana. Good choices for small standards in containers (2 to 4 feet) are euryops, lantana, rosemary, roses, and Southern Indica azalea. Larger specimens (4 to 6 feet) include camellia, hibiscus, lilac, Princess flower (Tibouchina urvilleana), staghorn sumac, and witch hazel. In mild-winter areas, bottlebrush and tea tree (Leptospermum) make perfect patio or street standards.

To prevent the tree from reverting to shrub form, it will need continued pruning and trimming to control growth, including the removal of any suckers that emerge along the trunk.

SHRUBS IN BORDERS

Borders filled with several plant types show shrubs to their greatest advantage. All shrubs, but especially evergreens, lend permanence to flowering borders that change with the seasons; in cold climates, shrubs may be the only source of winter interest. They can be focal points and accents or, conversely, serve as backgrounds for showier plants. Shrubs that reflect the color or texture of nearby trees link the planting scheme to the surrounding landscape. The weight and substance of many shrubs contrast with more delicate herbaceous plants. Flowering shrubs furnish color and fragrance, as well as attract birds and butterflies.

Many shrubs need not be staked, deadheaded, cleared away, or lifted for winter storage. The border at right contains shrubs, subshrubs, and shrubby perennials that exhibit blooms from early spring (magnolia) into fall (abelia, butterfly bush, and roses).

The border is filled with color, including purple-leafed barberry; the gray or gray-green foliage of lavender, lavender cotton, sage, and wallflower; and the yellowish leaves of blue mist and spiraea. Greens vary from bright green broom to dark green germander to apple green plumbago. Bronze-purple tints infuse the foliage of abelia and heavenly bamboo. In fall, deciduous barberry, plumbago, and spiraea, and evergreen heavenly bamboo present good color.

A. This shady corner is brightened with shrubs such as golden-leafed box honeysuckle *(Lonicera nitida* 'Baggesen's Gold'). Its color is complemented by the rosy lavender of flowering onion *(Allium)* and echoed by the chartreuse flowers of euphorbia in the foreground. Various hostas add bold foliage contrasts.

B. Along the path perennials grow. Shrub roses dominate borders on both sides of the walkway. The bluish green leaves of sea kale *(Crambe maritima)* and *Sedum spectabile,* each displaying masses of flowers in season, combine well with the silvery grasses *(Festuca* and *Miscanthus)* and the teal garden shelter.

C. Shrubby lavenders star in this dry California garden, with both French and Spanish species promising a long season of color. Their gray foliage is repeated in the silvery leaves of lavender cotton *(Santolina chamaecyparissus);* floral color appears again in the broad-leafed sea lavender *(Limonium perezii).* Rosemary and scented pelargoniums offer additional fragrance.

A MIXED PLANTING

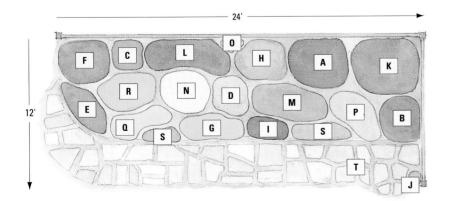

24'

12'

The Plants

A. Abelia grandiflora 'Sherwoodii'
GLOSSY ABELIA (**1**)

B. Berberis thunbergii 'Cherry Bomb'
JAPANESE BARBERRY (**1**)

C. Buddleia davidii 'Black Knight'
BUTTERFLY BUSH (**1**)

D. Caryopteris clandonensis 'Worcester Gold'
BLUE MIST (**1**)

E. Ceratostigma plumbaginoides
DWARF PLUMBAGO (**3**)

F. Erysimum 'Bowles Mauve'
WALLFLOWER (**1**)

G. Genista lydia
BROOM (**2**)

H. Lavandula angustifolia
ENGLISH LAVENDER (**3**)

I. L. a. 'Munstead'
ENGLISH LAVENDER (**2**)

J. Lonicera heckrottii
GOLD FLAME HONEYSUCKLE (**1**)

K. Magnolia 'Randy'
HYBRID MAGNOLIA (1)

L. Nandina domestica 'Woods Dwarf'
HEAVENLY BAMBOO (**3**)

M. Potentilla 'Katherine Dykes'
CINQUEFOIL (**2**)

N. Rosa 'Fair Bianca'
ROSE (**1**)

O. Rosa 'New Dawn'
ROSE (**1**)

P. Salvia officinalis 'Berggarten'
COMMON SAGE (**2**)

Q. Santolina chamaecyparissus 'Nana'
LAVENDER COTTON (**3**)

R. Spiraea bumalda 'Limemound' (**2**)

S. Teucrium chamaedrys 'Prostratum'
GERMANDER (**5**)

T. Thymus pseudolanuginosus
WOOLLY THYME

GARDEN-FRIENDLY ROSES

B e bold with roses and you can create a spectacularly colorful land-scape. But first, you may have to change the way you think about these familiar plants. Many gardeners grew up in the heyday of hybrid teas—long-stemmed beauties with perfectly formed buds that make wonderful cut flowers but so-so landscape plants. But lately, western gardeners are trying floribundas, grandifloras, and English roses, as well as rediscovering old roses for hedges and borders.

The best roses for landscape use are repeat bloomers—attractive, compact plants with clean-looking foliage and strong resistance to pests. While many roses meet these criteria, some stand out for particular uses.

'Mary Rose'

SMALL HEDGES, BORDERS. As a group, floribundas are probably the finest landscape roses. They bear large clusters of flowers atop compact 2- to 5-foot-tall plants that are covered with glossy green leaves. Spaced 18 to 24 inches apart, they make excellent hedges, borders, or edgings along garden paths. Dependable varieties include white 'Iceberg', pink 'Simplicity', yellow 'Sun Flare', and red 'Europeana'. The polyantha rose, a parent of many modern floribundas, carries abundant small flowers in big clusters, making it too an excellent hedge. Particularly attractive are 'The Fairy' and 'China Doll'.

GROUND COVERS. For low raised beds, banks, and sunny parking strips, roses that grow no taller than 2 feet and spread their canes widely are perfect. Choose vigorous, disease-resistant growers such as 'Flower Carpet', with its bright pink flowers.

FENCE DRAPES. Some climbers (leaners, really, that do not cling to surfaces on their own) are particularly beautiful against weathered split-rail fences. Easy-care types include red 'Blaze', 'White Dawn', coral 'Cl. Mrs. Sam McGredy', and multicolored 'Joseph's Coat'.

MIXED BORDERS. Some roses combine handsomely with perennials in mixed borders. 'Graham Thomas' (a yellow English rose), 'Sally Holmes' (a pale pink to white shrub rose), and 'Dainty Bess' (a rose pink hybrid tea) pair well with perennials like catmint, cranesbill, lavender, and *Salvia superba* 'East Friesland'.

TRELLISES, ARBORS. Some climbing roses are quite vigorous, and are at their best when supported on sturdy trellises or redwood arches. Two climbers to consider are 'Cl. Cécile Brunner', a polyantha with pale pink flowers that has a romantic old-fashioned look (especially when trained against white lattice), and the evergreen Lady Banks' rose, with large clusters of small yellow or white flowers that are stunning against a sun-splashed adobe wall.

COTTAGE GARDENS. For a soft, romantic look, try old roses (see facing page)—notably the mounding, shrubby types with long, graceful canes, such as hybrid perpetuals and some Bourbons. In cold mountain areas, rugosa roses are good choices.

Rosa banksiae

WHAT'S OLD IS NEW

Antique roses are those belonging to classes that were developed before 1867, the year that the first hybrid tea rose was introduced. Variously categorized by parentage into albas, Bourbons, Chinas, hybrid perpetuals, Noisettes, moss roses, Portlands, and early teas, their virtues have been rediscovered, and they are likely to be found where modern roses are sold, though specialist growers offer wider selections.

Some old roses bloom only in spring. They are superb for tumbling over a fence, or filling in a mixed border, or providing a green backdrop for later-blooming summer flowers. To ensure an abundant crop of petals for homemade potpourri, plant fragrant varieties in a corner of a vegetable garden. Other old roses (hybrid perpetuals, for example) are repeat bloomers and are more suitable for highly visible areas.

Growth habits of old roses range from compact, 4-foot shrubs (China roses) to tall, 5- to 8-foot shrubs with opulent, often very fragrant flowers (hybrid perpetuals). You'll also find vigorous, somewhat gangly shrubs with cup-shaped blooms (Bourbons).

If you like the look of old roses but want to try something new, consider the modern English roses, which were created by British hybridizer David Austin. These vigorous, and often disease-resistant, roses were developed by crossing old roses with modern hybrid teas and floribundas. The resulting roses combine the charming form and fragrance of old roses with the repeat flowering and color range of modern hybrids. Plants vary from 2-foot shrubs to shrubby climbers.

'Belle Story'

'Abraham Darby'

A. **'Pink Bells'** repeats its profuse bloom to make it a colorful and low-maintenance ground cover. Its compact dimensions (2½ by 4 feet) are ideal for a small, sunny spot.

B. **Full bloom in spring.** A cream-colored rose and purple clematis entwine above brilliant pink peonies. With proper pruning of the rose and clematis, the show repeats yearly.

C. **Spilling over** a rustic fence, the thornless canes and huge blooms of the Bourbon rose 'Zéphirine Drouhin' dress up an otherwise plain barrier.

DISPLAYING VINES

Lightweight wooden or metal trellises of different sizes can hold only lightweight climbers such as clematis. The strongest types have posts that can be anchored in the ground or in a large pot.

Freestanding trellises and arbors support permanent vines with hard, woody stems, such as grape or wisteria. The stems twirl up the posts, and the spreading foliage provides shade.

A sturdy fence or wall bears the weight of vigorous vines such as *Rosa banksiae*, bougainvillea, or trumpet vine. Prune and tie to prevent the plants from sprawling.

VINES

Whether framing an entry, draping a pillar, or just rambling along the ground, vines can bring dazzling color to western gardens. The fast growth of many vines makes them ideal plants for temporary screens and permanent structures alike. They can cover a large area such as a fence, or weave a delicate tracery on a wall in a small garden. Trailing vines can be planted in hanging containers on a small deck or balcony to shield the space from view. And because many vines are evergreen or feature variegated foliage and decorative fruits, they can provide year-round interest.

Not only do vines have a softening effect on walls, they also greatly improve the appearance of other garden structures, such as arbors, gazebos, and spa surrounds. Keep in mind that plants climbing on vertical supports need less frequent clipping and training than those that are trained horizontally. The latter tend to bloom more heavily, however, because their stems are more exposed to sunlight.

Wisteria, which looks equally at home in an oriental setting or a cottage garden, can be grown as tree, shrub, or vine. In this Seattle garden, its exceptionally abundant flower clusters embellish an arbor.

VINES CAN DO MANY THINGS

Soften a fence. Weave vigorous growers such as clematis (above), passion vine, or honeysuckle through an openwork fence to hide unsightly chain link or disguise old or sagging wood.

Another option is to plant vines beside the fence and allow them to grow and dangle over the top in lavish sprays. Danglers with showy flowers include rambler roses, potato vine, and clematis.

Brighten an entry. Train woody vines such as wisteria, trumpet vine, climbing roses, or bougainvillea (above) to frame entryways, gables, and balconies. Their beautiful flowers can dress up plain house walls or soften an angular deck or unattractive railings. Wires fastened to eye screws will hold main branches to the wall, or the vine may be run up porch or deck posts.

Screens and boundaries. Quick climbers such as morning glory or more permanent perennials such as ivy, trumpet vine (above), or Virginia creeper can cover plain fences and walls with color. Vines covering a boundary fence increase the feeling of enclosure on the garden side, while the thick cover of greenery also serves as an attractive windbreak or privacy screen.

Shade and fragrance. A sturdy arbor becomes a haven when used as a support for vines that cast cooling summer shade. Fragrant vines suitable for arbors include Carolina jessamine, honeysuckle, jasmine, roses, and wisteria. Tie the growing vines to the structure with tree tape or strips of soft cloth until the plant has established good contact with the frame. To shade porches during hot summers, train annual vines such as moonflower or morning glory up lengths of twine or garden netting.

LAWNS

Although the lawn is usually the most conspicuous feature of a home landscape, it need not be large to enhance the overall beauty of the property. A well-designed small lawn can be just as functional and handsome as a big expanse of grass, and since both must be regularly fertilized, irrigated, and mowed, a small lawn requires much less work.

Some water-conscious gardeners question the need for a grass lawn at all, but it can have many advantages. Grass is one of the best planting materials to keep the ground attractively covered, and it provides a uniquely safe and inviting surface for children's play and for recreational activities.

Studies done for the Arizona Department of Water Resources show that 600 square feet of lawn is sufficient for most family activities. So unless you plan to play football, a patch 20 by 30 feet is plenty. In parts of California where drought is a problem, cities and counties often have regulations restricting the size of lawns in new landscapes.

Lawns in the landscape

Lawns combine handsomely with flower borders, naturalistic plantings, and paved entertainment areas. Don't think of a lawn as a simple rectangle or square; a small circle of lawn, ringed by trees and flowers, for example, can be the centerpiece of a formal garden, while a curved or kidney-shaped lawn can direct the eye to a focal point, such as a tree or sculpture. A grassy pathway can lure a visitor around a stand of shrubs to a secret garden waiting beyond. And squares of turf alternated with paving can create a cool and interesting space for patio tables and chaises.

When designing or redesigning a lawn area, give some serious thought to the amount of care the grass will need. A shady spot under a tree may be better off planted with a ground cover such as ivy. And if you prefer playing tennis to mowing the front lawn, be selective about the type of grass you plant (see pages 206–207).

To eliminate tedious hand-trimming, install mowing strips along the perimeter of your lawn. A ribbon of concrete, brick, or flat pavers, just wide enough to accommodate the wheels of a mower, will allow you to cut right to the edge of the grass. Lawns with rounded or simple geometric shapes are quicker to mow.

Use edgings (plastic, metal, or wood benderboard) when you want to contain your lawn, as well as any plantings on the other side. If you plant a grass that spreads by stolons, or runners, 8-inch edging will keep it from invading nearby flower beds.

Finally, make sure you have a plan for irrigating your lawn. Will a simple hose and hose-end sprinkler serve your purposes? Or do you have an existing system that needs upgrading or repair? A built-in automatic sprinkler or drip irrigation system is simplest to install *before* the turf has been laid (see pages 328–329).

A. This small garden in the Pacific Northwest is filled with species rhododendrons and hostas, and the undulating grass path acts as a subtle foil for the various colors and textures of their flowers and foliage. Stepping-stones in strategic places prevent worn spots from appearing in the grass and provide a handsome pathway. The region's natural heavy rainfall helps to keep the grass lush.

B. A central lawn offers an area of tranquility in this densely planted landscape; its smooth surface looks restful, especially when viewed from the deck. Mower lines reveal how the lawn is graded to gently slope from the center to the edges, so that excess water can run off into the thirsty flower beds.

C. Contained by formal hedges, this grassy area becomes an open-air seating nook. The sense of seclusion is heightened by surrounding conifers and roses. A gap is left between them to permit viewing of passersby as they follow the curved strip of lawn that serves as a passageway through the garden "rooms."

D. The grassy median between two paving strips softens the driveway to this rustic country home. The turf can be easily mowed, and is prevented by the concrete from spreading into the daylily beds that line the drive.

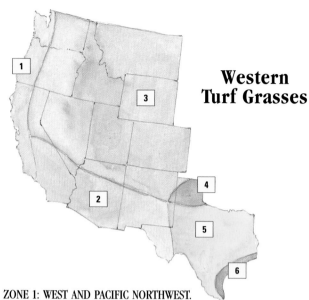

Western Turf Grasses

ZONE 1: WEST AND PACIFIC NORTHWEST. Climate is cool; rain is plentiful except during the summer. Cool-season grasses (bent grasses, fine and tall fescues, Kentucky bluegrass, and perennial ryegrass) do well here.

ZONE 2: SOUTHWEST. Temperatures are high, rainfall is scarce, and soils are dry. Bermuda grass dominates the region, along with some zoysia and St. Augustine. Dichondra is common in Southern California. Where temperatures are not torrid, tall fescues can provide year-round turf with adequate irrigation. Perennial ryegrass is used for overseeding of dormant warm-season grasses.

ZONE 3: MOUNTAINS, PLAINS. Climate is dry and semi-arid, with a wide temperature range. Drought-tolerant native grasses, such as buffalo grass, do well. With irrigation, fine fescues and Kentucky and rough-stalked bluegrasses succeed in northern areas. Tall fescues, Bermuda grass, St. Augustine grass, and zoysia are preferred in southern regions, where the winters are mild.

ZONE 4: MIDCENTRAL. Summers are warm and humid, with abundant rainfall; winters are generally mild. Bermuda grass, tall fescues, and zoysia perform well; ryegrasses and Kentucky and rough-stalked bluegrasses are also used.

ZONE 5: CENTRAL SOUTH. Climate is warm and humid, with abundant rainfall; winters are mild. Bermuda grass, centipede grass, tall fescues, and zoysia do well. Kentucky bluegrass is used in cool areas; St. Augustine is favored in southern areas.

ZONE 6: GULF COAST AND HAWAII. Semitropical climate offers a year-round growing season and generally high rainfall. Bahia, Bermuda, centipede, St. Augustine, and zoysia grasses grow well throughout most of the region. Bent grass, fine fescues, and ryegrasses are used for winter overseeding of dormant warm-season turfs.

CHOOSING THE RIGHT

*M*any lawn grasses are now available, including modern hybrids and native grass strains. Some of these are shown below and are widely sold in the West. None is perfect, but together they indicate a movement toward more climate-sensible lawn grasses. Climate plays a critical role in determining which grass type is best for your garden. Of course, in many regions, gardeners must also consider water demand.

For years, such cool-season grasses as bent grass, bluegrass, and the fine fescues were favored because of their velvety, green look. While these thirsty grasses perform well in parts of the country with abundant summer rainfall, such as the East Coast, they are not always the best choice for more arid western gardens.

In dry-summer climates, the less-thirsty tall fescues have become the most popular of the cool-season grasses. In warm-winter climates, they stay evergreen year-round. New hybrids, including the dwarf tall fescues such as 'Bonsai' and 'Twilight', have been bred to be drought tolerant, with finer, softer blades than the rough-textured tall fescues of the past. In regions where droughts are common, dwarf tall fescues are usually the first choice for home lawns. Tall fescue turf is fairly successful in shady areas, and it bounces back quickly from foot traffic.

Fine fescues and Kentucky bluegrass are still recommended for cool mountain regions, although such drought-tolerant native grasses as buffalo grass are ideal for rustic, informal settings. Once established, buffalo grass forms a dense turf that can be clumpy. Gray-green in color from spring to frost, it turns golden tan in winter.

Crested wheatgrass, blue grama grass, and similar native grasses are found in seed mixes with ryegrass or fescue—best for creating a meadow. Other "wild" mixes combine low-growing flowers such as English daisy or clover with ryegrasses and fescues. The turf is softer and less uniform, but can be mowed and tolerates foot traffic.

GRASS FOR YOUR LAWN

In Southern California, where winters are mild and summers quite hot, the top performers are warm-season grasses (Bermuda grass, St. Augustine grass, zoysia). Although Bermuda grass has a reputation for being weedy and invasive, it thrives in heat and is the best type for desert climates. Hybrid varieties such as 'Santa Ana' can even endure smog. Both commercial and hybrid Bermuda grasses can survive on less water and fertilizer than most lawns, but they do not tolerate shade.

Because Bermuda grass always turns brown during its winter dormant season, a common practice in the South is to overseed Bermuda lawns each fall with perennial ryegrass. This cool-season grower does not compete with Bermuda's strong root system, but it contributes good green color to lawns over the winter months.

St. Augustine grass is the most shade tolerant of the warm-season grasses. Hybrids are well adapted to either dry or humid summer climates, but all are sensitive to cold. Temperatures under 55°F cause St. Augustine grass to turn brown. This grass will also become dormant if water is withheld in the summer, but will readily turn green again when it is watered.

Dichondra, a low, creeping, cloverlike member of the morning glory family, has small, rounded leaves and resembles grass from a distance. It is still used for lawns in warm-winter regions, but it is fading from popularity because it requires ample water and constant vigilance against weeds, cutworms, flea beetles, snails, and slugs.

Zoysia is a tougher option, especially in areas where summers are hot and humid. The drawback to this grass is its long winter dormancy; it remains brown for several months. This grass is slow growing, although hybrids such as 'El Toro' spread faster from plugs (small clumps) or sprigs. Zoysia sod is sometimes available, but beware of zoysia plugs offered in newspaper advertisements by eastern sources; they are not adapted to western climates.

Seed or Sod?

If you are planning a new lawn, should you plant grass seed or lay down a carpet of sod? Although lawns grown from seed require a great deal of work to install and even more care to establish, they do have several advantages over sod. Seeded lawns are much less expensive to plant. The wide variety of seed available allows you to choose the grass or grass mixture that will do best in the soil and sunlight conditions of your property.

Also, because seeded lawns establish deep roots, they're generally more durable than sod for heavy traffic use and are likely to last longer. But it does take more time to create a seeded lawn, including several weeks of keeping the ground moist and weed-free while the grass sprouts and grows.

The primary advantage of sod is its easy installation. It doesn't demand much care to establish itself: new sod must be watered daily, but you don't need to fight weeds, seedling diseases, washouts, or seed-eating birds, as you do with seeded lawns. In fact, when you lay sod, you bury the weed seeds already in the soil. Another persuasive argument for sod is that it gives you a lush green lawn immediately. Sod lawns can be planted at any season, except when the ground is frozen.

The main disadvantage of laying sod is that it is more expensive than seed. And the choice of turf mixes available as sod may be limited in your area. Also, sod does not always bond well with local soils and can fail to thrive.

Whether you choose seed or sod, the end result will be more successful if the lawn area is tilled, weeded, amended, fertilized, and leveled; in other words, the ground must be well prepared before planting begins.

To calculate how much seed or sod to buy, measure the size of the lawn area and calculate its square footage. Boxed or bagged lawn seed will have coverage listed on the label; sod generally comes in foot-wide strips from 5 to 9 feet long.

Left to right: St. Augustine, dwarf fescue, blue ryegrass, 'Santa Ana' Bermuda, 'El Toro' zoysia.

LAWN ALTERNATIVES

If the only person who walks across your lawn is the one who mows it, you should consider an alternative ground cover that does not require so much care for so little return. You should also think seriously about lawn substitutes if your property has places where turf grass will be difficult to establish and maintain, such as on slopes or in damp or darkly shaded areas, or if you live in a hot zone where irrigation is impractical or too expensive. Today, many western gardeners treat the traditional grass lawn as just one option in an expanded palette of low-growing landscape plants.

Whether you want to fill broad areas or uninteresting corners, or install edges for walks or borders, ground covers offer numerous possibilities in foliage texture and color. A wide range of ground covers can be both handsome and tough. Even ice plant, commonly seen along freeways, can be stunning when in full bloom.

For a low-maintenance lawn alternative, choose a ground cover adapted to the conditions in your area—the soil, sunlight, and available irrigation. Consider as well the amount of foot traffic the plant can tolerate. Although a grass lawn is best for active play, many tightly matted grass substitutes can bounce back from light foot traffic. Resilient low-growing herbs such as chamomile, woolly thyme, and Corsican mint are often grown between paving stones because they emit fragrance when stepped on.

An ecological alternative to a turf-grass lawn is a meadow of native grasses. However, although a meadow makes an adventurous play area for children, the wild look of grasses allowed to grow tall could be too unkempt for a front yard.

Despite its wild appearance, a meadow lawn requires the same preparation as an all-grass type. Before planting, you must rid the area of weeds by rotary tilling, solarizing the soil to "bake" the weed seeds, or applying an herbicide. You must then dig in organic matter and fertilizer. In midautumn or early spring, native grasses can be introduced by seeding or by setting out plugs of each species. Both methods demand extra watering and weeding until the grasses are established; after that, however, they need to be mowed and fertilized just once each spring.

If you decide to incorporate a meadow planting, do it in stages. The first year, a native grass "border," about 6 feet wide, can be established alongside a traditional mowed lawn; the next year it can be widened to 10 feet. For more color, intersperse the grasses with showy perennial wildflowers such as coneflowers, yarrow, Shasta daisies, and liatris. At the end of the first year, let the grasses ripen their seedheads; the airy plumes will add interest to the winter garden, and the seeds, usually dispersed by the wind, will provide extra coverage, as well as food for wildlife.

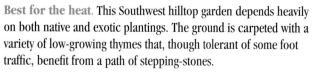

Best for the heat. This Southwest hilltop garden depends heavily on both native and exotic plantings. The ground is carpeted with a variety of low-growing thymes that, though tolerant of some foot traffic, benefit from a path of stepping-stones.

Best for cooler climates. This Northwest garden takes advantage of the cool, damp shade beneath the towering conifers with a ground cover of mosses. A strip of bare soil separates them from a shade-tolerant lawn of creeping fescue and bluegrass.

A GROUND COVER SAMPLER

NAME	LIGHT	BLOOMS	DESCRIPTION/LANDSCAPE USES
Ajuga reptans Carpet bugle	Sun or partial shade	Spring to summer	Forms thick, quick-spreading mat. Foliage ranges from green to bronze to reddish purple; some variegated. Spikes of mostly blue flowers.
Aptenia cordifolia	Sun	Spring to summer	Trailing stems to 2 ft. long. Inch-wide, heart-shaped or oval, bright green, fleshy leaves. Flowers purplish red.
Cerastium tomentosum Snow-in-summer	Sun or partial shade	Early summer	Silvery gray mat covered with white flowers. Needs good drainage. Fine contrast to dark green foliage. No foot traffic. Not for large areas.
Chamaemelum nobile Chamomile	Sun or partial shade	Summer	Grows quickly into an aromatic mat of finely textured, lacy, bright green leaves. Bears numerous buttonlike yellow flowers.
Coprosma kirkii Coprosma	Sun or partial shade		Grows to a bushy, springy shrub covered with yellow-green, narrow, glossy leaves. Bears insignificant flowers. Tolerates sea wind and salt spray.
Cymbalaria aequitriloba Cymbalaria	Shade		Forms 1-inch-thick mat . Bears insignificant purple flowers. May be invasive. Takes occasional foot traffic; recovers quickly from damage.
Erodium reichardii Cranesbill	Sun or partial shade	Spring to fall	Forms dense tufts of dark green foliage. Bears many small, white or pink, cup-shaped flowers.
Herniaria glabra Green carpet	Sun or shade		Vigorous trailing plant with thick mass of tiny, bright green foliage; turns reddish bronze in cold weather. Insignificant flowers.
Lampranthus Ice plant	Sun	Late winter to spring	Blooms of 2 to 2½ inches in oranges, yellows, pinks, reds, and purples. Fleshy, succulent leaves; erect or trailing habit.
Mentha requienii Corsican mint	Sun or partial shade	Summer	Dense mat of tiny, round, bright green leaves; fragrant when crushed. Bears tiny, light purple flowers. Spreads moderately.
Phyla nodiflora Lippia	Sun	Spring to fall	Dense mat of elongated gray-green leaves. Bears small lilac to rose flowers. Dormant and shabby looking in winter.
Potentilla verna Spring cinquefoil	Sun; partial shade in heat	Spring and summer	Grows quickly as tufted creeper with dainty, bright green leaves. Small, roselike, yellow flowers. Not invasive. More moisture tolerant than other potentillas.
Pratia pendulata Blue star creeper	Sun or partial shade	Late spring to summer	Creeping plant with thick covering of small, oval, pointed leaves. Bears many pale blue, starlike flowers. Takes light foot traffic.
Soleirolia soleirolii Baby's tears	Shade; sun near coast	Summer	Produces dense mat of tiny, round leaves. Insignificant white flowers. Tender stems and leaves, easily damaged, but resume growth quickly. May be invasive.
Thymus praecox arcticus Creeping thyme	Sun or partial shade	Summer to fall	Forms carpet of round, aromatic, dark green leaves. Bears small, purplish white flowers. Takes occasional light foot traffic.
T. pseudolanuginosus Woolly thyme	Sun or partial shade	Summer to fall	Forms dense mats. Small, aromatic leaves are gray and woolly. Seldom bears its tiny, pinkish lilac flowers. Slightly tolerant of foot traffic.

Pratia pendulata   *Cerastium tomentosum*   *Aptenia cordifolia*   *Lampranthus*

BUILDING A BORDER

A successful flower border is largely a matter of good marriages between plants. Whether you use traditional perennials and annuals or plants chosen for the arid West, good borders are a blend of plant "bones," "binders," and "bursts."

The easy border pictured at right shows how these three groups of plants work together to ensure a long season of bloom. The "bones" are sizable shrubs or perennials around which the composition is built. They include *Lavatera thuringiaca* 'Barnsley', English lavender, and penstemon *(Penstemon gloxinioides* 'Apple Blossom' and *P. g.* 'Midnight'); all are nearly evergreen in the mild California climate. Other perennials mound and billow around them, their flowers coming and going throughout summer. Because they go dormant in winter, they form the supporting cast of the bones, which include aster, blue mist *(Caryopteris clandonensis* 'Dark Knight'), Russian sage *(Perovskia* 'Blue Spire'), salvia (sky blue *S. azurea grandiflora* and cornflower blue *S. guaranitica),* and purple coneflower *(Echinacea purpurea).*

Echinacea purpurea

Between the bones are the "binders," low-growing, spreading perennials such as catmint, Swan river daisy, and Santa Barbara daisy. They ramble around the taller perennials, creating a sea of bloom that binds the border together.

In winter and early spring when the binders are dormant, spaces are left between the bones for clumps of 'Palomino' daffodils to "burst" forth in their season of glory. Later in spring, another burst—a red-hot poker—shoots up its candlestick spires.

What makes this border work is the limited color palette of its flowers. Pink, blue, and lemon yellow are the predominant colors; purple and lavender play a supporting role. An edging of silvery lamb's ears gives the border definition in twilight.

Before the other spring plants fill out, some spaces between the bones and the binders are occupied by temporary plantings in pots—golden 'Sunspray' rose or 'Graham Thomas', a David Austin English rose.

Perennial borders are best planted in midautumn, when the soil is still warm, but before the rains have come. After choosing your plants, prepare the soil by digging and amending it down to 2 feet. Install a drip irrigation system at this point, if desired.

During the blooming season, clip off faded flowers and shear back trailing plants to ensure a succession of blossoms. To help smother weeds, lay 3 to 4 inches of mulch around plants.

A. The border at right, pictured in July, is orchestrated for bloom over a long season. Summer bloomers include catmint, tree mallow (pink), lavender, penstemon (pink), and santolina (yellow). In July and August, after the penstemons have faded, purple coneflower (center) puts out its lavender pink daisylike flowers. September and October bring asters in white and lavender blue, and sky blue *Salvia azurea grandiflora.*

B. This container adds sculptural elements between plantings. It combines thyme with golden sage. Yellow Swan river daisies ramble around it; 'Apple Blossom' penstemon grows behind.

LANDSCAPING WITH PERENNIALS

Perennial flowers are long-lived bloomers prized because they come back year after year. Most are easy to grow, although it may take a few years to get them established and they vary in the length of time they can grow in one spot without revitalization. Most need periodic rejuvenation by division or other methods.

There are perennials suitable for every location and condition. Some are hardy in the snowiest mountain areas, many live in the driest deserts. Most die down to the ground after blooming, only to reappear the following year. Others are evergreen in mild weather climates, including lily-of-the-Nile and some daylilies. A few, such as coral bells, live most of the year as low-key foliage plants, then explode in brilliant color. With deadheading, many perennials offer repeat shows throughout the season. Becoming familiar with the various characteristics of perennials will help guide your selections.

A border composed entirely of perennials can provide a spectacular display as well as an engaging challenge for the gardener who wants to orchestrate plantings for color and form. Consider decorating one side of a garden with a kidney-shaped or large, rectangular border. Another dramatic option is the island bed, which is placed in an open space in the garden and then surrounded by paving or lawn. It has the added advantage of being viewable from all sides. Still another choice is the double border, which flanks two sides of a walk or lawn.

Many gardeners like to create "mixed" borders, which can include small trees and shrubs, bulbs, roses, ornamental grasses, and annual flowers, in addition to perennials. The perennials supply successive color throughout the year, lengthening the borders' period of attraction and lending it enormous variety in color and form.

Long-lasting color is provided here by the globular yellow flowerheads of Jerusalem sage, which are repeated in a different form on the airy stalks of 'Bowles Mauve' wallflower. The tropical foliage of canna provides a dramatic accent.

BARGAINS FOR BORDERS

Filling this border with plants from small containers can dramatically cut its cost.

Smart nursery shopping

In the course of buying perennials, you can easily spend more than you expected. But careful planning and selective shopping can help you stay within your budget. For example, you'll get better value from a plant that has a lengthy flowering period than from one with a brilliant but short-lived display.

For the longest possible period of bloom, buy plants before they flower. This does not mean that you should never buy blooming plants. Some prized perennials are available at nurseries only during their flowering season.

Small plants are also a better value. In most cases, when perennials are transplanted from 1-gallon containers, 4-inch pots, and six-packs, the plants in the smaller containers will catch up to the growth of the 1-gallon plants within 6 weeks (as shown below).

Why? Healthy plants in small containers, if not root-bound, experience less transplant shock and establish their roots faster than larger, more mature plants.

The border shown above contains 14 perennials: 3 hybrid penstemons, 2 dwarf Shasta daisies, 3 coreopsis, 4 Swan river daisies, and 2 catmint. If you plant the penstemons, daisies, and coreopsis from jumbo six-packs and the Swan river daisies and catmint from 4-inch containers (the most likely available size), you'll spend a quarter of the amount it would have cost if you had bought all the plants in 1-gallon containers.

Moreover, it pays to shop around. The cost of the same 4-inch container plant can triple from one nursery to another—a big difference in cost when you want to fill an entire border with flowers.

SIX WEEKS AFTER PLANTING

Six-pack

4-inch

1-gallon

BLOOMS FOREVER

To ensure successive color through the growing season, plant an assortment of flowering plants that bloom in spring and summer. This border plan, designed in the English country style, makes it easy. Two white-flowered shrubs, deutzia and mock orange, and the heirloom shrub rose 'Baronne Prévost' anchor the composition. A combination of sun-loving spring- and summer-flowering perennials fills out the rest of the border in medium tones of blue and pink, with accents of creamy pale yellow and white. The arrangement will suit any sunny spot in the garden, and offers a display that repeats year after year.

A. This late-summer perennial combo for a moist, partly shaded area matches the unfolding spires of bright pink astilbes with clusters of starry pink asters at the rear; leafy silver lamb's ears add soft texture.

B. From summer to fall, common yarrow supplies soft color that blends beautifully with purple wallflower *(Erysimum* 'Bowles Mauve').

C. A long season of interest—from spring until fall—can be provided by green and variegated grasses. In summer, the strong tones of rosy-flowered stonecrops *(Sedum)* and lavender blue Russian sage *(Perovskia* 'Blue Spire') transform this arrangement.

The Plants

A. Achillea ageratifolia
GREEK YARROW **(6)**

B A. millefolium
COMMON YARROW **(2)**

C. Anchusa azurea 'Loddon Royalist' (2)

D. Aquilegia McKana Giants
COLUMBINE **(3)**

E. Aster frikartii 'Mönch' (8)

F. Campanula glomerata 'Joan Elliott'
CLUSTERED BELLFLOWER **(3)**

G. Delphinium elatum
CANDLE DELPHINIUM **(3)**

H. Deutzia elegantissima
'Fasciculata' (1)

I. Filipendula rubra 'Venusta'
QUEEN OF THE PRAIRIE **(5)**

J. Geranium himalayense
CRANESBILL **(1)**

K. Iris, Siberian hybrid (light blue) (7)

L. Iris, border bearded (apricot) (3)

M. Kniphofia 'Maid of Orleans'
TORCH-LILY **(3)**

N. Lavandula angustifolia 'Munstead'
ENGLISH LAVENDER **(1)**

O. Nepeta faassenii
CATMINT **(3)**

P. Paeonia 'Festiva Maxima'
PEONY **(1)**

Q. Papaver orientale
ORIENTAL POPPY **(1)**

A SPRING-SUMMER SHOW

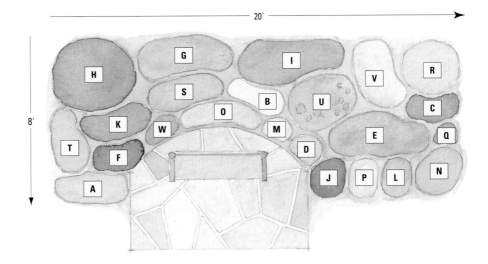

R. Philadelphus purpureomaculatus 'Belle Etoile'
MOCK ORANGE **(1)**

S. Phlox carolina 'Miss Lingard' and P. paniculata 'Mt. Fiji'
THICK-LEAF PHLOX **(2)**
SUMMER PHLOX **(1)**

T. Platycodon grandiflorus
BALLOON FLOWER **(4)**

U. Rosa 'Baronne Prévost'
ROSE **(1)**

V. Sidalcea malviflora 'Elsie Heugh'
CHECKERBLOOM **(3)**

W. Stachys byzantina
LAMB'S EARS **(2)**

PERENNIALS UNBOUND

More than any other plants, the wild forms of annuals, biennials, and perennials lend a look of authenticity to cottage gardens. With softer, wispier growth habits and smaller blossoms than modern hybrids, these rangy beauties were once mainstays of the garden and, like old roses, they have been rediscovered for their color, form, and scent.

Western cottage gardens take their cues from both climate and regional history. A wooden clapboard house looks great fronted with single hollyhocks and native herbs such as butterfly weed *(Asclepias tuberosa)* and bee balm. Prairie homes are still decorated with coneflowers and iris descended from plants brought by pioneers. Western adobes have their cottage tradition too, in Spanish-inspired courtyards where jasmine and lilies grow among olive and citrus trees.

A true cottage garden needs an enclosure, such as a fence, hedge, or wall. The garden could hold herbs, small fruit trees, a climbing vine, and any number of self-seeding flowers that weave in and out of more permanent specimens. Love-in-a-mist, Cupid's dart, and kiss-me-over-the-garden-gate are just a few self-seeders with romantic names that you will discover when you set out to create a cottage garden of your own.

A. Vertical accents in this western cottage garden are supplied by blue delphinium, peach foxglove, and bright yellow mullein *(Verbascum)*. Roses and other shrubs soften the enclosing fence; dusty miller and borage *(Borago officinalis)* tie together the other plantings with their silver foliage or silvery blue flowers.

B. Cool and hot tones play off each other: lime green nicotiana and gray-leafed lamb's ears frame scarlet 'Flanders Field' poppies. The annual poppies reseed themselves; the other two plantings live through the winter in mild climates.

C. The perfect flowers for partially shaded cottage gardens are self-sowing columbines. Their airy blooms play in the breeze, drawing hummingbirds to their nectar. Here, their flowers contrast with the bold petals of iris and campanula and the billowy drifts of creamy white coral bells *(Heuchera)*.

A Cottage Garden

The Plants

A. Achillea ptarmica 'The Pearl'
YARROW **(9)**

B. Campanula glomerata 'Alba'
BELLFLOWER **(6)**

C. Convallaria majalis
LILY-OF-THE-VALLEY **(30)**

D. Delphinium elatum 'Summer Skies' and 'Galahad'
CANDLE DELPHINIUM **(9)**

E. Digitalis purpurea Excelsior
COMMON FOXGLOVE **(7)**

F. Filipendula rubra 'Venusta'
QUEEN OF THE PRAIRIE **(5)**

G. Gypsophila paniculata 'Bristol Fairy'
BABY'S BREATH **(6)**

H. Lavandula angustifolia 'Hidcote'
ENGLISH LAVENDER **(6)**

I. Linum perenne
PERENNIAL BLUE FLAX **(14)**

J. Monarda didyma 'Croftway Pink'
BEE BALM **(4)**

K. Nigella damascena 'Persian Jewels'
LOVE-IN-A-MIST **(19)**

L. Rosa gallica 'Versicolor' ('Rosa Mundi')
FRENCH ROSE **(2)**

M. Rosa 'Cécile Brunner' (2)

N. Viola wittrockiana Imperial Antique Shades
PANSY **(35)**

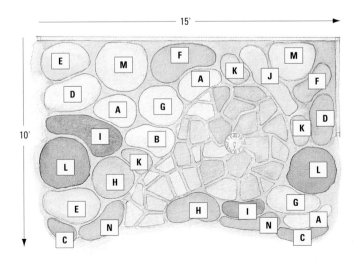

SAVING WATER

Gardeners in many western regions face a particular challenge: a short annual rainy season that is followed by many dry months. Whether in the hot inland deserts or along the cool coast, plants receive no rain in summer and no water except by artificial means. In drought years, some communities may severely limit the water supplied for local gardens.

Fortunately, many fine plants will thrive with little or no water during a normal dry season, once their root systems are established. Star performers include showy native species, such as wild lilac *(Ceanothus)* and brilliant yellow flannel bush *(Fremonto-dendron)*. These plants have evolved to survive dry summers in much the same way cacti have evolved to live in desert zones.

Many favorite dry-summer plants for flower beds come from the Mediterranean region, southern Africa, or Australia—the other parts of the world where dry summers are the norm. Blue iris, agapanthus, lavender, juniper, bougainvillea, and eucalyptus trees are all drought-tolerant species from overseas.

Combine Mediterranean and native perennials to make an unthirsty flower border that will need no extra irrigation after the first year. In fact, it is a good idea to group together the unthirsty plants in your garden; most perform better without summer irrigation, and you can save time and money by not watering those sections of your yard.

When designing islands of plants with low water needs, choose those areas of the garden where summer irrigation would be difficult to install or maintain.

A. The traditional English border gets a western twist when all the perennials are tough and drought tolerant. Blue catmint, golden yarrow, dwarf purple lavender, and scarlet penstemon bloom throughout the summer without much supplemental irrigation.

B. Many drought-tolerant plants are fragrant; their scent is even more concentrated when their essential oils are not diluted by additional water. This fragrant patch in a raised-bed garden includes rosemary, lemon thyme, and purple butterfly bush.

C. Big, rugged shrubs with low water needs give strength and permanence to the garden. Here, pink-flowered mallow, which spreads into clumps 10 feet by 10 feet, is surrounded by a variety of herbs around a simple birdbath.

A WATERWISE BORDER

The Plants

A. **Achillea filipendulina 'Coronation Gold'**
FERNLEAF YARROW **(2)**

B **A. 'Moonshine'**
YARROW **(7)**

C. **Asclepias tuberosa**
BUTTERFLY WEED **(7)**

D. **Catananche caerulea**
CUPID'S DART **(2)**

E. **Coreopsis lanceolata 'Goldfink' (2)**

F. **Echinacea purpurea 'Bright Star'**
PURPLE CONEFLOWER **(1)**

G. **Erigeron karvinskianus**
SANTA BARBARA DAISY **(4)**

H. **Euphorbia epithymoides**
CUSHION SPURGE **(12)**

I. **Geranium endressii 'Wargrave Pink'**
CRANESBILL **(1)**

J. **Lavatera thuringiaca 'Barnsley'**
TREE MALLOW **(2)**

K. **Liatris spicata 'Kobold'**
GAYFEATHER **(6)**

L. **Pennisetum alopecuroides**
FOUNTAIN GRASS **(9)**

M. **Penstemon gloxinioides 'Apple Blossom'**
BORDER PENSTEMON **(3)**

N. **Perovskia 'Blue Spire'**
RUSSIAN SAGE **(6)**

O. **Stachys byzantina 'Silver Carpet'**
LAMB'S EARS **(5)**

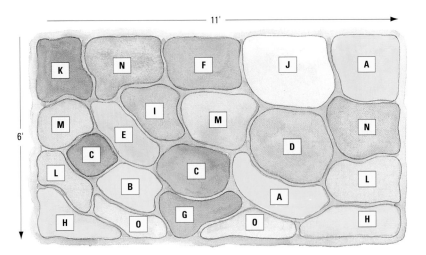

JEWELS OF THE CHAPARRAL

There's a trail to hike each spring, after the late-season rains have swept in to scrub Southern California clean. It's no walk in the wilderness—turn around and you see most of the Los Angeles Basin. But it's one of those trails that makes you feel better about living in a place with thrust faults and bad traffic. At one turn blooms an orange spray of monkey flower *(Mimulus).* At the next, ceanothus's blue blossoms create the illusion that you're walking

Southern California chaparral

through clouds. You may see a hawk; you may hear the dry scuttle of a lizard. The one thing that's certain is that every breath will carry a sharp sage aroma that connotes Southern California as powerfully as the smell of sea spray at Point Dume. This is chaparral.

Asked to name plants that are emblematic of California, you'll probably think of palms, an orange grove, or a Cabernet grapevine. But these are interlopers, transplanted here, like so many Californians, from around the globe. Chaparral is truly native—fossils show that it's been here for some 17 million years.

Early Spanish explorers gave chaparral its name after noting the resemblance of California scrub oak to *chaparro,* the native scrub oak of Spain. Today, however, chaparral refers not to any single plant but to a community of dense brush that makes up one of the most ubiquitous habitats in California; along with its close relative, coastal sage scrub, it can be found in the Coast Range as far north as Oregon. But it achieves real dominance in Southern California's Transverse and Peninsular Ranges.

Trichostema lanatum

Romneya coulteri

Zauschneria

The three robust chaparral plants at left have gorgeous flowers. But, like cats, none will ever be truly domesticated; they are best at the backs of wide borders, on sunny hillsides, or in wild fringes of the garden where they won't crowd out less vigorous plants. Also give them ample drainage.

Arctostaphylos uva-ursi
'Wood's Compact'

While Southern California's climate is paradise for golfers and movie directors, and even gardeners with a ready supply of imported water, it's tough on plants dependent on rainfall. The dry season is long, hot, and punishing, the rainy season brief. Chaparral is above all a habitat adapted to scarce water supplies: its plants go dormant in summer and grow during the rainy season. Leaves are designed to limit evaporation. Many species of manzanita, one of the dominant plants in upper-level chaparral (3,000 to 5,000 feet), have leaves that tilt vertically, minimizing the leaf surface exposed to sunlight.

Chaparral plants are brilliant in spring. Smothered with yellow flowers, flannel bush *(Fremontodendron)*—native to the Sierra Nevada foothills and the inland slopes of Southern California's mountains—is almost its own parade float. And lavender *Salvia clevelandii* provides much of chaparral's pungent fragrance.

The qualities that make these plants survivors in the wild also make them some of the best choices for western gardens. Several —such as Matilija poppy *(Romneya coulteri)* and some ceanothus—also do well in the Northwest. Take your design cues from nature. You'll need the conditions that embrace these plants in the wild—gritty, sun-baked soil, well drained slopes, and full sun. Give them room to grow; many, such as woolly blue curls *(Trichostema lanatum)*, hate to be crowded. Use them together or mix them with plants from other Mediterranean climates. Plant them in fall; let winter rains establish them.

Flannel bush, cloaked in spring with golden blooms, brightens a wine-country garden near Napa, California.

The small flowers of the three plants at right give them a well-mannered appearance. *Ceanothus* 'Ray Hartman', a big shrub to 20 feet tall, can be trained as a small tree. *Mimulus,* unlike the other plants shown here, needs shade (but full sun on the coast). Use *Salvia clevelandii* at the back of a sunny border.

Ceanothus 'Ray Hartman'

Mimulus

Salvia clevelandii

ANNUALS

Flowering annuals provide quick and showy color that can bring instant drama to an otherwise quiet corner of the garden. Grown easily from seed, annuals come into bloom rapidly but die at the end of a single season, after their flowers are spent. In spring and early summer (plus fall and winter in low elevations), nurseries are filled with rows of annuals in flats and small containers in a rainbow of colors. The roster usually includes some frost-tender perennials or biennials that are often sold as annuals (foxgloves and *Salvia farinacea*, for example).

Use annuals to fill spaces between shrubs in mixed borders, set them out for temporary color in a newly planted rose garden or perennial flower border, or put them in pots or window boxes where you want continuous color.

For the best effect in beds and borders, group at least three plants (six are better) of a single color together. Certain annuals, however, seem to look most natural in a confetti-mix of colors—pastel cosmos, Shirley poppies, and State Fair zinnias for example.

Limit annuals to a single shade and species where you would like broad sheets of color. A long, sweeping bed of pink petunias or bright red salvias can be an attention-getter in front of an evergreen hedge or along a brick patio.

In low-elevation regions you can have two different color shows with annuals: cool-season annuals such as forget-me-nots flower in late winter and early spring, and warm-season annuals such as marigolds and sunflowers are planted after the last frost for blossoms from summer to late fall.

Consider seeding annuals in a kitchen garden; they will add color and fragrance. And many annuals provide a supply of cut flowers for indoor arrangement. Those that keep their color when dried (*Limonium* is an example) are ideal for floral crafts.

A. Spring: Golden California poppies (*Eschscholzia californica*) glitter among purple dwarf verbenas and trailing petunias. This informal planting would be perfect for a sloping site in full sun or even for a parking strip.

B. Summer: If you want to grow your own floral fireworks, it's easy to find plenty of hot-colored annuals. Dwarf French marigold 'Aurora Red' and cockscomb 'Forest Fire', shown here, are easy to grow from seed and will bloom into fall with regular watering and a monthly dose of fertilizer. Remove spent flowers to keep the plants bushy and blooming.

C. Winter: Mixed Shirley poppies (*Papaver rhoeas*) mingle lavishly with dwarf toadflax (*Linaria maroccana* 'Fairy Bouquet'), an annual related to the snapdragon. Such combinations bring a carefree look to mixed borders and containers.

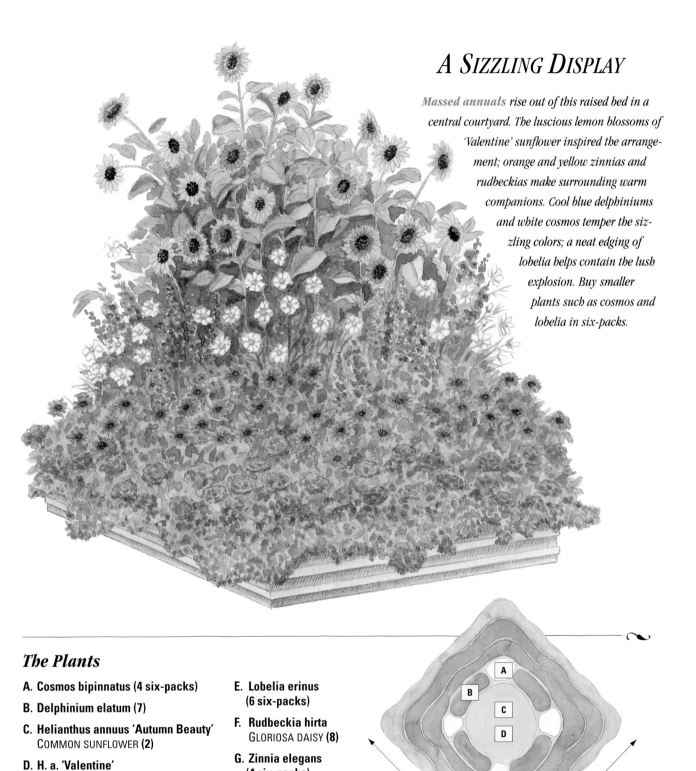

A Sizzling Display

Massed annuals rise out of this raised bed in a central courtyard. The luscious lemon blossoms of 'Valentine' sunflower inspired the arrangement; orange and yellow zinnias and rudbeckias make surrounding warm companions. Cool blue delphiniums and white cosmos temper the sizzling colors; a neat edging of lobelia helps contain the lush explosion. Buy smaller plants such as cosmos and lobelia in six-packs.

The Plants

A. **Cosmos bipinnatus (4 six-packs)**

B. **Delphinium elatum (7)**

C. **Helianthus annuus 'Autumn Beauty'**
   COMMON SUNFLOWER **(2)**

D. **H. a. 'Valentine'**
   COMMON SUNFLOWER **(2)**

E. **Lobelia erinus (6 six-packs)**

F. **Rudbeckia hirta**
   GLORIOSA DAISY **(8)**

G. **Zinnia elegans (4 six-packs)**

5'   5'

BULBS

Some of the best-loved garden flowers, such as tulips and daffodils, arise from bulbs—or from corms, tubers, rhizomes, or tuberous roots. Although traditionally associated with spring, some bloom in late winter, summer, or fall, making bulbs ideal for single displays and for mixed borders.

Bulbs are inexpensive, and to get a good splash of color, you should plant them by the dozens. Bulbs that multiply and spread from year to year, such as grape hyacinths, can be naturalized under trees or in meadows.

In naturalized settings, grassy cover disguises bulb foliage, which must be left until it has yellowed and can easily be pulled away. In formal gardens, oversow newly planted bulbs with annuals. The flowers will bloom simultaneously, but the long-blooming annuals will camouflage the wilting bulb foliage.

In fall, plant bulbs in containers, in flower boxes, or along a walkway or path for spring color. Spring-planted bulbs such as gladiolus can be set out in 4-week intervals to provide an ongoing source of cut flowers. Autumn-blooming bulbs, such as autumn crocus, saffron crocus, and spider lily, offer special bursts of late-season color.

A. When thickly massed, a display of tulips requires hundreds of bulbs. Here, annual blue forget-me-nots, their seeds sown just after the tulip bulbs were planted, furnish a lacy filler and extend the color as the tulips fade. When the show is over, both plants can be dug out and the bed refilled with summer annuals.

B. Yellow-throated daffodil flowers stand out against their strappy green leaves. Polyanthus primroses bloom over a longer period than do the daffodils, and add another touch of spring to this informal setting.

C. Tall, single white tulips rise elegantly above pink forget-me-nots. A few dozen tulips of a single color also make a striking statement tucked at the edge of a flower border or alongside a walkway, but this two-color planting scheme is even more effective when carried out on a large scale in formal island beds.

A SPRINGTIME SHOW

The Plants

A. Artemisia schmidtiana 'Silver Mound'
ANGEL'S HAIR (**12**)

B. Hyacinthus 'Gypsy Queen' and 'Blue Giant'
HYACINTH (**16, 12**)

C. Iris 'Apple Blossom Pink' (10)

D. Iris 'Heavenly Rapture' (10)

E. Iris 'Wedgwood' (30)

F. Myosotis
FORGET-ME-NOT (**10**)

G. Papaver rhoeas 'Mother of Pearl'
SHIRLEY POPPY (**22**)

H. Petunia hybrida (white) (5)

I. Primula polyantha
POLYANTHUS PRIMROSE (**15**)

J. Rosa 'Iceberg'
ROSE (**1**)

K. Tulipa 'Apricot Beauty'
TULIP (**18**)

L. Viola wittrockiana Imperial Antique Shades
PANSY (**24**)

M. Viola wittrockiana (white)
PANSY (**10**)

N. Wisteria sinensis 'Alba'
CHINESE WISTERIA (**4**)

Peach, blue, and white dominate this springtime garden corner. The roses and wisterias serve as a sparkling backdrop for hyacinths, irises, and tulips. As the bulbs die back after flowering, artemisias, poppies, and annuals will fill in around them, extending the life of the border.

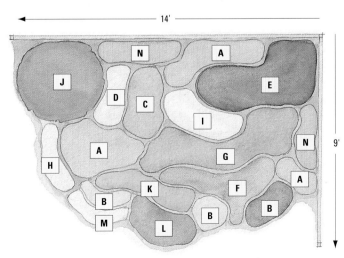

COLOR IN

Color gives a garden its personality. The success of a garden's overall plan depends to a large extent on how well plant color arrangements harmonize and how well they fit the site. Like beauty, pleasing color combinations are in the eye of the beholder; there are no hard-and-fast rules for using color successfully, so feel free to experiment in your own borders.

You can mass flowers of a single color for elegant simplicity or mix several different shades of one color together for subtle plays of light against dark. Combine hot colors like red, orange, and yellow for sizzle in sunlight, or slow the pace and soothe the eye with

Sizzlers

Bright gold, yellow, orange, and red look spectacular in bright sunlight. Against a quiet background, they combine well with each other, and individually each pairs well with blue. The sizzlers are for emphasis, color, and warmth.

Primary colors

All colors derive from red, yellow, and blue. These combine well together, especially when tempered with gray.

Neon brights

Brilliant scarlet, hot pink, and orange are dazzling in sunlight. Together they make a strong statement, if used carefully—in a big pot against an adobe wall, for example. The neon brights don't work well with softer colors, because they steal the spotlight.

Midnight shades

Dark purple, burgundy, and near black are regal yet somber colors that combine well. However, they disappear in shade. At dusk they glow next to lighter colors, such as lime green or white.

THE GARDEN

cool pastels. Tame aggressive colors with gray, add sparkle with white, or wake up somber burgundies or deep purples with lime green. Make sure that flowers with contrasting colors, such as red and white, bloom at the same time, or pair plants with blue and yellow for a classic combination.

When choosing your palette, take a cue from the colors of surrounding walls, garden furnishings, or the landscape beyond your garden. Pick a flower of one color and hold it next to other plants to see what works. Or plant a container with likely combinations, and, if the colors are pleasing, try them in beds and borders.

Cool pastels
Pale lavender, pink, blue, and apricot are romantic colors. They're excellent in cottage gardens and billowy perennial borders. All harmonize with soft blue, silver, and pale yellow.

Earth tones
Green, straw, gold, and amber, the colors found in nature, are most effective in gardens by the seashore, near oak woodlands, or on grassy hillsides—or in naturalistic gardens near wild land.

The Anchors

These are a color gardener's best friends. They play a variety of roles in the garden, and are capable of enhancing a wide array of other colors with equal aplomb.

Snow white
White keeps pastels from fading into oblivion and prevents jewel tones from losing their richness in the sun's glare. In the shade or twilight, it supplies welcome illumination and adds sparkle to greens.

Gray
The temperers, gray or silver-foliaged plants, mellow the heat of reds, oranges, yellows, and magentas. They're diplomats. Flower colors that would war if planted directly next to each other co-exist peacefully separated by a buffer zone of gray.

Lime green
Yellow-green foliage is handsome as a foil, backdrop, or spotlight. It brightens somber colors like deep purple or blue. And it provides a lively backdrop for marine blue flowers, such as summer forget-me-nots (Anchusa capensis) or clear pink flowers.

Blue
From sky-colored to royal hues, blue blends well with most colors, even strong ones like scarlet. It complements yellow and enhances lavender. Sky blue and soft coral, the colors of a Southwest sky at dusk, combine especially well.

HERBS

Gardeners have known the culinary and medicinal value of herbs for thousands of years. Today, herbs are equally valuable as adornments—planted in a kitchen window box, mixed with other plants in a scented garden, or used as hedges along a garden path. Most herbs are easy to grow, and many develop a more intense flavor and fragrance when given little water.

The compact herb garden below, which edges a patio just outside a kitchen, was designed to look good and to deliver snippets for flavoring soups, salads, and grilled meats. It pairs foliage and flowers in a classic yellow and blue combination. A terracotta pot adds a Mediterranean touch, and the miniature rose 'Sunsplash' supplies a colorful accent from May through August.

A Fragrant Nook

The Plants

A. Allium schoenoprasum
CHIVES **(3)**

B. Artemisia dracunculus
FRENCH TARRAGON **(4)**

C. Nepeta faassenii
CATMINT **(3)**

D. Origanum majorana
SWEET MARJORAM **(1)**

E. Origanum vulgare
OREGANO **(2)**

F. Rosa 'Sunsplash'
ROSE **(1)**

G. Rosmarinus officinalis 'Collingwood Ingram'
ROSEMARY **(3)**

H. Salvia officinalis 'Icterina'
COMMON SAGE **(3)**

I. Santolina chamaecyparissus 'Nana'
LAVENDER COTTON **(3)**

J. Thymus citriodorus 'Aureus'
LEMON THYME **(1)**

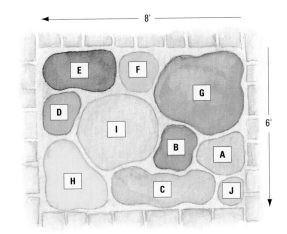

A Formal Circle

The Plants

HERBS

A. Chamaemelum nobile
CHAMOMILE **(22)**

B. Salvia officinalis 'Icterina'
COMMON SAGE **(8)**

C. Salvia officinalis 'Purpurascens'
COMMON SAGE **(16)**

D. Salvia officinalis 'Tricolor'
COMMON SAGE **(16)**

E. Thymus citriodorus
LEMON THYME **(16)**

F. Thymus vulgaris
COMMON THYME **(16)**

G. Thymus vulgaris 'Argenteus'
SILVER THYME **(16)**

SHRUB

H. Buxus sempervirens 'Suffruticosa'
TRUE DWARF BOXWOOD **(40)**

Formal herb plantings vary in design, from intricate "knot" gardens filled with geometrical planting beds and gravel paths to "sundial" gardens composed of flowering herbs that open at different times of the day. Formal gardens require precision in planting: begin hedges with small plants spaced closely, and place herb plants according to a carefully designed pattern. Maintaining such an orderly garden requires more work than for informal borders, but an arrangement of neatly edged plants creates a uniquely peaceful setting.

A formal herb garden need not be large, but it must be sunny for the herbs to thrive. In the formal circle shown above, the different textures and tones of the foliage—yellows, greens, and grays—offer interesting contrasts and harmonies, creating a "stained-glass window" effect. The warm tones of flagstone and brick, traditional paving materials for this type of garden, blend well with the herbs and lend an air of antiquity to the site.

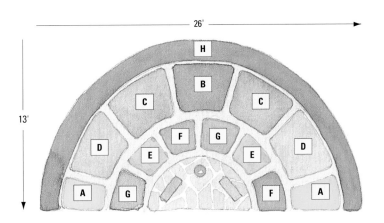

FRUITS AND VEGETABLES

Creating a garden that is both edible and attractive is well within the reach of even novice gardeners. Fortunately, most nurseries in the West supply a wide range of fruit trees, vegetables, and herbs, and a number of these plants have ornamental appeal. In the garden, it is possible to mix edibles with flowering perennials and annuals. Using vegetables as ornamentals in the landscape allows you to enjoy small amounts of home-grown produce without a big commitment of time and garden space.

Herbs, with their distinctive fragrances and interesting colors, can line pathways. Long-lived vegetables such as cabbages can fill decorative containers. The colors and textures of leafy greens such as Swiss chard enliven late-season borders, while the sculptural images of plants such as artichoke or rhubarb lend an exotic touch to a border.

For best effect when mixing vegetables and flowers, cluster plants in groups of three or more. Vary plant heights and add accents such as fennel or dill. To avoid a busy look, repeat the same plants throughout the bed.

Many vegetables and fruits require extra cosseting, generally in spring; others are virtually maintenance-free. Do not plant disease-susceptible ornamentals—that require spraying—with edible plants.

A. The bright flowers and circular leaves of nasturtiums add a peppery flavor to salads. This annual vine looks best when allowed to grow unchecked; it will quickly cover any object left in its way.

B. A river of gold signet marigolds winds among blue-green and red cabbages, curly-leafed Savoy cabbages, and smoky colored kale, blurring the line between decorative and edible.

C. Lettuces and herbs develop into interesting plant sculptures when allowed to go to seed in this desert garden. Squash plants in the background will soon fill in for the heat-tender greens.

A KITCHEN GARDEN

The Plants

A. Apple, dwarf (**2**)

B. Asparagus (**4**)

C. Blueberry (**2**)

D. Calendula officinalis
POT MARIGOLD (**8**)

E. Chives (**6**)

F. Monarda didyma
'Cambridge Scarlet'
BEE BALM (**2**)

G. Pepper (**5**)

H. Rhubarb (**2**)

I. Rosmarinus officinalis
'Prostratus'
DWARF ROSEMARY (**1**)

J. Salvia officinalis
'Icterina'
COMMON SAGE (**1**)

K. S. o. 'Purpurascens'
COMMON SAGE (**1**)

L. S. o. 'Tricolor'
COMMON SAGE (**1**)

M. Sweet basil
'Dark Opal' (**6**)

N. Thymus citriodorus
'Aureus'
LEMON THYME (**4**)

O. Tropaeolum majus
GARDEN NASTURTIUM (**4**)

Accessible and varied, this richly textured garden contains a cornucopia of herbs, vegetables, and fruits. The focal point is the "living fence" created by two espaliered apple trees, easily reached from the pathway. The other plants are also edible. The garden is shown here in late spring.

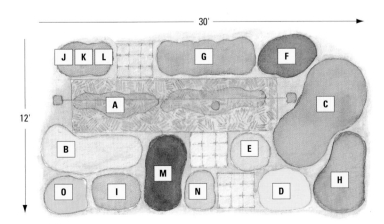

ORNAMENTAL GRASSES

I f you are looking for special effects in your garden, consider planting ornamental grasses. These versatile plants offer beauty and grace while demanding minimal care in return. Once used almost exclusively in prairie or native gardens, they are now finding their way into elegant and even formal landscapes.

Ornamental grasses can be divided into two types, according to their growth habit. Runners, such as ribbon grass *(Phalaris arundinacea)*, spread by rhizomes and can be invasive. If contained, these grasses make wonderful ground covers. The growth of clumpers, such as fountain grass and blue fescue, is not rampant. With their handsome upright or tufted shapes, they blend well in perennial flower borders with irises, daylilies, and plants that have softly spired or daisy-shaped flowers.

Massed groups of clumping grasses, as shown here, can create the same color impact as landscape shrubs. The taller plants, such as zebra grass *(Miscanthus sinensis* 'Zebrinus') or giant reed *(Arundo donax)*, can make effective hedges and privacy screens.

In small gardens, use ornamental grasses as specimens or as accents in borders. In large gardens, fill wide borders with grasses that have airy textures and interesting colors. If you have a pond in your garden, try planting some moisture-loving grasses such as purple moor grass *(Molinia caerulea)* close to the water's edge, where they will help to establish a naturalistic setting.

Most ornamental grasses are perennial and live for many years. Consult the chart at right for help in finding choices that would be suitable for your garden.

The showy, plumelike flower clusters of maiden grass lend an imposing presence to the summer border.

AN ORNAMENTAL GRASS SAMPLER

	NAME	LIGHT	BLOOMS	DESCRIPTION/LANDSCAPE USES
UNDER 2 FEET ▼	*Arrhenatherum elatius bulbosum* 'Variegatum' Bulbous oat grass	Sun or partial shade	Summer	White-striped foliage. Showy, erect, oatlike flower spike. Short-lived in hot inland areas. Dormant in summer. Effective as accent in perennial borders and large rock gardens.
	Briza media Quaking grass	Sun or partial shade	Spring	Heart-shaped florets resemble rattlesnake rattles; good for cutting. Green foliage. Evergreen. Use as accent or in groups in shrub and perennial borders.
	Calamagrostis acutifolia 'Stricta' Feather reed grass	Sun	Late spring to fall	Bright green foliage. Tall, erect flower spikes, but bloom varies, depending on climate. Good for cutting. Deciduous in colder areas; semi-evergreen in mild areas. Makes strong vertical accent plant; in groups, plant at rear of a border.
	Carex buchananii Leather leaf sedge	Sun or partial shade		Coppery red-brown foliage with curled leaf tips. May be short-lived. Evergreen. Use as accent, in groups, or combined with blue, gray, or dark green foliage.
	C. morrowii 'Goldband' 'Goldband' Japanese sedge	Shade or partial shade		Lustrous, bright yellow-striped foliage. May be short-lived. Evergreen. Use as accent, alone or in groups, in borders, or spilling over rocks or walls.
	Festuca amethystina, F. cinerea Blue fescue	Sun or partial shade	Spring	Foliage may be green, blue, or gray. *F. a.* 'Superba', with blue-green weeping foliage and pink flowers, is best bloomer. Evergreen. Use as ground cover, in groups, or as a single accent. Makes good edging for borders.
	Imperata cylindrica 'Rubra' Japanese blood grass	Sun; partial shade in heat		Leaves are bright green with blood-red tips; turn reddish brown in fall. Spreads slowly.
	Stipa tenuissima Mexican feather grass	Sun or partial shade	Summer	Fine-textured green foliage clumps. Tall, tan in winter. Flowers fine-textured, filmy, green turning tan. Can become invasive.
2 TO 4 FEET ▼	*Helictotrichon sempervirens* Blue oat grass	Sun	Late summer to fall	Blue-gray foliage with sharply pointed tips. Showy flowers; blooms best in cool areas. In hot areas, in wet, heavy soil, root rot may occur. Evergreen. Makes good accent alone or in groups, in borders and rock gardens.
	Miscanthus sinensis 'Gracillimus' Maiden grass	Sun or shade	All year	Narrow, green foliage. Showy beige flowers; good for cutting. Evergreen. Use as a specimen or plant at back of a border.
	Pennisetum setaceum 'Rubrum' Purple fountain grass	Sun	Summer to fall	Purple foliage topped by red-purple plumes; good for cutting. Evergreen to deciduous. Cold-hardiness varies greatly. Noninvasive type. Effective as accent or in groups in perennial or shrub borders. Striking with blue and gray plants.
	Stipa gigantea Giant feather grass	Sun	Summer	Gray-green foliage, golden flower spikes dangle from stems; good for cutting. Evergreen. Use as a specimen or in groups, particularly in perennial borders.
OVER 4 FEET ▼	*Cortaderia selloana* 'Gold Band' or 'Sun Stripe' Yellow pampas grass	Sun	Late summer to fall	Yellow-green leaves with yellow stripes. Erect, creamy white flower spikes; good for cutting. Noninvasive type. Evergreen. Use as dramatic accent with shrubs or in background plantings.
	Miscanthus sinensis Eulalia grass	Sun or shade	Summer to fall	Green foliage, some with white or yellow. Cultivars differ greatly. Showy plumes; good for cutting. Deciduous. Use as specimen or in groups.

Calamagrostis acutifolia 'Stricta'   *Imperata cylindrica* 'Rubra'   *Stipa tenuissima*   *Helictotrichon sempervirens*

GRASSY BORDERS

Though a solitary clump of ornamental grass can create a focal point among other garden plants, you can enliven an entire border—or a whole garden—by skillfully combining several or even a dozen kinds of grasses. The photographs at left present some particularly showy types, illustrating the color range of these plants and offering ways to combine them together or to mix them with more traditional border plants such as shrubs and perennials.

A. Massed grasses bring excitement to this wild-looking garden. These undemanding plants would also work well at a waterfront or pond edge. Clockwise from the top: tawny red switch grass *(Panicum virgatum* 'Haense Herms'), bluish Lyme grass *(Elymus condensatus* 'Canyon Prince'), red Japanese blood grass, and a wiry green rush.

B. A soft look is achieved by mixing drifts and clumps of ornamental grasses with small-flowered pink shrub roses. Red Japanese blood grass, blue wild rye *(Elymus glaucus),* and large bursts of golden sedge *(Carex elata* 'Bowles Golden') create a colorful year-round display. The roses, allowed to ramble, offer a brief but glorious midsummer show of profuse blossoms.

C. Like bursts of fireworks, the flower spikes on giant feather grass *(Stipa gigantea)* shoot skyward. The yellowish flowers shimmer on 3- to 4-foot stems in late spring, set off against blue-beard *(Caryopteris).* They show off especially well when backlit by early morning or evening light, and the slightest breeze makes them wave softly to and fro.

A MEDLEY OF GRASSES

The Plants

A. Briza media
PERENNIAL QUAKING GRASS **(5)**

B. Calamagrostis arundinacea 'Karl Foerster'
FOERSTER'S FEATHER REED GRASS **(5)**

C. Festuca amethystina 'Superba'
AMETHYST-FLOWERING FESCUE **(13)**

D. Festuca cinerea 'Blausilber'
BLUE-SILVER FESCUE **(11)**

E. Helictotrichon sempervirens (Avena sempervirens)
BLUE OAT GRASS **(5)**

F. Imperata cylindrica 'Rubra'
JAPANESE BLOOD GRASS **(13)**

G. Miscanthus sinensis 'Gracillimus'
MAIDEN GRASS **(1)**

H. Miscanthus sinensis 'Yaku Jima' ('Yakushima')
JAPANESE SILVER GRASS **(1)**

I. Pennisetum alopecuroides 'Moudry'
BLACK-FLOWERING PENNISETUM **(1)**

J. Stipa tenuissima
MEXICAN FEATHER GRASS **(13)**

This all-grass island planting, seen here predominantly from one side, demonstrates the variety that can be found among a single group of plants. Heights vary from under 1 foot to nearly 5 feet; colors range from silvery blue to blue-green to deep green with red tints. The airy floral panicles bring the entire composition alive with movement.

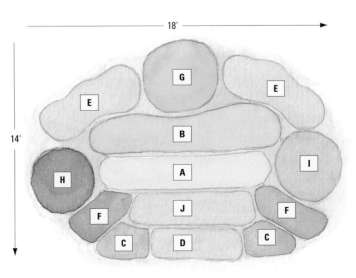

DWARF CONIFERS

Much of the West is prime country for growing conifers, and winter is the season when we appreciate how much they contribute to the landscape. But many conifers are forest giants; having them in your garden would be akin to keeping a whale in a bathtub. Fortunately, a group of smaller plants—the dwarf conifers—is ideally suited to home gardens.

You can buy dwarf conifers at nurseries in 1- and 5-gallon cans. They are typically classified into four sizes: miniature (plants that seldom grow taller than a foot); dwarf (plants that will be between 3 and 6 feet tall in 10 years); intermediate (6 to 15 feet); and large (more than 15 feet tall). The dwarf types fit best into home gardens or containers. They stay compact, are long-lived, and remain relatively free of diseases and pests.

When choosing a conifer for your landscape, consider the plant's form and color. Do you want a species that grows upright or one that cascades or sprawls near the ground? Would you prefer a plant with foliage that's green, gold, or blue?

Also take into account the seasonal colors of neighboring plants: a 'Blue Star' juniper or golden cedar may be a handsome focal point in a winter landscape, but would look insipid and out of place in summer surrounded by pink petunias.

Use a colorful conifer to anchor a perennial planting, to dress up an entryway, or to provide contrast in a mixed border. Or cluster several conifers in a large pot for a low-maintenance, year-round spectacle. Some gardeners in cold-winter areas like Denver or Anchorage use dwarf conifers beautifully as backbones of a border, then fill in around them with spring and summer annuals and perennials that have compatible colors. In winter, a light dusting of snow turns conifers into a magical presence in the garden.

A. This poolside mix of colors and textures is provided by a bonsai black pine (right), a weeping deodar cedar (upper left), and various species of pine and *Chamaecyparis*.

B–D. Choice specimens include *Chamaecyparis obtusa* 'Fernspray Gold' backed by *Picea lukiagensis* 'Purpurea' with *Chamaecyparis thyoides* 'Andelyensis' in front (**B**); mounding *Pinus mugo* 'White Bud' (**C**); and graceful, spreading *Cedrus deodara* 'Prostrate Beauty' (**D**).

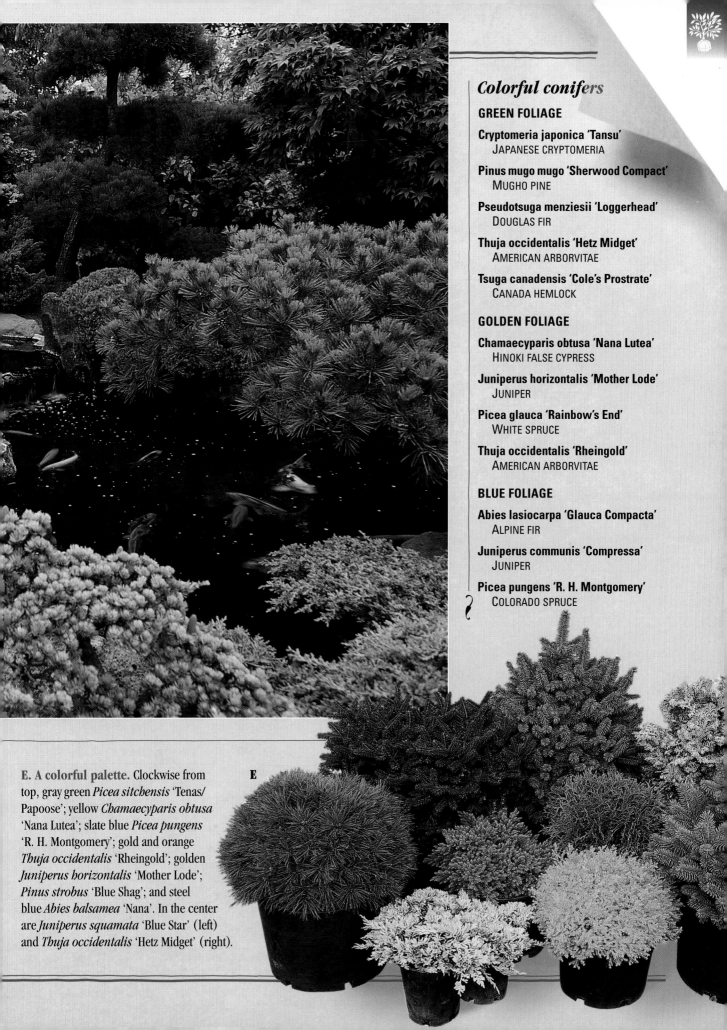

Colorful conifers

GREEN FOLIAGE

Cryptomeria japonica 'Tansu'
JAPANESE CRYPTOMERIA

Pinus mugo mugo 'Sherwood Compact'
MUGHO PINE

Pseudotsuga menziesii 'Loggerhead'
DOUGLAS FIR

Thuja occidentalis 'Hetz Midget'
AMERICAN ARBORVITAE

Tsuga canadensis 'Cole's Prostrate'
CANADA HEMLOCK

GOLDEN FOLIAGE

Chamaecyparis obtusa 'Nana Lutea'
HINOKI FALSE CYPRESS

Juniperus horizontalis 'Mother Lode'
JUNIPER

Picea glauca 'Rainbow's End'
WHITE SPRUCE

Thuja occidentalis 'Rheingold'
AMERICAN ARBORVITAE

BLUE FOLIAGE

Abies lasiocarpa 'Glauca Compacta'
ALPINE FIR

Juniperus communis 'Compressa'
JUNIPER

Picea pungens 'R. H. Montgomery'
COLORADO SPRUCE

E. A colorful palette. Clockwise from top, gray green *Picea sitchensis* 'Tenas/ Papoose'; yellow *Chamaecyparis obtusa* 'Nana Lutea'; slate blue *Picea pungens* 'R. H. Montgomery'; gold and orange *Thuja occidentalis* 'Rheingold'; golden *Juniperus horizontalis* 'Mother Lode'; *Pinus strobus* 'Blue Shag'; and steel blue *Abies balsamea* 'Nana'. In the center are *Juniperus squamata* 'Blue Star' (left) and *Thuja occidentalis* 'Hetz Midget' (right).

ROCK GARDEN PLANTS

Rock gardens are landscapes in miniature, simulations of boulder-strewn mountain slopes, rocky outcrops of coastal bluffs, or windswept high plains—all created with diminutive flowering or evergreen plants. Columbines and tulips just 2 inches tall and pines and willows that barely reach 1 foot in height are some plants that thrive in rock gardens.

True alpine plants grow beneath a winter blanket of snow on high mountain slopes. Low and ground-hugging, they send deep roots into rocky crevices and put forth brilliantly colored, and often surprisingly large, flowers. Fortunately, some alpines also tolerate climates at lower elevations, if their need for good drainage is met. Rock garden enthusiasts in coastal areas of the West can grow small flowering bulbs, perennials, and dwarf shrubs that originated in windy and dry summer areas of the Mediterranean and regions of similar climate.

Your property may be suitable for a rock garden if it contains natural outcroppings of rock or slopes with thin, gravelly soils that make it difficult to prepare the deeply dug beds needed for perennials and shrubs. Because the flowers and foliage of most rock garden plants are best seen at close range, try to incorporate them in and around stone steps or along the tops of retaining walls.

In the mountainous regions of the West, gardeners may enjoy rock gardening on a large scale, setting alpine plants among huge boulders and gravelly scree (a rocky soil common to these areas). In this type of landscape, dwarf pines and contorted shrubs create dramatic effects.

If you import stone for your rock garden, make sure the rocks are all of a similar type and that they are laid so that the grain of each one runs in the same direction. Because they form the backbone of such a garden, most of the rocks should be buried halfway in the soil and should blend in with their surroundings.

A. The variegated form of *Sedum kamtschaticum* dominates this rockery planted mostly with succulents such as hen and chickens *(Sempervivum tectorum)* and various species of stonecrop. The simple repetition of small-leafed and rosette-forming succulents helps to tie together the grouping of rounded boulders.

B. Crevices in these granite boulders create a fine setting for the vigorous moneywort *(Lysimachia nummularia)*. Its light green foliage and bright yellow flowers offer a pleasing contrast to the rosy pink blooms of stonecrop.

C. The bright flowers of *Penstemon pinifolius* make a delightful addition to a rock garden. Growing here in a sunny scree pocket, this Southwest native is adaptable to most western climates.

AN ALPINE NICHE

The Plants

A. Achillea 'Moonshine'
YARROW **(3)**

B. Armeria maritima
COMMON THRIFT **(3)**

C. Asteriscus maritimus
(Odontospermum maritimum)
GOLD COIN **(3)**

D. Cerastium tomentosum
SNOW-IN-SUMMER **(3)**

E. Chamaecyparis obtusa 'Torulosa'
HINOKI FALSE CYPRESS **(1)**

F. Dianthus knappii
HARDY GARDEN PINK **(3)**

G. Eriogonum umbellatum
'Polyanthum'
SULFUR FLOWER **(3)**

H. Imperata cylindrica 'Rubra'
JAPANESE BLOOD GRASS **(3)**

I. Rosmarinus officinalis
'Collingwood Ingram'
ROSEMARY **(3)**

J. Santolina chamaecyparissus
LAVENDER COTTON **(3)**

K. Sisyrinchium bellum
BLUE-EYED GRASS **(3)**

L. Stipa tenuissima
MEXICAN FEATHER GRASS **(3)**

M. Thymus praecox arcticus
'Reiter's'
CREEPING THYME **(5)**

R. Rock

A gentle, rocky slope is the perfect setting for this group of shrubs and perennials with low water needs. The majority of these plants are particularly suited to low elevations and coastal gardens, but would also do quite well in other areas of the West. Some are California natives; others are Mediterranean in origin. Their foliage textures and flowers will supply interest throughout the year.

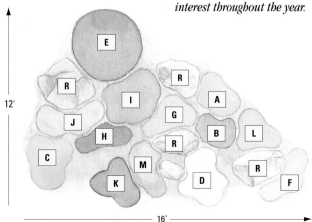

SUCCULENTS

Spaced uniformly—and unimaginatively—in a conventional bed of rocks or gravel, succulents have had their reputation unfairly maligned. But with water conservation a priority in much of the West, gardeners are discovering new ways to use them as landscaping plants, either in the ground or in a variety of containers. Many succulents are almost tropically lush, with rich leaf textures and spectacular flowers.

One of the most appealing features of succulents is the color they offer. Leaves can range from the bronze red of pork and beans *(Sedum rubrotinctum)* to the nearly black rosettes of some aeoniums. Subtle shades of green extend from deep forest hues to soft-tinted yellow greens, gray greens, and blue greens.

For flowering succulents, many of which are quite showy, the blooming period typically lasts from early winter until late spring. Some mature plants send out slender stems up to 2 feet high, bearing blossoms in rich yellows, purples, and reds.

To make a strong impact in a landscape setting, mass plants of the same kind, taking care to vary the leaf color and shape of each adjacent succulent group. For added height and bulk in a succulent garden, try using a few taller drought-tolerant plants, such as agave, jade plant, or euphorbia.

In small gardens, cluster creeping or trailing succulents along stone steps, between paving stones, or on rock walls. These plants will brighten odd, dry corners around the base of a house wall, and can produce a colorful display along a parking strip.

Nearly all succulents can survive several weeks without water, but most will have a plumper, lusher look if given regular watering during dry summers. Some succulents, such as *Sedum telephium* 'Autumn Joy', are perfectly at home in an irrigated flower bed. Verify the water needs of succulents before planting them.

A. Outcrops of a rocky berm: succulents mingle with tufted mounds of pink-flowered common thrift *(Armeria maritima)*, California poppies, and sweet alyssum. These tough succulents will not be overwhelmed by the aggressively self-seeding annuals.

B. The blue-green rosettes of aloes provide the perfect foil for their brilliantly colored flowers, which rise above the leaves on tall, often branched stems. Here, the light green leaves of a *Tylecodon* provide a striking contrast to the aloes.

C. The adaptability of sedums is illustrated here, where the popular hybrid 'Autumn Joy' is in full flower alongside a geranium, silvery artemisia, and clumps of grasses.

D. Simple but bold, this composition features a clump of rosette-forming aeoniums. Their red-edged leaves repeat the floral color of a delicate *Crassula.* Like most succulents, both look well against a boulder.

Echeveria

Showy Succulents

FOR LEAF COLOR

Aeonium arboreum
Green
A. a. 'Atropurpureum'
Dark purple
A. a. 'Zwartkop'
Nearly black

Cotyledon orbiculata
Gray-green, edged red

Crassula argentea 'Sunset'
Yellow, tinged red
C. a. 'Tricolor'
Green, white, pink

Echeveria agavoides
Pink, gray-green, blue-gray,
lavender blue

Kalanchoe pumila
Lavender
K. fedtschenkoi
Lavender gray

Sedum adolphii
Orange-brown
S. rubrotinctum
Reddish brown

Senecio mandraliscae
Blue-gray
S. serpens
Blue-gray

FOR FLOWER COLOR

Aloe species
Red, orange, yellow

Crassula falcata
Scarlet

Delosperma cooperi
Purple
D. nubigenum
Yellow

Echeveria species
Yellow, pink, orange-red, red

Lampranthus species
Orange, yellow, pink, purple, red

Sedum telephium 'Autumn Joy'
Rose, turning bronze in autumn

D

A SUCCULENT DISPLAY

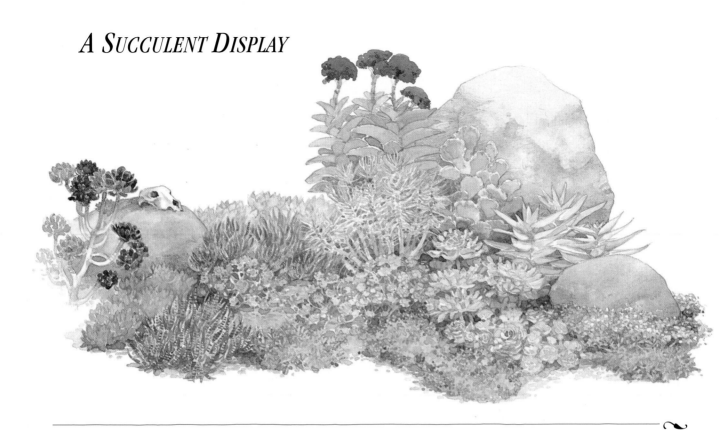

The Plants

A. **Aeonium arboreum 'Zwartkop'**
   BLACK AEONIUM **(3)**

B. **A. urbicum (3)**

C. **A. decorum (3)**

D. **Aloe aristata**
   TORCH PLANT **(3)**

E. **A. striata**
   CORAL ALOE **(1)**

F. **Cotyledon undulata**
   SILVER CROWN **(1)**

G. **Crassula falcata**
   PROPELLER PLANT **(3)**

H. **Dudleya brittonii**
   SILVER DOLLAR
   PLANT **(1)**

I. **Echeveria agavoides**
   WAX AGAVE **(3)**

J. **E. imbricata**
   HEN AND CHICKS **(5)**

K. **Haworthia fasciata**
   ZEBRA HAWORTHIA **(3)**

L. **Sedum album (3)**

M. **S. rubrotinctum**
   PORK AND BEANS **(3)**

N. **S. spathulifolium**
   'Purpureum' (5)

O. **Senecio mandraliscae (1)**

R. **Rock**

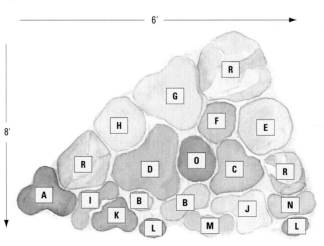

*Lush, yet drought tolerant, this
small garden is filled with some
of the many succulents that thrive
in well-drained soils. The repetition
of rosette-forming succulents unifies the composition. The silver and
grey foliage of the aeoniums and*
Aloe striata *enlivens the green
palette, while brilliant red* Crassula
falcata *and nearly black* Aeonium
arboreum *'Zwartkop' provide dramatic accents.*

A SUCCULENT SAMPLER

NAME	DESCRIPTION
UNDER 1 FT.	
Aloe brevifolia, A. nobilis, *A.* hybrids	Neat rosettes of fleshy leaves, often with spines or marks in a contrasting color. Clusters of long-lasting orange, yellow, cream, or red flowers. Mature plants hardy to the mid 20s.
Dudleya brittonii, *D. virens*	Rosettes of narrow, fleshy leaves coated with a powdery bloom. Small, starry, white-to-yellow and red flowers in spring.
Echeveria elegans Hen and chicks	Grayish white rosettes edged pink. Pink flowers lined with yellow. Can burn in hot summer sun.
E. 'Doris Taylor'	Hairy rosettes tinged deep rose. Shiny red and yellow flowers. Grows well in mild coastal areas.
Sedum album	Tiny green leaves sometimes tinted red. Small white to pinkish white flowers.
S. rubrotinctum Pork and beans	Green leaves resemble jelly beans, turn coppery-red in sun. Flowers are reddish yellow.
Sempervivum arachnoideum Cobweb houseleek	Small rosettes of gray-green leaves connected by fine white hairs that give a cobweb-covered look to plant. Red flowers (seldom blooms).
S. tectorum Hen and chickens	Rosettes of gray-green leaves with pointed red-brown tips. Star-shaped red flowers. Good in rock gardens.
1 TO 3 FT.	
Aeonium arboreum 'Zwartkop', *A. decorum,* *A. haworthii*	Green, gray, purple, or black rosettes of slick-skinned, powdery, or downy leaves—the brighter the light, the deeper the leaf color. Starry, small, pink, white, or bright yellow flowers.
Crassula falcata Propeller plant	Gray-green, fleshy, sickle-shaped leaves. Masses of showy, small, scarlet flowers in late summer.
Euphorbia milii Crown of thorns	Roundish, thin, light green leaves. Clustered bright red flower bracts nearly all year. Grows outdoors in zones 21–24; elsewhere, a pot plant.
Kalanchoe blossfeldiana and hybrids	Hybrids bear orange, gold, salmon, or hot pink flowers. Fleshy, glossy, dark green leaves with a red edge. Big clusters of small, bright red flowers. Some hybrids hardy outdoors in mildest coastal climates.
Senecio mandraliscae, *S. serpens*	Both have cylindrical, curved, blue-gray leaves. *S. mandralisca,* a widely used ground cover, reaches 1½ ft. tall; *S. serpens* reaches 1 ft. tall. May be sold as *Kleinia.*
OVER 3 FT.	
Aloe arborescens, *A. bainesii, A. ferox,* *A. plicatilis*	Fleshy, long, pointed, green or gray-green leaves. Clusters of orange, yellow, cream, pink, or red flowers bloom mostly from February to December. Slow growing, some reach 15 ft. tall or more. Hardiest of these big aloes are *A. arborescens* and *A. ferox* (to 16°F).
Crassula argentea Jade plant	Fleshy, glossy, bright green leaves, sometimes edged with red. Clusters of tiny, star-shaped, pink flowers bloom from November to April. A landscape shrub in mild climates; elsewhere, a pot plant.
Portulacaria afra Elephant's food	Small, fleshy, bright green leaves; similar to those of jade plant. Rarely blooms in western states where hardy; can be used as informal screen. Variegated form is best suited to Southern California coast.

Dudleya anthonyi   *Aeonium arboreum* 'Zwartkop'   *Kalanchoe fedtschenkoi*   *Echeveria* 'Violet Queen'

WILDFLOWERS

Miner's lettuce, milk maids, sugar-scoops, and shooting stars—these are just a few of the many wildflowers that grow in the West. With their evocative names and brilliant colors, wildflowers offer the gardener a chance to bring pioneer history, Native American lore, and ecological conservation into the garden. For example, you can sow wildflowers in a 4- to 8-foot border to create a cheery transition between lawn and woods; you can sprinkle wildflowers in gaps between ground covers; or you might simply designate a corner or circle of your property as a "wild" patch where children can explore and play. Although wildflowers are often naturalized in the garden, don't be afraid to include such flowers as the delicate western columbine *(Aquilegia formosa)* in formal borders. And feel free to intersperse native species with their modern hybrid offspring (such as Pacific Coast irises, hybrids of *Iris douglasiana)* and other garden flowers.

The wildflower gardens sold in cans at garden centers typically contain wildflowers along with annuals for immediate color and a smattering of perennials. Specialty seed companies offer regional mixes, and there are plenty of showy western natives to make these worthwhile.

Hot colors in the desert. Under a palo verde, the reddish spikes of Parry's penstemon and gold Mexican poppies (Eschscholzia mexicana) *put on a spring show.*

After the Show

Weeds are the primary cause of failure for wildflower gardens. So whether you are seeding a wildflower border or painstakingly planting an area with small starts of perennial grasses and flowers, you must prepare the planting bed as carefully as you would for any flower border.

With luck, you will get a good display the first year. (Continue to remove weed seedlings as they start

to emerge.) But once the plants have finished blooming, your natural meadow may take on a ragged, or even weedy, appearance.

Let all the plants in your wildflower garden set seeds, allowing them to dry out on the plants. The seeds will spill onto the ground and sprout new plants the following year. And they'll attract wild birds. You can gather some seeds by hand, too, and save them for later plantings or to fill out any bare spots.

In early winter or very early spring, mow or cut the dry stems down to 6 to 8 inches. At the same time, pull out any weeds, such as oxalis or dandelion. This once-a-year trim will give perennial wildflowers room and light to spread, before the next crop of annuals has emerged from their seeds. In regions that typically have a lot of rain in winter, irrigate a wildflower patch only when rains are light.

A WILDFLOWER SAMPLER

	NAME	LIGHT	BLOOMS	DESCRIPTION
YELLOW	*Baileya multiradiata* Desert marigold	Sun	Late spring to fall	Bright, daisylike flowers; grows 1 to 1½ ft. tall. Thrives in hot-summer areas.
	Coreopsis tinctoria Annual coreopsis	Sun	Spring	Bright, daisylike flowers with purplish brown centers; good for cutting; grows 1½ to 3 ft. tall.
	Layia platyglossa Tidytips	Sun	Late spring	Daisylike flowers with white tips; grows to 1 ft. tall.
	Mentzelia lindleyi Blazing star	Sun	Spring to early summer	Bright, showy, saucer-shaped flowers; grows 2 to 4 ft. tall.
RED AND ORANGE	*Dimorphotheca sinuata* African daisy	Sun	Winter and spring	Masses of daisylike flowers, orange to white; grows to 1 ft. tall.
	Eschscholzia californica California poppy	Sun	Winter to summer	Orange, cup-shaped flowers, also available in red, pink, yellow, and white; grows to 1½ ft. tall.
	Gaillardia pulchella Indian blanket	Sun	Summer	Masses of daisylike flowers with yellow tips; good for cutting; grows 1 to 2 ft. tall.
	Papaver rhoeas Shirley poppy	Sun or partial shade	Spring to summer	Crinkled, saucer-shaped flowers in range of reds; long blooming; grows 2 to 5 ft. tall.
	Penstemon eatonii Firecracker penstemon	Sun	Spring to summer	Grows 1½ to 3 ft. tall, with tubular scarlet flowers in spikelike clusters.
	Ratibida columnifera Mexican hat	Sun	Summer	Drooping, red-ray flowers touched with yellow surrounding a black central cone. Grows to 3 ft. tall.
BLUE AND VIOLET	*Centaurea cyanus* Cornflower	Sun or partial shade	Spring to summer	Bright, button-shaped flowers; good for cutting; grows 1 to 2½ ft. tall.
	Clarkia amoena Farewell-to-spring, godetia	Sun	Late spring to summer	Large, cup-shaped flowers; good for cutting; grows 1 to 2 ft. tall.
	Iris douglasiana hybrids Pacific Coast iris	Light shade; sun in cool areas	Spring	Sword-shaped evergreen foliage; blue, white, and yellow flowers on 8 to 24 in. stems.
	Nemophila menziesii Baby blue eyes	Sun or partial shade	Spring	Small, cup-shaped flowers with a white eye; grows ½ to 1 ft. tall.
	Phacelia campanularia California desert bluebells	Sun	Spring	Long-blooming, brilliant, bell-shaped flowers; grows ½ to 1½ ft. tall.
	Sisyrinchium bellum Blue-eyed grass	Sun	Spring to summer	Grassy leaves, ½-in. blue flowers on 6 to 24-in. stems.
WHITE	*Oenothera pallida* Evening primrose	Sun	Summer	Large, fragrant, saucer-shaped flowers; grows to 1 ft. tall.

Iris douglasiana hybrid

Ratibida columnifera

Sisyrinchium bellum

Penstemon eatonii

FINISHING TOUCHES

A garden's personality doesn't come from plants and structures alone. Much depends on the gardener's knack for adding finishing touches: a copper lantern, a bright glazed pot, a collection of folk-art birdhouses. Picture a weathered teak bench nestled among old-fashioned roses or a lacy hammock in the shaded corner of a rustic wooden deck.

Luckily, garden accessories have never been as plentiful and as varied as they are today. Furniture is available in various styles—from English to Grecian to Mission. Umbrellas come fitted with lights or with canvas walls that block the wind. Outdoor galleries sell everything from leaf-shaped pavers to giant metal flowers. Resourceful gardeners are turning humble boulders and saguaro "skeletons" into striking sculptures and adding drama with colorfully painted walls and outdoor lighting.

Whatever the piece, how you use it in your garden is limited only by your imagination.

BIRDBATHS

If you set out a birdbath, it's a sure bet feathered visitors will come flocking—especially on warm summer days. While birds will gladly frolic in a streambed or puddle, a birdbath is their preferred watering hole.

Birdbaths run the range from utilitarian to eccentric. Some are basic bowls that either sit atop pedestals or hang from chains. Others are designed as much for people to look at as for birds to splash in; you can display them as sculpture among garden plants.

Once birds discover your bath as a reliable water source—in the right spot, kept filled and clean—your garden will come alive with their color, music, and activity. And you'll discover the quiet pleasure of watching finches, wrens, and other songbirds swoop into the bath for a splashing good time.

While a bath cools birds in summer, it can also help them keep warm in winter: frequent bathing insulates birds by keeping their feathers clean and fluffed up.

Birdbath Basics

Keep it shallow but roomy. *Ideally, baths should be 2 to 3 inches deep and 24 to 36 inches across. The sides should slope gradually .*

Consider materials. *Plastic and metal are often too slippery for birds. Some plastics can crack with age; metal dishes should be stainless steel or other rust-resistant material.*

Keep it clean. *Use a strong jet of water from the hose to clean the bowl. If the bottom is dirty, scrub it.*

Keep it safe. *Put the birdbath next to shrubs or trees that provide cover and escape routes. Place ground-level baths*

where they have 10 to 20 feet of open space around them—but no more, or you'll leave damp birds exposed to hawks, owls, and cats.

Keep it moving. *Running water attracts birds. Some baths come with built-in fountains. Or you can create a small fountain by adding a submersible pump with a spray head.*

Keep it from freezing. *In cold climates in winter, add a heating element to keep the bath water thawed.*

A. **Native perennials** and a birdbath invite feathered passersby in this cottage garden.

B. **This fanciful stone bowl,** embellished with salamanders, can rest on a pedestal or a boulder.

C. **As much sculpture** as birdbath, this copper basin stands out against a fountain of ornamental grasses.

D. **A homemade bath** is a glazed terracotta saucer resting atop a straight-sided pot.

E. **A steel sundial** encircles the copper basin in this dual-purpose structure.

F. **A granite basin,** of the type used in Japanese tea ceremonies, welcomes birds to perch on its rim.

G. **Suspended** near a window, this glazed stoneware bath provides a delightful show of songbirds.

BIRDHOUSES

Like weathervanes and sundials, birdhouses can be as much garden art as accessory. They come in many styles, from gaily painted wooden antiques to late-model metal. Flashy or whimsical houses are fun to look at, but may not work as living spaces for birds.

Only cavity-nesting birds (those that nest in tree hollows) use birdhouses. This group includes bluebirds, chickadees, nuthatches, swallows, and wrens. The kind of house you install determines the kinds of birds you'll attract, but this is a most inexact science: while a birdhouse may be intended for a wren or a bluebird, it will be fair game for any birds of similar size.

Small birds like chickadees, nuthatches, and most wrens prefer a hole that's 1⅛ inches across. Medium-size birds like bluebirds and swallows need a nest box with a hole of 1½ inches. White-breasted nuthatches need 1¼ inches; mountain bluebirds need 1⁹⁄₁₆ inches.

Tree swallows and violet-green swallows accept a wider variety of habitats, often stealing houses from bluebirds. Larger birds such as purple martins and flickers take boxes with 2¼- and 2½-inch entry holes, respectively. Flickers usually like to dig out their own nests, but sometimes you can attract them with a large nest box. Fill it with wood chips; they'll dig it out.

A. **Is it a stork** or a birdhouse?

B. **This collection** of fanciful birdhouses includes (left to right) a funky false front of found materials, goofy feline, white saltbox, rough-hewn bungalow for chickadees, and avian version of the Taj Mahal.

C. **Bird chalet** has a thatched roof and a rustic bark body.

D. **Geometric birdhouses,** made to Audubon specifications, sit atop tall poles.

Birdhouse Basics

To keep birdhouses safe from raccoons and cats, mount the houses atop metal poles. If you want to put a birdhouse in a tree, hang it from a branch.

Keep houses away from feeders (the mealtime bustle makes nesting birds nervous).

Face the entrance away from prevailing weather, and remove any perch your birdhouse came with (it's unnecessary, and house sparrows use it to heckle birds inside).

Birdhouses should be made from materials that insulate well, like 1-inch-thick wood (plastic milk bottles and milk cartons are too thin and have poor ventilation; heat can bake chicks inside or make them fledge too early).

Nest boxes need an openable side or top for easy cleaning, drain holes on the bottom, and, in hot-summer areas, ventilation holes high in the sides.

If you put up more than one, keep houses well separated and out of sight of one another. Houses must go up early, since migrant birds start returning in late February and look for nest sites soon after they arrive.

E. Wren house has a 1⅛-inch entry hole and a short chain to minimize swinging.

F. Chickadee house mimics the birds' favored hollow conifer.

G. This terracotta "bird bottle" accommodates wrens, sparrows, and swallows.

H. Purple martin condos are built to hold a crowd.

I. Bluebird box with 1½-inch entry hole has a removable side for easy cleaning at season's end.

AN AVIAN PARADISE

For birds, heaven is one enchanted acre in Rancho Santa Fe, California. Once a neglected citrus orchard, this garden has all the elements that birds like. Tall trees such as birch, liquidambar, oak, and sycamore offer shelter. Water—in birdbaths, in a fountain, in two big Japanese pots—is readily available for

sipping and bathing. Folk art birdhouses perch atop tall posts entwined with potato vines. Nectar-rich plants such as milkweed and penstemon flaunt their colorful blooms over a long season. Paths covered with cedar bark chips serve as duff for birds to scratch around in.

Figuring out how to make wildlife so at home wasn't difficult, says the garden's owner and creator, Agatha Youngblood. "Nature teaches us what to do." Youngblood uses no chemicals on her property; she relies instead on manure for fertilizer and insecticidal soap for pests.

And so the songbirds flock to this Eden. Hummingbirds and butterflies flit among the blossoms. An owl often sits in the fountain on warm mornings, his feathers afluff beneath the cooling spray. The garden draws people, too—family, neighbors, even strangers who fall under its spell and become friends.

A. This high-gabled house comes complete with a slate foundation.

B. Colonial-style, this birdhouse offers tenants a grand view of surrounding blooms.

C. A birdbath nestles among blossoms, including columbine and 'Betty Prior' rose.

BOULDERS

With all its geologic faults, volcanoes, and glacial features, the West is full of rocks. Yet they seldom occur naturally in urban landscapes, so we bring them into our yards—to use as accents among plants, to create rock gardens, and to build walls, paths, and benches.

Quarries and rock yards can supply a great variety of decorative rock, from small flagstones and cobblestones to huge boulders and columns.

Before you buy, consider your site. (Put a 2-ton rock in the wrong place, and you're stuck.) It's wise to work with a landscape architect, designer, or contractor with plenty of experience in installing rock. And if you live on a sloping lot, you may need to consult a landscape contractor or architect to ascertain the ability of the slope to hold the rocks securely.

A. Statice, fescue, and other drainage-loving plants thrive among the stones set beneath rock sculptures.

B. When cut, boulders can take on the sharp planes of modern sculpture.

C. An artificial stone slab, "planted" vertically, creates a new type of growth.

Boulder Basics

Try to work with rock naturally available in your region. It's relatively inexpensive and more likely to suit your landscape.

At the rock yard, flag the rocks you want with colored ribbon. Figure out exactly where each will go in the garden—and which side will go up (taking snapshots of the rocks can help you place them at delivery time).

Most rock is sold by the ton, though some is also sold by shape (slabs and columns, for example). If you want rocks covered with moss or lichen, expect to pay extra, but beware: moss doesn't always survive the move from mountain canyon to backyard patio.

Don't put large rocks on top of small ones. Unless you do it artfully, the large rocks will look unstable. Rocks with flat tops are useful as informal benches or for holding container plants.

Allow for the settling of large rocks (the amount can be significant).

Rocks look better with time. Scars from transport and handling disappear, and lichen grows if you live where the air is relatively unpolluted.

Artificial boulders offer a lighter-weight alternative, but they can be more expensive. Typically made of concrete over metal lath, they're shaped, colored, and textured to look like the real thing.

D. Rocks vary from region to region. The boulders below should give you an idea of options. Shown from left to right: Sonoma fieldstone, red cinder, Sonoma fieldstone, waterwashed flagstone, Sonoma fieldstone, feather rock, desert cloud, desert paint, imagination stone, and holey fieldstone.

CONTAINERS

Almost any container that will hold soil can be used to grow plants. But those that make the biggest statements in the landscape are large, artfully crafted, and full of character. Smaller vessels can make their mark, too, if they're clustered to form a single focal point.

Nurseries offer plenty of good pots in wood, terracotta, and concrete. Styles range from elegant urns to whimsical terracotta frogs. Specialty pottery stores—with containers from places such as China, Greece, Italy, Mexico, and Thailand—have sprung up in many urban areas. And mail-order catalogs are offering more and more selections, from cheerful handpainted vessels to sophisticated, lightweight fiberglass pots. Some of the best containers can be found in antique shops and even at garage sales.

Choose containers that complement your home or that accent your landscape. Then plant them with flowers and shrubs that offset the pots' style.

B

A. Trio of terracotta includes a Cretan urn, an Italian urn with glazed interior, and an Italian fluted flower pot.

B. Bougainvillea bursts out of an urn in this protected alcove.

C. Textured tile shards form a mosaic on this 11-inch-high planter.

D. This glazed Asian urn, nestled in a clump of bamboo, serves as an ornament.

E. Moss lines this hanging wire container; lobelia spills out and over its sides.

F. Fully glazed, these painted Italian terracotta jardinieres feature a grapevine design.

G. Cast-iron urn will acquire a light coating of rust over time.

H. This terracotta kangaroo embraces pinks in her pouch. Next to her is a footed container holding a hydrangea.

I. Cast terracotta has surface decoration ranging from basket weave to floral design.

CONTAINERS FOR SHADE

Many of the most colorful warm-season flowers are sun worshipers. But not all—a careful search of nurseries will turn up a surprising variety of shade plants to make attractive and showy container arrangements.

Some of the most striking effects come from plants with captivating leaf markings and colorful foliage. Gray, red, and yellow foliage can be used as a stunning foil for bright flowers and lush green leaves. Use textures as well in your designs: bold leaf shapes, such as those of hostas, can contrast handsomely with fine-textured foliage, and strap-leafed plants can add drama and soften the harsher lines of other plantings.

A. Delicate maidenhair fern *(Adiantum)* is placed with a lace cap hydrangea, pink polka-dot plant *(Hypoestes phyllostachya),* and snow bush *(Breynia nivosa)* in a 13-inch-wide Italian terracotta pot.

B. This yellow-flowered abutilon *(Abutilon hybridum)* has been trained as a standard and set in a 29-inch-wide Italian terracotta pot. At its base are crotons *(Codiaeum variegatum)* and orange-flowered Hiemalis begonias.

Displaying Big Pots

When they're bursting with blooms, big containers can command as much attention as flower beds. But to show them off to best advantage, you need to put them in the right spot. Usually that means against a plain background—such as paving, walls, lawns, or foliage—that enhances their colors and shapes.

Big plant-filled pots are useful in many situations. They can adorn structures, add interest in front of a hedge, break up open spaces, or serve as portable color to hide a work in progress. They can direct traffic and serve as barriers and focal points.

They're perfect solutions for paved-over areas where plants otherwise won't grow, such as beside a front door, along an expanse of paving, or where a pavement meets a house or garage wall.

Two containers can make a welcoming display on either side of a front walk, entry, or doorway. A single, large container planting makes a handsome focal point in the corner of a deck or patio, or at the end of a pond where its image reflects in the water.

Nestle a big pot among flowering perennials in a border, and you can fill out a temporary bare spot or add height to low plantings.

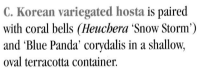

C. Korean variegated hosta is paired with coral bells (*Heuchera* 'Snow Storm') and 'Blue Panda' corydalis in a shallow, oval terracotta container.

D. This brightly colored bowl, 34 inches across and 9 inches tall, holds Hawaiian ti plants (*Cordyline terminalis*), *Browallia speciosa* 'Blue Bells Improved', pink impatiens, coleus, and variegated wax flower (*Hoya*).

CONTAINERS FOR SUN

Choosing plants for sun pots is a challenge, simply because so many spectacular flowering or fruiting plants grow beautifully in sun. You can combine flowering annuals like marigolds with shrubs such as princess flower *(Tibouchina urvilleana);* trees such as citrus with perennials like gloriosa daisy; or grasses with vines.

Choose your container first, because its shape and size will help determine the plants you'll grow. If the pot is simple, the plants it holds can dominate. But if the container is strong in character, you may want to fill it with a simple plant—a single rose, for example.

For large mixed plantings, select the foundation plant first—one with year-round foliage, such as a conifer or New Zealand flax. Then choose plants with flowers that complement its colors.

A. Striking New Zealand flax *(Phormium tenax* 'Maori Maiden') is surrounded by 'Barbara Karst' bougainvillea and purple heliotrope *(Heliotropium arborescens)* in a 20-inch-wide Italian urn.

B. Nagami kumquat *(Fortunella margarita)* stands above gold-flowered Becky Mix dwarf gloriosa daisy *(Rudbeckia hirta)* and *Scaevola aemula* 'New Blue Wonder' in this 22-inch-square concrete container.

C. Arching branches of weeping cedar *(Cedrus deodara)* rise out of this stoneware urn, 22 inches wide by 28 inches deep. Also planted are carex, blue fescue *(Festuca glauca)*, *Phygelius* 'African Queen' (red flowers), and *Loropetalum chinense* (greenish white flowers).

D. A hand-thrown stoneware pot, with a sculpted and glazed surface, holds *Bidens ferulifolia* 'Gold Marie' and cinquefoil *(Potentilla)*. Behind the 20-inch-wide pot is pink corn cockle *(Agrostemma githago)*.

E. Tall 'Red Eye' verbascum rises from surrounding Transvaal daisy *(Gerbera jamesonii)* and zinnias. The pot is hand-thrown, glazed stoneware, 20 inches wide by 19 inches deep.

FURNITURE

There's an enduring graciousness to outdoor furniture. It evokes images of rolling lawns, intimate gardens, and lemonade in the afternoon. But deciding which furniture to buy can be a challenge.

Many styles are available in materials that include teak, woven willow, and cast iron. Rustic furniture blends well with natural surroundings. Other styles are more finely crafted to complement patios and decks. Still other outdoor "furniture" comes not from a showroom but from a gardener's imagination: well-placed boulders, stones, or wooden planks can also provide outdoor seating.

Manufactured lounges, chairs, and tables are often designed in sets, with pieces priced individually. The price range can be wide. In general, wooden furniture is more expensive than its cast-resin or metal counterparts.

Whichever type you choose, keep in mind that outdoor furniture must be suited to year-round use outdoors; sun, rain, insects, fungus, smog, and people dole out heavy wear and tear.

A–B. Two welcoming benches hewn from nature blend with their surroundings. When not in use, the granite bench set on a coastal hilltop doubles as garden sculpture. The wooden bench looks right at home in the surrounding leafy landscape.

C. The granite table and cast concrete bench angle over a reflecting pond. Carved boulders that complement the grouping provide additional places to sit.

D. This rustic wooden bench fits right into the rugged landscape.

E. A cozy pair of rattan lounges becomes a threesome by adding another cushion to the cube tabletop.

F. Carved and cushioned, these fanciful wooden pieces prompt a second look and invite a long stay.

G. The gently curved seat of this teak garden bench ensures comfort.

H. A wrought-iron chaise longue delivers an invitation to relax or take some sun.

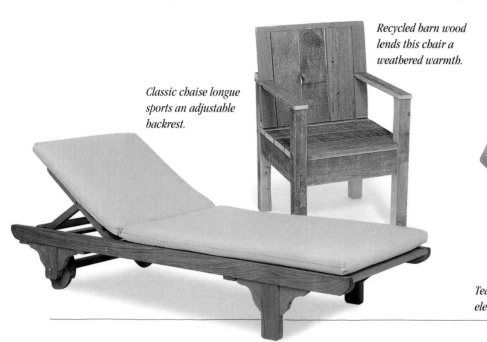

Classic chaise longue sports an adjustable backrest.

Recycled barn wood lends this chair a weathered warmth.

Teak folding chair withstands the elements with no maintenance.

Furniture Materials

With so many styles available, the choice of garden furniture can bewilder even decisive shoppers. One good way to narrow the field is to narrow your range of materials.

METAL. If you like heavy metal but your budget doesn't, you can buy cast aluminum or steel that looks like wrought iron. Consider also enameled or powder-coated, aluminum-frame furniture. It won't rust, and it's durable and lightweight.

WOOD. Teak and redwood are favored for their beauty, strength, and resistance to insects and rot. (To avoid depleting natural supplies, purchase only plantation-grown teak or recycled redwood.) Other woods include jarrah, a member of the eucalyptus family that performs and weathers like teak; Honduran cedar, the pink-brown wood with the distinctive "cigar-box" smell; and jatroba (also known as courbaril), a tight-grained wood from the West Indies and Central and South America. Willow and cypress also appear in outdoor furniture. Willow is less durable; a yearly application of water sealer will extend its life.

As woods weather, they turn to shades of gray unless you seal them with marine varnish or semitransparent stain.

SYNTHETICS. Synthetic wicker looks and feels like natural wicker, but it's made of cellulose, resin, or latex-coated fibers and is undaunted by weather. Wicker and rattan made of natural fibers are less durable and are better suited to sheltered patios or enclosed porches.

Matching table and chair set is rolled steel. Perforations on the seat prevent water from pooling.

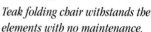

This teak chair brings a flourish to formal settings.

Both bistro chair (left)
and teak steamer chair
(below) fold for storage.

Wicker's natural flexibility creates a
chair with the right amount of give.

Cast aluminum has
the wrought-iron look
without the weight.

This stately cedar chair recalls
design elements of the Arts
and Crafts movement.

Joinery 101

When shopping for outdoor
furniture, pay close attention to the joinery. A good
joint—where a chair leg
or arm meets the seat, for
example—looks nearly
seamless. And it is strong:
it gives a chair, bench, or
table the strength needed
to withstand weight and
lateral movement.

The photographs at left
show three types of quality
joinery on wooden furni-
ture. Brass hexagonal head
bolts and barrel nuts (top)
reinforce joints at critical
points. Mortise-and-tenon
joints held in place with
dowels (middle) create a
strong interlocking bond.
Screws and blocking join
and reinforce a redwood
chair (bottom).

GARDEN ART

Like icing on a cake, the right garden art—in the right place—can transform a seemingly ordinary garden into a magical hideaway. An outdoor sculpture can serve as a visual oasis among a riot of blooms or as a focal point that breaks up long stretches of foliage. It may be a playful gargoyle standing guard over a pond, or small leaf-shaped rocks nestled on the ground among baby's tears. Even a topiary can turn a humble herb garden into a charming outdoor room.

Shopping for garden art is half the fun. Where you begin is mostly determined by your resources. Size, shape, and cost vary as much as the art itself. The key is to select pieces that fit your garden's style. For larger, more expensive pieces, look in outdoor sculpture galleries. Major metropolitan areas and small towns known as artists' havens usually have at least one such gallery. Some artists also sell out of their studios. Specialty garden shops and interior design/gift stores are other places to hunt.

For the budget-minded, mail-order catalogs offer a good selection of sundials, birdhouses, painted or sculpted wall plaques, and sculptures of wood, metal, or stone. And wonderful surprises are always awaiting discovery in salvage yards, antique shops, and thrift stores.

A. This sampling of garden art includes (from left) a tin-and-glass lantern, steel acrobat, carved redwood sphere, wooden birdhouse, concrete gargoyle, glass gazing balls, mosaic guitar, mosaic teacup planter, concrete pineapple finial, and carved stone heads.

B. Surprise is key in a whimsical garden. Consider this 6-foot metal plant.

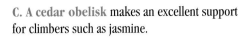

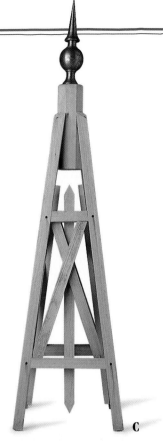

C. A cedar obelisk makes an excellent support for climbers such as jasmine.

D. This cast-iron sundial, made to stand atop a pedestal, reproduces one found at George Washington's estate.

E. Like a good garden spirit, this stone gargoyle stands watch over plants.

F. A trio of ceramic vases, filled with sunflowers, adds an artistic touch on a table.

G. This gentle friar of carved wood welcomes birds and other guests.

H. A topiary gardener, clutching a rake, leaps among rows of flowers. The chicken-wire frame was custom-designed.

D

E

F

G

H

Display Basics

The size and shape of the piece help determine how best to set it off. Large sculptures can sit on the ground, stand on a pedestal or platform, or bask in the center of a fountain or pool.

If you collect a variety of objects, vary their positions and heights in the garden. A carved rock placed on the ground or a birdhouse hanging from a branch can add cheerful touches in otherwise overlooked parts of the garden.

Keep the backdrop simple. No matter where you put garden art, make sure the surroundings are simple enough to display it properly (hedges and solid-colored walls work well).

Check it out. After you buy a piece of art and take it home, place it in different locations to see where it looks best. If the piece is too heavy to move around, walk around the garden and imagine it in various positions.

Keep scale in mind. A massive piece requires plenty of space to stop it from dwarfing its neighbors. A small piece can get lost in a jungle of foliage.

B

D

A

C

A. **A surplus** of terracotta pots creates a humorous work of garden art. The "hair" is dusty miller.

B. **A saguaro skeleton** is a natural sculpture in a planting of desert marigolds.

C. **Colorful fish** of painted wood and plastic poke into pots or flower beds.

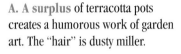

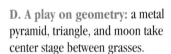

D. **A play on geometry:** a metal pyramid, triangle, and moon take center stage between grasses.

E. **A "tree-trunk" planter,** of shaped and textured concrete over a metal form, adds a sculptural element in the center of a pool.

F. **Steel maple leaves** accent foliage.

G. **Leaves** of stone rest among ivy and asparagus fern.

H. **A "green man" plaque** enlivens a tree trunk.

AN ARTIST'S GARDEN

Keeyla Meadows's garden in Albany, California, is a bit like a fairy tale. The riot of pinks, purples, blues, and yellows; the cheerful-looking plants and paving; the pots, plaques, and furnishings cast an enchanting spell.

"I approach the landscape as I do a painting, working with colors, textures, shapes, and composition," Meadows says. Lush plantings tumble in showers of color from beds and planters. Fanciful benches and handmade urns attract the eye. A copper arbor topped by giant morning glory flowers entices visitors to the back of the garden.

The curving planters give height, depth, and dimension to the small space. Meadows painted the planters bright pink and trimmed them with handmade blue tiles. The tiles reappear in the patchwork brick-and-flagstone paving that meanders around the flower beds.

Plants cover every inch of ground, discouraging weeds and creating a wondrous jumble of foliage and color.

A. This glazed ceramic urn, brushed with soft pastels, holds pink-flowered *Clematis* 'Duchess of Albany'.

B. A rose pink bench, a pinkish copper "morning glory" trellis, and cobalt blue tiles add artful touches to this colorful garden. Pink twinspur, pink foxgloves, and blue delphiniums contribute matching hues. A clematis embellishes the trellis with starburst blooms of deep rose pink.

C. A whimsical bench painted heavenly blue provides cozy seating. A pink-and-white clematis and a pink climbing rose embellish the picket fence behind.

HAMMOCKS

The world slows down when you stretch out in a hammock. Suspended and supine, you notice more keenly the pleasures of summer: the soft air wafting across your cheeks, a swaying view into the branches of a tree, chirping birds, the scent of sun-warmed flowers.

Today's hammocks have evolved well beyond the trusty versions made of cotton rope. New synthetic materials are softer, more comfortable, and more durable than traditional materials. The variety of colors and patterns can be easily coordinated with contemporary outdoor furniture. Sizes now range from subcompact to behemoth.

If your garden lacks trees or posts at just the right distance apart (12 to 15 feet) to hang a hammock, you can choose from sturdy frames made of such materials as wood or aluminum.

Sources include outdoor furniture dealers, home supply stores, and mail-order companies.

A. The classic cotton rope hammock comes in various lengths and widths. This one is large enough for two.

B. Quilted and padded hammock is covered with acrylic fabric that resists fading and mildew.

C. Hammock chair hangs from a single 36-inch oak crossbar. Plump cushions are covered in washable acrylic.

D. Brazilian-style hammock, of handwoven and crocheted cotton thread, is finished with lacy fringe.

E. Hybrid hammock combines fabric for comfort under your torso with rope for air circulation around your legs.

F. Multicolored Mayan hammock looks delicate but is durable. This one contains almost 2 miles of string.

Hammock Basics

Hammocks take many forms:

Synthetic rope hammocks *are usually made of durable, soft-spun materials such as polyester that resist moisture and are available in a range of colors. As with any woven rope, this type will emboss its pattern on your arms and legs if you lie on it for a while.*

Cloth hammocks *are often made of the same fabric that covers contemporary umbrellas and outdoor chairs. It's strong and mildew resistant, and it stands up to harsh sun.*

Screen or mesh hammocks *are made of a soft shade-cloth-type material that allows good air circulation, can be cleaned easily, and is water and stain resistant.*

Quilted hammocks *are typically made of two layers of weather-resistant polyester with batting between.*

Most hammocks *come with sturdy metal chains, S-hooks, and oversize threaded hooks you can attach to posts. Some suppliers sell these separately. Frames enable you to place a hammock almost anywhere—on a deck or patio or in the middle of a lawn. Other hammock extras include storage bags, canopy tops, and add-on wheels for the frames.*

A

LIGHTING

When night falls, the garden becomes a perfect stage for outdoor lighting. Each spot, beam, and burst of light brings daylight to darkness, yet it does so in a selective fashion: by controlling the source of light, you can accentuate the positive in your garden while leaving the negative in darkness or deep shadow.

Outdoor lighting can also visually enlarge indoor rooms. If at night you peer out at an unlighted garden, your windows seem little more than black holes or dark mirrors. Landscape lighting makes the windows transparent again, and your home feels more spacious because the eye is drawn outdoors.

Good outdoor lighting has a practical use, too. Lights can outline paths for safe and easy walking, and they can brighten dark areas to discourage intruders.

Lighting can be subtle, dramatic, and anything in between. Lighting a pond underwater or silhouetting a single shrub or tree can add ethereal magic to nighttime gardens. Carefully placed lights can even mimic the play of moonlight and shadow across pavings.

A. Recessed lights add drama to patio walls.

B. Upward-facing lights placed at the base of trees define trunks and leaves without calling attention to themselves.

C. Careful illumination expands the space in this two-level garden. Because several points of interest are lighted, the view is "stretched."

Lighting Basics

Outdoor lighting fixtures are either decorative or functional. Decorative lights—lanterns, hanging and post- or wall-mounted units, path lights, and strip lights—can add some fill light, but they're primarily meant to be seen and to set an architectural tone.

A functional fixture's job is to light the garden unnoticed. Although some manufacturers make attractive versions, the less visible these fixtures are, the more successful your lighting will be.

Backlighting a lacy shrub makes it glow delicately.

Path lights can flank walks or go high under eaves.

Sidelighting dense trees defines their details.

Shadowing magnifies plant silhouettes on walls.

"Moonlighting" casts soft pools of light below trees.

"Grazing" lights aim upward to highlight architecture.

Uplighting trees reveals form; canopy reflects glow.

A

Standard Current or Low-Voltage?

Outdoor lighting can be powered by standard 120-volt current or by low-voltage systems with transformers that reduce household current to 12 volts.

Standard current

Well suited for large projects or for lighting tall trees with a strong blast of light, standard-voltage fixtures are often better built and longer lasting than low-voltage models. However, they're also larger, harder to hide, more costly to install, more difficult to move, and harder to aim.

Any standard-voltage installation requires a building permit, and codes require that circuits be wired through ground fault circuit interrupters (GCFIs). Wires must be encased in rigid conduit unless they're at least 18 inches underground, and all junctions must be encased in approved outdoor boxes.

Low voltage

Advantages include energy conservation, greater safety, easier installation, portability, and more control of light beams. Some are solar powered.

On the down side, low-voltage fixtures are often simply staked in the ground and can be upset easily. They're expensive. And the number of lamps that can be attached to one transformer is limited.

B

C

A. Because it's lightweight, this low-voltage copper cylinder is easy to hang from trees.

B. Graceful lines mark this Craftsman-style copper lantern.

C. This low-voltage, hand-crafted copper lantern hangs from a curved staff.

D. A "mushroom" path lamp lights the way for safe passage.

E. This two-tiered pagoda stands tall among shrubs.

F. Unobtrusive and ideal for "grazing," this low-voltage unit casts light upward.

D

E

F

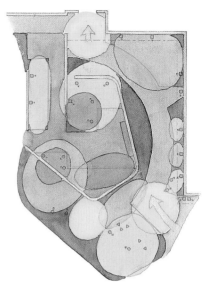

G. This wall-mounted decorative spot provides a vertical shaft of light.

H. The swivel spot casts a narrow beam wherever you need it.

I. Mounted on a wall or ceiling, this low-voltage square spot supplies a pale glow.

J. Designed to illuminate steps and decks, this 12-volt light measures only 3½ inches across.

K. This flush-mounted light tucks beneath steps, staying out of harm's way.

L. Placed under water, this low-voltage unit may be aimed upward at statues, plants, or small waterfalls.

Light Placement

Whether your garden is large or small, start by determining how much of it you want to light. Most lighting designers divide the garden into three zones: a foreground, which is usually given midlevel brightness; a middle ground, with low-level light and an interplay of shadows; and a background—often the brightest of all—to draw the eye through the garden.

The concept plan above shows these different zones. Pathways are marked and arrows indicate entryways. Individual lights are indicated with triangles (tree mounts), circles (ground lights), and squares (wall mounts); arrows show the direction of the light they will cast. Fine-tuning for placement and brightness should be done under actual conditions.

Lighting should never be spotty. It should define, not disguise. For example, uplighting gives the mantle of a tall tree a dramatic form, but it can also make the top appear to hover ghostlike above the earth. To visually anchor the trunk, have the light (or an additional one) illuminate the trunk near ground level.

Finally, be aware of how your lights may affect your neighbors. Some communities even have ordinances regulating "light trespass."

PORTABLE LIGHTING

Special occasions such as holidays or outdoor parties often call for temporary lighting that can be put into place nearly instantly. A broad range of lanterns is available, from hurricane lamps that burn oil to glass-sided lanterns that house candles. Classic New Mexican luminarias—open paper bags that contain votive candles set in sand—have now been electrified, adding to the growing field of specialty outdoor lighting. Tiny hat lights on strings can bring a carnival atmosphere to a patio or deck. And lanterns on stakes can add drama along the path to a gate or door.

A sampling of lights you might find in stores and catalogs that sell home accessories is pictured here. Keep in mind that selections change from year to year.

No matter which lantern you choose, you'll need to place it with care; this is especially true for lanterns with open flames. Unless snow covers the ground around them, avoid placing lanterns along a path or among foliage where they can pose a fire hazard. Also, make sure that they're sturdy and will not topple in a breeze. And avoid putting metal lanterns that could become hot near dry plant material.

A. Weatherproof luminarias contain clear bulbs locked into plastic frames. Flanges molded into each base secure frames to the wall. Bags can be slid onto the frames upside down to keep out rain.

B. Galvanized steel-hat lights dance across a patio.

C–H. Variations on the hurricane theme, these lanterns protect candles from evening breezes. All are glass and metal, except for the terracotta "beehives" (**E**).

I. A cast-iron Japanese lantern casts a flickering glow across night gardens.

PAINT

When you're looking to enhance your garden, consider the power of paint. Imagine a sky blue wall behind a row of bright yellow and orange nasturtiums and blue cornflowers. Or a mint green wall behind a cluster of metal cafe chairs painted the color of strawberry sherbet. Such arresting color schemes are at home in Mexico and southern Arizona—especially in gardens that surround Mediterranean, contemporary, or adobe-style houses.

Color can highlight many garden features. A low white wall, for example, might more readily invite sitting if you paint its top azure blue or another color that blends with your garden's decor and the color of your house. Paint can brighten pots, outdoor furniture, or other garden accessories. It can add texture to a plain wall by mimicking brick or wood. It can embellish a wall with a delicate tracery of faux vines.

Walls painted with garden scenes can visually enlarge sites too small or too dark (narrow side yards, for example) to accommodate real plants.

Artful painting transforms successive concrete walls into a lush, tropical scene. Potted plants add to the illusion.

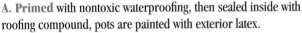

A. **Primed** with nontoxic waterproofing, then sealed inside with roofing compound, pots are painted with exterior latex.

B. **The trompe l'oeil gate** in this Palo Alto, California, garden welcomes visitors to an imaginary land beyond the wall.

C. **Purple patches** and shades of blue enliven this urchin's domain.

D. **A wash of color** sets off the rich hues of geranium in a figured wall pot.

Paint Basics

*For **plaster and stucco**, use exterior latex or acrylic paint. Rolling will force paint into crevices for a more uniform surface. (You may also mix tint into wet stucco.)*

*For **new wood**, first seal all exposed surfaces with one or two coats of latex or exterior wood primer. Then paint with flat latex acrylic or vinyl exterior enamel or house paint in the desired sheen.*

***Make sure surfaces** are free of dirt, grease, rust, and paint flakes (scrape and sand the surface, if necessary, to achieve this).*

***Paint in fair** (above 50°F), dry weather, out of direct sun.*

*To **avoid wrinkling**, fading, or loss of gloss in solvent-thinned paints and streaking of latex paints, apply after morning dew and at least two hours before evening damp.*

*To **paint faux bricks** on a white stucco wall, glue a horizontal row of three brick-size sponges onto a piece of scrap wood, leaving 1/2-inch spaces between them. Then dip them into a tray of paint and stamp them onto the wall.*

STENCILS

Colorful wall paintings can set the stage for plants, pools, patios, and outdoor parties. They can also make small gardens seem larger, add interest to blank walls in tight or dark places where plants won't grow, and provide colorful backdrops for wall-mounted pots of flowers.

If you're not an artist, never fear: a wide variety of stencils with garden themes can help you easily embellish outdoor walls or furnishings with bright images of flowers, vines, pots, or trees. Patterns of twining ivy, wisteria, or even large flower pots are now available through mail-order suppliers (to find suppliers, check the directory sections of home-decorating magazines). You can use a single stencil to create a delicate tracery of vines along a wall or combine many different stencils to make a picture on a blank wall.

Stencils are usually made of plastic film with a cut-out image in the center; you tape them onto the surface you wish to paint with masking tape, then apply paint inside the cutout to create your image. Exterior latex paint—which comes in small cans and many colors—is the best choice for painting stucco or adobe walls.

Stencil Basics

Stenciled images can be applied to most outdoor surfaces such as stucco, concrete, wood, metal, stone, even porch or patio decking. You can combine them with plants, pots, or other garden elements to create a three-dimensional mural.

Start with a clean, dry surface and an exterior latex paint.

Many stencils come in sections or overlays. Mix and match these elements to produce unique designs.

For crisp images and edges, use a clean, dry stencil brush with a flat top and firm but not stiff natural bristles. A sponge works best for creating soft images or textures. On some designs, you may want to alternate between these two techniques.

Apply paint from the outside of the stencil cutout to the center.

To enhance plant images, add hand-painted details such as vines, veins, and tendrils.

A. **Several stenciled images** come together in this "courtyard garden."

B. **Hand-painted veins** enhance the heart-shaped leaves of this lilac garland.

C. **Grape ivy "planting"** in a clay pot is created from elements of a vine stencil.

D. **Hand-painted vine** and tendrils help to create a realistic-looking grapevine.

E. **Teardrop-shaped leaves** cascade from a vine of wild myrtle.

F. **Waving fronds** of a sword fern require two overlays.

A PAINTED GARDEN

A medley of Caribbean color saturates the walkways, walls, and planters in this Northern California garden. Concrete and stucco have abandoned their traditional background roles here and usurped the job of flowers by filling the landscape with eye-catching hues and distinctive forms.

Topher Delaney, a San Francisco landscape designer, created the garden on a lot that offered no privacy from neighbors. It had a driveway for a front yard and a long rear area with less than 30 feet between the house and fence. The house needed a sense of entry to break up the expanse of concrete that led to the front door.

The revised spaces are sculptural and whimsical. Playful colors and geometric shapes bring them alive. The paved surfaces and plastered and painted walls mix ocher, terracotta, red, pink, dark blue, sky blue, gray, and celadon. Some areas of concrete walls are smooth while others are scored and brushed. Delaney credits the owner, artist and craftsman Pedro Castillo, with many of the texture and color decisions.

A. **The blue wall** is a brilliant foil for embedded teacups afloat with bougainvillea blossoms.

B. **Color and light** play in this small-lot garden. A panel of glass blocks divides and brightens the two long sections of privacy wall.

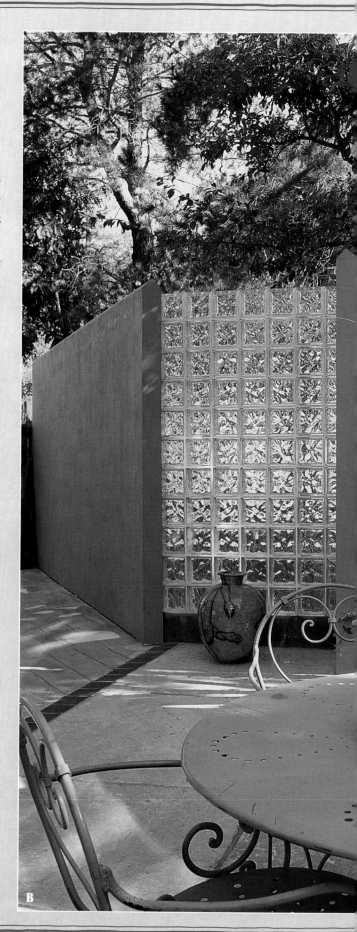

C. **Muted colors** mark the concrete around the pool's edge. Colored grout joins handmade trapezoids of faded blue and purple. At one end of the pool, a purple wall frames a whimsical ceramic bench.

D. **The colorful planter** masks the house foundation and brings drought-tolerant plants up to waist level along the poolside patio.

UMBRELLAS

I f the backyard is as much a part of the house as the family room or kitchen, it makes sense that a shade structure should look as if it belongs in that yard, not at a flea market or in a campsite.

Many good-looking shade structures are now available, including sleek, high-quality fabric gazebos and crisp, pyramid-shaped canvas parasols like those that dot the Italian and French Mediterranean coasts. Some umbrellas come with fabric walls designed to filter low sunlight; others are equipped with tiny lights that add sparkle over a table long after the sun has set. Some umbrellas are designed to hang, with no center pole to block a view.

The freestanding structures that support their fabric roofs with perimeter posts can create an outdoor "room." Corner supports don't require the large weighted bases that center-supported umbrellas must have, and, of course, the center of the shaded area isn't taken up with a post. Although they set up and knock down easily, these structures can be fixed in place on a lawn, deck, or patio for as long as you like.

A. The eight-foot umbrella adjusts to four positions. Sturdy brass fittings reinforce the hardwood pole and frame.

B. This canopy on four legs creates big shade for sunny days and a lovely garden room, day or night.

C. Even at night, an umbrella serves its purpose as backdrop or focal point.

D. This old-fashioned parasol, made of rain-repellent cotton, angles to give shade wherever it's needed. Side drapes provide privacy and shelter from the sun.

E. Canvas canopies make fine poolside companions to a bevy of steamer chairs.

F. Octagonal umbrella casts cooling shade by day and warm reflected light by night. Four lamps nestle at the top of the center pole.

G. This homemade umbrella has no center pole to interfere with cross-table conversation. It hangs from an arm of welded steel tubing that extends from a 16-foot-long pole bolted to the deck's side.

Umbrella Basics

When shopping for an umbrella or a shade structure, keep the following in mind:

__The pole__ should fit the opening in your table. Measure the opening before you shop for an umbrella.

__Look for fabrics__—natural or synthetic—that resist fading, rot, and mildew. Some also repel rain, although even the most water resistant aren't entirely waterproof.

__Check the workmanship__ of the umbrella's frame and struts (canopy ribs). Whether hardwood or metal, the frame should firmly snap the struts into place, and the struts should hold the canopy taut. Metal fittings should have an anticorrosion finish.

__Look for a guarantee__ that covers mechanical parts for the duration of the umbrella's life.

__To create__ a comfortable outdoor "room," go for a canopy fabric that not only shades but also "breathes," allowing air to pass through its weave. Otherwise, heat can be trapped inside the structure.

__If portability is important__, check the structure's weight. An umbrella or shade structure that combines a woven polyethylene canopy with an aluminum frame will be easier to move than one made with heavier materials.

WATER FEATURES

S parkling, splashing, dripping, or still, water brings tranquillity to a garden. Even the smallest water feature can calm the surroundings. And the sounds of falling water can mask traffic and other neighborhood noises.

A pleasing water feature can be as modest

as a wall-mounted terracotta basin from a nursery or as big and pricey as a 6-foot granite sculpture that dribbles water into a pool. You can convert a wooden planter box, metal basin, or large pot into a small fountain. Coat the inside of a wooden container with asphalt emulsion or epoxy paint, or use a liner of heavy-gauge plastic sheeting. If you're using an unglazed pan or clay pot, coat the interior with asphalt emulsion, epoxy, or polyester resin. Then drop in a submersible pump and add water.

A. This pair of Chinese water bowls creates a small oasis in a shaded corner.

B. The serpentine sides of this water channel reflect the ripples that it contains. The circular pool acts as a catch basin and a soothing focal point.

C. A sculpted orb shimmers with a thin sheet of water. The sphere takes on a more pronounced patina over time, as does the copper container box.

D. This galvanized watering can pours a gentle arc into a whiskey barrel half. A small submersible pump in the barrel sends water up through clear plastic tubing to a hole drilled near the top of the can, which is held in position with a length of heavy nylon cord running from its handle to a nearby fence.

E. Water pipe directs a steady flow into a rustic basin.

F. Cast-stone fountain mounts on a wall.

G. English birdbath fountain of cast stone is fitted with a plug-in pump. Water bubbles out of the orb's top.

A. Recirculating water animates this black granite sculpture. Water burbles from a shallow reservoir in the top, then trickles through a bed of stones to a below-ground reservoir constructed from a rubber pond liner.

B. An urn fountain, set on a low pedestal in a lily-filled pool, welcomes visitors to this California garden.

C. A trio of penguins brings polar whimsy to a desert setting.

D. This tile fountain and cushioned bench create an ideal spot for quiet contemplation.

E. A textured stainless steel sculpture drips sheets of water over its carved surfaces.

A Pond in a Pot

A glazed ceramic pot at least 30 inches in diameter, without a drain hole, makes a simple, handsome water feature. Fill it about two-thirds full with water, then add plants—each in its own pot (set plants on inverted pots to raise them). Choice plants include water lilies and water irises. The size of the container dictates the number of plants you need. Once they're in place, fill the rest of the tub with water.

To control mosquito larvae, add mosquito fish (gambusia) or goldfish. The fish will also feed on algae in the tub. To acclimate the fish before releasing, place them, still in their plastic bag, in the tub garden for about 20 minutes. A 30-inch-diameter tub can accommodate about six fish.

Once a year, without emptying the water, scrub the plant pots and the inside of the tub with a stiff brush. Remove loose algae. Drain when 2 inches of decomposed matter accumulates on the bottom (every few years). Scrub the inside surfaces and divide plants.

REGIONAL PROBLEMS AND SOLUTIONS

Lofty mountains, vast deserts, and long stretches of ocean-front make the West's scenery among the most magnificent on the planet. But this terrain —and the climate that comes with it—also give birth to violent acts of nature.

Homeowners in the West need to plan for everything from floods and landslides to wildfires in residential areas. Drought is a fact of life here. And every so often, freezing air pushes south from the Arctic and kills tender plants. In new housing developments, privacy is often an issue. Air quality can also cause problems, whether the source is natural or manmade. Certain plants aggravate allergies, for example; others do not grow well in smog.

But every problem brings an opportunity for a whole new approach. Thoughtful landscape design and maintenance can help prevent the West's worst natural calamities.

EROSION

Rolling hills and rugged mountains give the West beauty and character, but they can also be the source of dangerous problems. At the top, the bottom, and the sides of hills, rain, melting snow, saturated soil, or earth movement can send a lifetime's investment sliding off its lot.

Vast areas of the West are underlain with clay soils that often expand and heave when wet and shrink and crack when dry. Other areas have easily eroded silty and sandy soils. The Pacific Coast strip and western Colorado are two of the most landslide-prone areas of the country, but housing development there continues to sprawl up hillsides that may be unstable.

When the terrain is cut and graded (flattened or reshaped for construction, see page 397), weighed down by houses and swimming pools, and soaked by landscape irrigation, it needs special care. If you already have an erosion-prone property, maintenance can prevent costly problems. But if you are a prospective buyer, carefully examine a house and its surrounding property for the following indications of past or future earth movements and potentially dangerous site conditions.

Perennials such as lavender-blue catmint *(Nepeta faassenii)* cloak this slope, which rises above a 3-foot-tall stone retaining wall.

Danger signs

AROUND THE HOUSE

Are outside stairs or paving pulling away from the walls?

Can you see cracks, hairline cracking, or patched repairs in concrete, masonry, or plaster? Look for cracks radiating from the top corners of doors and windows.

Have interior or exterior doors been planed and rehung?

Are there cracks around pool coping or in the pool wall?

Has moisture accumulated around the foundation? Look for calcite deposits or wet stains on the concrete or wood of lower walls.

ON THE PROPERTY

How close to the slope are structures, including a swimming pool, if any? Ideally, they should be at least 15 feet away.

Is cut-and-fill grading in a smooth slope steeper than the natural terrain?

Is the slope above or below the house or the house site?

Ideally, a house should be higher than the street so it doesn't receive runoff from the road. But if the property is downhill from the street, the condition of the curb and sidewalk indicates the slope's stability—if they are cracked or damaged, the slope may be unstable. A sturdy retaining wall erected downslope from the street is another sign of past problems.

If the street is below the property, is the curb at the base of the slope being overturned by shifting earth?

If the slope is undisturbed by grading, is there a watercourse that could overflow and flood the property?

Do runoff and debris have a clear channel to the street?

Are there signs of past mudflows, particularly where brush fire has burned the natural cover, or does the area have a history of fire followed by mudflow or flooding? You'll see swaths of earth surrounded by surviving vegetation. If roots are not flaring from the bases of tree trunks, it could mean they are covered with sediment deposited by mudflow.

Are there gullies on the base of a slope? These indicate poor drainage, which may be caused by erosion from insufficient ground cover, improperly compacted fill, or bedrock fractures below the face of the slope.

Is there surface "ponding" on flat ground? It so, it may mean poor grading or uneven soil settlement. It may also be due to obstructed pipes or drainage channels.

Do poorly placed downdrains empty into gardens unintentionally (washes and water channels are exceptions)? Are surface drains cracked or distorted?

THREE DEGREES OF SLOPE

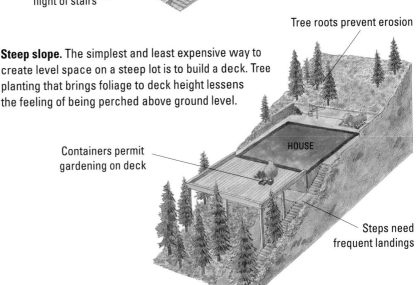

Shallow slope. To create a level lawn area in front, the grade has been raised at the street and lowered in front of the house. Ground cover has been planted on the slopes edging the driveway and entrance walk.
In the backyard, terraces with steps between create level areas for a lawn, play yard, and planting beds.

Streetside
retaining wall

HOUSE

Entrance walk and
driveway are ramps

Medium slope. Low retaining walls in front create five different levels; four levels solved the slope problem in the backyard. Lawn is a gentle slope, so that the mower need not be lifted or pulled up and down steps.

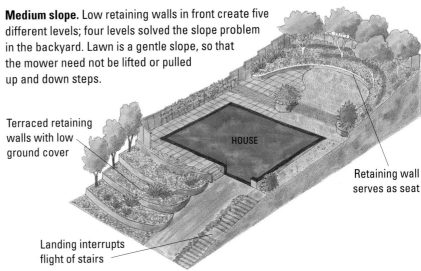

Terraced retaining
walls with low
ground cover

HOUSE

Retaining wall
serves as seat

Landing interrupts
flight of stairs

Tree roots prevent erosion

Steep slope. The simplest and least expensive way to create level space on a steep lot is to build a deck. Tree planting that brings foliage to deck height lessens the feeling of being perched above ground level.

Containers permit
gardening on deck

HOUSE

Steps need
frequent landings

Are slopes flecked with softball-size holes? The burrows of gophers and ground squirrels can increase a slope's susceptibility to saturation and slumping.

IN THE NEIGHBORHOOD

Can you spot any new or previously repaired cracks in street, sidewalk, or ground?

Are there large areas of slumping earth? They will be detectable by the curvature of tree trunks; downhill-tilting fences and utility poles; unusual, bumpy-looking terrain (particularly at the bottom of a hill); and cracked, broken, or tilted retaining walls.

Are pipes stretched along the side of the road? They may mean that utility companies deal frequently with damaged lines.

Preventing erosion

Surface drains, berms, retaining walls, and terraces are all effective erosion controls, as illustrated by the property at right.

Many plants—including California buckwheat, ceanothus, Japanese honeysuckle, kinnikinnick, and periwinkle—are fast growing and have dense, strong roots. These plants can be installed on slopes to help hold soil in place (a complete list of erosion-control plants is in the *Sunset Western Garden Book*).

Careful maintenance can help stop erosion, too. Make sure all the soil beside the house slopes away from the foundation and regularly clear debris from drains, gutters, and weep holes in retaining walls. Contact your municipal flood control authority to find out your responsibilities for slopes and drains.

Above all, if you suspect a serious erosion problem on your property (or a neighboring one), seek professional advice from a private or public structural or soils engineer, an erosion control specialist, or an engineering geologist.

Holding a Slope

Jute is a biodegradable netting, usually sold in 4-foot-wide rolls, that can be found at irrigation supply stores and some nurseries. When installed on a slope with erosion-control plants, jute prevents surface erosion until the plants get established. Over time, the jute degrades and the plants grow large enough to take over the job of erosion control.

To install jute, unfurl the rolls on the slope so they run across the grade; secure them to the ground with U-shaped galvanized or plastic-coated pins (usually sold along with the jute). Cut small, X-shaped holes in the jute and plant the seedlings or young plants through them into the ground beneath. Use drip irrigation to minimize runoff.

LANDSCAPING FOR EROSION

House is at least 15 feet from the back slope

Driveway channels slope runoff toward the street

Ground-cover plants are large, dense, and deeply rooted

THREE SURFACE DRAINS

Well-engineered retaining wall braces the slope

Terrace drain and downdrains carry runoff from upper slope

Garden walk doubles as drain channel, directing water and debris to driveway

Eighteen-inch-high berm keeps landscape irrigation and rain from sheeting down the slope and causing erosion on downhill neighbor's property

With one hillside above and sloping ground below, this property required several different strategies to control erosion. The well-constructed, terraced slope behind the house includes horizontal drains that intercept water and debris and carry them across the face of the slope. Vertical channels (downdrains) steer runoff downslope to the street, safely past the house. A berm prevents runoff from spilling onto the neighbor's property.

Stream beds of river rock can channel water to a drain in winter and remain decorative in summer.

This brick walk has edges higher than its center. It carries off downslope surface drainage.

To drain two banks, a flume of wooden 2 by 12s was fitted with a top grate made of 1 by 1s.

FIRE

Wildfires have devastated many parts of the West. By late summer and fall, the highly flammable vegetation that cloaks wilderness areas has been stressed by drought, low humidity, or drying winds. It can ignite and quickly build into a raging inferno.

Ironically, the most wildfire-prone areas have some of the characteristics that define the "good life" in the West. They tend to be on hillsides, surrounded by thick stands of trees and brushy open spaces, or packed close together in canyons. Firefighters have difficulty reaching properties up narrow, curvy, tree-lined (even overgrown) roads or dead-end side streets with little bridges that can't support fire engines.

One of the most important things you can do to prevent your house from going up in smoke is to landscape properly. Fire offi-cials claim that you can halve the odds of your home being destroyed if you clear the brush within 30 to 400 feet of the house—the exact distance is determined by slope, wind, neighborhood density, and house architecture and materials.

For years, the common wisdom was to landscape with fire-retardant plants. Fire specialists, horticultural consultants, and landscape architects now say that this practice is misleading, even dangerous. The Oakland hills, California, fire of 1991 showed that the use of fire-retardant plantings gave people a false sense of security, especially when those plants were affected by drought or poorly maintained, or adjacent to a house with a wooden roof.

In a high-intensity fire everything burns. But some gardens are safer than others. Follow the guidelines described on the following pages. Be sure to avoid highly flammable plants (right) that contain high levels of oil or resin, have foliage with low moisture content, or can accumulate large amounts of dead foliage.

Above a scrubby canyon, this Santa Barbara garden has been landscaped for fire safety. The lawn is a buffer between the house and fire that might encroach up the canyon. Fire-resistant jade plants and low-fuel-volume perennials grow around its perimeter.

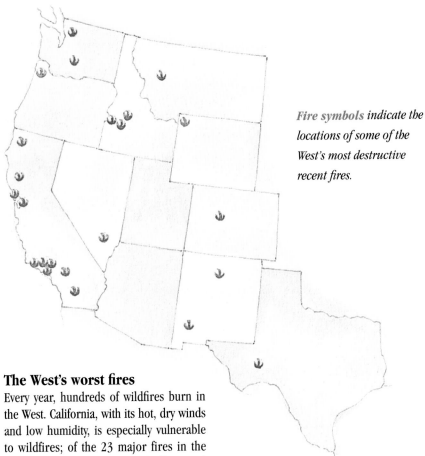

Fire symbols indicate the locations of some of the West's most destructive recent fires.

Highly flammable plants

Abies
FIR

Acacia

Adenostoma fasciculatum
CHAMISE

Arctostaphylos
MANZANITA

Artemisia californica
CALIFORNIA SAGEBRUSH

Cedrus
CEDAR

Cortaderia selloana
PAMPAS GRASS

Cupressus
CYPRESS

Cytisus scoparius
SCOTCH BROOM

Eriogonum fasciculatum
CALIFORNIA BUCKWHEAT

**Eucalyptus camaldulensis,
E. globulus, E. rudis, E. viminalis**
RED GUM, BLUE GUM, FLOODED GUM, MANNA GUM

Heteromeles arbutifolia
TOYON

Juniperus
JUNIPER

Palms

Picea
SPRUCE

Pinus
PINE

Pseudotsuga menziesii
DOUGLAS FIR

Rhus laurina
LAUREL SUMAC

Rosmarinus officinalis
ROSEMARY

Taxus
YEW

Thuja
ARBORVITAE

Umbellularia californica
CALIFORNIA LAUREL

Cedrus

The West's worst fires

Every year, hundreds of wildfires burn in the West. California, with its hot, dry winds and low humidity, is especially vulnerable to wildfires; of the 23 major fires in the West in recent times, almost half ravaged the Golden State. Between 1991 and 1995 alone, almost a million acres of California burned. And all across the West, 1996 was one of the worst fire years. Below are some factors that occur or combine to create a disastrous fire season.

RAINFALL. Heavy rains encourage abundant grass growth, which increases the hazard of grass fires later in the summer. Low rainfall increases the amount of dead foliage (known as dead fuel).

FREEZE. In open spaces, killing freezes turn live-fuel plants into crackling-dry fuel.

GROWTH. Some fast-growing communities have ignored fire threats in the rush for development, creating an excess of incendiary flora and structures. More thoughtfully designed, fire-safe subdivisions reduce fire hazards by providing buffers between wild land and houses.

WIND. Foehns, sundowners, monos, Santa Anas—these hot, dry winds start in the interior and blow out to the coast. Heavy onshore winds, though cooler and moister, can fan small fires in coastal sage and chaparral, creating infernos.

FUEL LOADING. Coastal sage becomes tinder 7 to 10 years after a burn (chaparral 15 to 20 years after a burn). Unless this crackling-dry growth is trimmed or burned, it builds up, creating conditions that favor more damaging fires. Mount Tamalpais in Marin County, for example, now has a fuel load three to four times greater than typical loads in Southern California.

LIGHTNING. Warm air, cooling as it rises into the western mountain ranges, creates thunderstorms. As lightning strikes at higher elevations, it sparks fires.

A FIRE-RETARDANT HOUSE AND GARDEN

A. Hydrant. Near the street, you can install a standpipe for fire-fighters' use; check size with fire department. Make sure it's accessible. If possible, use a gravity feed from pool.

B. Siding. Nonflammable material such as stucco is preferred. Avoid shingles or other wooden siding.

C. Eaves and vents. Eliminate eaves or enclose them with stucco or other nonflammable material. Place vents at outer edge of soffit and cover them with ¼-inch wire mesh. If feasible, when fire approaches, block the vents with precut plywood panels.

D. Roof. Use noncombustible materials.

E. Glass. Thermal-pane and safety glass are the most resistant to heat-caused damage. If fire threatens, cover the glass outside with shutters, fire curtains, or plywood panels.

F. Pump. Have a well-maintained pump (gas, diesel, or propane) of at least 100-gpm capacity, with standard 1½-inch threaded standpipe. Keep a plastic or cotton-jacket fire hose (long enough to reach far side of house) and nozzle at hand.

G. Walls, fences, and railings. Use nonflammable masonry, wrought iron, or chain-link—particularly adjoining the house; fences of flammable materials can act like fuses. Make wooden arbors or trellises of 4-by-4 or larger lumber.

H. Deck. Nonflammable brick, tile, or concrete decking is safest. If you use wood, recommended 1-hour fire ratings require overscaled decking—at least 1½-inch-thick tongue-and-groove boards over a solid substructure.

I. Substructure. Decks in wild-land areas should either be enclosed with a nonflammable solid skirt—concrete block, gypsum board, stucco, or other exterior sheathing—or built with oversize timbers (at least 6-by-6 posts and beams).

J. Pool, hot tub. Can serve as a ready reservoir for you and the fire department (a typical hot tub holds about 500 gallons—as much as a tank truck). If possible, make the water source drainable to an accessible hydrant or pumphouse.

K. Two hundred-foot reduced fuel zone. Plant low-growing, deep-rooted, drought-tolerant ground covers. Prune them regularly to remove woody undergrowth and encourage new growth.

L. Access. Keep fire lanes (preferably on both sides of the house) clear enough for fire fighters to bring in trucks and other equipment.

Landscaping for Fire

Eliminate fire "ladders"—*plants of different heights that form a continuous fuel supply from the ground up into the tree canopy.*

Create a transition zone, *if your lot size allows it, 30 to 50 feet from the house. Remove most major plants, but leave enough shrubs to stabilize a slope. Hydroseed (apply a combination of mulch and seed through a high-pressure hose) with native grasses and wildflowers or plant low-volume herbaceous perennials like gazania, poppy, and common yarrow.*

Arrange plants into islands, *50 to 300 feet from the house. The distance between shrubs should be three to five times their height.*

Cut out weak or diseased trees *in heavily wooded areas; thin healthy ones, if needed.*

Get rid of stumps, *except when slope stability is a concern. Paint stumps thoroughly with 1 part glyphosate to 3 parts water.*

Regularly clean up leaves *and other plant litter and remove brush that grows with winter rains.*

Clean off all vegetation and debris *from the roof and gutters several times during the year.*

Keep plants well irrigated *and well maintained, especially those within 30 feet of the house (if water supplies permit). Keep grasses watered and green year-round, or let them dry out and cut them back to 4 inches.*

Prune vegetation *next to the house to under 1½ feet high. In early spring, prune or mow down low ground covers, such as ceanothus and* Coprosma kirkii. *Fertilize and water afterward.*

Periodically cut back chaparral *plants hard.*

Thin crowns of clustered trees, *trim limbs up off the ground to 20 feet or more, and cut back any branches to 15 or 20 feet from the house. Prune out all dead branches; remove all dead plants.*

Clear out overhanging tree branches *along the driveway, and prune back bushy shrubs (so that fire trucks have easy access).*

FROST AND SNOW

Mild winters are one of the main reasons that people choose to live at low elevations in the West. But frosts can occur almost anywhere, at any time, even in the mildest climates. Arctic air that flows south can cause low temperatures that last for days, killing even hardy plants. At high elevations, cold winters with heavy snows consistently threaten plant survival. If you live in a zone that regularly experiences frost, choose hardy plants. But no matter where you live in the West, protect your plants during cold weather, especially tender plants like citrus and early blooming fruit trees like Japanese plum.

Preparing for frost

Local weather reports tell you when to expect cold weather. But a common type of freeze can occur in isolated spots on clear, still, dry nights. Known as "radiation" freezes, these happen when warmth that was stored in the ground during the day rises quickly and is replaced by cold air. Frost pockets are most likely to develop just before dawn and in low-lying areas.

To protect plants from radiation freezes, cover them with plastic or burlap, which slows the loss of heat and insulates against the cold. Prop up the material so it doesn't touch plant leaves. You can add sources of heat, such as outdoor lights, under the covers.

On cold nights, run sprinklers under vulnerable plants like citrus. As the water cools or freezes, it releases heat that warms the air around the plant. (Do this only if there are no restrictions on your water supply and if the tree can support a coating of ice.)

The following precautions will go a long way toward reducing winter damage to your garden.

PRECONDITION PLANTS. As winter approaches, slow down growth and harden plants by withholding nitrogen fertilizer, gradually watering less, and avoiding heavy pruning. Let plants form seeds or fruit to force slower growth.

KEEP SOIL MOIST AND WEEDED. Dry winter winds and cold temperatures hasten evaporation from the soil and from leaf surfaces, causing them to wilt. Plants weakened by wilting are more susceptible to damage from freezing temperatures. Bare soil absorbs more heat than weedy soil, so remove weeds often.

MULCH. Mulching prevents soil from alternately freezing and thawing, which can damage roots. However, mulching also reduces the amount of heat stored in the soil, and can increase the chance of frost damage to foliage. Apply a 4- to 6-inch layer of loose organic material such as leaves, straw, or compost around the base of plants. But if you are expecting frost, remove the mulch so the sun can warm the soil beforehand.

PROTECT FROM SUN. If plants are frozen overnight, protect them from damage by quick-thawing in morning sun with shade cloth, sheets, or burlap. Paint tree trunks (see page 323) or wrap them.

Frost-damaged banana plant has crackling dry foliage.

Tender citrus are easily injured by frost. This one has shriveled leaves and fruit.

Ice plant in exposed area is damaged; a nearby tree protected the other bed.

After a freeze

In mild-climate areas, rare freezes can leave gardens with wilted foliage and split bark. When this occurs, what can you do? The best advice is to be patient and wait until new growth starts before you pick up the pruning shears. The longer you wait, the more obvious the actual damage will be.

Look for live buds (they will be greenish rather than withered and brown). If you can't find buds, look for healthy plant tissue: carefully scratch through the bark with your thumbnail, starting near the branch tips and working inward. Greenish or whitish wet tissue is still alive.

For ground covers, look under dead or discolored leaves. Green pieces with roots attached may have survived. If there's enough green growth below, the plants may recover.

Wait to prune conifers and broad-leafed evergreens until they are actively growing. The pruning cuts will heal better than if the plants are dormant, and old wood and foliage helps protect live tissue until the chance of frost damage is past.

Twigs and small branches that are blackened, misshapen, soft, or shriveled, however, are almost certainly dead. Remove them; otherwise, they could invite botrytis or other fungi that attack dead or weakened plant tissue (and can later spread to live tissue) when air is still and moist. Grayish or brown fuzz on damaged leaves or other plant parts is a symptom of fungal infection.

If bark is split, there is little you can do except leave the cracks alone and see how they close. If pruning or dropping leaves reveals bark on sun-sensitive trees such as citrus and avocado, paint the exposed areas with white latex paint.

Irrigate frost-damaged plants immediately and continue with a regular watering pattern. But don't water severely damaged soft-stemmed plants like banana until the new growth starts; wet soil could cause them to rot. In all cases, wait until new growth starts to mature before fertilizing. Scale back the amount of fertilizer in proportion to the amount of foliage lost.

Severely damaged plants

Some plants killed to the ground by frost may have undamaged root systems that will resprout, so before removing the plant, wait a year to see if it revives. It may take two or three years to determine the full extent of damage on old, established trees.

If a budded or grafted plant shows signs of life, make sure the new growth is from the grafted portion, not the rootstock.

WINTER PROTECTION

Snow. To prevent heavy, wet snow from breaking upright branches, wrap conifers with a spiral of twine (left). A tent of bamboo stakes covered with burlap (right) shelters plants from snow and wind.

Roses. Protect the bud union from the cold. After pruning for winter, mound up soil around the base, covering the bud union, then surround with straw (left). Wrap with netting or hardware cloth (right).

Frost. Insulate the trunks of frost-sensitive plants with corrugated cardboard, newspapers, or batting (left). Or cover the plant and raise the temperature around it with trouble lights (right).

PESTS

Many western gardeners share their land with animals that still claim the territory. Deer, raccoons, and other four-legged creatures—however beautiful or cute they may be—regularly visit suburban and even urban gardens to munch on prized plants. A single gopher can raise havoc with an entire landscape. But animal pests become especially troublesome in mountainous or agricultural areas, or on the borders of wild land. Of course, many people prefer to invite wild creatures to their gardens, instead of trying to keep them out. But how do you create a landscape that both meets your goals for the garden and is safe from marauding animals? It takes persistence, planning, and ingenuity.

Before landscaping a new garden, consult your neighbors and your local Cooperative Extension Service to find out which animals are common in your area and what their favorite plants are. Next, decide how far you are willing to go to protect your garden. Some simple techniques can be effective (a household dog can sometimes scare away deer and rabbits, for example), but truly hungry animals are difficult to deter completely. For some pests, you need to use more aggressive controls, such as traps or barriers.

Raccoons. These nocturnal bandits raid koi ponds, muddy garden pools, and dig holes in lawns and garden beds in their search for grubs. Raccoons overturn garbage cans and strew refuse around. They eat many fruits and vegetables, especially corn and melons.

Pocket gophers. Rarely will a garden have a single gopher; where present, these rodents are ubiquitous. They dig tunnels 6 to 18 inches below the soil's surface, pushing up fan-shaped mounds of loose dirt. They eat roots, bulbs, and occasionally plant foliage.

Moles. As these animals burrow tunnels just below the soil surface, the plants above are heaved up out of the ground. Tender roots are severed and lawns disrupted. Moles do the garden a service, however, by eating larvae and other bugs, and they rarely eat garden plants.

Pest-proofing your garden

RACCOONS. Protect koi ponds with electric fences that can be turned on at dusk and off at dawn, and provide places in the pond for fish to hide. Control grubs in lawns with parasitic nematodes or diazinon. Don't throw kitchen waste into the compost or leave pet food outdoors. Secure garbage cans. Harvest ripe fruits, and keep fallen fruit picked up. Prune back tree limbs or woody vines that overhang the house and provide access to the roof or attic.

GOPHERS AND MOLES. Traps, repellents, and other products are available (refer to the *Sunset Western Garden Book* for specifics). Line planting holes and raised beds with wire mesh. Try planting ▶

Deer. The most notorious garden pests, these hungry animals live around many communities, especially on the edge of wild land. They eat prized garden plants, especially vegetables and roses. Deer like to browse, establishing trails and feeding mainly at dawn and dusk.

Wild rabbits. Wherever residential neighborhoods adjoin chaparral, woods, or desert, these little opportunists dart into gardens to eat young seedlings and tender shoots, as well as summer flowers, shrubs, and fruit tree bark. They're a threat to vegetable gardens, too.

Squirrels. Familiar sights in most neighborhoods, squirrels bury acorns or other nuts in pots, lawns, and flower beds—then leave them to sprout. They also nibble tender buds of camellias, grapevines, fruit trees and fruits, nuts, and sometimes roses.

the following plants that these herbivores don't seem to like: ceanothus, natal plum, lantana, lavender, catmint, oleander, mature penstemons, rhaphiolepis, rosemary, salvia, strawberry tree, and toyon.

DEER. Planning a deer-proof garden is challenging because this animal's diet differs from place to place—what deer snub at one garden they may devour a few miles away. The *Sunset Western Garden Book* lists plants that are considered best bets in deer country; some of those are planted in the gardens shown below and at right. Protect vegetable gardens with fences.

RABBITS. Clean up thickets and brush piles, which rabbits use as nests. Protect vegetable gardens with fences of wire mesh (2 feet tall and 6 inches below ground, with a mesh smaller than 1½ inches). Loosely wrap the trunks of young tress and shrubs with wire mesh or plastic cylinders.

SQUIRRELS. Protect the soil around container plants from lost acorns and nuts—and digging—with fine wire mesh or a mulch of small river rocks. In early spring, drape bird netting over grapevines, roses, and deciduous fruit trees; wrap individual fruits with nylon stockings. Don't plant notorious squirrel hangouts, such as walnut trees, near patios.

A. This herb garden in deer country is filled with borage, thyme, and oregano. In bloom are various irises and, in the background, flannel bush.

B. Deer on this woodland pathway will pass right by *Ceanothus* 'Julia Phelps', New Zealand flax, and *Ribes sanguineum*.

C. Smooth river rocks serve as a deterrent to squirrels. Water and liquid plant food can be poured through the rocks, which are easy to remove when you change soil.

PEST PROTECTION

Fence should be at least 2 feet high above ground and 1 foot below ground to stop rabbits, gophers, and moles.

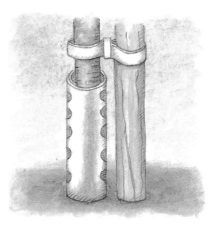

Tree guards of hardware cloth or plastic prevent rabbits from gnawing on the tender bark of young trees.

Wire basket set inside planting hole is an effective barrier, keeping tender bulbs out of reach of gophers.

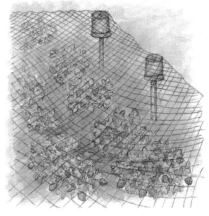

Nylon netting placed on sticks or PVC pipes keeps birds and deer away from seed beds and kitchen gardens.

Deer fence may be the only way to keep these animals out of the garden. It must be at least 7 feet tall.

Nets of string or nylon encircling the canopy of a young fruit tree can foil birds and squirrels during harvest season.

POLLEN

Arbutus unedo

Itchy eyes, a runny nose, near-constant sneezing—to many allergy sufferers, this is what spring and summer bring. Airborne pollen causes about 60 percent of all allergy problems, and most of it comes from flowers and summer-blooming grasses.

Pollen is an increasing problem in parts of the West. According to one recent study, pollen counts in Tucson, Arizona, have increased by 1,000 percent over the past 20 years. Similar statistics are coming from other western cities. Most of the increase can be attributed to exotic grasses, shrubs, and trees brought here from moister climates.

Reducing pollen

The very nature of airborne pollen makes it difficult to escape. You can't replace all the trees and shrubs growing in your neighborhood or tear out the walnut orchard down the street, for example.

You can, however, choose plants for your own garden that are known not to produce airborne pollen and avoid the ones that do. Then at least you can enjoy your own garden without aggravating your allergies. And tell your neighbors and municipal officials, too. In fact, some communities prohibit the planting of the worst pollen producers.

What to plant?

The worst pollen producers actually represent only a small percentage of the plants available in nurseries in the West. In fact, the most colorful flowering plants don't produce airborne pollen—they have sticky pollen that is distributed by insects. Among the plants listed at right are those that produce little pollen, as well as some of the most notorious troublemakers. An allergist can tell you about other nonallergenic plants for your area.

Nonallergenic plants

TREES

Arbutus unedo
STRAWBERRY TREE

Catalpa speciosa
WESTERN CATALPA

Celtis
HACKBERRY

Cercis occidentalis
WESTERN REDBUD

Chilopsis linearis
DESERT WILLOW

Cornus
DOGWOOD

Eriobotrya
LOQUAT

Eucalyptus sideroxylon 'Rosea'
RED IRONBARK

Fouquieria splendens
OCOTILLO

Ginkgo biloba
MAIDENHAIR TREE

Jacaranda mimosifolia
JACARANDA

Lagerstroemia indica
CRAPE MYRTLE

Leptospermum laevigatum
AUSTRALIAN TEA TREE

Liriodendron tulipifera
TULIP TREE

Magnolia soulangiana
SAUCER MAGNOLIA

Maytenus boaria
MAYTEN TREE

Pittosporum phillyraeoides
WILLOW PITTOSPORUM

Podocarpus gracilior
FERN PINE

Tips for a Sneeze-free Garden

DISPATCH WEEDS REGULARLY
Many weeds are highly allergenic. Keep them mowed, spray with an herbicide, or hand-pull or hoe them before they bloom.

TRIM GRASSES
Lawn grasses, particularly Bermuda grass, are among the most common causes of allergies. Mow your lawn frequently at the proper height so that seedheads don't form. Keep grass growing vigorously with regular water and fertilizer to prevent it from going to seed. Try to avoid mowing the lawn yourself. If grass causes
your allergies to flare up too much, replace the lawn with a substitute ground cover (see pages 208–209).

USE A RAKE
Nothing makes dust, pollen, and fungal spores spread faster than leaf blowers. Try a rake instead.

CONSIDER OTHER CAUSES
Fungal spores, dust mites, and animal dander cause many allergies, particularly in fall. Consult an allergist to identify the cause of your symptoms before you undertake any relandscaping.

Prunus caroliniana
CAROLINA LAUREL CHERRY

P. subhirtella 'Pendula'
SINGLE WEEPING CHERRY

Pyrus
ORNAMENTAL PEAR

Sapium sebiferum
CHINESE TALLOW TREE

Sequoia sempervirens
COAST REDWOOD

Umbellularia californica
CALIFORNIA LAUREL

Vitex agnus-castus
CHASTE TREE

SHRUBS AND PERENNIALS

Alcea rosea
HOLLYHOCK

Aquilegia
COLUMBINE

Arctostaphylos
MANZANITA

Aucuba japonica
JAPANESE AUCUBA

Berberis thunbergii
JAPANESE BARBERRY

Caesalpinia

Calluna vulgaris
SCOTCH HEATHER

**Camellia japonica,
C. sasanqua**

Campanula
BELLFLOWER

Canna

Carpenteria californica
BUSH ANEMONE

Cassia artemisioides
FEATHERY CASSIA

Chaenomeles
FLOWERING QUINCE

Choisya ternata
MEXICAN ORANGE

Cistus
ROCKROSE

Clematis armandii
EVERGREEN CLEMATIS

Dianthus caryophyllus
CARNATION

Dicentra
BLEEDING HEART

Escallonia

Ferns

Gelsemium sempervirens
CAROLINA JESSAMINE

Gladiolus

Hemerocallis
DAYLILY

Heteromeles arbutifolia
TOYON

Hibiscus

Hydrangea macrophylla
BIGLEAF HYDRANGEA

Ilex aquifolium
ENGLISH HOLLY

Impatiens
BALSAM

Iris

Leucophyllum frutescens
TEXAS RANGER

Mahonia aquifolium
OREGON GRAPE

**Myrtus communis
'Compacta'**
DWARF MYRTLE

Nandina domestica
HEAVENLY BAMBOO

Oenothera berlandieri
MEXICAN EVENING
PRIMROSE

Penstemon

Phormium
NEW ZEALAND FLAX

Platycodon grandiflorus
BALLOON FLOWER

Plumbago auriculata
CAPE PLUMBAGO

Potentilla
CINQUEFOIL

Rhaphiolepis indica
INDIA HAWTHORN

Rhododendron

Romneya coulteri
MATILIJA POPPY

Spiraea

Strelitzia reginae
BIRD OF PARADISE

Tradescantia virginiana
SPIDERWORT

Verbena peruviana
DESERT VERBENA

Zantedeschia
CALLA

CACTI AND SUCCULENTS

Agave

Dasylirion wheeleri
DESERT SPOON

Yucca elata
SOAPTREE YUCCA

Y. gloriosa
SPANISH DAGGER

Y. rigida

Liquidambar

Allergenic plants

TREES AND SHRUBS

Acacia

Acer
MAPLE

Adenostoma fasciculatum
CHAMISE

Almond

Alnus
ALDER

Betula
BIRCH

Carya illinoensis
PECAN

Castanea
CHESTNUT

C. pumila
CHINQUAPIN

Ceanothus
WILD LILAC

Cupressus
CYPRESS

Fraxinus
ASH

Juglans
WALNUT

Juniperus
JUNIPER

Lamium
DEAD NETTLE

Ligustrum
PRIVET

Liquidambar
SWEET GUM

Morus
MULBERRY

Olea europaea
OLIVE

Platanus
PLANE TREE

Populus
POPLAR

Quercus
OAK

Rhamnus

Salix
WILLOW

Sambucus
ELDERBERRY

Schinus molle
CALIFORNIA PEPPER TREE

Syringa vulgaris
COMMON LILAC

Ulmus
ELM

OTHER PLANTS

Amaranthus
AMARANTH

Carex
SEDGE

Chrysanthemum

Dahlia

Helianthus
SUNFLOWER

Rudbeckia hirta
GLORIOSA DAISY

Trifolium
CLOVER

Vicia
VETCH

Zinnia

PRIVACY

Privacy is becoming an increasingly valuable commodity. Noisy streets and bright lights shining through your bedroom window at night—these are just some of the intrusions brought by houses that are built close together, on small lots, or near roadways.

Fortunately, most privacy problems can be solved with creative landscaping. Well-positioned hedges, fences, or walls can shield your house from the street or from neighbors. A tree or an arbor can block the view of your property from the hillside above. A combination of walls or berms, plants, and maybe a fountain or other water feature can even soften the noise of the busy street nearby.

In addition to shielding you from the outside world, creating privacy has some extra benefits. Walls and berms, carefully placed, can create outdoor "rooms" and add interest to the garden.

Identify the intrusions

Before you can create privacy, you must determine exactly what you want to block out or be shielded from. Walk around your property, identifying areas that require covers or screens. Also try to evaluate how plantings and additional structures will affect your neighbors, the patterns of sun and shade in your garden, and any views you want to preserve.

A really annoying privacy problem might seem to call for fast-growing, closely spaced trees or shrubs. But don't over-do it. You may end up replacing or removing such plants because fast-growers are often not long-lived. You can, however, plan for selective removal, such as every other shrub in a closely spaced hedge. Or combine both fast- and slow-growing plants, knowing that you'll remove the less desirable ones as the better species mature.

A. Behind this fence and a screen of dense plantings lies a lush garden. The drivewaywide trellis frames the garage door, softening its appearance.

B. The wall of flowers shields the occupants of this house from passersby and blocks noise. The height of a front wall or fence is often restricted by building codes; adding a lattice panel and arbor, as was done here, can make it taller.

C–D. Hidden from the street by stepped walls and raised beds, this house still presents an attractive front (**C**). To blend with the house, the wall is of matching slumpstone covered with a plaster slurry. Flagstone caps the wall and beds. Behind the wall is a 32-foot-deep patio (**D**) as wide as the house. A granite-backed fountain conceals noise. The patio is paved with Mexican tile to match the interior, visually extending the living area.

What can you do to foster quiet in the garden? Plants alone won't deflect noise generated by street traffic or neighbors. It takes a solid barrier—a fence, earth, or even a thick wall. But keep security concerns in mind. If barriers create shadows near entrances, for example, install outdoor lights for night visibility.

Berm. A mound of soil planted with shrubs and trees buffers sound from a neighbor's garden or a busy street. It also provides a leafy privacy screen. Dense evergreen plants are best for this use.

Wall fountain. The soothing burble of falling water is effective in masking nearby noise. The water doesn't so much drown out other sounds as focus attention on gentler ones nearer by.

Fence shields the view when it is at least slightly higher than eye level, or approximately 6 feet. To add privacy without extending a fence, mount a trellis or flower box on top. Another option, for a long side yard, for example, is to stagger a fence with sections of clipped hedge.

BUFFERING NOISE

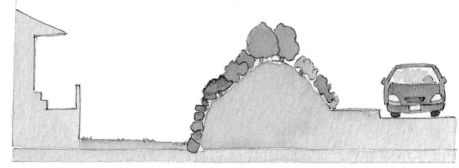

Berm

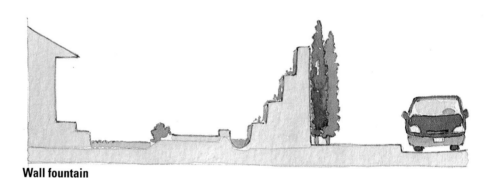

Wall fountain

PRIVACY SCREEN

Fence

Good-neighbor gardening

Always think about your neighbors before you begin any building, planting, or pruning along shared property lines.

First, find out exactly where the boundaries of your property are, so you don't end up building or planting on your neighbors' property. Also check local ordinances, restrictions, and easements that could affect your plans (see page 23). Many communities have guidelines that protect solar access or beautiful views.

Any fences, hedges, or plantings on the property line belong to both you and your neighbor as tenants-in-common. So before you begin, talk to your neighbor about what you'd like to do and how it will look or be maintained. If you can't come to an agreement, you may need to install your fence or screen just inside the boundary of your property.

Under certain circumstances, you can prune branches and roots that extend over your property from a neighbor's tree, but only up to the boundary line. You may not trespass on your neighbor's property to prune a tree.

If the construction or pruning you do on your property affects the health of plants on your neighbor's property or alters the integrity of their shapes, you may be liable for damages.

Use common sense when planting near property lines. Don't plant trees or shrubs that will eventually outgrow their space or extend too far into neighbors' yards or rob them of sunlight. Avoid planting species that drop a lot of debris (such as fruit trees, Monterey pine, privet, silk tree, and sycamore) and those that have weak branches (poplar and Monterey cypress) or aggressive roots (camphor tree and coral tree).

CREATING PRIVACY

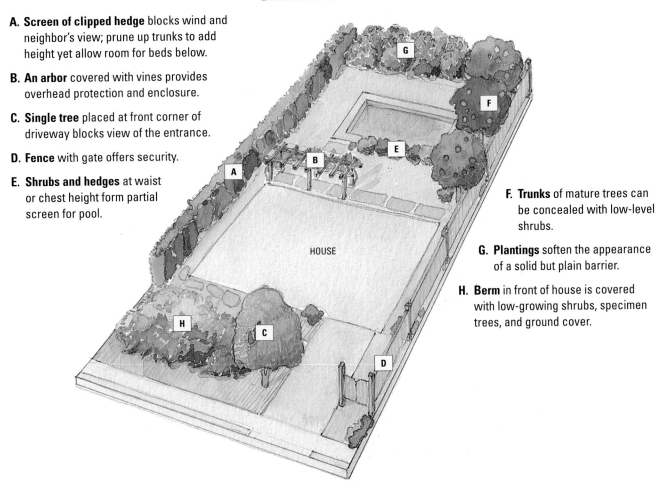

A. Screen of clipped hedge blocks wind and neighbor's view; prune up trunks to add height yet allow room for beds below.

B. An arbor covered with vines provides overhead protection and enclosure.

C. Single tree placed at front corner of driveway blocks view of the entrance.

D. Fence with gate offers security.

E. Shrubs and hedges at waist or chest height form partial screen for pool.

F. Trunks of mature trees can be concealed with low-level shrubs.

G. Plantings soften the appearance of a solid but plain barrier.

H. Berm in front of house is covered with low-growing shrubs, specimen trees, and ground cover.

HOUSE

Roadside Pollution

Airborne particulates—small particles of dust and debris from cars, trucks, and buses—can sometimes harm plants growing close to busy streets or highways. When the particulates settle on plants, they reduce the amount of light that reaches the leaves and provide breeding grounds for insect pests, such as mites. To help keep roadside plants healthy, wash them off frequently with strong jets of water from the hose, thoroughly rinsing both the top and bottom surfaces of leaves.

Auto exhaust can also harm plants growing too close to roadways; avoid planting smog-sensitive plants right along busy streets.

In cold-winter climates, salts used to melt snow and ice on roads and walkways can accumulate in the soil nearby and damage plants growing there. If the soil is well drained, heavy irrigation in spring may help leach out salts and reduce damage to plants. Ask a local nursery about plants that resist salt damage and use them beside roadways and driveways. Apply sand or sawdust to control ice, rather than salt. If you must use salt, try to avoid it in late spring, when plants are emerging from dormancy. Don't pile salted or dirty snow around plants.

SMOG

P lants use the same air people do. They take it in through leaf pores. And when the air looks dingy, smells oily, stings your eyes, and hurts your lungs, plants suffer too. Even though air quality has improved in the West over the past 20 to 30 years, the signs of smog damage to plants is still evident, particularly in the more densely populated areas of California. Smog can affect a plant's appearance, growth, bloom, or fruiting—or all of these. It can weaken or stunt plants and cause small, blighted or bleached-looking areas on the leaves. Flowers and fruit may drop and fruit production can be lowered. The general decline of a plant may make it more susceptible to attack by insects and diseases.

Home gardeners find the damage to plants from smog disconcerting, but it can be truly serious for commercial growers. Consequently, most research into smog damage has focused on the susceptibility of crop plants.

At present, the plants considered most tolerant of smog are those that grow well in smoggy areas. In the absence of scientifically established resistance, this implied resistance is your best guide. Ask a reputable local nursery or your local Cooperative Extension Service to suggest plants that have survived smog in your area. Plants propagated in the local nursery trade are likely to be among the most resistant.

Smog-damaged plants exhibit various symptoms, depending on the species, and the growing season and conditions. Leaves become yellow or bleached; the needles of conifers (left and above) may discolor or drop off, leaving the plant half-bare.

Smog-susceptible plants

Smog is most harmful to herbaceous plants, especially young, rapidly growing ones. Here are some plants that have shown sensitivity to smog, as reported by commercial growers and by research performed in greenhouses at the Los Angeles State and County Arboretum. You don't need to avoid these plants completely—reduced yields are more serious for commercial growers than home gardeners. But if you are having difficulty growing certain plants, it may be smog that is at fault. And you may want to avoid altogether the annuals in the list below.

Rhododendron 'Bow Bells'   *Philadelphus*

FRUITS AND VEGETABLES

Almond	Onion
Apple	Parsley
Apricot	Peach
Avocado	Pepper
Beans	Plum
Broccoli	Prune
Cantaloupe	Radish
Carrot	Spinach
Cherry	Tomato
Citrus	
Corn	
Cucumber	
Fig	
Grapes	
Lettuce (head and romaine)	
Nectarine	

Can you help a plant recover from smog damage?

No. But if you keep it otherwise healthy, the plant may outgrow the damage and recuperate later in the year.

ORNAMENTALS

Acer saccharinum
SILVER MAPLE

Adiantum
MAIDENHAIR FERN

Ageratum houstonianum
FLOSS FLOWER

Antirrhinum majus
SNAPDRAGON

Begonia

Betula alba
WHITE BIRCH

Browallia
AMETHYST FLOWER

Calceolaria
SLIPPER FLOWER

Calendula officinalis

Catalpa speciosa
WESTERN CATALPA

Chrysanthemum

Coleus hybridus

Cyclamen

Dahlia

Dianthus caryophyllus
CARNATION

Hibiscus rosa-sinensis
CHINESE HIBISCUS

Impatiens

Lantana

Liquidambar
SWEET GUM

Lobularia maritima
SWEET ALYSSUM

Matthiola
STOCK

Mentha
MINT

Morus
MULBERRY

Orchid

Petunia hybrida

Philadelphus
MOCK ORANGE

Philodendron

Pinus
PINE

Platanus
PLANE TREE

Primula
PRIMROSE

Rhododendron

Rosa
ROSE

Salvia splendens
SCARLET SAGE

Schinus molle
CALIFORNIA PEPPER TREE

Senecio hybridus
CINERARIA

Tagetes
MARIGOLD

Viola
VIOLA, VIOLET, PANSY

Zinnia

Lettuce is susceptible to damage from smog, as are many other vegetables. These have shriveled and discolored leaves.

SOILS

The West has soil problems that can present gardeners with their most frustrating dilemmas. Not always easy to recognize, these problems may be caused by microscopic disease organisms such as oak root fungus or Phytophthora. Or the problem may be well below the surface—an impenetrable hardpan that prevents water drainage, for example. Or the topsoil may have been removed during construction of your home.

The key to dealing with a soil problem is to know exactly what it is before you begin planting. Then you can choose whether to correct the problem or select plants that will grow despite it.

SOIL TEXTURE. The soil in your garden may be too sandy or too clayey. Sandy soils absorb water quickly, dry fast, and don't hold onto nutrients. If you pick up a handful of moist, sandy soil and squeeze it into a ball, it will break apart easily when you let it go.

Clay soils are the opposite of sandy soils. Water is slow to be absorbed, but once it is, the soil stays wet for a long time—often too long for healthy root growth. If you form a handful of wet clay soil into a ball, it will hold its shape.

The only way to improve sandy soils and clay soils is to add organic matter and work it as deeply into the ground as possible, but at least 6 to 8 inches.

DRAINAGE. Soils that drain poorly reduce the availability of air to roots. And without air, roots suffocate and the plant can't absorb water and dies; molds and rots can take over.

Overwatering can suffocate plant roots growing in clay soils, but often a further problem lies below the soil's surface. Hardpan is an impervious layer of hard soil or clay that does not allow water to drain through. Caliche, a common type of hardpan in the Southwest, is a layer of white calcium carbonate, or lime.

The map on page 20 will tell you if hardpan is common in your region. Your nursery or Cooperative Extension Service can tell you about other local drainage problems. To evaluate drainage, dig a hole 12 to 24 inches deep and fill it with water. If the hole does not drain in 24 hours, drainage is poor.

If you discover that you have hardpan, a landscape professional can sometimes bring in special equipment that will break up a thin layer. Another option is to dig a drainage "chimney" through the hardpan at the base of each planting hole.

Thick hardpans may require the installation of subsurface drainage, usually by a landscape contractor. Or you can plant in raised beds or mounds (see pages 404–405). Raised mounds are less expensive and can be made of topsoil, firmly tamped down, and amended with organic matter.

SALINITY. Where annual rainfall is low, soils are alkaline and irrigation water is on the saline side—all common conditions in the Southwest. Excess salts accumulate in the soil and damage plants. Yellowing foliage and burnt leaf edges, especially on acid-loving plants like azaleas and camellias, are signs of salinity.

Leaching the salts out of the soil with heavy irrigation is effective only if you have good drainage. You can help to lower the soil's pH by adding organic matter and acidifying fertilizers, such as ammonium sulfate, sulfur, or gypsum.

TOPSOIL. The top layer of native soil, which is usually best for plant growth, is often redistributed or removed during grading and construction of a new home. What's left is a problem soil: rocky, hard, sandy, or slippery, and low in organic matter and nutrients. The addition of organic matter will help if the problem is not severe, but often the best solution is to replace the topsoil that was removed. Choose a replacement soil that is as close as possible to your native soil and that is free of weeds, salts, and herbicides. Put the topsoil down in layers, tilling each layer into the ground. If the ground is sloping, you may have a problem with erosion as well (see pages 294–297).

Soil amendment mixed with fertilizer is blown through a giant hose over tilled soil. Such heavy equipment requires two people to operate, but can cover an entire site quickly.

Amending soil

Adding organic amendments is the most effective way to improve your soil's texture, giving water- and nutrient-holding capacity to sandy soil and aerating and loosening clay soils. There are many amendments to choose from, including compost, composted manure, wood shavings, ground bark, and peat moss. Locally available agricultural byproducts such as grape and apple pomace are also useful and usually inexpensive.

To get the best results, use generous amounts—about 25 to 50 percent of the total soil volume to be amended. For example, to amend soil to a depth of 6 to 8 inches, you should add 2 to 4 inches of organic matter. The chart below can help you estimate how much soil amendment you'll need for large areas.

Most soil amendments can be purchased in bags or in bulk. If you need a lot, buying in bulk is usually less expensive. Most nurseries and garden centers carry amendments in bags, some in bulk. For additional sources, look in the Yellow Pages under Topsoil, Soil Amendments, or Building and Garden Supply.

Adding organic matter to soil does more than improve soil's texture. In general, most organic matter acidifies the soil (lowers the pH), which in much of the West has a positive effect. But as it breaks down, some raw organic matter, like wood shavings and ground bark, can rob the soil of nitrogen—an element important for plant nutrition. To counter this, some amendments are nitrogen fortified. If you use one that isn't, dig in 1 pound of ammonium sulfate for each 1-inch layer of raw organic matter spread over 100 square feet. A year later, apply about half as much ammonium sulfate. After that, watch for nitrogen deficiency (yellowing, stunted growth) and amend as necessary. Alternatively, you can simply plant species that are native to alkaline soil.

How Much to Amend?

TO COVER THIS AREA	2 INCHES DEEP	3 INCHES DEEP	4 INCHES DEEP
100 sq. ft.	⅔ cu. yd.	1 cu. yd.	1⅓ cu. yd.
250 sq. ft.	1⅔ cu. yd.	2½ cu. yd.	3⅓ cu. yd.
500 sq. ft.	3⅓ cu. yd.	5 cu. yd.	6⅔ cu. yd.
1,000 sq. ft.	6⅔ cu. yd.	10 cu. yd.	13⅓ cu. yd.

Testing Your Soil

A soil test may be in order if you're planning to put in a new lawn, a vegetable plot, or ornamentals. The time to correct fertility, pH, or other soil problems is before you put plants in the ground.

Before getting a test, ask neighbors about any problems they've had with their soil. Your county's Cooperative Extension Service or local nursery can let you know about soil problems common to your area. If your lawn or ornamental plants are dying, check first to make sure the cause is not overwatering, poor drainage, insects, or disease.

In some western states, you can have your soil tested through the Cooperative Extension Service. In other areas, the service can recommend a private soil laboratory. Before sending your sample, find out what tests are available, their cost, and whether the lab will recommend specific soil improvements.

Laboratory soil testing can be expensive. A basic fertility test by a commercial lab can cost more than $50, so be sure to get a reliable sample:

Dig samples *from different areas of the garden separately, using a soil probe or shovel and scraping away surface residue such as rocks.*

Cut a ½-inch-thick vertical slice; *dig down about 12 inches for unplanted areas, 3 to 6 inches for turf. Cut out a 1-inch-wide core from each shovel slice. Place the samples in clean paper or plastic bags.*

Collect 5 to 10 samples *for each area, all similar in texture and type, per 1,000 square feet.*

Thoroughly mix samples *from one area, breaking up any clods. If soil is too wet to mix, spread it out to air-dry.*

Label the sample *with your name, address, phone number, general sample location, the types of plants that grow in the sample location, date and depth of sample, and any special problems you know about. Generally, the more information you provide, the more specific remedies the tester will provide.*

SOIL-BORNE DISEASES

Four soil-borne diseases—oak root fungus, verticillium wilt, Phytophthora, and Texas root rot—are serious problems in various parts of the West. Each is aggravated by overwatering or poor drainage. While certain practices can help plants that are already infected, planting species that have known resistance to a disease is the best way to prevent problems.

Oak root fungus

This fungus (*Armillaria mellea*) infects the soil in many parts of the world, but for various reasons it is more of a problem in California than elsewhere in the West. The fungus organism sustains itself on buried wood, mostly dead roots, but it also gets into the tissues of living plants, where it can kill them. Some plants are able to resist this infection, but gardeners in *Armillaria*-infested neighborhoods can play it safe by choosing plants that are known to be resistant to the disease.

Symptoms of oak root fungus include dull yellow leaves, wilting, entire dead branches, and distinctive brown mushrooms, shown here.

Plants resistant to oak root fungus

TREES

Abies concolor
WHITE FIR

Acer ginnala
AMUR MAPLE

A. macrophyllum
BIGLEAF MAPLE

A. palmatum
JAPANESE MAPLE

Ailanthus altissima
TREE-OF-HEAVEN

Arbutus menziesii
MADRONE, MADRONA

Avocado

Brachychiton populneus
BOTTLE TREE

Broussonetia papyrifera
PAPER MULBERRY

Calocedrus decurrens
INCENSE CEDAR

Carya illinoensis
PECAN

Castanea sativa
SPANISH CHESTNUT

Catalpa bignonioides
COMMON CATALPA

Celtis australis
EUROPEAN HACKBERRY

C. occidentalis
COMMON HACKBERRY

Ceratonia siliqua
CAROB

Cercis occidentalis
WESTERN REDBUD

C. siliquastrum
JUDAS TREE

Cryptomeria japonica
JAPANESE CRYPTOMERIA

Cupaniopsis anacardioides
CARROT WOOD

Cupressocyparis leylandii

Cupressus arizonica glabra
SMOOTH ARIZONA CYPRESS

Elaeagnus angustifolia
RUSSIAN OLIVE

Eucalyptus camaldulensis
RED GUM, RIVER RED GUM

E. cinerea

**Fig (edible) 'Kadota',
'Mission'**

Fraxinus angustifolia

F. uhdei
EVERGREEN ASH

F. velutina 'Modesto'
MODESTO ASH

Geijera parviflora
AUSTRALIAN WILLOW

Ginkgo biloba
MAIDENHAIR TREE

**Gleditsia triacanthos
'Shademaster'**

Gymnocladus dioica
KENTUCKY COFFEE TREE

Ilex aquifolium
ENGLISH HOLLY

I. opaca
AMERICAN HOLLY

Jacaranda mimosifolia
JACARANDA

Liquidambar orientalis
ORIENTAL SWEET GUM

Cercis occidentalis

L. styraciflua
AMERICAN SWEET GUM

Liriodendron tulipifera
TULIP TREE

Macadamia
MACADAMIA NUT

Maclura pomifera
OSAGE ORANGE

Magnolia

Malus
CRABAPPLE

Maytenus boaria
MAYTEN TREE

Melaleuca styphelioides

Metasequoia glyptostroboides
DAWN REDWOOD

Pear

Persimmon

Pinus canariensis
CANARY ISLAND PINE

P. monticola
WESTERN WHITE PINE

P. nigra
AUSTRIAN BLACK PINE

P. patula
JELECOTE PINE

P. radiata
MONTEREY PINE

P. sylvestris
SCOTCH PINE

P. torreyana
TORREY PINE

Pistacia chinensis
CHINESE PISTACHE

Pittosporum rhombifolium
QUEENSLAND PITTOSPORUM

Prunus mume
JAPANESE FLOWERING PLUM

P. cerasifera

Pseudotsuga menziesii
DOUGLAS FIR

Pyrus calleryana

Quercus ilex
HOLLY OAK

Q. lobata
VALLEY OAK

Quillaja saponaria
SOAPBARK TREE

Sapium sebiferum
CHINESE TALLOW TREE

Sequoia sempervirens
COAST REDWOOD

Sophora japonica
JAPANESE PAGODA TREE

Taxodium distichum
BALD CYPRESS

Ulmus parvifolia
CHINESE ELM

Walnut (Juglans hindsii)
CALIFORNIA BLACK WALNUT

SHRUBS

Acacia longifolia
SYDNEY GOLDEN WATTLE

A. verticillata

Brugmansia suaveolens

Buxus sempervirens
COMMON BOXWOOD

Calycanthus occidentalis
SPICE BUSH

Carpenteria californica
BUSH ANEMONE

Chamaecyparis lawsoniana 'Ellwoodii'
PORT ORFORD CEDAR

Clerodendrum bungei
CASHMERE BOUQUET

Cotinus coggygria
SMOKE TREE

Dais cotinifolia
POMPON TREE

Erica arborea
TREE HEATH

Exochorda racemosa
COMMON PEARL BUSH

Hibiscus syriacus
ROSE OF SHARON

Hypericum beanii
ST. JOHNSWORT

Ilex aquipernyi
HOLLY

Nandina domestica

Lonicera nitida
BOX HONEYSUCKLE

Mahonia aquifolium
OREGON GRAPE

M. nevinii
NEVIN MAHONIA

Myrica pensylvanica
BAYBERRY

Nandina domestica
HEAVENLY BAMBOO

Phlomis fruticosa
JERUSALEM SAGE

Prunus caroliniana
CAROLINA LAUREL CHERRY

P. ilicifolia
HOLLYLEAF CHERRY

P. lyonii
CATALINA CHERRY

Psidium cattleianum
STRAWBERRY GUAVA

Rhus aromatica
FRAGRANT SUMAC

Sambucus canadensis
AMERICAN ELDERBERRY

Shepherdia argentea
SILVER BUFFALOBERRY

Vitex agnus-castus
CHASTE TREE

VINES

Hedera helix
ENGLISH IVY

Wisteria sinensis
CHINESE WISTERIA

Magnolia grandiflora

Pyrus calleryana

Carpenteria californica

Phytophthora

Several types of Phytophthora are common in western soils, causing diseases known as collar, foot, root, and crown rot. One of the most common, *P. cinnamomi,* kills the roots of a plant, causing wilting, yellowing, stunting, and dropping of the leaves. Plants grow poorly and twigs and branches die back. Eventually, the entire plant may die. The list of plants below is only a guideline. Some may resist *P. cinnamomi* but be susceptible to other Phytophthora species.

Plants resistant to Phytophthora

Ginko

Fraxinus
ASH

Ginkgo biloba
MAIDENHAIR TREE

Liquidambar
SWEET GUM

Liriodendron tulipifera
TULIP TREE

Tilia
LINDEN

Zelkova serrata
SAWLEAF ZELKOVA

Texas root rot

This fungus thrives in the high temperatures and alkaline soils of the Southwest. It destroys the outer roots of a tree, cutting off water and causing plants to wilt and often die.

Plants immune to Texas root rot

TREES

Bambusa
BAMBOO

Ensete
ORNAMENTAL BANANA

Palms, all species

SHRUBS

Agave

Arundo donax
GIANT REED

Cortaderia selloana
PAMPAS GRASS

Dracaena
YUCCA

Strelitzia
BIRD OF PARADISE

Plants resistant to Texas root rot

TREES

Acacia farnesiana
SWEET ACACIA

Celtis pallida
DESERT HACKBERRY

Cercidium
PALO VERDE

Chilopsis linearis
DESERT WILLOW

Citrus (on sour orange rootstock)

Cupressus arizonica
ARIZONA CYPRESS

C. marcrocarpa
MONTEREY CYPRESS

C. sempervirens
ITALIAN CYPRESS

Eucalyptus

Lysiloma microphylla thornberi
FEATHER BUSH

Morus alba
WHITE MULBERRY

Pinus halepensis
ALEPPO PINE

Platanus occidentalis
AMERICAN SYCAMORE

P. wrightii
ARIZONA SYCAMORE

Prosopis
MESQUITE

Tamarix aphylla
ATHEL TREE

T. chinensis
SALT CEDAR

Walnut (Juglans major)
NOGAL

Pyracantha

SHRUBS AND VINES

Cacti

Caragana arborescens
SIBERIAN PEASHRUB

Dodonaea viscosa
HOP BUSH

Elaeagnus angustifolia
RUSSIAN OLIVE

Fouquieria splendens
OCOTILLO

Jasminum
JASMINE

Juniperus
JUNIPER

Lagerstroemia indica
CRAPE MYRTLE

Larrea tridentata
CREOSOTE BUSH

Lonicera japonica
JAPANESE HONEYSUCKLE

Nerium oleander
OLEANDER

Punica granatum
POMEGRANATE

Pyracantha
FIRETHORN

Rosmarinus officinalis
ROSEMARY

Sambucus mexicana
BLUE ELDERBERRY

Chilopsis linearis   *Sambucus mexicana*

Verticillium wilt

The fungi that cause verticillium wilt can persist in the soil for many years. Fumigation of the soil may make it safe for growing shallow-rooted plants, but wilt-susceptible, deep-rooted shrubs and trees still will be at risk. In regions where verticillium wilt is a problem, your safest landscape selections will come from the list of wilt-resistant plants below. Some varieties of tomato are also resistant; look for a "V" by the plant's name.

Plants resistant to verticillium wilt

TREES

Betula
BIRCH

Carpinus
HORNBEAM

Cedrus
CEDAR

Cercidiphyllum japonicum
KATSURA TREE

Citrus

Cornus
DOGWOOD

Crataegus
HAWTHORN

Eucalyptus

Fig (edible)

Gleditsia triacanthos
HONEY LOCUST

Ilex
HOLLY

Liquidambar styraciflua
AMERICAN SWEET GUM

Malus
CRABAPPLE

Morus
MULBERRY

Pinus
PINE

Platanus
SYCAMORE

Pyrus
ORNAMENTAL PEAR

Quercus
OAK

Salix
WILLOW

Sorbus aucuparia
EUROPEAN MOUNTAIN ASH

Tilia
LINDEN

Umbellularia californica
CALIFORNIA LAUREL

Walnut (Juglans)

SHRUBS

Arctostaphylos
MANZANITA

Buxus
BOXWOOD

Ceanothus
WILD LILAC

Cistus hybridus
WHITE ROCKROSE

C. salviifolius
SAGELEAF ROCKROSE

Cornus
DOGWOOD

Hebe menziesii

Ilex
HOLLY

Lantana

Nerium oleander
OLEANDER

Pyracantha
FIRETHORN

PERENNIALS AND BULBS

Alcea rosea
HOLLYHOCK

Alyssum

Anemone
WINDFLOWER

Aquilegia
COLUMBINE

Begonia (semperflorens)

Dianthus
PINK

Erysimum cheiri
WALLFLOWER

Gaillardia grandiflora
BLANKET FLOWER

Geum

Gypsophila paniculata
BABY'S BREATH

Helianthemum nummularium
SUNROSE

Helleborus niger
CHRISTMAS ROSE

Heuchera sanguinea
CORAL BELLS

Iberis sempervirens
EVERGREEN CANDYTUFT

Mimulus
MONKEY FLOWER

Nierembergia hippomanica violacea
DWARF CUP FLOWER

Oenothera
EVENING PRIMROSE

Penstemon
BEARD TONGUE

Platycodon grandiflorus
BALLOON FLOWER

Potentilla
CINQUEFOIL

Primula
PRIMROSE

Ranunculus asiaticus
PERSIAN RANUNCULUS

Vinca minor
DWARF PERIWINKLE

Viola
PANSY

ANNUALS

Ageratum houstonianum
FLOSS FLOWER

Calendula officinalis
POT MARIGOLD

Dianthus barbatus
SWEET WILLIAM

Gaillardia pulchella

Iberis
CANDYTUFT

Impatiens wallerana

Nemesia strumosa
NEMESIA

Portulaca grandiflora
MOSS ROSE

Scabiosa atropurpurea
PINCUSHION FLOWER

Tropaeolum majus
GARDEN NASTURTIUM

Verbena hybrida
GARDEN VERBENA

Zinnia

Zinnia elegans

SUN

The sun is a powerhouse that fuels plant growth. But too much sun can damage plants and make the outdoors unbearable for people, as well. Summer sun also heats up houses, requiring additional air conditioning, which raises electrical bills and overtaxes the West's supply of power. Fortunately, there are some easy ways you can reflect or block the sun's heat.

Plant protection

Plants that are adapted to the climate in which they are grown are seldom damaged by the sun if they are well maintained and well irrigated. But seedlings or plants that have recently undergone changes in growing conditions, such as transplanting or heavy pruning, can be harmed or even killed by strong sun. Signs of such damage include scorched leaves, especially at the edges, leaf drop, blistered fruit, and split or cracked bark.

Consider sun patterns when you choose sites for trees and shrubs. Plants that face south, southwest, or west, or those that receive plenty of afternoon sun are in the most danger of sunburn. And those that are placed beside heat-reflecting driveways and patios or that are in exposed positions are more vulnerable.

Young seedlings of flowering annuals and perennials need protection from the sun until they can establish their roots in the ground. This is especially true if they have been planted during warm weather. Methods of protecting young seedlings are shown at right. Also, harden off young seedlings for a week or so by exposing them to increasing intervals of time outdoors.

The bark of young trees is sensitive to sunburning, even in cool weather. Strong sunlight can kill exposed bark, causing it to split, which weakens the wood beneath. Likewise, the bark of recently pruned trees (especially evergreens like citrus and avocado) is highly sensitive. Protection can be provided by painting the trunk or branches white or wrapping with a light-colored commercial tree wrap, available at nurseries.

A concrete corner can become unbearably hot, but a casual overhead structure of peeled logs laid atop a beam filters sun. The rafters' placement affects the shade cast (see page 375).

Misty arbor. Even a west-facing courtyard in California's Central Valley can house ferns. An automatic misting system, built into the lattice overhead, both waters plants and cools the air.

SUN PROTECTION

Plant grafted trees with the bud union (where the tree has been grafted onto the rootstock) away from afternoon sun.

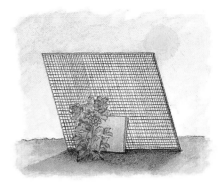

Lightweight window screen can provide temporary shade for new plantings. Prop it against a stake or board.

Hot spells

Periods of intense heat in late spring and early summer can hit plants when they are at a vulnerable stage. They are still producing tender new growth and haven't yet become conditioned to hot, dry weather. Take steps to protect them.

BEFORE THE HEAT. On warm summer days, plants wilt slightly because their leaves lose water faster than their roots can take it up. During the night the plants recover—if their roots have water to absorb. Make sure that water is available to the entire root zone (usually the entire area beneath the leaves) so that plants can recover after an extremely hot day. When you irrigate, give plants plenty of water—don't just sprinkle. Roots that were encouraged by winter rain and previous watering will have spread deeply into the ground and will help a plant survive through hot weather.

Mulching helps soil retain moisture and cools roots near the surface. For shallow-rooted plants such as azaleas, begonias, and camellias, mulch is essential. Apply an organic material such as compost or ground bark in a layer at least 2 to 3 inches thick around the root zones of these plants.

DURING A HOT SPELL. When temperatures begin rising toward 100 degrees, it's important to cool off plants and protect them from the scorching, intense direct rays of the sun. Newly planted flowers and vegetables need the most help. Sprinkle overhead throughout the day until shade covers the leaves or the sun goes down. If a sudden rise in temperature finds you without any kind of protection, throw a sheet or some newspaper over vulnerable plants until cooler weather arrives.

The soil in containers quickly dries out. Moving planters and pots into the shade can be easier than trying to keep them wet throughout the day.

Coat trunks with white tree paint or a white latex paint diluted with an equal amount of water.

A bamboo mat or window shade can guard a tree trunk from sun. Simply wrap the mat around the tree and tie in place.

Floating row covers protect against both heat and cold. Lightweight cloth filters sun, saving seedlings from scorch.

Sturdy frame of 2 by 2s supports 4-inch lath. Wire sections together at top; move as needed to shield young plants.

PROVIDING SHADE

Planting shade trees is one of the best ways to cool your home and garden. Public utilities have estimated that properly positioned deciduous trees can cut home energy costs for summer cooling by more than 20 percent.

Nature's air conditioners

For most houses, the ideal shade tree has a slightly spreading canopy and reaches between 25 and 45 feet in height. It must be deciduous so sun can shine through its leafless canopy in winter, warming the home (and thus reducing heating bills) during the cool months. Fifteen good candidates are given at right.

The east-facing and west-facing sides of the house are the most important ones to shade. Trees on the east side block the morning sun, while ones on the west side shade your house during the hottest part of the day, the afternoon. Trees should be planted no closer than 5 to 10 feet from the foundation of the house, depending on the size of the tree; larger trees must be farther away. At that distance roots won't burrow down to damage the foundation, and the canopy will still be able to reach far enough to shade some of the roof. In most cases, you will have to plant several trees on each side of the house to provide adequate shading. Direct sun shining through windows can warm the inside of a house in a hurry, so make sure you position trees where they'll shade windows but won't block desirable views from inside.

COOLING THE AIR

A. Morning sun comes from the east, so trees planted close to the east wall of the house shade and cool the interior, preventing heat from building up indoors.

B. The north side of the house will be cool, so no trees are needed here for shade. A single ornamental tree graces the corner.

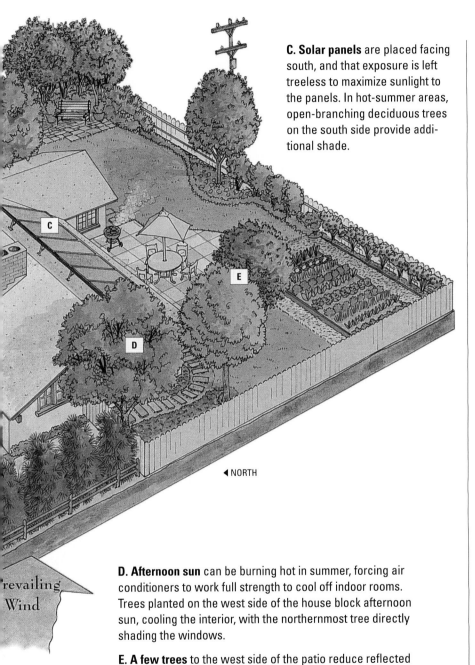

◄ NORTH

C. Solar panels are placed facing south, and that exposure is left treeless to maximize sunlight to the panels. In hot-summer areas, open-branching deciduous trees on the south side provide additional shade.

D. Afternoon sun can be burning hot in summer, forcing air conditioners to work full strength to cool off indoor rooms. Trees planted on the west side of the house block afternoon sun, cooling the interior, with the northernmost tree directly shading the windows.

E. A few trees to the west side of the patio reduce reflected heat off the paving, creating a more comfortable environment for relaxing and entertaining. They also reduce late-afternoon glare through the windows.

Prevailing Wind

Trees for Shade

Here are 15 deciduous trees for shading western gardens. Before making a selection, ensure that the species is adapted to your region and will not outgrow your site.

Celtis sinensis
CHINESE HACKBERRY

Cercidium
PALO VERDE

Chilopsis linearis
DESERT WILLOW

Crataegus oxyacantha
ENGLISH HAWTHORN

Fraxinus
ASH

Gleditsia triacanthos inermis
HONEY LOCUST

Koelreuteria paniculata
GOLDENRAIN TREE

Lagerstroemia indica
CRAPE MYRTLE

Pistacia chinensis
CHINESE PISTACHE

Platanus acerifolia
LONDON PLANE TREE

Prunus
FLOWERING FRUIT TREES

Pyrus calleryana
ORNAMENTAL PEAR

Robinia ambigua 'Purple Robe'
LOCUST

Sapium sebiferum
CHINESE TALLOW TREE

Tilia cordata
LITTLE-LEAF LINDEN

WATER

Dry summers, recurring drought, and a limited supply of water for a population that is constantly growing are just a few of the reasons that water is the West's most precious resource. Water conservation should be a part of every westerner's lifestyle. And landscapes should be designed to be as water-thrifty as possible.

Eight fundamental principles for a water-wise garden are given below. Information on irrigation systems can be found on the following pages and on pages 402–403.

USE WATER-CONSERVING PLANTS. Some plants need a lot of water to survive; others perform better with less. You can find water-thrifty trees, shrubs, flowering plants, ground covers, and even some grasses for your garden. Some provide seasonal color, others year-round green. The key is to choose plants that are well adapted to the natural conditions of your region. Lists of low-water-use plants are in the *Sunset Western Garden Book*.

GROUP PLANTS WISELY. Place thirsty plants together and drought-resistant plants elsewhere. Then put plants that need regular watering on a separate irrigation system and schedule.

LIMIT TURF AREAS. A lawn requires more irrigation than almost any other landscape feature. Limit its size to just what you need for your purposes and choose a grass or grass mix adapted to your climate (see pages 206–207). Consider replacing at least part of your lawn with hardscape materials or alternative plants.

IRRIGATE EFFICIENTLY. Make sure that your watering practices and devices use water as efficiently as possible.

IMPROVE YOUR SOIL. Routinely cultivate your soil and incorporate organic matter. You'll improve the soil's ability to resist evaporation and retain moisture.

MULCH. Place a layer of organic or mineral material over soil and around plants. Mulch greatly reduces moisture loss through evaporation, reduces weeds, and slows erosion.

MAINTAIN YOUR GARDEN. Tighten faucets so they don't drip. Water plants only when needed, not by the clock or calendar. Avoid runoff, which wastes water.

CONTROL WEEDS. These garden intruders consume water needed by more desirable plants.

ARIZONA'S OASIS IDEA

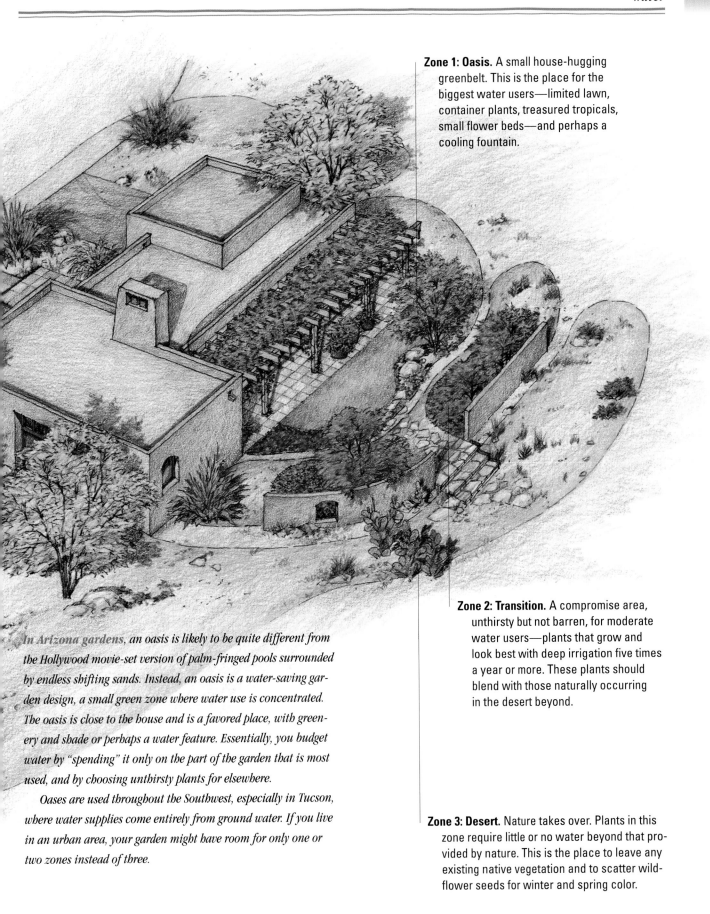

Zone 1: Oasis. A small house-hugging greenbelt. This is the place for the biggest water users—limited lawn, container plants, treasured tropicals, small flower beds—and perhaps a cooling fountain.

Zone 2: Transition. A compromise area, unthirsty but not barren, for moderate water users—plants that grow and look best with deep irrigation five times a year or more. These plants should blend with those naturally occurring in the desert beyond.

Zone 3: Desert. Nature takes over. Plants in this zone require little or no water beyond that provided by nature. This is the place to leave any existing native vegetation and to scatter wildflower seeds for winter and spring color.

In Arizona gardens, an oasis is likely to be quite different from the Hollywood movie-set version of palm-fringed pools surrounded by endless shifting sands. Instead, an oasis is a water-saving garden design, a small green zone where water use is concentrated. The oasis is close to the house and is a favored place, with greenery and shade or perhaps a water feature. Essentially, you budget water by "spending" it only on the part of the garden that is most used, and by choosing unthirsty plants for elsewhere.

Oases are used throughout the Southwest, especially in Tucson, where water supplies come entirely from ground water. If you live in an urban area, your garden might have room for only one or two zones instead of three.

CHOOSING AN IRRIGATION SYSTEM

An irrigation system should fit the lay of your land and the arrangement of your plants. But you should also choose a system that doesn't demand more time than you have to spend in the garden. Choose wisely and watering becomes a leisurely and rewarding process, paid off by healthy, good-looking plants. Choose poorly and watering becomes a dreaded task, an obligation that takes away from the joys of gardening. Worse, a poorly designed irrigation system results in unhealthy plants and a lot of wasted water.

A wealth of equipment—from micro-sprinklers to automatic timers to soil moisture sensors—can help you water your garden efficiently, even when you're busy or out of town.

The most common irrigation devices are pictured on these pages; for step-by-step instructions on installing drip and sprinkler systems, see pages 402–403.

Hoses

A hose can make the task of watering your garden easy or difficult. If you buy an inexpensive type that is prone to kinking, you'll spend more time cursing than watering. But if you purchase a durable, kink-free type, it will last much longer and work more efficiently.

Unreinforced vinyl hoses are inexpensive and lightweight, but they are also the least durable and most prone to kinking. Reinforced vinyl hoses are less likely to kink and lightweight—important if you have to move the hose around a lot. Rubber hoses, which have dull surfaces, are the heaviest and toughest types. They kink in hot weather but work well in cold weather. Reinforced rubber-vinyl hoses are flexible, kink resistant, moderately heavy, and durable.

Hoses are sold by length and have various inside diameters ($\frac{1}{2}$-inch, $\frac{5}{8}$-inch, and $\frac{3}{4}$-inch hoses are common). Though the difference in hose diameter may seem slight, the water volume each carries varies greatly. If you have low water pressure or if you must run your hose uphill, you'll need all the pressure and flow you can get. Buy the largest diameter, shortest hose that is practical for your situation.

Hose-end sprinklers

These come in a variety of forms, from large impulse sprinklers that can cover hundreds of square feet to small bubblers ideal for watering shrubs or containers. Choose models with a spray pattern that matches the areas you'll be watering. If you have clay soil or sloping ground that is slow to absorb water, select models that apply water slowly to avoid wasteful runoff.

The downside of hose-end sprinklers is that they have to be moved around by hand to cover large areas and they deliver water unevenly; some areas they cover get wetter than others. To get an idea of how much and how evenly your sprinklers apply water, place five identical, straight-sided cups randomly in the area of coverage. Run the sprinklers for 15 or 30 minutes,

A. Soaker hose with factory-drilled holes lets water slowly drizzle out.

B. Water from emitter line spreads slowly through soil to irrigate grass roots.

C. Porous polyvinyl tubing soaks soil at high pressure; at low pressure, water seeps.

D. Delivery tubes for irrigation systems range from (left to right) $\frac{1}{2}$-inch-diameter tube, spaghetti tube, and two soaker tubes.

E. Other components of an irrigation system include (left to right) emitters, mini-sprinklers, and piping that leads from the water source.

F. Hose is good-quality, reinforced type that bends without kinking.

D

E

then measure the water accumulated in each cup. The cups nearest and farthest from the sprinkler will probably have the least water. In any case, both the amount of water and the unevenness of the distribution will give you an idea of how long to run the sprinklers (use timers so you don't forget the sprinklers are on) and how to move them so that patterns overlap and everything is watered evenly.

Soaker hoses

One of the simplest and least expensive ways to water plants is with soaker hoses. Unlike sprinklers or a complete drip irrigation system, they attach to hose bibs quickly and with little fuss.

Of the two types of soaker hoses available, one applies a fine spray, the other small droplets. Both are generally sold in 50- and 100-foot lengths.

Perforated plastic emits streams of water from uniform holes drilled along one side. The hose can be used face down, so water goes directly into the soil, or turned up for broader coverage. Output depends on pressure and how far you turn the hose. This type of soaker hose is very useful for irrigating narrow areas of lawn or bedding plants, or around the bases of trees that need slow, deep irrigation.

Ooze tubing is made from recycled tires. The water seeps out of tiny pores. It requires a filter to prevent clogging, and applies water slowly—as little as 4 gallons per minute per 100-foot length. If you don't use a pressure regulator, turn on the water until it seeps out of the pores. If you see pinhole sprays, turn down the faucet. To prevent mineral deposits from clogging tubing, bury the tubing 2 to 6 inches deep or cover it with mulch.

This tubing can be used like perforated plastic pipe or it can be run out in rows (spaced about 2 to 3 feet apart) to irrigate large beds.

Drip irrigation

For any size garden and all kinds of plantings except lawns, drip irrigation is the most efficient way to get water down to plant roots. Drip irrigation applies water at slow rates so it can be absorbed without runoff. Because the water is applied directly where it is needed, it results in greater conservation and fewer weeds.

Even though a drip irrigation system may look intimidating, it is easy to install, even for a beginner. The key is good planning and design. Laying out the water lines requires only cutting with pruning shears and punching holes for emitters.

Start your design with a detailed drawing of your garden, including the positions and spacing of plants. Learn the water needs of your plants. Are they drought tolerant or do they need frequent irrigation? If you are starting a new garden, group the plants according to their water needs.

Rough out your plan on paper, and take it to an irrigation supply store for some expert help with the design and installation of your system.

Rigid-pipe sprinkler systems

Traditionally used for watering lawns, underground pipe systems with risers for sprinkler heads remain the best method for watering medium-size to large lawns and low-growing ground covers. For the greatest water savings, however, use drip irrigation for trees, shrubs, perennials, annuals, and vegetables. With a good electronic controller, both systems can be run automatically.

The basic components of a rigid-pipe system are shown on pages 402–403. Residential water lines seldom have enough water pressure to service the house and water the entire garden at one time. Unless you have only a small area to water, you'll need to divide your sprinkler system into several circuits, each serving only part of the lawn or garden and operated by its own valve. You then operate one circuit at a time to avoid exceeding the maximum flow rate for your water supply. Valves can then be operated by an automatic controller.

Automated irrigation

An automatic sprinkler system is the most efficient way to water. Manufacturers now offer a dazzling array of equipment that can make it work even better.

CONTROLLERS. Electronic controllers are far more accurate than mechanical timers —and most have useful features that mechanical timers do not offer.

Controllers capable of daily multiple cycles reduce runoff. When water is applied faster than the soil can absorb it, some will run off the property. If you have this problem, set a repeat cycle to operate the sprinklers for 10 or 15 minutes at, for example, 4, 5, and 6 A.M.

Dual- or multiple-program controllers let you water a lawn on a more frequent schedule than that needed for ground covers, shrubs, and trees.

SPRINKLERS. New low-precipitation-rate nozzles reduce runoff, improve spray uniformity, and allow a large area to be irrigated at one time. They are particularly useful on sloping ground or on soil that absorbs water slowly.

MOISTURE SENSORS. Linked to an electronic controller, a moisture sensor in the open air or in the ground takes the guesswork and day-to-day decisions out of watering. Sprinklers equipped with moisture sensors won't go on if it's raining or if the ground is sufficiently moist.

WATER HARVESTING

Water scarcity calls for ingenuity. Harvesting, channeling, and storing rainwater in barrels or cisterns (large tanks or reservoirs), like those in ancient Egypt, help keep gardens watered in times of drought. Harvested rainwater is a high-quality "tonic" for house plants, seedlings, orchids, and other plants that may be sensitive to chemicals and salts found in some water supplies.

In the driest parts of the West, such as in the Arizona deserts, you can mimic nature by re-creating desert washes in

Water collected from the roof comes out through pipes to irrigate plants in the garden. The rock wash collects this runoff, slows its flow, and channels it to the plants that most need irrigation.

your garden. Normal rainfall is channeled from roofs through downspouts and along washes to planting areas. When heavy monsoons hit, the washes carry excess rains away from the house.

Natural washes contain various rock sizes: large ones, too heavy for the current to move, stay in the center; small ones wash to the sides. Gravel settles in flat areas and bends, and in crevices between rocks. When making your own wash, work with at least three sizes of native rock that fit the scale of your garden.

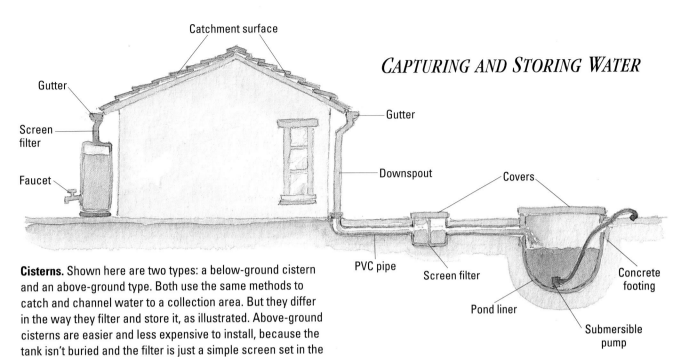

CAPTURING AND STORING WATER

Catchment surface

Gutter

Screen filter

Faucet

Gutter

Downspout

Covers

PVC pipe

Screen filter

Pond liner

Concrete footing

Submersible pump

Cisterns. Shown here are two types: a below-ground cistern and an above-ground type. Both use the same methods to catch and channel water to a collection area. But they differ in the way they filter and store it, as illustrated. Above-ground cisterns are easier and less expensive to install, because the tank isn't buried and the filter is just a simple screen set in the gutter system. Underground cisterns, on the other hand, are more permanent.

NATIVE AMERICAN TECHNIQUES

Planting mounds

4 ft.

3 ft.

Water applied to highest terrace filters down to lower beds

2 ft.

Ancient farming techniques that conserve water, practiced by Native Americans of the Southwest, can be adapted to modern planting beds. Planting large crops in basins, insulating roots with straw mulch and manure, and constructing raised, terraced beds that channel water from highest to lowest beds (left), are all methods used to distribute sparse water supplies. For individual seedlings and young plants, build planting "mounds" (above). Scoop out the center of the mound to keep plants from washing away during flood irrigation.

About Those "Monsoons"

Late summer is "monsoon" season in the Southwest. Clouds suddenly darken desert skies (often in the afternoon) and dump heavy rain. Then, almost as suddenly, the rain stops, leaving garden plants freshened and their leaves quivering with moisture. The clouds disappear, unveiling the hot sun again. While not true monsoons, which are more common in tropical climates, these rains—the result of warm, moist air carried northward by trade winds into Arizona, New Mexico, and Texas from the Gulf of Mexico—can be a garden's best friend. They can irrigate your garden—for free—with high-quality water. But you must catch, store, and disperse this sudden bounty of rainwater, using washes, cisterns, or other techniques.

WIND

Strong winds can raise havoc in the garden. Irrigation from sprinklers blows everywhere but on plants, foliage dries out, and trees grow irregularly, their limbs subject to breakage.

But if you live in one of the West's many windy areas, you can protect your plants. Listed below are some temporary solutions to wind problems. More permanent solutions are shown in the illustrations on the facing page.

STAKES AND TIES. Make sure plants are properly staked and tied, especially newly planted trees (see page 334). Tie loosely, using flexible materials that don't cut into the trunk or branches.

TEMPORARY WINDBREAKS. When the ground is frozen, cold winter winds can dry out plants, even though the ground contains plenty of moisture. At other times, new plants may need wind protection to help get them established. For temporary wind breaks, encircle plants with wire or plastic screen and fill in around them with straw; or protect with burlap, shade cloth, or lath supported on a sturdy frame. You can redirect blowing snow or sand with snow fences. Some of these solutions are similar to those found in the section on Frost, pages 302–303.

MULCHES. To prevent excess drying of the soil around plants, mulch with organic matter such as straw, ground bark, or bark chips (the larger sizes are less likely to blow away). Cover the mulch with chicken wire, landscape fabric, or burlap, pegged at the corners to hold it down securely. Or place a layer of gravel, rocks, or moist soil over the mulch. If you soak the mulch thoroughly before a windy period, it is less likely to blow away.

WATERING. In windy areas, drip irrigation, soaker hoses, and bubbler sprinkler heads are more effective than overhead sprinklers. For lawns, use sprinklers that apply water in heavy streams close to the ground, and, if possible, wait until wind dies down to irrigate.

After a strong wind, irrigate trees and shrubs. Newly planted lawns may need sprinkling several times a day during extremely windy periods. Set container plants in a protected area; soak thoroughly and sprinkle overhead. Wooden and plastic containers are slower to dry than clay pots. To prevent moisture from evaporating too quickly from clay pots, set each one in a larger pot, or plunge single pots in the ground.

A properly placed windbreak of trees or shrubs buffers cold winds and diminishes blowing dust, which in turn slows soil erosion. It can lower home energy consumption and make gardening easier. A windbreak also reduces noise, which makes the outdoors more pleasant.

If positioned perpendicular to prevailing winds, a windbreak reduces winds on the leeward side (the side facing away from wind) by up to 50 percent, depending on the density and height of the plants used. In open areas (a Wyoming ranch, for example), maximum wind reduction occurs on the leeward side for a distance of 10 to 20 times the height of the tallest trees. To protect homes in residential areas, windbreaks should be planted no farther away than four times the height of the tallest tree.

The ideal windbreak consists of fairly fast-growing, upright trees or shrubs that can be planted close together. Suitable species include some eucalyptus, junipers, pines, pittosporum, privet, and poplars.

This clear barrier, just a few feet high, retains views while blocking wind on this low-level deck. Panels of tempered glass are best for such outdoor use.

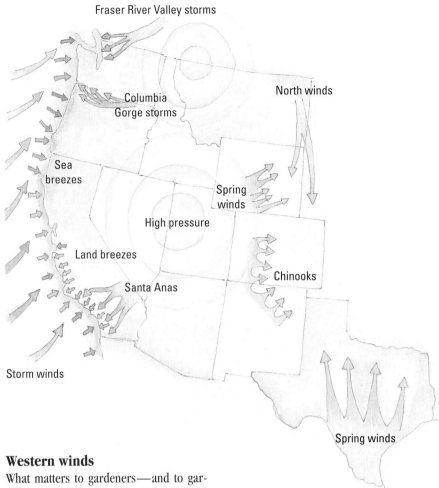

Fraser River Valley storms

North winds

Columbia Gorge storms

Sea breezes

Spring winds

High pressure

Land breezes

Chinooks

Santa Anas

Storm winds

Spring winds

Western winds

What matters to gardeners—and to garden plants—is when winds come and how strong they are. In many areas, fortunately, winds are generally predictable.

COASTAL WINDS. As the land heats up on clear days during the warm months, the air over it also heats and rises. To replace it, cool, humid air flows onto the land in a northwesterly direction from the ocean. Called "sea breezes," these steady winds start in midmorning, reach their peak in the afternoon, and taper off in the evening.

As the land cools after sunset—but only if it becomes cooler than the ocean—the flow reverses and cooler, drier air runs down canyons and valleys and out to the sea (see pages 20–21). These "land breezes" are most pronounced in winter and in California, where the ocean is relatively warm.

STORM WINDS. Pacific storms that strike the coast are fronted by strong southerly winds. As these winds are squeezed between the advancing storm and the coastal moun-

tains, they intensify and can cause catastrophic damage.

ICE STORMS, SANTA ANAS, AND CHINOOKS. When air pressure builds in the intermountain states during fall and winter, it pushes past the Sierras, Cascades, and Rockies toward lower-pressure areas to the east and west. In the Northwest, this creates powerful ice storms as winds roar out of the Columbia Gorge and Fraser River Valley. In Southern California, it creates Santa Anas—hot, dry winds. On the eastern flank of the Rockies, these winds are milder and known as chinooks.

TEXAS SPRING WINDS. In spring, the showery convergence zone (where cool northern air meets warm southern air) moves north. Air blows across Texas to this zone, creating persistent winds.

WIND BARRIERS

Effective control. A solid screen or fence isn't necessarily the best barrier against wind; angled baffles or lattice-type fencing are better choices. A fence-top baffle aimed into the wind offers the most shelter; a lattice-type screen provides diffused protection near the fence.

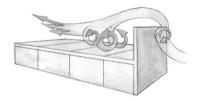

Solid barrier. Protection drops at distance roughly equal to barrier's height.

Louvered screen. Wind diffused near screen; best protection at 6 to 12 feet.

Solid barrier, angled into wind. Good protection near barrier.

Solid barrier, angled away from wind. Protects best up to 8 feet from barrier.

PROTECTING TREES

B y the very nature of their growth habits—tall and spreading—trees are highly susceptible to wind damage. Special care should be taken when planting trees in windy locations to make sure they become firmly rooted and develop a strong structure. Regularly examine mature trees and take steps to prevent a tree or broken limbs from falling—both can be extremely hazardous to people and property.

Windy sites

The first step is to choose a species that can withstand windy conditions (many are listed in the *Sunset Western Garden Book)*. When choosing a tree at the nursery, select one with a strong trunk that doesn't need much staking for support. The canopy should be symmetrical, making up about two-thirds of the height of the tree. Look for specimens with branches along the entire trunk; these will further strengthen the tree as it grows. Be sure to avoid any root-bound trees grown in containers.

As you set the tree in the hole, position the side with the most branches into the wind. If planting a bare-root tree, place the largest roots toward the wind to improve anchoring. Stake the tree securely (below).

Young trees growing in windy sites can be stunted by as much as 25 percent and usually grow lopsided, most of their branches and foliage growing away from the wind. Consequently, they need careful pruning to develop a strong structure and a pleasing shape. Mature trees also need regular pruning to withstand strong winds. Consult a certified arborist for help.

Staking a Young Tree

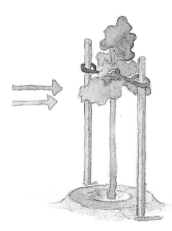

When planting a tree in a windy area, careful staking is especially important. Select two sturdy stakes at least as tall as the tree's lowest branches, plus 18 inches. Position the tree so that the side with the most branches faces into the wind to counteract the tree's natural tendency to grow away from the wind. At planting time, position the stakes on either side of the tree at right angles to the prevailing wind. Tie the trunk to the stakes once, near the top of the stakes. The ties should be flexible, yet keep the trunk from rubbing against the stakes.

Seven Danger Signs

Tree experts agree that most storm damage to trees is predictable. These signs indicate trouble.

A. Too dense a crown. A top-heavy canopy of foliage can act like a sail, catching wind and causing the tree to blow over or limbs to break. To thin the foliage, remove at least half the volume of leaves. You can do this yourself if the tree is small enough. Arborists say that you should be able to see light through the tree canopy.

B. Too narrow a crotch. A narrow crotch can split, letting the limb break. Installing the necessary hardware and cables to prevent splitting is a job for a professional. You can prune off the limb if it isn't too large to handle and if removing it doesn't destroy the tree's shape.

C. Too wide a crotch. An almost horizontal limb can break under the stress of wind or the weight of rainwater on foliage. Shorten or remove the limb if it isn't too large to handle, or have a professional install a cable between the limb and trunk.

D. Dead or weakened wood. In winds, these branches often break. Prune them off yourself if they are small enough and low enough to handle; otherwise, hire a professional.

E. Trunk cavity. The bigger the cavity, the more it can weaken the structural integrity of the tree. Carve out rotted wood; smooth the edges of the bark. If the cavity is collecting water or there are complications involving live wood, consult a tree professional; the cavity will need a drain or foam filling to keep it dry.

F. Shallow or weak root system. Inadequate anchoring in soil makes a tree susceptible to blowing over. However, it's not always easy to determine whether the root system is weak. Thin foliage as necessary to reduce the wind's effect. Water deeply and infrequently to encourage deep rooting. Drill holes in the ground 3 inches wide or wider and 24 to 30 inches deep, so that water can penetrate to the deep-root zone; fill the holes with gravel. (If the tree is old, stimulating deeper rooting may be difficult.)

G. Climbing ivy. Eventually, climbing stems will girdle the trunk, interfering with the flow of vital fluids. Ivy foliage adds weight and harbors pests. Roots compete for water and nutrients. Remove all the ivy as far up as you can reach, and keep it from growing up in the future.

SEACOAST PLANTINGS

Salt-laden winds, fog and humid air, and low sun intensity are among the special conditions seacoast gardens impose on plants. They prevail whether you have a cool Northwest coastal garden or a subtropical location in *Sunset Western Garden Book's* zone 24. Coastal soil is sandy and salty, and it retains very little moisture. But for gardens directly or largely influenced by the ocean, the tough plants listed here can take these inhospitable conditions. Some, including ceanothus, echium, *Lavatera assurgentiflora,* myoporum, rosemary, and statice, can survive even if they suffer direct hits of spray-laden wind. Others such as rockrose can't tolerate salt spray, so surround them with taller plants.

Buffeted by constant winds, plants on a coastal slope need to be tough to survive. This illuminated pathside garden is filled with a mix of colors and textures that includes the purple flowerheads of statice and the striking form of aloe.

Seacoast plantings

TREES

Albizia distachya
PLUME ALBIZIA

Casuarina stricta
MOUNTAIN SHE-OAK

Cordyline australis

C. indivisa
BLUE DRACAENA

Corynocarpus laevigata
NEW ZEALAND LAUREL

Cupaniopsis anacardioides
CARROT WOOD

Cupressus macrocarpa
MONTEREY CYPRESS

Eucalyptus (some)

Ficus rubiginosa
RUSTYLEAF FIG

Melaleuca quinquenervia
CAJEPUT TREE

Metrosideros excelsus
NEW ZEALAND
CHRISTMAS TREE

Myoporum laetum

Pinus (some)
PINE

Quercus ilex
HOLLY OAK

Vitex lucens
NEW ZEALAND
CHASTE TREE

Vitex

Tecomaria capensis

Phormium hybrid

SHRUBS

Acacia longifolia
SYDNEY GOLDEN WATTLE

A. verticillata

Arbutus unedo
STRAWBERRY TREE

Atriplex
SALTBUSH

Calothamnus
NET BUSH

Carissa

Cistus
ROCKROSE

Coprosma

Corokia cotoneaster

Correa
AUSTRALIAN FUCHSIA

Cytisus
BROOM

Dodonaea viscosa

Echium fastuosum
PRIDE OF MADEIRA

Elaeagnus

Escallonia

Euonymus japonica
EVERGREEN EUONYMUS

Garrya elliptica
COAST SILKTASSEL

Gaultheria shallon
SALAL

Genista
BROOM

Griselinia

Hakea

Halimium

Hebe

Juniperus
JUNIPER

Lagunaria patersonii
PRIMROSE TREE

Laurus nobilis
SWEET BAY

Lavatera assurgentiflora

Leptospermum
TEA TREE

Leucodendron argenteum
SILVER TREE

Lonicera nitida
BOX HONEYSUCKLE

L. pileata
PRIVET HONEYSUCKLE

Melaleuca (most species)

Myoporum (some)

Myrica

Pittosporum crassifolium

Rhamnus alaternus
ITALIAN BLACKTHORN

Rhaphiolepis

Rhus integrifolia
LEMONADE BERRY

Rosa rugosa
RAMANAS ROSE

Rosmarinus officinalis
ROSEMARY

Westringia fruticosa

VINES AND GROUND COVERS

Abronia
SAND VERBENA

Arctostaphylos uva-ursi
KINNIKINNICK

Arctotheca calendula
CAPE WEED

Atriplex semibaccata
AUSTRALIAN SALTBUSH

Baccharis pilularis
DWARF COYOTE BRUSH

Bougainvillea

Carpobrotus
ICE PLANT

Ceanothus gloriosus
POINT REYES CEANOTHUS

C. griseus horizontalis
CARMEL CREEPER

Delosperma
ICE PLANT

Drosanthemum

Juniperus conferta
SHORE JUNIPER

Lampranthus
ICE PLANT

Muehlenbeckia complexa
MATTRESS VINE

Osteospermum fruticosum
TRAILING AFRICAN DAISY

Polygonum aubertii
SILVER LACE VINE

Solandra maxima
CUP-OF-GOLD VINE

Tecomaria capensis
CAPE HONEYSUCKLE

PERENNIALS AND ANNUALS

Aloe arborescens
TREE ALOE

Aurinia saxatilis
BASKET-OF-GOLD

Calocephalus brownii
CUSHION BUSH

Centaurea cyanus
CORNFLOWER

Cerastium tomentosum
SNOW-IN-SUMMER

Chrysanthemum (some)

Erigeron glaucus
BEACH ASTER

E. karvinskianus
SANTA BARBARA DAISY

Eriogonum
WILD BUCKWHEAT

Eschscholzia californica
CALIFORNIA POPPY

Euryops

Felicia amelloides
BLUE MARGUERITE

Impatiens oliveri
POOR MAN'S RHODODENDRON

Lavandula angustifolia
ENGLISH LAVENDER

Limonium perezii
STATICE

Pelargonium
GERANIUM

Phormium
NEW ZEALAND FLAX

Santolina chamaecyparissus
LAVENDER COTTON

Tropaeolum majus
GARDEN NASTURTIUM

Gaultheria shallon

Cistus

LANDSCAPE PLANS

A garden reflects your interests as well as your needs. Perhaps you love to cook, and want a steady supply of fresh greens, fruits, and vegetables. Perhaps you have an active family, with children who like to romp on lawns, jump on play structures, eat barbecue fare, and swim. Perhaps you prefer a wild garden of rambling shrubs, trees, and flowers that attract butterflies and birds. Or maybe you're not a gardener at all, and want just a patio, a water feature, and a few containers.

In any case, you need a plan. The following plans show a variety of garden styles; they were created by landscape designers and architects from Seattle to San Francisco to Phoenix. Follow one exactly, or adapt a few features to your own plan.

Once you know exactly what you want, you're ready to start, whether that means peeling up sod to make room for flower beds and a path, or building a new garden from the ground up.

The Plants

A. Acer palmatum
JAPANESE MAPLE

B. Arbutus unedo
STRAWBERRY TREE

**C. Arctostaphylos uva-ursi
'Point Reyes'**
KINNIKINNICK

D. Celtis sinensis
CHINESE HACKBERRY

**E. Fraxinus velutina
'Modesto'**
MODESTO ASH

**F. Hardenbergia
violacea**

G. Leptospermum scoparium
NEW ZEALAND TEA TREE

H. Malus
CRABAPPLE

I. Melaleuca nesophila
PINK MELALEUCA

J. Nerium oleander
OLEANDER

K. Phormium tenax 'Yellow Wave'
NEW ZEALAND FLAX

L. Pittosporum tobira
TOBIRA

M. Sapium sebiferum
CHINESE TALLOW TREE

N. Scaevola 'Mauve Clusters'

TWO ENTRY GARDENS

The area in front of a house is often too public for sitting, entertaining, or other more typically backyard pursuits. But these two plans show what is possible when homeowners decide to take back the front for themselves.

In the design above, landscape architect Lisa Moulton of Redwood City, California, created a private enclave by surrounding the garden with a 5-foot-high fence, which is softened by an open grid and climbing vines. Inside this space, the garden makes a series of transitions from the public to the private world. The first transition occurs at the gate, to the left of the driveway. The second is at the front steps, where visitors can either enter the patio or continue to the front door.

Lush growth surrounds the patio. A Chinese hackberry and Chinese tallow tree provide shade for most of the day. Their fall leaves add seasonal interest; in winter, their bare

A Second Entry Garden

An alternative plan for the same property is shown below. Here, landscape architect Alan Burke of Preview, in Seattle, has created a low-maintenance design filled with shrubs, ornamental grasses, and natural boulders. Most of the shrubs are broad-leafed evergreens; deciduous shrubs provide colorful accents in fall. 'Bonsai' fescue is a good water-thrifty choice for the small lawn.

Leyland cypresses, planted in a row along the southwest side of the garden, create a sense of enclosure. A 6-foot-wide walk, accented with brick steps and clusters of large terracotta pots, creates a welcoming transition in a short space.

The Plants

A. Agapanthus 'Peter Pan'
LILY-OF-THE-NILE

B. Armeria maritima
COMMON THRIFT

C. Cercis occidentalis
WESTERN REDBUD

D. Cupressocyparis leylandii
LEYLAND CYPRESS

E. Dietes vegeta
FORTNIGHT LILY

F. Euonymus alata
WINGED EUONYMUS

G. E. fortunei 'Emerald Gaiety'

H. Hebe 'Patty's Purple'

I. Hedera helix 'Needlepoint'
ENGLISH IVY

J. Ilex cornuta 'Burfordii'
BURFORD HOLLY

K. Juniperus chinensis procumbens 'Nana'
JAPANESE GARDEN JUNIPER

L. J. sabina 'Tamariscifolia'
TAMARIX JUNIPER

M. Lagerstroemia indica 'Chica Red', L. i. 'Chica Pink'
CRAPE MYRTLE

N. Lantana montevidensis

O. Lavandula angustifolia
ENGLISH LAVENDER

P. Melaleuca quinquenervia
CAJEPUT TREE

Q. Pennisetum alopecuroides, P. setaceum
FOUNTAIN GRASS

R. Pittosporum tobira
TOBIRA

S. Quercus robur 'Fastigiata'
ENGLISH OAK

T. Rhaphiolepis indica
INDIA HAWTHORN

U. Salvia nemorosa 'East Friesland'

V. S. splendens
SCARLET SAGE

W. Verbena peruviana 'Little Pinkie'

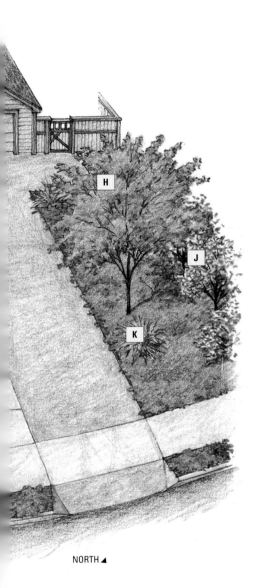

NORTH ▲

silhouettes allow sun to warm the patio. Perennials along the patio edges provide further seasonal color. Beside the driveway, a line of white-flowered oleanders softens the property line, and a flowering crabapple signals the arrival of spring.

A key element of the design was Moulton's innovative use of brick, which was set in a woven pattern in colored concrete. The front steps and raised planters are also of brick.

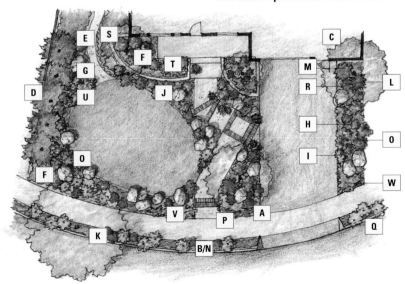

TWO SIDE-YARD GARDENS

S ide yards are design challenges— long, narrow spaces that are difficult to make attractive, let alone useful. In these two—one sunny, one shady— designer David Kato of Katoscapes in Los Gatos, California, rose to the challenge.

On the sunny east side of the house, the side yard is only 6 feet wide, except for an alcove off the kitchen. In the plan shown at left, Kato took advantage of the wonderful morning light there by creating a breakfast nook large enough to hold a table and a passageway. Connecticut bluestone surfaces the area, while the rest of the side yard is paved with brick to match a brick wall, and inset with bluestone. Raised brick planters bring colorful plants such as impatiens to eye level and further define the nook. A Japanese maple *(Acer palmatum* 'Arakawa') provides seasonal interest.

Trees cast dense shade on the west side of the house, and here Kato developed a serene garden filled with shade-loving plants (illustrated at right). French doors from the living room face symmetrical wrought-iron arches that echo the arched entrances to both side yards. The square grid running the length of the garden wall is also wrought iron. Stone fountainheads spout water into limestone bowls, sending a burbling sound indoors. Lush greenery, including sasanqua camellias, ferns, salal, and Japanese spurge, spills from a raised bed along the fence and fills ground-level planting areas. Dark green creeping fig softens the stucco wall. The side yard is paved with waterwashed flagstone; cranesbill grows between the stones.

NORTH
▼

The Plants

A. Acer japonicum 'Aconitifolium'
A. palmatum 'Arakawa'
FERNLEAF FULLMOON MAPLE
JAPANESE MAPLE

B. Anemone hybrida
JAPANESE ANEMONE

C. Asplenium bulbiferum
MOTHER FERN

D. Buxus microphylla japonica
JAPANESE BOXWOOD

E. Camellia sasanqua
SASANQUA CAMELLIA

F. Erodium reichardii
CRANESBILL

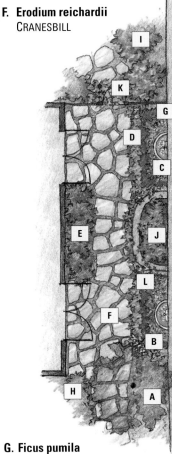

G. Ficus pumila
CREEPING FIG

H. Gaultheria shallon
SALAL

I. Hydrangea macrophylla
BIGLEAF HYDRANGEA

J. Impatiens wallerana

K. Jasminum polyanthemum
PRIMROSE JASMINE

L. Pachysandra terminalis
JAPANESE SPURGE

GARDENS FOR SMALL SPACES

Limited space is no barrier to successful design, as the plans shown here and on the following pages illustrate for three western climates. Each plan draws on a lively mix of plants, paving, water features, and overhead structures.

Lavish use of wood and rich textural interest characterize the Pacific Northwest retreat shown on page 346. The cedar deck, made of 2 by 4s set in a pattern inspired by the shape of Japanese fans, takes up almost half the 25-by 40-foot space. Containers planted with perennials, bulbs, and herbs fill in close to the house. A wooden seating area along one edge of the deck overlooks a fan-shaped "lawn" of Irish moss bordered by a pathway of stepping-stones set in river rock. Vine maples and a trellis mask intrusive views and white blossoms brighten the often gray climate. A fountain in the southwest corner has three basalt

columns, with the lowest drilled for a recirculating bubbler. Harvard & Associates, Seattle, designed the garden.

In a Southern California version of the same space (page 347), water-frugal plants such as agave, Carmel creeper, creeping thyme, fountain grass (*Pennisetum setaceum* 'Cupreum'), and mondo grass fill a garden that is defined by flagstones, native boulders, and a stucco wall. Changes in level, including a step-down patio, make the garden seem larger; boulders bordering the planting beds hold the patio excavation in place. Walls clad with trumpet vine and a two-story bougainvillea-covered trellis ensure privacy, as do Leyland cypress trees that block a shed and the neighbors' second-story deck. Finishing touches in the garden include a sculpture on the rear wall and a waterfall. Designer: EPT Landscape Architecture, Pasadena.

Southwest garden

The Southwest courtyard illustrated at left and below is the work of landscape architect Carol Shuler of Scottsdale, Arizona, who created a desert oasis in a formerly barren patio. To make the tiny space seem larger, she carefully coordinated a limited number of plantings and furnishings. The courtyard's L shape separates the seating and dining areas.

Shade is cast by a shoestring acacia planted in a cutout in the concrete slab; Saltillo tile covers the remaining surface. The surrounding fence was painted a light peach. Brick planters contain liriope, Myers asparagus, *Muhlenbergia capillaris* 'Regal Mist' (a clumping perennial grass), and *Ruellia brittoniana* 'Katie'. Color is provided by pots of geraniums, lobelia, and petunias. Colorful throw pillows and a whimsical birdhouse collection provide bright accents.

The Plants

A. Acacia stenophylla
SHOESTRING ACACIA

B. Asparagus densiflorus 'Myers'
MYERS ASPARAGUS

C. Citrus
CALAMONDIN

D. Cycas revoluta
SAGO PALM

E. Euryops pectinatus

F. Gelsemium sempervirens
CAROLINA JESSAMINE

G. Justicia spicigera
MEXICAN HONEYSUCKLE

H. Liriope muscari 'Variegata'

I. Lobelia

J. Muhlenbergia capillaris 'Regal Mist'

K. Pelargonium
GERANIUM

L. Petunia hybrida

M. Ruellia brittoniana 'Katie'

N. Salvia clevelandii
SAGE

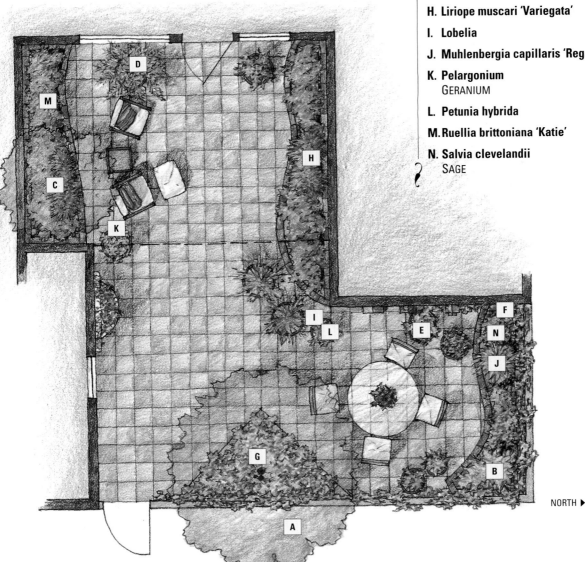

NORTH ▶

A NORTHWEST RETREAT

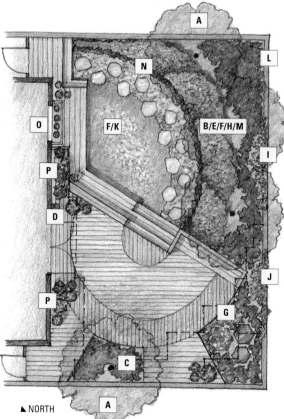

▲ NORTH

The Plants
Pacific Northwest

A. Acer circinatum
VINE MAPLE

B. Anemone blanda 'White Splendor'

C. Bulbs: 'Thalia' and 'Golden Cheerfulness' daffodils, Tulipa tarda

D. Clematis armandii
EVERGREEN CLEMATIS

E. Cornus canadensis
BUNCHBERRY

F. Crocus speciosus 'Alba', C. vernus 'Snow Storm'

G. Cyclamen persicum

H. Gaultheria procumbens
WINTERGREEN

I. Hydrangea anomala
CLIMBING HYDRANGEA

J. Passiflora 'Incense'
PASSION VINE

K. Sagina subulata
IRISH MOSS

L. Sarcococca hookerana humilis

M. Trillium ovatum
WAKE ROBIN

N. Viola cucullata 'Freckles'
SWEET VIOLET

O. Mixed herbs

P. Mixed perennials

A CALIFORNIA PATIO

The Plants
Southern California

A. Agave attenuata

B. Bougainvillea

C. Ceanothus griseus horizontalis
CARMEL CREEPER

D. Cupressocyparis leylandii
LEYLAND CYPRESS

E. Distictis buccinatoria
BLOOD-RED TRUMPET VINE

F. Helichrysum petiolare 'Limelight'
LICORICE PLANT

G. Mahonia aquifolium
OREGON GRAPE

H. Ophiopogon japonicus
MONDO GRASS

I. Pennisetum setaceum 'Rubrum'
FOUNTAIN GRASS

J. Pistacia chinensis
CHINESE PISTACHE

K. Succulents

L. Thymus praecox arcticus
CREEPING THYME

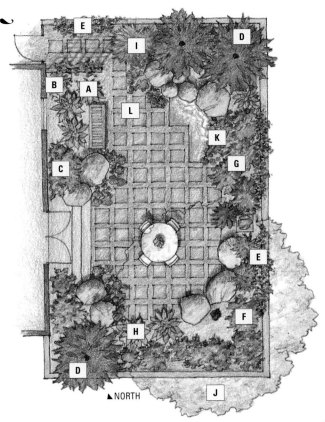

▲ NORTH

A GARDEN FOR CUTTING

Bouquets by the dozen come almost year-round from Dariel and Ken Alexander's garden in Lafayette, California. Not just flowers, but shrubs and trees provide the raw material for both fresh and dried arrangements.

Most of the flowers grow in two large beds facing the house and separated by a grape arbor. At the back of the beds, roses help screen from view raised vegetable beds, as well as fruit trees, pussy willow, bulbs, and more flowers. Tightly trimmed feverfew defines the front of the beds.

Spring favorites include native shrubs (California buckeye, flannel bush, forsythia, red flowering currant), flowering dogwood, French pussy willow, lilac, sweet mock orange, and four kinds of spiraea. Summer blooms include hollyhock, roses, and yarrow (fernleaf, common, and 'Coronation Gold'). In fall, the colorful foliage and berries of currant and dogwood, and the interesting branch patterns of corkscrew willow, supply material for inventive floral displays.

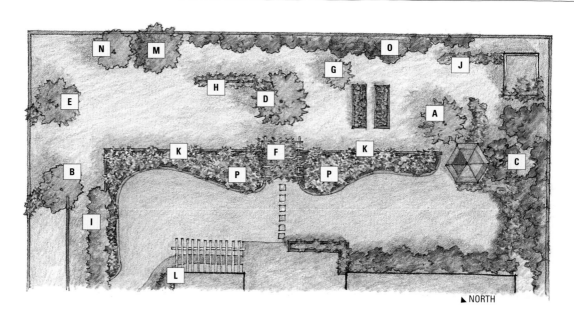

NORTH

The Plants

TREES

A. Apricot

B. Morus alba
FRUITLESS MULBERRY

C. Pinus contorta
BEACH PINE

D. Prunus americana
WILD PLUM

E. Peach

SHRUBS AND VINES

F. 'Concord' grapes

G. Fremontodendron 'California Glory'
FLANNEL BUSH

H. Lonicera
HONEYSUCKLE

I. Philadelphus coronarius
SWEET MOCK ORANGE

J. Raspberries

K. Roses: 'Ballerina', 'Dolly Parton', 'Chrysler Imperial', 'French Lace', 'Gold Badge', 'Graham Thomas', 'La Reine Victoria', 'Queen Elizabeth'

L. Roses, climbing: 'Cl. Cécile Brunner', 'Cl. Lady Forteviot', 'Climbing America', Lady Banks' rose

M. Salix caprea
FRENCH PUSSY WILLOW

N. S. matsudana 'Tortuosa'
CORKSCREW WILLOW

O. Mixed shrubs: California buckeye, 'Cloud Nine' dogwood, forsythia, lilac, red flowering currant, spiraea, viburnum

FLOWER BEDS

P. Perennials: Campanula, coreopsis, dianthus, feverfew, foxglove, geum, gloriosa daisy, heliopsis, hollyhock, penstemon, phlox, purple coneflower, purple loosestrife, salvia, scented geranium, veronica, yarrow

Annuals: Cosmos, larkspur, phlox, sweet pea, zinnia

Bulbs: Daffodil, Dutch iris, tulip (spring); crocosmia, dahlia (summer)

A FOUR-SEASON GARDEN

Even in climates with a well-defined winter, the garden needn't shut down from fall frost to spring awakening. If plants are chosen for interest in more than one season, the garden can bring the view indoors—if not the viewer outdoors—year-round, as in this Northwest garden designed by landscape architect Robert Chittock of Seattle.

Colors and points of interest change as the months pass, yet the garden's overall character and structure remain constant. Large trees around the perimeter include fir, bamboo, pink-flowered dogwood (*Cornus florida* 'Rubra'), Chilean fire brush, and deciduous magnolia. Set against them is a wide range of plants: azaleas (including 'Gumpo', 'Sekidera', and 'Treasure') and rhododendrons ('Sir Charles Lemon' and 'Unique') for spring bloom, and perennials such as long-flowering lily-of-the-Nile and yellow red-hot poker. The Japanese snowdrop tree brings fall color, as do the magnolia and dogwood, whose branch patterns also create sculptural forms in winter.

Amid this profusion, the regularity of 18-inch buff-colored pavers lends a sense of order to the open area and walkways. An obelisk and rectangular pond are visible from many angles. Around the pond, giant feather grass and variegated *Miscanthus sinensis* contribute interesting silhouettes, as do eight species of sea holly, whose steel blue or amethyst flowerheads and blue bracts are particularly striking. From the house, an arbor leads straight to a viewing area overlooking unlandscaped areas beyond.

The Plants

A. Agapanthus Headbourne hybrids
LILY-OF-THE-NILE

B. Ajuga reptans 'Crispa'
CARPET BUGLE

C. Alchemilla mollis
LADY'S-MANTLE

D. Carex: six species

E. C. opnopta

F. Cornus 'Eddie's White Wonder', C. florida 'Rubra'
DOGWOOD

G. Daphne odora
WINTER DAPHNE

H. Embothrium coccineum
CHILEAN FIRE BRUSH

I. Enkianthus perulatus

J. Eryngium: eight species
SEA HOLLY

K. Euphorbia: three species

L. Hakonechloa macra 'Aureola'
JAPANESE FOREST GRASS

M. Helleborus foetidus, H. orientalis
HELLEBORE

N. Hypericum 'Ruby Glow'
ST. JOHNSWORT

O. Iris sibirica 'Snow Queen'
SIBERIAN IRIS

T. **Mitella breweria**

U. **Ophiopogon planiscapus
   'Nigrescens'**

V. **Oxalis oregana**
   REDWOOD SORREL

W. **Phyllostachys aurea**
   GOLDEN BAMBOO

X. **Pieris japonica**
   LILY-OF-THE-VALLEY SHRUB

Y. **Polygonatum**
   SOLOMON'S SEAL

Z. **Prunella grandiflora**
   SELF-HEAL

AA. **Rhododendron**
    RHODODENDRON AND AZALEA

BB. **Rubus tricolor**

CC. **Rudbeckia fulgida**

DD. **Sarcococca hookerana humilis**

EE. **Saxifraga rosacea**

FF. **Sisyrinchium striatum**

GG. **Stipa gigantea**
    GIANT FEATHER GRASS

HH. **Styrax japonicus**
    JAPANESE SNOWDROP TREE

II. **Tolmiea menziesii**
    PIGGY-BACK PLANT

JJ. **Waldsteinia fragarioides**

KK. **Zantedeschia aethiopica
    'Green Goddess'**
    COMMON CALLA

P. **Kniphofia uvaria**
   RED-HOT POKER (YELLOW HYBRIDS)

Q. **Lilium auratum, L. 'Pink Perfection',
   L. regale**
   LILY

R. **Magnolia denudata**
   YULAN MAGNOLIA

S. **Miscanthus sinensis**
   EULALIA GRASS

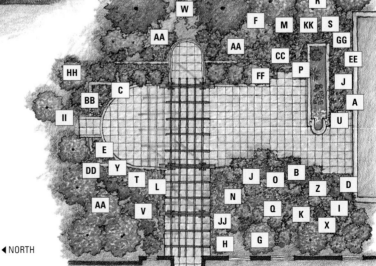

◀ NORTH

A GARDEN FOR WILDLIFE

F ood, shelter, and water—provide these in your garden, and birds and butterflies will come. In the garden illustrated above, various features and diverse plant combinations create a hospitable and welcoming habitat.

Butterflies like sunny, sheltered spots with plenty of long-blooming, nectar-rich flowers (and perhaps food crops to nourish caterpillars), some moist or damp areas, and maybe a rocky area for basking. Birds need shelter, plants that supply nectar, seeds, or berries, and a lawn for hunting worms. Put out a birdbath, feeders, and (especially if you live in the Pacific Northwest) nesting boxes.

At the back of flower beds, plant taller shrubs and trees to provide a windscreen for butterflies and shelter for birds as well as nectar and food for them.

The middle section of the beds is the visual focal point, the best place to put colorful perennials and annuals. In front, plant the lowest growers—lavender and salvia, for example. Place plants that attract butterflies where they'll get full sun between 11 and 3, when these insects are most active.

Keep three things in mind when designing your wildlife garden. First, do not use insecticides. Most birds eat spiders, and insecti-

The Plants

FOR BUTTERFLIES

A. Acer circinatum
VINE MAPLE

B. Achillea taygetea
YARROW

C. Alcea rosea
HOLLYHOCK

D. Asclepias tuberosa
BUTTERFLY WEED

E. Buddleia davidii
BUTTERFLY BUSH

F. Diascia
TWINSPUR

G. Gaillardia grandiflora
BLANKET FLOWER

H. Helianthus
SUNFLOWERS

I. Lavandula
LAVENDER

J. Vaccinium ovatum
EVERGREEN HUCKLEBERRY

K. Zinnia

FOR BIRDS

L. Arbutus menziesii
MADRONE

M. Arctostaphylos uva-ursi
MANZANITA

N. Ceanothus
WILD LILAC

O. Cornus stolonifera
DOGWOOD

P. Foeniculum vulgare
FENNEL

Q. Gaultheria shallon
SALAL

R. Heteromeles arbutifolia
TOYON

S. Lobularia
SWEET ALYSSUM

T. Lonicera
HONEYSUCKLE

**U. Penstemon gloxinioides
'Apple Blossom'**
BORDER PENSTEMON

V. Pinus radiata
MONTEREY PINE

W. Salvia
SAGE

X. Typha
CATTAIL

OTHER PLANTS

Y. Water lilies

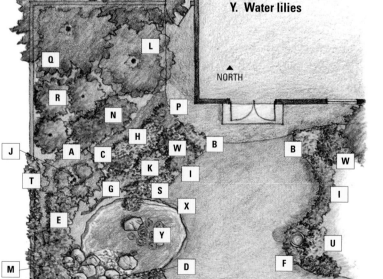

cides kill them off, along with desirable butterflies and caterpillars. Second, discourage predators such as cats by keeping feeders and birdbaths high up or otherwise inaccessible. Finally, because the best wildlife habitats are not overly manicured, try to be an unfastidious gardener. The less you rake under bushes, the better it is for birds. When possible, leave small brush piles in out-of-the-way places.

A KITCHEN GARDEN

Mixing practicality and beauty, this garden puts food crops at center stage. In just 40 by 60 feet, Jeff Dawson of Sebastopol, California (who is garden director for Kendall–Jackson Winery), found space for more than two dozen kinds of vegetables and herbs, as well as for fruit trees and vines.

The central walkway (paved with loose material such as straw or crushed rock) gives physical and visual access to the whole garden. Overall, however, the garden's layout draws visitors to its center, whether for a moment of reflection or to set up a barbecue and create a garden meal on the spot. The garden is productive all year; gardeners adapting this plan in cold-winter areas could sow cover crops.

To save space, the semidwarf apple trees, which reach only 5 to 6 feet, are espaliered. Likewise, grapes and berries are trained on trellises of 4-by-4 posts with horizontal heavy-gauge wire; 2-by-2 cross-pieces would also work. Concentric semicircles contain raised beds of perennial and annual herbs in the center and eggplant, tomatoes, melons, and sunflowers toward the outside. Taller crops, such as corn and pole beans, grow in the long beds at each corner where they won't shade other plants.

A compost bin hidden by the apple trees takes all garden waste and provides mulch for later crops. The double-dug raised beds are drip-watered: in-line emitters for the circles, perforated tubing for the long beds.

The varieties listed at right are Jeff Dawson's favorites, but feel free to plant your own instead.

The Plants

A. **Apples:** 'Pink Pearl'

B. **Beans, bush:** 'French Filet', 'Maxibel', 'Romano', 'Royalty' (purple)

C. **Beans, runner:** Annelino, scarlet runner

D. **Beets:** 'Chioggia', golden, 'Red Ace'

E. **Berries:** Boysenberry, raspberry, thornless blackberry

F. **Carrots:** 'Minicor', 'Nantes Scarlet'

G. **Corn:** 'Silver Queen', 'Sugar Buns'

H. **Eggplant:** 'Dusky', 'Japanese', 'Rosa Bianca'

I. **Grapes (seedless):** 'Canadice' (red), 'Himrod' (greenish white), 'Venus' (blue-black)

J. **Greens:** Arugula, lettuce, mizuna, Russian red kale

K. **Herbs:** Basil, chiso, chives, cilantro, dill, fennel, oregano, parsley, savory, sweet marjoram, tarragon, thyme (English, lemon, silver)

L. **Melons:** Charentais, 'Orange Blossom'

M. **Onions:** Cipollini, pearl, leeks

N. **Peppers, hot:** 'Habanero', poblano (ancho)

O. **Peppers, sweet:** Green, purple, red; 'Corona' (orange), 'Cubanelle', 'Italian Gourmet', 'Orobelle' (yellow)

P. **Potatoes:** 'Caribe'

Q. **Radishes:** 'French Breakfast'

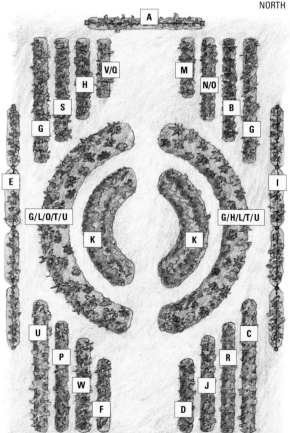

NORTH

R. Squash, summer: 'Peter Pan', 'Sunburst', zucchini

S. Squash, winter: 'Delicata', 'Table Gold Acorn', 'Waltham Butternut'

T. Sunflowers: Both tall kinds and shorter ones such as 'Lion's Mane'

U. Tomatoes: 'Coustralee', 'Georgia Streak', 'Green Zebra', 'San Marzano' (paste), 'Sun Gold' (cherry)

V. Turnips: 'Tokyo Cross'

W. Winter crops: Cabbage, cauliflower, garlic, leeks, lettuce, onions; or sow cover crops

INSPIRED BY NATURE...IN SEATTLE

Prolonged droughts across the West have converted gardeners to the water-saving benefits of native plants, as well as to their beauty in home landscapes. The regional gardens shown here and on the following pages use predominantly local plants in settings that take their cues from nature—with stunning results.

An angled walk and gentle berm give form, privacy, and an element of surprise to the shallow entry of the garden shown here. As you approach from the driveway, the 35-foot-deep, 60-foot-wide garden—designed by landscape architect Robert Chittock of Seattle—reveals itself in stages, offering meandering paths and planting pockets, as well as a shaded, private patio. Chittock covered the berm primarily with Northwest natives to create privacy and a woodsy atmosphere. He enhanced this natural look by punctuating the berm with large, low boulders, and planted multi-stemmed vine maples, which are native to the area.

The garden was designed for both viewing and cutting. Beneath the taller maples, midsize plants provide additional screening and color: azaleas, lilacs, Oregon grape, and rhododendrons. Plants with arresting leaf and flower textures add interest: columbine, euphorbia, false spiraea, ferns, hostas, lamb's ears, sedge, and Siberian iris. Lush sweet woodruff and redwood sorrel cover the spaces in between.

As a contrast to the garden's soft foliage and Northwest palette, the paths are hard-edged and neutral in tone. Precast 18-inch squares of buff-colored concrete were set on a bed of compacted gravel and sand.

The Plants

A. Acer circinatum
VINE MAPLE

B. Acer palmatum
JAPANESE MAPLE

C. Aquilegia
COLUMBINE

D. Arbutus menziesii
MADRONE

E. Astilbe
FALSE SPIRAEA

F. Carex
SEDGE

G. Dicentra spectabilis
COMMON BLEEDING HEART

H. Enkianthus

I. Epimedium

J. Euphorbia

K. Ferns

L. Galium odoratum
SWEET WOODRUFF

M. Helleborus foetidus
HELLEBORE

N. Hosta

O. Iris sibirica
SIBERIAN IRIS HYBRIDS

P. Lavandula
LAVENDER

Q. Mahonia aquifolium 'Compacta'
OREGON GRAPE

R. Oxalis oregana
REDWOOD SORREL

S. Pachysandra terminalis
JAPANESE SPURGE

T. Papaver orientale
ORIENTAL POPPY

U. Plum

V. Polygonatum
SOLOMON'S SEAL

W. Prunus serrulata 'Shirotae'
JAPANESE FLOWERING CHERRY

X. Pseudotsuga menziesii
DOUGLAS FIR

Y. Rhododendron species
AZALEA AND RHODODENDRON

Z. Sarcococca

AA. Stachys byzantina
LAMB'S EARS

BB. Syringa vulgaris
COMMON LILAC

CC. Thalictrum
MEADOW RUE

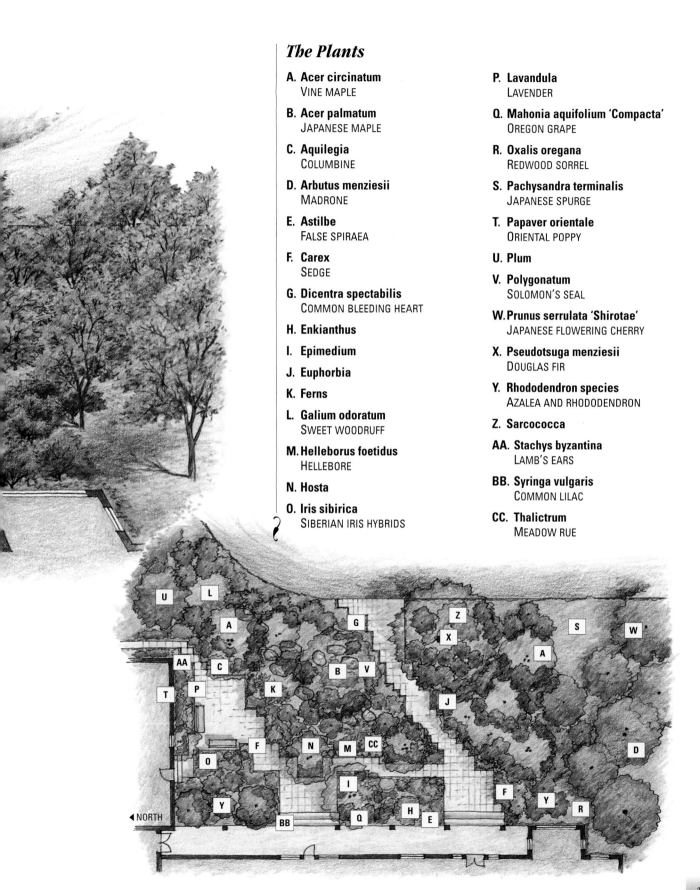

NORTH

INSPIRED BY NATURE... IN BERKELEY

The southwest-facing frontage of this house in the Berkeley hills is the location for a garden based on California's coastal chaparral. In this ocean-influenced region of winter rains, evergreen shrubs such as ceanothus, flannel bush, and manzanita dominate, and scrub oak is the main deciduous tree. Summer fog and the existing large trees (coast redwood, magnolia, deodar cedar) around the edges of the garden create a temperate microclimate suitable for shade dwellers such as Lenten rose to thrive.

Landscape architect Ron Lutsko of San Francisco included a broad palette of California plants native to this region, as well as ones from similar climates in Europe (bush germander, herbs, salvia, and santolina) and Australia (cordyline).

Wide beds that slope down between low retaining walls are covered with a chaparral-like mix of plants that brings forth alternating hues of red, yellow, and blue throughout spring and summer. Stairs that lead to the street alternate from one side of these beds to the other, allowing a longer look at the garden and breaking up the climb. Semicircular viewing areas at center of the walls are framed by tall *Arctostaphylos manzanita* 'Dr. Hurd'. Pathways are paved with sandstone and the walls are coated with stucco.

The garden's design demonstrates that native plants work just as well in broad beds neatly edged with walks and walls as they do on the edge of wild land.

The Plants

A. **Arctostaphylos hookeri 'Wayside'**
   MONTEREY MANZANITA

B. **A. 'Lutsko Pink'**

C. **A. manzanita 'Dr. Hurd'**

D. **A. nummularia**
   FORT BRAGG MANZANITA

E. **A. uva-ursi**
   KINNIKINNICK

F. **Beschorneria yuccoides**

G. **Bougainvillea 'San Diego Red'**

H. **Ceanothus maritimus**

I. **C. thyrsiflorus 'Skylark'**

J. **Cedrus deodara**
   DEODAR CEDAR

K. **Cordyline australis**

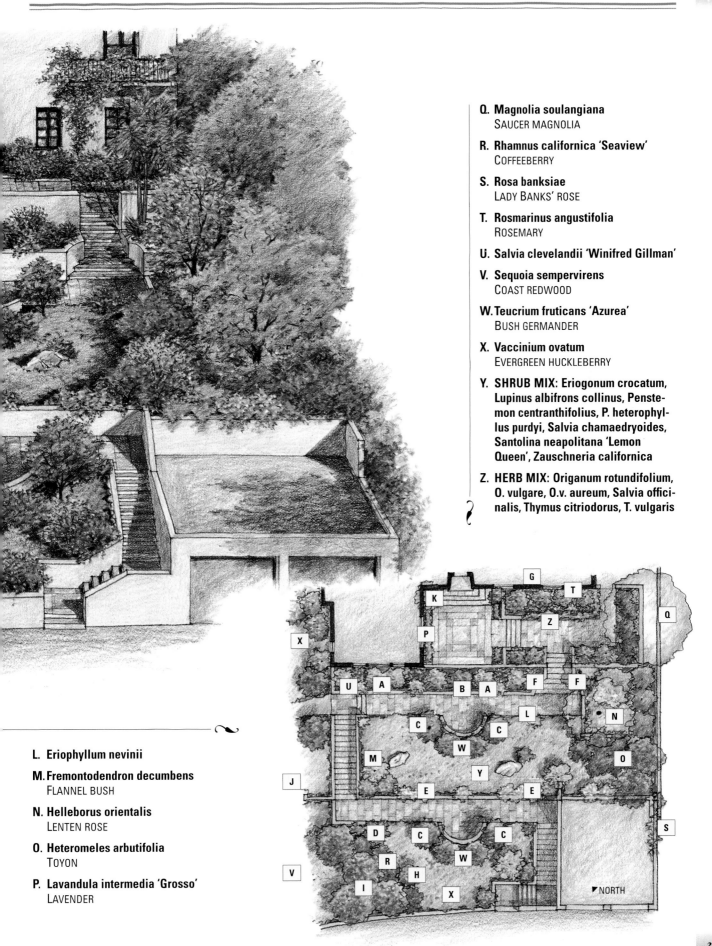

Q. **Magnolia soulangiana**
   SAUCER MAGNOLIA

R. **Rhamnus californica 'Seaview'**
   COFFEEBERRY

S. **Rosa banksiae**
   LADY BANKS' ROSE

T. **Rosmarinus angustifolia**
   ROSEMARY

U. **Salvia clevelandii 'Winifred Gillman'**

V. **Sequoia sempervirens**
   COAST REDWOOD

W. **Teucrium fruticans 'Azurea'**
   BUSH GERMANDER

X. **Vaccinium ovatum**
   EVERGREEN HUCKLEBERRY

Y. **SHRUB MIX: Eriogonum crocatum, Lupinus albifrons collinus, Penstemon centranthifolius, P. heterophyllus purdyi, Salvia chamaedryoides, Santolina neapolitana 'Lemon Queen', Zauschneria californica**

Z. **HERB MIX: Origanum rotundifolium, O. vulgare, O.v. aureum, Salvia officinalis, Thymus citriodorus, T. vulgaris**

L. **Eriophyllum nevinii**

M. **Fremontodendron decumbens**
   FLANNEL BUSH

N. **Helleborus orientalis**
   LENTEN ROSE

O. **Heteromeles arbutifolia**
   TOYON

P. **Lavandula intermedia 'Grosso'**
   LAVENDER

INSPIRED BY NATURE...IN PHOENIX

Native plants let this Phoenix garden blend into the surrounding desert, yet the design supplies enough color and form to keep the garden attractive in all seasons.

A courtyard between two parts of the 1920s adobe house functions as an outdoor living room in the mild winters. To accentuate this roomlike feeling, landscape architect Christine Ten Eyck paved the courtyard with colored brown concrete. To create a "ceiling," she planted blue palo verde and Mexican bird of paradise bushes. Stone from the site was inlaid in the concrete around a simple stone bowl fountain, hand carved in Mexico.

Beyond the courtyard walls, plantings of creosote bush, desert ironwood, and littleleaf palo verde create more shade. Their interesting branch patterns help the visual transition from the oasislike courtyard to the native desert. Paths are of compacted decomposed granite.

Below and around the trees grow flowering perennials and succulents, including Baja ruellia and sage in the courtyard, and desert marigold, globe mallow, and moss verbena outside. The result is a lush garden with lots of shade and year-round color that evokes the feeling of the Sonoran Desert.

The Plants

A. Agave weberii
SMOOTH-EDGED AGAVE

B. Baileya multiradiata
DESERT MARIGOLD

C. Buddleia marrubifolia
WOOLLY BUTTERFLY BUSH

D. Caesalpinia mexicana
YELLOW MEXICAN BIRD OF PARADISE

E. Carnegiea gigantea
SAGUARO

F. Cercidium floridum
BLUE PALO VERDE

G. C. microphyllum
LITTLELEAF PALO VERDE

H. Justicia spicigera
MEXICAN HONEYSUCKLE

I. Larrea tridentata
CREOSOTE BUSH

J. Leucophyllum frutescens 'Green Cloud'
TEXAS RANGER

K. L. laevigatum
CHIHUAHUAN SAGE

L. Olneya tesota
DESERT IRONWOOD

M. Opuntia ficus indica
INDIAN FIG PRICKLY PEAR

N. Ruellia peninsularis
BAJA RUELLIA

O. Salvia coccinea, S. greggii
SAGE

P. Sphaeralcea ambigua
GLOBE MALLOW

Q. Verbena pulchella gracilior
MOSS VERBENA

NORTH

A FAMILY GARDEN

Often, a range of family interests (seating, dining, and play areas, a pool or spa, and both flower and vegetable beds) compete with one another for limited space in the garden. This design achieves the seemingly impossible, fitting all these elements into a single garden about 55 by 65 feet.

Landscape designer Nick Williams of Tarzana, California, put a covered patio and umbrella table close to the house, convenient to a barbecue area. The free-form lawn is large enough for games, lounging, or playing with the family dog.

To create a feeling of continuity in the condensed space, the landscape contains a relatively small selection of plants. The main border plants are star jasmine, punctuated with *Rhaphiolepis,* tobira, and *Xylosma.* Camphor tree, Indian laurel fig, jacaranda,

and strawberry tree provide shade and seasonal color, as do red trumpet vine and wisteria. Baby's tears, coral bells, and iris are spotted around the garden. The coral bells, dwarf periwinkle, and lily-of-the-Nile bloom over a long period.

Herbs grow next to the house (at the bottom of the plan) and a vegetable garden fits into one back corner. Around the vegetable beds, fast-draining pea gravel provides a walkable surface in all weather; bark chips would also work well.

The play structure, positioned in the other back corner, was constructed from a kit, and includes swings, a slide, and a small playhouse—complete with a low-voltage light. For safety, both pathway and high-intensity lights are spotted around the pool and throughout the garden.

The Plants

A. Agapanthus africanus, A. orientalis
LILY-OF-THE-NILE

B. Arbutus unedo
STRAWBERRY TREE

C. Cinnamomum camphora
CAMPHOR TREE

D. Citrus
'IMPROVED MEYER' LEMON

E. Coprosma repens 'Marble Queen'
MIRROR PLANT

F. Distictis buccinatoria
BLOOD-RED TRUMPET VINE

G. Ficus microcarpa nitida
INDIAN LAUREL FIG

H. Herbs

I. Heuchera sanguinea
CORAL BELLS

J. Iris

K. Jacaranda mimosifolia

L. Limonium perezii
STATICE

M. Pittosporum tobira 'Variegata'
TOBIRA

N. Rhaphiolepis 'Majestic Beauty'

O. Soleirolia soleirolii
BABY'S TEARS

P. Trachelospermum jasminoides
STAR JASMINE

Q. Vinca minor
DWARF PERIWINKLE

R. Wisteria sinensis
CHINESE WISTERIA

S. Woodwardia fimbriata
GIANT CHAIN FERN

T. Xylosma congestum

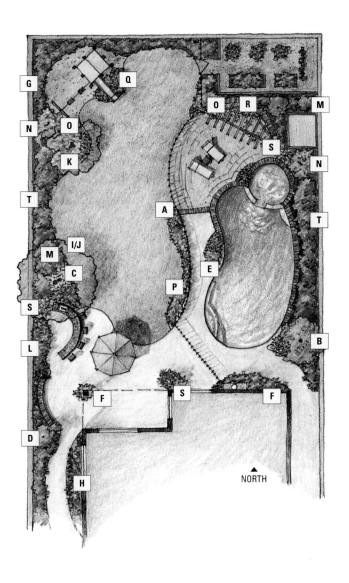

Most of the paving has an economical washed-concrete finish, but to set off a seating area by the pool and spa, Williams used weathered brick. Blue tile that matches the pool trim also tops the barbecue area.

Williams says the key to this design is to keep it simple. It's important when including so much in so little space that the plant palette be limited in its texture and color. And patterns and color selections for tile and other hardscape materials were chosen to subtly complement the plants' natural hues.

MATERIALS AND TECHNIQUES

You've dreamed, schemed, and planned your new landscape. Now it's time to lay some brick and pound a few nails. When it comes to garden structures, just what's involved? What kind of lumber is best for raised beds? How do you make a gravel pathway? Which fasteners are best for overheads? Is homemade concrete best?

Whether you use tried-and-true materials like wood and flagstone, or try out new products like recycled glass tiles and colored concrete, remember that a little local knowledge goes a long way. After you have read the step-by-step instructions given here, seek advice at your local building department, lumberyard, or garden center.

Should you do the work yourself? Although it's satisfying and can be more economical, some projects take hard work and require construction or woodworking experience. If you decide to do it yourself, read over the safety guidelines given at the end of the chapter.

LUMBER

Many landscaping projects begin with lumber, including decks, fences, steps, and raised beds. Given here is an overview of lumber products you'll need for garden construction projects, along with the fasteners and finishes that are available for them. Step-by-step directions illustrate the most common wooden garden projects: an attached deck (see pages 370–371), a basic board fence (see pages 372–373), and a free-standing overhead (see page 374).

Lumberyard tools and materials

Because wood comes in so many sizes, species, and grades, a visit to a lumberyard can be a daunting experience for the beginning do-it-yourselfer. Busy salespeople may not be very helpful if you are unfamiliar with basic building terminology, so it's a good idea to familiarize yourself with the ones you'll need for your projects *before* asking an employee for help.

SOFTWOOD OR HARDWOOD? Lumber is divided into these two broad categories, which refer to the origin of the wood. Softwoods come from conifers, hardwoods from deciduous trees.

As a rule, softwoods are much less expensive, easier to tool, and more readily available than hardwoods. In fact, nearly all outdoor construction is done with softwoods. However, many lumberyards now stock more economical offerings of hardwoods, such as mahogany and ipe (a South American newcomer).

SPECIES. Woods from different trees have specific properties. Redwood and cedar heartwoods (the darker part of the wood, cut from the tree's core), for example, have a natural resistance to decay. This characteristic, combined with their beauty, makes them ideal candidates for decks, natural-finish lath roofing, and raised beds. But these woods are too expensive for structural members or for elements that will be painted or stained. As a result, many landscape professionals substitute less expensive woods,

such as Douglas fir or western larch, for those parts of an outdoor structure. You can also apply protective finish to make wood more durable (see page 369). Another option for reducing the cost of wood for outdoor projects is to work with pressure-treated lumber; for details, see the page opposite.

LUMBER GRADES. Wood is sorted and graded at a lumber mill according to several factors: natural growth characteristics (such as knots), defects resulting from milling errors, and commercial drying and preserving techniques that affect each piece's strength, durability, and appearance. A stamp on the lumber identifies its moisture content and its grade and species mark, as well as the mill that produced it and the grading agency (often WWP for Western Wood Products Association).

In general, the higher the grade, the more you will have to pay. One of the best ways to save money on a structure is to identify the best grade (not necessarily the highest grade) for each element.

Structural lumber and timbers are rated for strength. The most common grading system includes the grades Select Structural, No. 1, No. 2, and No. 3. For premium strength, choose Select Structural. Often, lumberyards sell a mix of grades called No. 2 and Better. Other grading systems used for some lumber (typically 2 by 4s) classify wood as Construction, Standard, and Utility, or as a mixture of grades called Standard and Better.

Redwood is usually graded for its appearance and the percentage of heartwood versus sapwood it contains: Clear All Heart is the best and the most expensive. B Heart, Construction Heart, and Merchantable Heart, in descending order of quality, are typical grades of pure heartwood; grades lower than these are likely to contain increasing amounts of knots, splits, and other flaws.

Cedar grades, starting with the highest quality, are Architect Clear, Custom Clear, Architect Knotty, and Custom Knotty. These grades don't indicate if wood is heartwood or sapwood.

Pressure-treated timbers and railroad ties (left) serve well as edging for raised beds or steps. Grades of redwood range from tough and knotty (center) to clear (far right). Higher grades of redwood are not only more attractive but also, because they contain higher percentages of heartwood, are more decay resistant.

BUYING LUMBER. Lumber is divided into categories according to size: *dimension lumber,* which is from 2 to 4 inches thick and at least 2 inches wide; *timbers,* heavy structural lumber at least 5 inches thick; and *boards,* which are normally not more than 1 inch thick and 4 to 12 inches wide.

Lumber is sold either by the *lineal foot* or by the *board foot.* The lineal foot, commonly used for small orders, considers only the length of a piece. For example, twenty 2 by 4s, 8 feet long, would be the same as 160 lineal feet of 2 by 4s.

The board foot is the most common unit for volume orders. A piece of wood 1 inch thick, 12 inches wide, and 12 inches long equals one board foot. To compute board feet, use this formula:

Thickness (in inches) $\times$ width (in feet) $\times$ length (in feet).

So a 1 by 6, 10 feet long, would be computed as follows:

1 inch $\times$ ½ foot (6 inches) $\times$ 10 feet =5 board feet.

When you place an order at a lumberyard, you must give the exact dimensions of the lumber you need.

NOMINAL SIZES. Remember that a "2 by 4" does not actually measure 2 by 4 inches. Its *nominal size* is designated before it is dried and surface-planed; the finished size is actually 1½ by 3½ inches. Likewise, a nominal 4 by 4 is actually 3½ by 3½ inches.

Rough lumber is usually closer to the nominal size because it is wetter and has not been surface-planed. If your measurements are critical, be sure to check the actual dimensions of any lumber you are considering before you buy it.

DEFECTS. Lumber is subject to a number of defects due to weathering and milling errors. When choosing lumber, lift each piece and look down the face and edges for any defects. The most common problems are cupping and bowing—warps and hollows on the board. In addition, be on the lookout for problems such as rotting, staining, splits, and missing wood or untrimmed bark along the edges or corners of the piece, called wane. Also look for insect holes and reservoirs of sap, or pitch.

Pressure-treated Lumber

Although redwood and cedar heartwoods have a natural resistance to decay and termites, most other woods that come in contact with soil or water will rot and lose strength. To avoid this problem, less durable types of lumber, such as Southern pine and western hem-fir, are often factory-treated with chemical preservatives that guard against rot, insects, and other sources of decay. These woods are less expensive and, in some areas, more readily available than redwood or cedar. They can be used for surface decking, gates, and steps, as well as for structural members such as posts, beams, and joists.

Pressure-treated wood is available in two "exposures": Ground Contact is required for lumber that will be close to the ground. Use Above Ground for applications such as decking.

Working with treated lumber has drawbacks. Unlike redwood and cedar, which are easy to cut and drive fasteners into, treated wood can be hard and brittle, and can warp or twist. Moreover, some people object to its greenish brown color (though applying a semitransparent stain can conceal it) and the staplelike treatment incisions that usually cover its surface (some newer types come without these marks).

The primary preservative used in pressure-treated lumber contains chromium, a toxic metal. As a precaution, therefore, you should wear safety glasses and a dust mask when cutting this type of lumber, and you should never burn the scraps. In addition, wear gloves when handling it for prolonged periods.

Is it safe to use pressure-treated lumber for outdoor structures such as vegetable beds and play yards? Studies suggest that it is, but you can opt for heartwood in potential contact areas, or line planters with impermeable plastic or sheet metal.

Some salvaged wood, such as railway ties, has been treated with creosote, a toxic chemical that is not recommended for garden construction.

Practical needn't be plain. Color surrounds these steps, which are fronted with heavy, pressure-treated timbers. The attractiveness of these risers belies their durability; they will last long after foot traffic and rain would have rotted untreated wood.

FASTENERS AND HARDWARE

Nails, screws, and metal framing connectors are essential for outdoor projects. Without them, it would be difficult to put boards or beams together.

NAILS. Hot-dipped galvanized, aluminum, or stainless steel nails are essential for outdoor construction because they assure rust resistance. Common and box nails are similar but the former have a thicker shank, making them more difficult to drive but increasing their holding power. Both types are sold in boxes (weighing 1, 5, or 50 pounds) or loose in bins. Standard nail sizes are given in "pennies" (penny is abbreviated as "d," from the Latin *denarius*). The higher the penny number, the longer the nail. Equivalents in inches for the most common nails are as follows:

4d=1½ in. 6d=2 in. 8d=2½ in.
10d=3 in. 16d=3½ in. 20d=4 in.

Choose nails that have a length two or three times the thickness of the material you will be nailing through. Most decking, fence, and overhead framing is secured with 8d and 16d nails.

DECK SCREWS. Although they're more expensive than nails, coated or galvanized deck screws have several advantages over nails: they don't pop as readily, their coating is less likely to be damaged during installation, and their use eliminates the possibility of hammer dents in the decking. Moreover, they are surprisingly easy to drive into soft woods, such as redwood and cedar, if you use an electric drill or screw gun with an adjustable clutch and a Phillips screwdriver tip. Screws are not given ratings for shear (or hanging) strength, so use nails, lag screws, or bolts to fasten joists to beams or ledgers, and posts to beams.

For decks, choose screws that are long enough to penetrate joists at least as deep as the decking is thick (for 2-by-4 or 2-by-6 decking, buy 3-inch screws). Screws are sold in small boxes, by the pound, or, at a substantial savings, in 25-pound boxes.

The heavy-duty lag screw, or lag bolt, has a square or hexagonal head and requires a wrench or a ratchet and socket to tighten it.

FRAMING CONNECTORS. The photo at right shows several framing connectors. Galvanized metal connectors can help prevent lumber splits caused by toenailing two boards together. Be sure to attach connectors with the nails specified by the manufacturer.

To eliminate visible fasteners, deck clips can be nailed to the sides of decking lumber and secured to joists. In addition to remaining hidden between the deck boards, these clips also elevate the boards slightly off the joist, discouraging the rot that wood-to-wood contact may breed. Unfortunately, the clips are more expensive to buy and more time-consuming to install than nails or screws.

BOLTS. For heavy-duty fastening, choose bolts. Most are zinc-plated steel, but aluminum and brass ones are also available. Bolts go into predrilled holes that are secured by nuts. The machine bolt has a square or hexagonal head that must be tightened with a wrench. The carriage bolt has a self-anchoring head that digs into the wood as the nut is tightened. Expanding anchor bolts allow you to secure wooden members to a masonry wall.

Bolts are classified by diameter (⅛ to 1 inch) and length (⅜ inch and up). To give the nut a firm bite, select a bolt ½ to 1 inch longer than the combined thicknesses of the pieces to be joined.

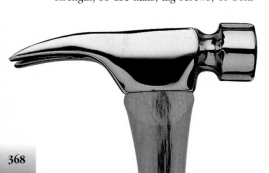

| Ring shank nail | Common nail | Finishing nail |

Wood Finishes

Structural elements that contact soil or are embedded in concrete do not require a finish. But to protect other parts of a structure and to preserve its beauty, apply a water repellent, a semitransparent stain, or a solid-color stain.

Finishes change a wood's color or tone and may mask its grain and texture. Whatever product you choose, it's best to try it on a sample board first. Always read labels: some products should not be applied over new wood; others may require a sealer first.

Water repellents, also known as water sealers, help prevent decking from warping and cracking. Clear sealers don't color wood but they allow it to gradually fade to gray; some types come in slightly tinted versions. You can buy either oil- or water-base versions, many of which include UV-blockers and mildewcides.

Don't use clear-surface finishes such as spar varnish or polyurethane on outdoor lumber. In addition to their high price, they wear quickly and are very hard to renew.

Semitransparent stains contain enough pigment to tint the wood's surface with just one coat, while permitting the natural grain to show through. They are available in both water- and oil-base versions. In addition to traditional grays and wood tones, you'll find products for "reviving" a deck's color or for dressing up pressure-treated wood.

Solid-color coverings include both deck stains and deck paint. The stains are essentially paints; their heavy pigments cover wood grain completely. Usually, any paint color can be mixed into this base. Even though these products are formulated for foot traffic, you'll probably have to renew them frequently. A word of caution: don't choose stains or paints intended for house siding; they won't last.

Shown here, from top to bottom, are: unfinished redwood, clear water sealer, tinted oil-base repellent, semitransparent gray stain, and red solid-color stain.

Framing connectors and hardware, clockwise from top right: post anchors, deck post tie, earthquake straps, rigid tie corner, joist hangers, rigid flat tie, and decorative post tops.

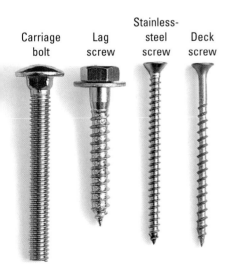

Carriage bolt   Lag screw   Stainless-steel screw   Deck screw

BUILDING A LOW-LEVEL DECK

A low-level, house-attached deck helps to extend the indoor living space. It is also a manageable and economical do-it-yourself project. Before you begin, review the advice given on pages 142–145 and check your local building codes. This type of deck can be completed in a few weekends' time, but it will require the work of at least two people.

Think ahead about benches or other items that may need to be integrated with the deck's framing. Be sure the completed deck will be at least 1 inch below adjacent access doors. If you're planning a freestanding deck, substitute an extra beam and posts for the ledger shown; extra bracing at the corners may also be necessary. For other deck plans, see Sunset's *Complete Deck Book*.

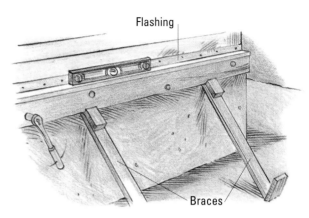

1. Determine the position of the ledger and prop it into place with 2-by-4 blocks or braces. Drill staggered holes for lag screws every 16 inches, then fasten ledger in place, making sure it is level. To prevent rot, either space the ledger off the wall with blocks or washers, or add metal flashing, as shown.

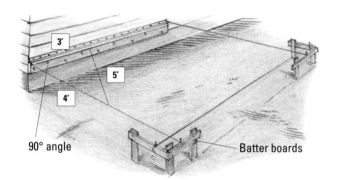

2. Batter boards mark height of deck; build them at outside corners, level with the ledger top. To mark deck edges, string mason's line from batter boards to ledger. Corners must be square; determine using the "3-4-5" triangle method shown.

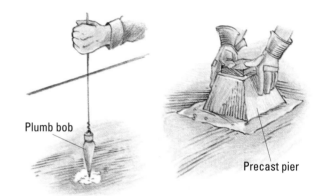

3. Dangle a plumb bob from mason's lines to mark footings. Dig holes to depths required by code; add gravel, then fill with concrete (see pages 372–373). Push piers into the concrete, level their tops, and let concrete set overnight.

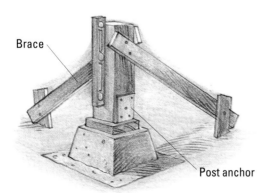

4. Unless piers have integral post anchors, add them now. Measure and cut posts—for this design, a joist's depth below the top of ledger. Check plumb on two sides of each post, temporarily brace each in place, and fasten to piers.

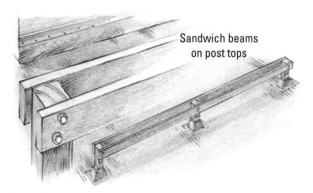

5. Position 2-by beams on each side of post tops, as shown. After leveling them with post tops, clamp them in place. Drill staggered holes, then fasten each beam to posts with bolts or lag screws.

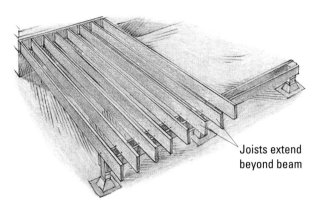

Joists extend
beyond beam

6. Position joists at predetermined span intervals and secure to ledger with framing connectors, as shown. Set them atop beams and toenail in place. Brace joists with spacers at open ends and, if required, at midspan. Add posts for any railings or benches, or an overhead anchored to deck framing.

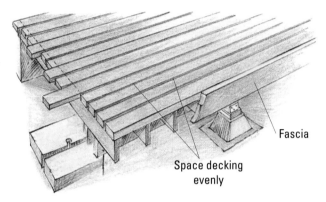

Fascia

Space decking
evenly

7. Align decking boards atop joists, staggering joints (if any). Space boards, leaving about ³⁄₁₆ inch—or the thickness of a 16d nail—for drainage. Fasten decking to joists with 16d common nails or deck screws. Trim edges with circular saw.

4-by-4 post

8. Finish decking ends and edges as desired with fascia boards or other trim. If you're planning benches, planters, steps, or railings that aren't tied directly to substructure, add them now.

Decking Patterns

Decks are designed from the top down, so one of your first decisions will involve selecting a decking pattern. The design you choose may affect how the deck's substructure is built. For a house-attached deck similar to the one shown, it's often simplest to run decking boards parallel to the house wall. Generally, the more complex the decking pattern, the smaller the joist spans required and the more complicated the substructure to support it.

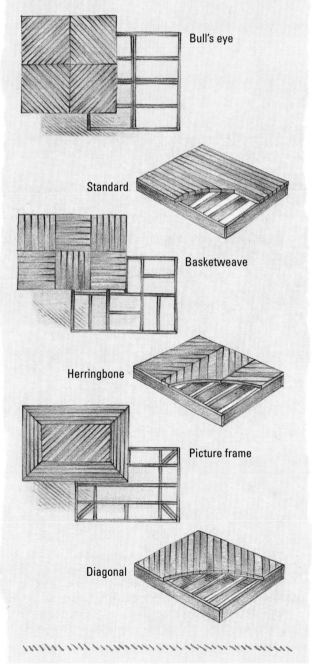

Bull's eye

Standard

Basketweave

Herringbone

Picture frame

Diagonal

BUILDING A BOARD FENCE

In general, fence building is a straightforward task. The hardest part is digging the postholes; the tools shown at right will make this easier. There are many design variations, but the procedure outlined below is a good one for putting up a basic board fence.

Before you set a post or pound a nail, check your local building and zoning codes, as they may influence style, material, setback, and other requirements. Then tackle the building stages: plotting the fence, installing posts, and adding rails and siding.

For fences from 3 to 6 feet tall, plan to set posts at least 2 feet deep—12 inches deeper for end and gate posts. For taller fences, the rule of thumb for post depth is one-third the post length. You can either dig postholes to a uniform depth or cut the posts once they are in the ground. Once the posts are installed, the rest of the job is easy, especially when you have one or two helpers.

If you're planning to hang a gate, too, see pages 148–149 for construction and design pointers.

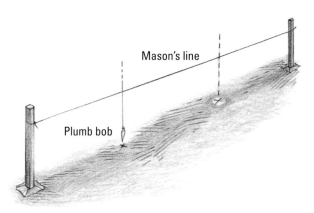

1. First, mark each end or corner post location with a stake. Run mason's line between the stakes, as shown. With chalk, mark remaining post locations on the line. Using a level or plumb bob, transfer each mark to the ground and drive in additional stakes. Then dig holes 6 inches deeper than post depth, making them 2½ to 3 times the post's diameter.

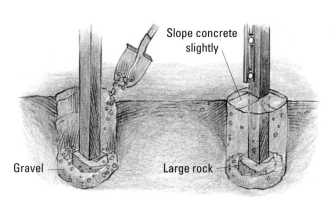

2. Place a rock at the base of each hole and add 4 to 6 inches of gravel. Place a post in a hole and shovel in concrete, tamping it down with a broomstick or capped steel pipe. Adjust the post for plumb with a level. Continue filling until the concrete extends 1 or 2 inches above ground level, and slope it away from the post to divert water.

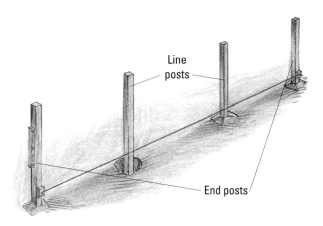

3. To align posts, first position two end or corner posts so their faces are parallel, then plumb them and set them permanently. Use spacer blocks and a mason's line to locate line posts, spacing each a block's thickness from the line. After setting posts in fresh concrete, you have about 20 minutes to align them before concrete hardens. Let cure for 2 days.

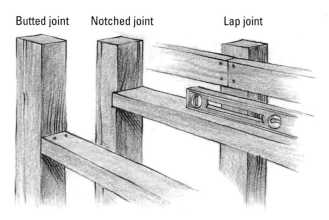

4. Brush on wood preservative where rails and posts will meet. Then fasten one end of each rail; check level with a helper and secure the other end. You can butt them against the post and toenail them, notch them in (cut notches before installing posts), or lap them over the sides or top of each post. If making lap joints, plan to span at least three posts for strength.

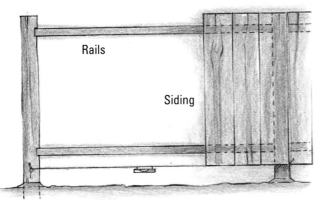

Rails

Siding

5. Cut siding boards to the same length. Stretch and level a line from post to post to mark the bottom of the siding. Check the first board for plumb, then secure it to rails with galvanized nails three times as long as the board's thickness. Add additional boards, checking alignment as you go.

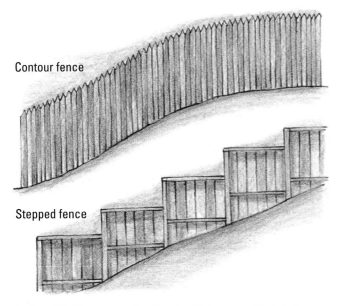

Contour fence

Stepped fence

6. On a hillside, post-and-rail and solid fences with pickets or grape stakes make good contour fences. Board, louver, basket-weave, and panel styles work better for stepped fences, which are more difficult to build. For both kinds, make sure that the bottoms of boards 6 inches or wider are cut to follow the contour of the hillside; otherwise, gaps will remain.

Digging Postholes

Although you could use a pick and shovel to dig post-holes for fences (or decks and overheads), some heavier equipment will save you time and effort. Two handy tools are shown below.

Posthole, or clamshell, diggers (below left) work in hard or rocky soil. Spread the handles to open and close the blades, which trap soil. This tool is difficult to use for holes more than 3 feet deep, as the sides of the hole interfere with the spreading of the handles.

A power auger, also known as a power digger or earth drill, is recommended whenever you have more than a dozen holes to dig. You can rent models for operation by one or two people (a two-person model is shown below right), and they may be freestanding or vehicle-mounted. Every so often, pull the auger out of the hole to remove the dirt; a posthole digger or a small spade may also be required.

When you turn the handle of a hand-operated auger, the pointed blades bore into the soil, scraping it up and collecting it in a chamber. Once the chamber is full, remove the auger from the hole and empty out the soil. This tool works best in loose soil.

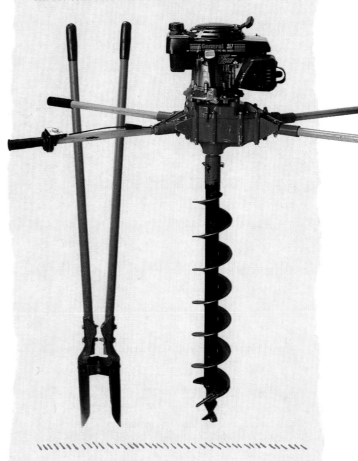

BUILDING AN OVERHEAD

Building an overhead is similar to building a deck, although you'll probably spend a lot more time on a ladder. These illustrations outline the sequence for erecting a freestanding overhead. For construction details on a house-attached overhead, see the facing page. An arbor is essentially a simple overhead; for design ideas, refer to pages 138–141.

If your overhead will span an existing patio, you can set the posts on footings and piers located outside the edge of the patio, or break through the existing paving, dig holes, and pour new concrete footings (and, if necessary, add piers). If you're planning to install a new concrete patio, then you can pour footings and paving at the same time, embedding the post anchors in the wet concrete.

1. Precut posts to length (or run a level line and cut them later). Set posts in anchors embedded in concrete footing or atop precast piers. Hold each post vertical and nail anchor to it.

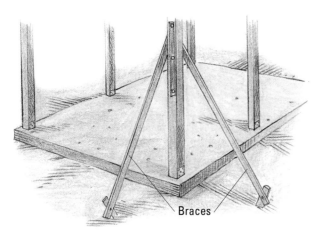

Braces

2. Continue to put up posts, plumbing each post with level on two adjacent sides. Secure each in position with temporary braces nailed to wooden stakes that are driven into ground.

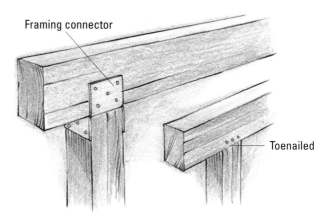

Framing connector

Toenailed

3. With a helper, position a beam on top of posts. Check that posts are vertical and beam is level (adjust, if necessary, with shims); then secure beam to posts.

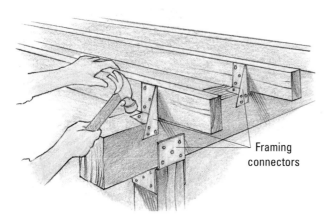

Framing connectors

4. Set and space rafters on top of beams and secure them with framing connectors (shown) or by toenailing to beams. For extra strength, install bracing between posts and beams.

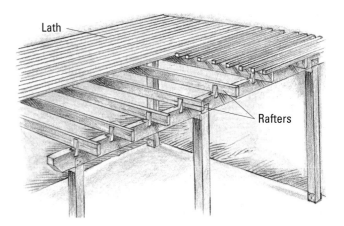

Lath

Rafters

5. Cover rafters with lath, either 1 by 2s or 2 by 2s. Space the lath for plant support or to achieve a specific amount of shade (see facing page).

Overhead alternatives

Although most overheads employ the same basic components (posts, beams, rafters or joists, and some type of roofing), there are many different ways to assemble them. Each, however, must conform to spans determined by local building codes, so be sure to check them before you start to build.

To attach an overhead to your house, you will need to install a ledger, much like a deck ledger (see page 370). Usually made from a 2 by 4 or a 2 by 6, the ledger is typically lag-screwed—either to wall studs, to second-story floor framing, or to the roof. If the house wall is brick or stone, however, you'll need to drill holes and install expanding anchors to bolt the ledger in place.

Rafters can be set on top of the ledger or hung from it with anchors, joist hangers, or rafter hangers. If your overhead's roof will be flat, simply square up rafter ends. Sloped rafters, however, require angled cuts at each end, plus a notch (as shown at right) where rafters cross the beam.

You can also opt for a solid roofing material such as shingles, siding, or even asphalt. If you leave the structure uncovered, treating it with a preservative or other finish can add years to its life.

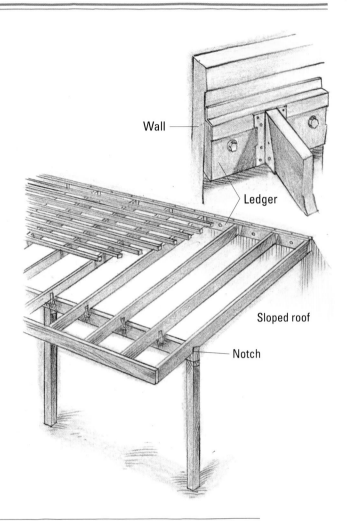

Designing for Shade

If you desire an open effect or plan to cover the overhead with vines, the rafters can act as a roof. For more protection, attach wood laths or louvers, arranged in a lattice pattern or placed at right angles to the rafters. Vary the wood thickness and spacing to cast the shade you desire—thin lath laid flat won't cast as much shade as thicker stock. The direction in which you run the lath depends on the time of day you need the most shade. If you want midday shade, run the lath east-west; for more shade in the morning and early evening, run the lath north-south.

Experiment with the width, spacing, and direction of overhead members by temporarily nailing different sizes to the rafters and observing the effect for a few days.

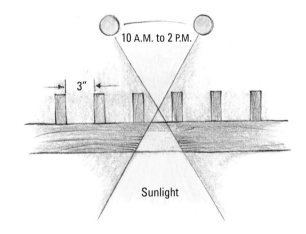

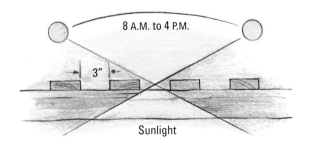

The same boards set 3 inches apart, but at different angles, will affect the extent of shade cast below an overhead. Lath or boards laid on edge diffuse early morning and late afternoon sun, but let in plenty of light at midday (above). The same members laid flat (left) allow in more sun in the early morning and late afternoon, but block more midday sun.

MASONRY

This section will guide you through the world of masonry materials and explain the basic techniques for building paths, patios, and walls. Although some stonework requires years of training, these basic masonry projects can be successfully completed by a do-it-yourselfer. The key is to proceed with patience.

However, you should seek advice from your local building department or garden supplier about the best concrete mix, brick types, or base treatment for use in your climate and soil. Speak with your neighbors about the masonry materials they have successfully used in their gardens, and browse through local offerings of masonry products before buying— new products constantly appear.

Loose stones and gravel. Clockwise from top: quartz, La Paz, ¼-in. dolomite, ¾-in. red lava, tumbled Japanese riverstone, ¼-in. pea gravel, aqua cove mix, ⁵/₁₆-in. red lava.

cubic yard, which simplifies ordering; others sell it by the ton. Most suppliers can help you calculate how much you need based on a square-foot estimate.

STONES FOR PAVING. Many stones are precut in square or rectangular shapes; these are fairly uniform in thickness and easy to lay in a grid pattern. Others, however, have random widths and thicknesses.

Granite and marble are both valued for their hardness and durability, though marble is too expensive for most garden construction. Sandstone, limestone, and other sedimentary stones are popular choices; they are more porous than other types and usually have a chalky or gritty texture. Slate, a fine-grained metamorphic rock

Shopping for stone

Stone is particularly appealing because it is a natural material, and most types are very durable. But the availability of stone types, shapes, sizes, and colors varies by locale, and its primary drawback is that it can cost up to five times as much as concrete or brick. Geography dictates price: the farther you live from the quarry, the more you'll have to pay. Some dealers sell stone by the

that is dense and smooth, is also an excellent choice for paving.

Flat flagstones and cut stone tiles are ideal for formal settings. Technically, flagstone is any flat stone that is either naturally thin or split from rock that cleaves easily. It blends well with plants and ponds or other water features. Furthermore, flagstone is one of the few paving materials that can be set directly on stable soil. However,

outdoor furniture and objects with wheels sometimes get caught on its irregular surface. Also, some types of flagstone become dirty easily and are difficult to clean.

Fieldstone, river rock, and pebbles are less expensive than flagstone or cut tiles. These water-worn or glacier-ground stones produce rustic, uneven pavings that make up in charm what they may lack in smoothness underfoot. Smaller stones and pebbles, for example, can be set or seeded into concrete (see page 382); cobblestones can be laid in concrete or on tamped earth to cover an entire surface; or narrow mosaic panels of very small stone can be used to break up an expanse of concrete or brick.

For economy, good drainage, and a more casual look, don't forget gravel or crushed rock, both of which can provide material for garden paving. Gravel is collected or mined from natural deposits; crushed rock is mechanically fractured and graded to a uniform size. Frequently, gravels are named after the regions where they were quarried.

When choosing a gravel, consider color, sheen, texture, and size. Take home samples as you would paint chips. Keep in mind that gravel color, like paint color, looks more intense when spread over a large area.

STONES FOR WALLS. There are two broad classes of stonework that work well for walls: rubble (untrimmed) and ashlar (trimmed). In addition, partially trimmed pieces such as cobblestones can create attractive effects.

The stones used in rubble walls are often rounded from glacial or water action; examples (often igneous in origin) include granite and basalt river rock and fieldstone. Since they are difficult to cut, it's usually easier to search for rocks that are the size you need. Rubblestone is frequently the cheapest kind available.

Fully trimmed ashlar stone is almost as easy to lay as brick. The flat surfaces and limited range of sizes make formal coursing possible and require less mortar than for rubblework.

Ashlar stone is usually sedimentary in origin; the most commonly available type is sandstone. When a tougher igneous stone, such as granite, is cut and trimmed for ashlar masonry, costs are likely to be quite high.

Left to right: Boquet Canyon, stardust flagstone, Idaho quartzite, California Mariposa slate, Lompoc flagstone, pink Arizona flagstone, chocolate Arizona flagstone, tan Arizona flagstone.

Artificial Rock

Rocks and boulders can lend a rugged texture to a residential landscape. However, big boulders can be hard to find and difficult to transport and install. In some gardens, the site conditions or the landscape design make it impossible to install them. So, some owners are turning to artificial rocks that are shaped, textured, and colored to resemble their natural counterparts.

One rock-forming method starts with a boulder-shaped frame of reinforcing bar. Wire mesh or metal lath is secured to the frame, then several layers of concrete are applied to the shell. To re-create the cracks and fissures of natural rock, the still-wet concrete may be carved with tools or embossed with crinkled aluminum foil, clear plastic wrap, or custom latex molds cast from actual rock formations.

Another popular rock-forming technique calls for latex models to be cast on real rocks. The models are sprayed with a mixture of concrete and strands of fiberglass or polypropylene. When the mixture dries, the forms are removed. The end product is a thin but sturdy panel with a rock-textured veneer. The models yield identical panels, which can be joined together horizontally or vertically so the viewer is not aware of the repeated shape.

True rock is often a pastiche of colors and may also be flecked with lichen or specks of soil. To imitate this look, installers color the concrete by brushing, spraying, or splattering on layers of diluted acrylic stains.

Artificial rocks offer other landscaping opportunities: they can form steps, waterfalls, and pockets for plants, lights, or ponds. Moreover, they can be used to hide pumps and electrical or water lines, as well as mask retaining walls.

Because of labor and materials, the cost of artificial rock is usually slightly higher than that of real stone or boulders.

These wide, slightly curved steps and low retaining walls are made of artificial cast stone formed directly on the hillside.

BRICK

Of the bewildering variety of bricks available, only two basic kinds are used for most garden construction: rough-textured *common* brick and smoother-surfaced *face* brick.

Most garden paving is done with common brick. People like its familiar, warm color and texture, and it has the advantage of being less expensive than face brick. Common brick is more porous than face brick and less uniform in size and color (bricks may vary up to ¼ inch in length).

Face brick, with its sand-finished, glazed surface, is not as widely available as common brick. More often used for facing buildings than for garden projects, this brick can be used to make elegant formal walls, attractive accents, edgings, header courses, stair nosings, and raised beds—all outdoor projects where its smoothness won't present a safety hazard.

Used brick has uneven surfaces and streaks of old mortar that can look very attractive in an informal pavement. Imitation-used, or "rustic," brick costs about the same as genuine used brick and is easier to find; it is also more consistent in quality than most of the older brick.

Low-density firebrick, blond-colored and porous, is tailor-made for built-in barbecues and outdoor fireplaces. It provides interesting accents but doesn't wear as well as common brick.

The standard brick is about 8 by 4 by 2⅜ inches thick. "Paver" bricks, which are solid and made to use underfoot, are roughly half the thickness of standard bricks. "True," or "mortarless," pavers are a standard 4 by 8 inches (plus or minus ⅛ inch) and can be invaluable for laying a complex pattern with tightly butted joints. To calculate the quantities of brick you'll need for a project, visit a building supplier first, with your measuring tape in hand.

All outdoor bricks are graded according to their ability to withstand weathering. If you live in a region where it regularly freezes and thaws, buy only bricks graded SW, which indicates they can withstand changing weather conditions.

A display of brick includes rough common bricks in various colors, smoother face bricks for accents and edgings, bullnose types (with rounded ends) for stairs and to cap walls, used or imitation-used bricks, and precut bricks (such as the triangle, above left) for patterns.

Precast pavers allow you to experiment with designs and shapes, and many imitate tile, brick, or adobe. An assortment is shown here, including those that interlock with puzzlelike shapes, stepping-stones, and turf blocks.

PAVERS

Available in many sizes, colors, and textures, concrete pavers are no longer limited to 12-inch squares. Easy to install, pavers are an ideal material for do-it-yourself masonry projects.

A simple square can form part of a grid or even a gentle arc. Squares or rectangles can butt together to create broad, unbroken surfaces, or they can be spaced apart and surrounded with grass, a ground cover, or gravel for textural interest.

Interlocking pavers fit together like puzzle pieces. They are made of extremely dense concrete that is mechanically pressure-formed. Laid in sand with closed (butted) joints, they create a surface that is more rigid than brick. No paver can tip out of alignment without taking several of its neighbors with it, and the surface remains intact even under substantial loads. Some interlocking shapes are proprietary, available at only a few outlets or direct from distributors. To locate these, check the Yellow Pages under Concrete Products.

Modern cobblestone blocks are very popular for casual gardens; butt them tightly together and then sweep sand or soil between the irregular edges.

Turf blocks, which leave spaces for plants to grow through, are designed to carry light traffic while retaining and protecting ground-cover plants. This special type of paver allows you to create grassy patios and driveways or side-yard access routes that stand up to wear.

Cast concrete "bricks," available in classic terracotta red as well as imitation-used, or antique styles, have become increasingly popular as substitutes for the real thing because, in many areas, they're significantly less expensive.

Some landscape professionals cast their own pavers in custom shapes, textures, and colors: adobe, stone, and imitation tile, for example. You can also make forms and pour your own pavers, but they won't be as strong as standard pressure-formed units.

A

TILE

Ceramic tile works well in both formal and informal gardens. It is also a good flooring choice for an indoor room that leads to an outdoor patio, as well as for the patio itself.

The first decision you'll need to make is whether to use glazed or unglazed tile. Glaze is a hard finish, usually colored, applied to the surface of a tile before its final firing. Most bright, colorful tiles are glazed. Unfortunately, unless a special grit is added to the surface of glazed tile, it can be slippery when wet, so for outdoor use choose unglazed tiles for paving and reserve the glazed ones for occasional accents, edgings, or raised planting beds.

Most outdoor tile, whether glazed or unglazed, falls into one of three categories: pavers, quarry tile, or synthetic stone.

Pavers are made by pouring clay into wooden or metal molds, drying or curing the tiles, and then firing them. They usually have a grainy, handcrafted look. Perhaps the best-known hand-molded pavers are Saltillo tiles (named for the city in Mexico where they are made). Pavers are not recommended for use outdoors in cool, wet climates, as mildew and moss are likely to become problems.

Quarry tiles are denser and more regular in shape than pavers. They come in natural shades of yellow, brown, and red, and are available with rounded edges and with varied finishes. These tiles are made by squeezing clay into forms under great pressure, then firing them until they are very hard.

Synthetic stone is now being developed by tile manufacturers impressed by the increasing popularity of real stone. These tiles, which mimic the look of granite, limestone, or sandstone, generally have enough surface bite to be safely used on patios. You can also buy concrete imitations of paver tiles; unlike concrete pavers (see page 379), these should be installed on a rigid mortar bed.

Sealer for tile

Some unglazed tiles are sealed at the factory; those that aren't should be coated with a penetrating sealer that allows the tile to "breathe" after installation. A sealer may darken a tile's surface or give it a shiny appearance, so you should try it first on an extra piece of tile. Some sealers require more maintenance than others. Ask your tile dealer to recommend the product most appropriate for your situation.

A. Glazed and unglazed tiles include unglazed embossed porcelain (top), unglazed ceramic (lion pattern), glazed painted ceramic (smallest tile), and tumbled stone (center).

B. From plain to painted, tiles come in a range of shapes and patterns, including concrete with inlay (center), antique French paver (top, center), painted Saltillo (sunflower pattern), glazed ceramic (hexagon), quarry tile (far right, bottom), and machine-tooled glazed border (far left, bottom).

B

This rustic stepped walkway combines adobe blocks with railroad ties. The ties hold the blocks in place; sand fills the joints.

Adobe

The famous mud brick of the Southwest, adobe is one of the world's oldest building materials. Modern adobe blocks are stabilized with portland cement or asphalt emulsions to make them impervious to water. Although sold mainly in Arizona, New Mexico, and Southern California, adobe can be used effectively throughout the West, though delivery charges can make it costly.

When spaced atop a bed of sand or soil with 1-inch open joints, irregular adobe can create a living floor; low-growing ground covers can fill the joints, softening the look and feel of a paved area. Rugged adobe walls also add color, texture, and—due to their thickness—coolness to an enclosed patio.

The most common block size is roughly 4 by 7½ by 16 inches, about the same size as four or five common bricks put together.

Concrete and Glass Blocks

The large size of concrete blocks—8 by 8 by 16 inches is standard—means that wall building progresses swiftly (see page 394). In addition to the standard size, blocks come in 4-, 6-, and 12-inch widths. Consider these if you are putting up a low wall or if you want to create a massive effect.

Two weights of block are suitable for residential projects. Standard blocks are molded with regular heavy aggregate and weigh about 45 pounds each. Lightweight, or cinder, blocks are made with special aggregates.

Whatever the size and weight of the standard block, a whole series of fractional units are available and the standard blocks can usually be found in stretcher (open end) and corner (closed end) forms. With a little planning and care in assembly, you should never have to cut a block.

Most manufacturers also make a variety of decorative blocks. Some units have patterns cast in relief on their face shells. Slump blocks are formed with the use of a press that gives them an irregular appearance similar to that of trimmed stone or adobe. Split-face blocks are broken apart when manufactured and resemble cut stone. Screen, or grille, blocks are often laid above a standard wall; they admit light and air while still affording privacy.

Glass blocks, popular during the '20s, '30s, and '40s, are currently staging a comeback. The photo above illustrates how a glass wall can be combined with other masonry materials. Typically, glass blocks come in 6- to 12-inch squares and in clear, wavy, or cross-hatch textures. Installation can be tricky, but several wall-building systems are aimed at do-it-yourselfers.

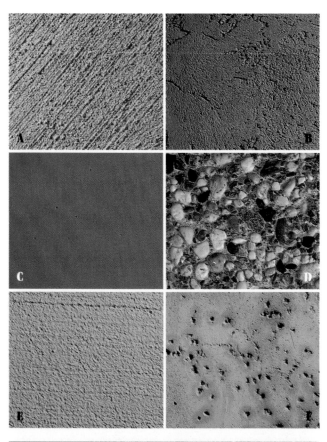

CONCRETE

Though sometimes disparaged as cold and forbidding, poured —or, more accurately, cast—concrete is even more variable in appearance than brick. Used with well-made forms, it can conform to almost any shape. Furthermore, it can be lightly smoothed or heavily brushed, surfaced with handsome pebbles, swirled or scored, tinted or painted, patterned, or molded to resemble another material. And if you eventually get tired of the concrete surface you have chosen, you can use it as a foundation for a new pavement of brick, stone, or tile set in mortar.

Concrete does have certain disadvantages. In some situations, it can seem harsh, hot, glaring, or simply boring. And if smoothly troweled, concrete can become slick when wet. Moreover, once its dry ingredients are combined with water, you have to work quickly before the mix hardens. A mistake could require an extensive and perhaps costly redo.

Concrete paving is usually given some surface treatment, both to improve its appearance and to improve traction. For example, you can spray it with a hose jet or sandblast it to uncover the aggregate, or you can embed colorful pebbles and stone in it. These finishes, generally known as exposed aggregate, are probably the most popular contemporary paving surfaces.

Other ways to modify a standard steel-troweled concrete surface include color dusting, staining, masking, acid washing, and salt finishing. Concrete can also be stamped and tinted to resemble stone, tile, or brick. The patterns simulate either butted joints or open ones, which can then be grouted to look like masonry units.

The standard slab for pathways and patios should be 4 inches thick. In addition, you will have to allow for at least a 2-inch gravel base in areas where frost and drainage are not problems, and a 4- to 8-inch base where they are likely to be cause for concern.

Forms for concrete are built in the same way as for wood edgings. For standard paving, you will need 2 by 4s on edge for forms and 12-inch 1 by 3s or 2 by 2s for stakes. If you plan to leave the lumber in place as permanent edgings and dividers, use rot-resistant redwood, cedar, or pressure-treated lumber. For curved forms, choose either tempered hardboard, plywood, or, if they will be permanent, redwood benderboard.

Be prepared to reinforce a concrete area more than 8 feet square with 6-inch-square welded wire mesh; install it after the forms are ready (see pages 392–393). If you're not sure whether your slab will need reinforcement, consult your building department or a landscape professional.

A–F. Six basic concrete finishes: broomed **(A)**, travertine **(B)**, slick surface **(C)**, exposed aggregate **(D)**, semismooth **(E)**, and rock salt **(F)**.

G. A river of colored concrete meanders past other areas of concrete that are alternately smooth and brushed and scored. Irregular "islands" mimic flagstone.

Weighty facts about concrete

Although many people think concrete is just "cement," it is actually a combination of portland cement, sand, aggregate (usually gravel), and water. The cement, which is a complex, finely ground material, undergoes a chemical reaction when mixed with water, and becomes a kind of "glue" that binds everything together. It also gives the finished product its hardness. The sand and aggregate act as fillers and control shrinkage.

Buying bagged, dry, ready-mixed concrete is expensive but convenient, especially for small jobs. The standard 90-pound bag makes ⅔ cubic foot of concrete, enough either to fill one post hole or to cover a 16-inch-square area 4 inches deep.

If your project is fairly large, order materials in bulk and mix them yourself, either by hand or with a power mixer. For small projects hand-mixing is less complicated, but it requires significant exertion. Large forms that must be filled in a single pour will warrant a power mixer, which can be rented.

Use this formula for regular concrete (the proportions are by volume):

1 part cement	2¾ parts aggregate
2½ parts sand	½ part water

Some dealers also supply trailers containing about 1 cubic yard of wet, ready-mixed concrete (about enough for an 8- by 10-foot patio). These trailers have either a revolving drum that mixes the concrete or a simple metal box into which the concrete is placed. Both types are designed to be hauled by car.

For a large patio, plan to have a commercial transit-mix truck deliver enough concrete to allow you to finish your project in a single pour. To locate concrete plants, look in the Yellow Pages under Concrete, Ready Mixed.

Molded Concrete

To create the look of stones by using concrete, you can dig holes or build shaped wooden forms and fill them with concrete. The resulting pads—with planting spaces in between—can be textured, smoothed, or seeded with aggregate. Commercial forms are also available, as shown below.

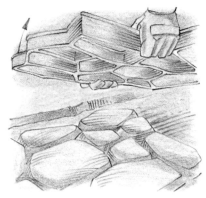

Plastic forms can be used to form a path of concrete "flagstone." Place the form on a clean, level surface (top); use a trowel to fill the mold with concrete (center), and smooth the top. When the concrete can hold its shape, remove the mold (bottom).

THE RECYCLED LANDSCAPE

At first glance, a wall, deck, or path of recycled materials may not look out of the ordinary. But take a closer look: those materials may surprise you. Pavers in the path may be made of glass. Or timbers around the planting beds may actually be plastic.

The stone pillars flanking an entryway might not be stone at all, but Milestone, a new material that is a combination of ground recycled glass, portland cement, and resins.

Patio pavers may not be masonry, but glass that was fashioned from reclaimed bottles. Paths or spaces between pavers may be filled with sparkling glass cullet, a gravel-like material that resembles fine beach pebbles. The glass, collected from recycled bottles, is crushed mechanically, then tumbled to smooth, sharp edges. The cullet comes in assorted colors—greens, deep amber, and clear.

One of the most surprising materials for landscaping is a lumber look-alike made from recycled plastic. It can be used as timbers for framing beds or as step risers. Much of this plastic stock is high-density polyethylene recycled from bottles that once held milk and liquid detergents. Large timbers are formed by injection molding—shooting hot plastic into a mold. Smaller ones are formed

To create this rammed earth barbecue, a mix of reddish soil, cement, and sand was moistened and compacted in a sturdy wooden form.

by extruding hot plastic from a mold. Then the boards and timbers are textured and colored so they resemble wood, or pigmented to look painted.

Other manufacturers are making fireproof thermoplastic shingles from cast-off computers, or taking landfill-bound wood along with waste plastic to produce a weatherproof composite wood called Trex. Though not meant for structural purposes, Trex can be used for decking, railings, and fencing. It can be painted or stained, and has the additional advantage for families with young children of being splinter-free.

You can also take common materials and give them new life in the garden: salvaged and remilled lumber for overheads, broken concrete for retaining walls, patio furniture made of scrap metal or wood taken from old barns, or a born-again wine barrel that's used as spill fountain or to catch rainwater from a downspout. Other items, such as a decorative plant trellis made of reinforcing bar, can demonstrate artistic ways to use existing materials.

You can find out more about recycled materials available in your area at lumber and building supply stores, or by calling your local Recycling Commission.

This sparkling walkway is formed by diamonds and triangles of glass pavers filled with ground-glass cullet.

Plastic timber edges a raised bed (left). The deck at right is made of composite wood that can be cut, drilled, sanded, and painted.

Broken concrete

Creating an elegant and enduring walkway or retaining wall out of concrete rubble is a satisfying recycling project that turns would-be trash into landscape art. Though large chunks of broken concrete can be set in mortar just like irregular flagstone or cut wall stone, they can also be set in sand. Another technique is to enclose raised beds or terrace an embankment by laying the material like a dry-stone (mortarless) wall (see page 396).

The most difficult part of the process may be scavenging the concrete pieces. If you're taking out a sidewalk, you'll have a supply at hand. Otherwise, keep an eye on nearby remodeling projects or check with demolition companies and masonry contractors.

Sidewalk concrete is the best for both walls and paving because it's strong, it has a consistent thickness of about 4 inches, and it's probably free of the reinforcing rods and mesh that are present in newer driveways and patio slabs.

Like stones, the concrete pieces may have to be shaped. For small adjustments, use a mason's hammer to chip away edges. For larger cuts, try a sledge and a brick set or cold chisel (see page 387). Whenever you're trimming concrete, wear long sleeves and pants and protect your eyes with safety glasses. Wear gloves when you handle the jagged chunks.

If space permits, spread out the concrete pieces before you begin construction. You'll avoid the difficulty of rummaging through piles of heavy chunks for the puzzle piece you need. For stability, choose concrete pieces that are approximately 12 inches wide. And check your local codes for height limitations and other restrictions before you begin building.

To build a simple wall, first roughly level and tamp soil about ¼ inch lower than the bottom of the first concrete course, then shovel in a ¼-inch layer of pea gravel. Set the first course so that front edges line up (a staked length of PVC pipe can serve as a guide for an even curve). Level the top of the pieces, then fill in any gaps with gravel. Offset pieces in successive courses, using chunks of equal thickness. Slope the wall inward an inch for every foot of height.

Concrete pieces also make great paving. To create a casual, cottage-garden look, lay irregularly shaped concrete chunks in a sand bed, with the spaces between them holding ground-cover plantings. Or set them in mortar like flagstone, filling the joints with a grout that is colored a contrasting hue.

A. Broken-concrete risers provide solid footing for these steps that meander up a sloping path. Gravel, loose stones, and the occasional tuft of greenery add to the casual look.

B. Concrete pieces stained with iron sulfate create a handsome foil for chartreuse, gold, and variegated foliage on a "rust patio." (Iron sulfate will stain anything it touches, and can harm plants, so it must be used according to label directions.)

LAYING BRICKS IN SAND

With careful preparation and installation, a brick-in-sand path or patio will prove to be as durable as bricks set in mortar. In addition, if you decide to change the surface later, you need chip out only one brick to remove the rest in perfect condition.

Typically, a bed of 1½- to 2-inch-thick sand or rock fines (a mix of grain sizes) is prepared and the bricks are laid with closed joints. If drainage is poor in your garden, you may also need to add a 4-inch gravel base (in areas where the ground freezes, 6 to 8 inches is advisable). An optional layer of landscape fabric will suppress the growth of weeds.

To hold both the bricks and sand firmly in place, build permanent edgings around the perimeter (see page 391). Install the edgings first; they serve as good leveling guides for preparing and laying the bricks. If you have a lot of cutting to do, or shaping of complex angles (along curved edgings, for example), rent a brick saw from a masonry supplier or tool rental outlet.

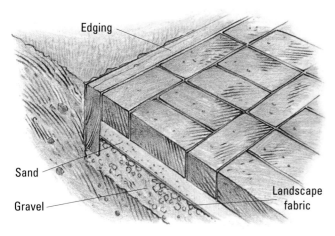

1. This typical brick-in-sand patio includes a gravel bed, a layer of landscape fabric, packed sand, and rigid edgings, which hold the bricks in place. Install edgings first.

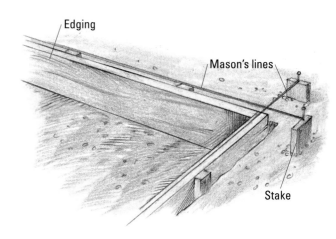

2. String mason's lines from stakes to serve as guides, first to mark edgings at the desired level and slope. Later, edgings can serve as a reference for leveling sand and bricks.

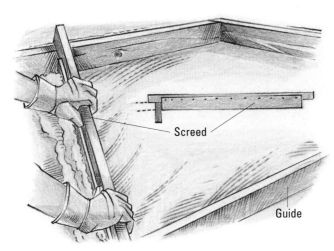

3. Lay down a 1½- to 2-inch-thick layer of dampened sand and level it with a bladed screed, as shown. If necessary, use a temporary guide on which to rest one end of the screed.

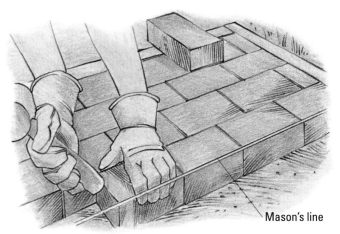

4. Another mason's line will help align courses. Begin at one corner; lay bricks tightly against one another, tapping each into place with a hand sledge or mallet. Check level frequently.

Concrete pavers can also be laid in sand much like bricks. With interlocking types, alignment is nearly automatic. After laying these units, it's best to make several passes with a power-plate vibrator to settle them. You can probably rent a vibrator locally; if not, you can use a heavy drum roller instead. Then spread damp, fine sand over the surface; when it dries, sweep it into the paver joints. Additional passes with either vibrator or roller will help lock the pavers together.

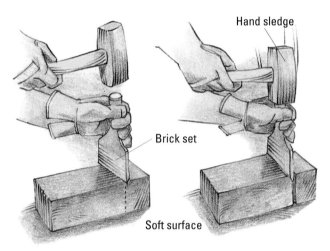

5. To cut bricks, score a line on all four sides (left); make the cut with one sharp blow (right). To cut angles, "nibble" at the waste area in several passes, a little at a time.

6. Throw fine sand over finished pavement, let dry for a few hours, and then sweep it with a stiff broom into joints. Spray lightly with water, so that the sand settles completely.

Brick Patterns

When choosing a brick pattern (also known as a bond), consider the degree of difficulty involved in laying it. Some bonds require not only accuracy but also a lot of brick cutting. The patterns shown below are some of the most popular; the jack-on-jack and running bonds are the simplest to lay.

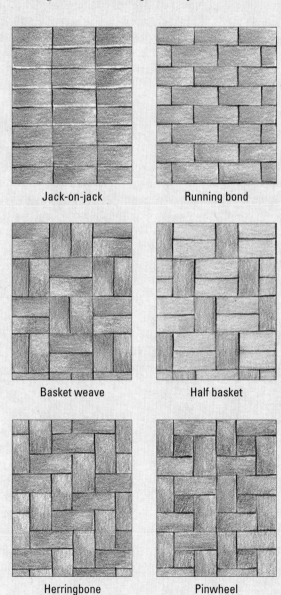

Jack-on-jack

Running bond

Basket weave

Half basket

Herringbone

Pinwheel

LAYING MASONRY IN MORTAR

The instructions below are for laying a flagstone path, but they are applicable to any masonry unit—ceramic tile, brick, or broken concrete—that you wish to set in mortar. You must allow a minimum slope for drainage off a path: 1 inch per 10 feet of run or ¼ inch per foot from side to side.

For the most permanent masonry surface, set stones, bricks, or tiles in a mortar bed over concrete that is at least 3 inches thick. If it is an existing slab, it must be clean and in good condition. Ask a concrete dealer whether you need to use a bonding agent for mortar on an existing or new concrete surface.

Mixing mortar

Mortar recipes vary according to their intended use, but the ingredients are usually the same: cement, sand, possibly lime (or fireclay), and water. Either make your own or buy more expensive ready-to-mix mortar. To build a wall, you will need a mix consisting of 1 part portland cement, ½ part hydrated lime or fireclay, and 6 parts sand. This mixture is much like Type N, commonly sold for general use. In contrast, a typical mortar for paving and most other below-grade installations contains only 1 part portland cement and 3 parts sand.

Small amounts of mortar can easily be mixed by hand, but mortar can be caustic, so be sure to wear gloves when you work

with it. Carefully measure the sand, cement, and lime into a wheelbarrow or similar container. Use a hoe to thoroughly mix the dry ingredients and form them into a pile. Make a depression in the center of the dry mix and pour some water into it. Mix, then repeat the process. When ready for use, mortar should have a smooth, uniform, granular consistency; it should also spread well and adhere to vertical surfaces (important when building a wall) but not "smear" the face of your work, which can happen when the mortar is too watery. Add water gradually until these conditions are met. Make only enough mortar to last a few hours; any more is likely to be wasted.

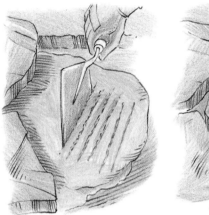

1. Dry-fit all stones, trimming if necessary. Then prepare a mortar mix just stiff enough to support the stones. Spread the mortar at least 1 inch deep, covering enough space to lay one or two stones at a time. Furrow the mortar with a trowel (left). Set each stone in place, bedding it with a rubber mallet (right), and checking for level. If a stone isn't level, lift it up and scoop out or add mortar as needed. Clean stones with a wet cloth as you work.

Mortar bag

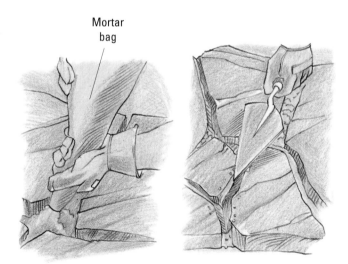

2. Let the mortar set for 24 hours, then grout joints with the same mortar mix (plus an optional ½ to 1 part fireclay for workability, but no lime). If stone is a nonstaining type, work grout across stones and into joints with a wet sponge. Otherwise, squeeze grout into joints, then smooth with a mason's trowel.

Trimming stone

Because most flagstones are irregular, you'll probably need to trim some pieces before setting them. You can keep this chore to a minimum, however, by carefully dry-fitting a design.

Wear gloves and safety glasses for even small trimming jobs. Chip off pieces with a mason's hammer or brick set and hand sledge. To make a major cut, use the adjacent stone as a guide and proceed with a brick set and sledge, as shown below. It is often difficult to keep a stone from splitting or shattering beyond the cut line, so have some extra stone on hand.

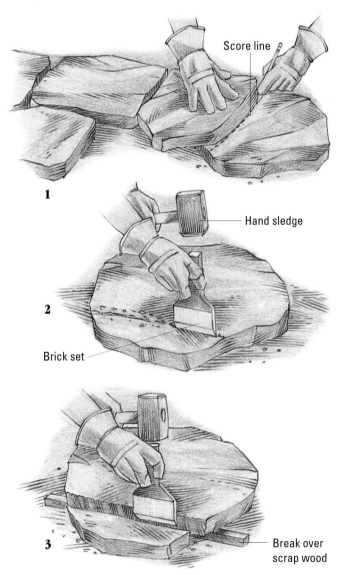

Score line

1

Hand sledge

2

Brick set

Break over
scrap wood

3

To cut flagstone, lay one block over its neighbor and trace its outline **(1)**. Then score a groove in the stone to be cut **(2)**. Finally, prop up the stone and split it with a sharp blow **(3)**.

Mosaics in Mortar

Large flagstones and tiles aren't the only masonry units that can be laid in mortar. You can set river rock, fieldstone, and pebbles in a mortar bed, or mix them with larger stones for a casual look (above).

Small pebbles or pieces of broken tile can be arranged mosaic-style in geometric or fanciful patterns; the bench below was fashioned from a mixture of beads, marbles, and broken tile. Lay out the complete design first before mixing any mortar.

To set mosaics in mortar, spread a 1:3 cement-sand mortar mixture over a concrete slab to a depth of ½ inch. The pieces must be placed in the mortar bed within 2 hours, so spread only as much as you can fill within that time; cut away any dry edges of mortar before spreading the next section. Keep the stones or tile in a pail of clean water and set them in the mortar while they're still wet, pushing them deep enough so the mortar gets a good hold on their edges—generally, just past the middle—then press down on them  *with a board to keep them level. Let the mortar set for 2 to 3 hours, then spread another thin layer over the surface and into the voids. Wash off any excess mortar before it sets.*

INSTALLING A GRAVEL PATH

Gravel—either smooth river rock or the more stable crushed rock—makes a low-cost, fast-draining path that can complement a wide variety of informal and formal planting schemes. The first step in laying a gravel path is to install wooden or masonry edgings to hold the loose material in place. Then put down landscape fabric to discourage weeds. Gravel surfaces tend to shift when walked on, but the movement will be minimized if you use a compacted base of crushed rock or sand.

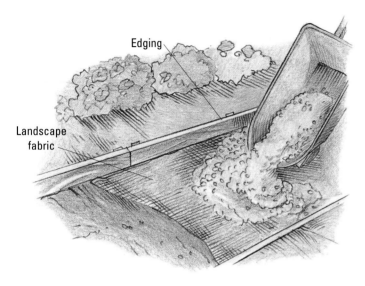

1. Install edgings first, then put down landscape fabric or plastic sheeting to protect against weeds. Pour decomposed granite or sand over the site, taking care not to dislodge the liner.

2. Rake the base material evenly over the path until it is a uniform 1-inch thickness. As you rake, wet the material with a fine spray.

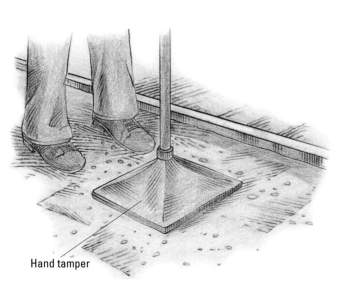

3. Using a drum roller or hand tamper, pass over the wet base several times, packing it down firmly. This firm base aids drainage and helps keep the topcoat from shifting underfoot.

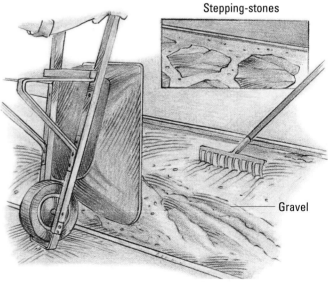

4. Spread the gravel at least 2 inches thick and rake it evenly over the base. If desired, place stepping-stones on the base so that their tops protrude slightly above the surrounding gravel.

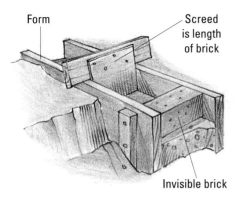

Form | Screed is length of brick

Invisible brick

Fieldstones

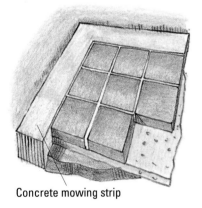

Concrete mowing strip

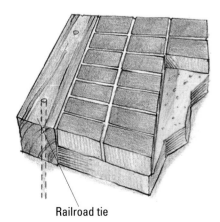

Railroad tie

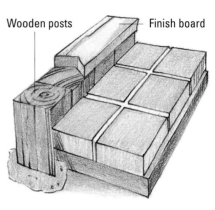

Wooden posts | Finish board

Plastic edging

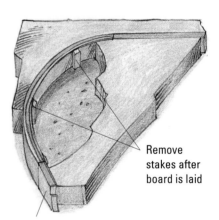

Remove stakes after board is laid

Benderboard

Bricks in soil

A look at edgings

Whether you lay it, hammer it, set it, or pour it in place, a patio or walk almost always requires an edging. In addition to visually outlining the surface, an edging confines the pavement within the desired area—which is especially important when you are pouring concrete, working with loose materials such as gravel, or setting bricks or pavers in sand.

Several tried-and-true edging options are illustrated here. The most popular are made of 2-by-4 or 2-by-6 lumber, but for emphasis, you can use 4-by-4 or 6-by-6 material. Heavy timbers and railroad ties make strong edgings and interior dividers, especially when drilled and threaded with steel pipe. If your design calls for gentle curves, try flexible redwood benderboard.

Another effective edging material is poured concrete. It is excellent for constructing invisible edgings underground, serving as a footing for mortared masonry units, or installing flush with a new walk. Bricks also establish a neat, precise edge. Set them directly in firm soil—horizontally, vertically, or even at an angle (but don't expect them to be very durable). And if you have random pieces of uncut stone, bear in mind that they make a perfect edging for a path in a rustic or naturalistic landscape.

Manufactured plastic or aluminum edgings are quite functional. These strips secure bricks or concrete pavers below finished paving height; they can be concealed with soil or sod. Flexible sections are convenient for tight curves.

For curbing paved areas, an edging is often installed after the base has been prepared and before the setting bed and paving are laid. String mason's lines around the perimeter, not only to mark the exact borders of the paving, but also to designate the outside top border of the edging. To achieve the correct edging height, you'll probably need to dig narrow trenches under the lines.

POURING A CONCRETE SLAB

Most of the work for a concrete path or patio lies in the preparation, which entails grading and formwork. Lay out stakes and mason's lines to mark the outline of the slab, allowing for at least a 1-inch drop for each 10 feet away from the house for drainage. If the exposed soil is soft, wet it and then tamp it firmly.

Wooden, steel, or copper dividers can be permanent partitions; they also serve as control joints to help prevent cracking and help break up the job into smaller, more manageable pours.

Be sure to add any required reinforcement to formwork before pouring. Check local building codes; usually, 6-inch-square welded wire mesh is the best choice for pavings.

See page 383 for instructions on mixing concrete. Pour large areas in sections and be sure to have helpers on hand to assist with hauling and spreading the wet concrete. You'll need gloves to protect your hands from the concrete's caustic ingredients; wear rubber boots if you have to walk on the wet mix.

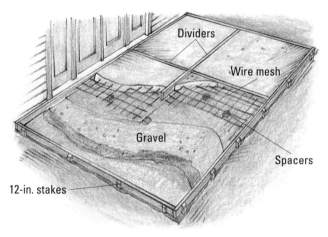

1. For rough grading, dig deep enough to allow for 4 inches of concrete plus 2 to 8 inches of gravel. Construct forms from 2 by 4s secured to 12-inch stakes, placing the form tops at finished slab height. Add welded wire mesh for reinforcement.

2. Begin pouring concrete at one end of form while a helper spreads it with a hoe. Work concrete up against form and tamp it into corners, but don't press it down too hard. A splashboard or ramp lets you pour the concrete where you want.

3. With a helper, move a 2-by-4 screed across the form to level concrete, using a rapid zigzag, sawing motion. A third person can shovel concrete into any hollows.

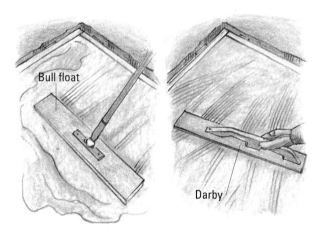

4. Initial floating smooths down high spots and fills small hollows left after screeding. As shown, use a darby for small jobs and a bull float with an extension handle for larger slabs.

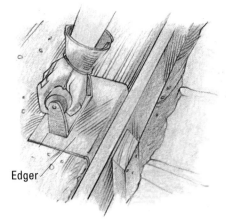

Edger

Guideboard

Jointer

5. Run the edge of a trowel between concrete and form. Then run an edger back and forth to create a smooth, curved edge (top). Make control joints every 10 feet with a jointer (bottom).

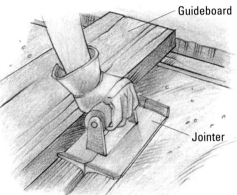

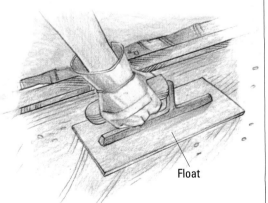

Float

6. Before the surface stiffens, give it a final floating with a wooden float. For a smoother surface, follow with a steel trowel. For a nonskid surface, drag a broom lightly across the concrete, without overlapping.

Pouring a Footing

You must provide a garden wall with a solid base, or footing. Very low walls (no more than 12 inches) and dry-stone walls (see page 396) may only require a leveled trench or a rubble base; but other walls require a footing fashioned from concrete that is twice as wide and at least as deep as the wall's thickness. In cold-weather areas, extend the footing below the frost line. Add 6 inches to the trench depth for a bottom layer of gravel.

If you need to pour a post footing for a deck, fence, or overhead, see page 372. Use bags of ready-mixed concrete for these small jobs.

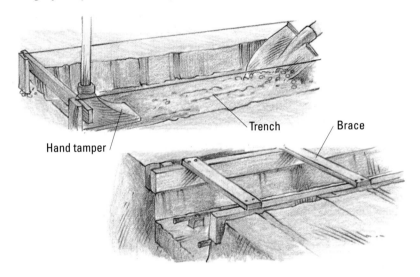

Hand tamper

Trench

Brace

1. Prepare a base for the footing by leveling and tamping the bottom of the trench and adding a 6-inch layer of gravel (top). Trenches in very firm soil may serve as forms; otherwise, build forms with 2-by lumber, stakes, and braces (bottom). Set any required reinforcing bars on a layer of broken bricks or other rubble.

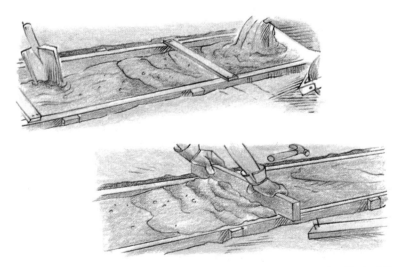

2. Pour concrete (top) and insert any vertical reinforcing bars required by building codes. Screed concrete level with tops of forms (bottom). Cover with a plastic sheet, leave to cure for 2 days, then remove the forms and begin to build the wall.

BUILDING A BLOCK WALL

For fast, inexpensive masonry wall construction, concrete blocks are the ideal material. Easy to work with, these rugged units make strong, durable walls.

First, lay out a dry course, or row, of blocks, spacing them ⅜ inch apart, and try to plan the wall so that no block cutting is necessary (you can also draw a plan on graph paper). If cutting is unavoidable, you can use the method described for bricks on page 387. Then you'll need to dig a trench for a strong, level concrete footing (for details, see page 393). Build the wall with a standard wall-building mortar (see page 388), but keep the mix slightly stiff. Otherwise, the heavy blocks may squeeze it out of the joints. A running bond pattern is the simplest to construct (see page 387).

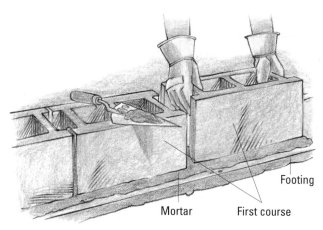

1. Spread a bed of mortar, 2 inches thick and wide enough for three blocks, over the footing. Then place the first-course corner block carefully and press it down to form an accurate ⅜-inch joint with the footing. Butter the ends of the next blocks with mortar, then set each one ⅜ inch from the previous block.

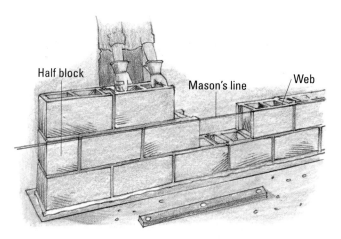

2. Check level often as you build up leads (at least three courses high) at both ends. String a mason's line between corner blocks as a guide to keep blocks straight. Start each even-numbered course with a half block. Butter both webs and edges, making full bed joints.

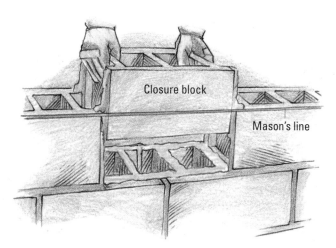

3. Fill in blocks between the leads, keeping ⅜-inch joint spacing. Be sure to check alignment, level, and plumb frequently. To fit the closure block, butter all edges of the opening and the ends of the block, then press it firmly into place.

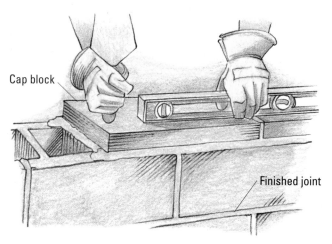

4. As you work, finish joints with a jointer or a wooden dowel. Solid cap blocks, available in various thicknesses, provide the simplest way to top off the last course. Simply mortar them in place on full bed joints, as shown. Tap into place and level.

Applying veneer to a block wall

Many people find concrete block boring or find that it doesn't blend well with their landscaping. If this is the case, consider dressing up a new block wall by applying a veneer to its surface.

Professional landscapers often take advantage of concrete blocks' low cost and speed of assembly to build a wall, then they cover it with plastering stucco for attractive texture and shape. Though plastering is an acquired technique, an accomplished do-it-yourselfer might reasonably tackle a small garden wall.

Plastering a block wall is a two-part operation. The first layer—or "scratch coat"—should be about 3/8 inch thick and must be applied after you have painted the wall with concrete bonding agent or covered it with wire lath. Then rough up the scratch coat with a commercial tool or a batch of wires held together (hence the name scratch) to help the finish coat's "bite." Apply the finish coat to a thickness of 1/4 inch; it may be precolored or painted

later. When the sheen has dulled, give texture to the plaster's surface by floating the finish coat with a steel trowel (with or without notches), a sponge, or a stiff brush.

For best results, buy plaster premixed. If the color is integral, consult with your supplier about coloring oxides, and plan to use a mix with white concrete and sand in it.

Another way to enhance a block wall is to apply a brick or stone veneer to it (see page 183). Although the resulting wall looks like solid masonry, it requires less labor and expense. You will need to place noncorrosive metal wall ties in the mortar joints in every other row of blocks, spacing them 2 to 3 feet apart. The ties must protrude beyond the blocks to help secure veneer units.

Lastly, mortar the veneer to the core. Bend the wall ties into the joints between the stones or bricks. As you build, completely fill the spaces between the wall and veneer with soupy mortar.

Plastering stucco creates a clean contemporary veneer atop a concrete block wall. Apply the plaster in two coats; the final coat may be precolored or painted when dry. Here, the neutral plaster finish matches the adjoining house wall.

Building a dry-stone wall

The key to building a stone wall is careful fitting; the finished structure should appear to be a unit rather than a pile of rocks. A dry-stone wall is constructed without mortar and depends upon the weight and friction of one stone on another for its stability. Not only is it simple to build, but also you can place soil and plants in the unmortared spaces as you lay the stones.

Use the largest stones for the foundation course and reserve the longer ones for "bond" stones—long stones that run the width of the wall. Set aside broad, flat stones to cap the top of the wall.

Most dry-stone walls slope inward on both surfaces; this tilting of the faces is called batter and helps secure the wall. To check your work, make a batter gauge by taping together a 2-by-4 board, a scrap block, and a carpenter's level, as shown below.

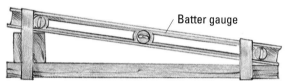

Batter gauge

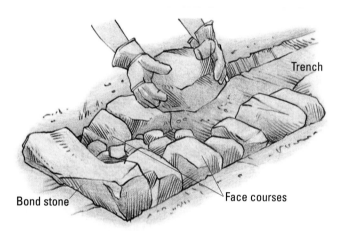

Trench

Bond stone

Face courses

1. Lay foundation stones in a trench about 6 inches deep. First, place a bond stone (one as deep as the wall) at one end; then position the two face courses at both edges of the trench. Choose whole, well-shaped stones for the face courses. Fill in the space between face courses with tightly packed rubble.

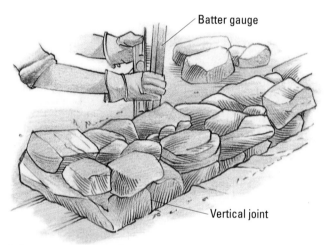

Batter gauge

Vertical joint

2. Lay stones atop the first course, staggering vertical joints. Select stones that fit together solidly and tilt the stones of each face inward toward one another. Use a batter gauge on faces and ends of the wall to check the tilt. Place bond stones every 5 to 10 square feet to tie the wall together.

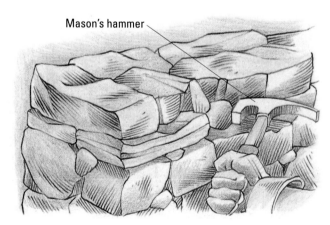

Mason's hammer

3. Continue to add courses, staggering vertical joints and maintaining the inward slope, so that gravity and the friction of the stones set one upon another will help hold the wall together. Gently tap small stones into any gaps with a mason's hammer.

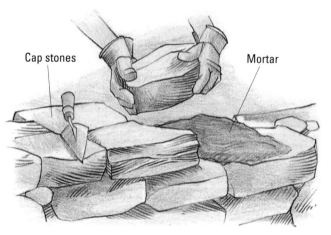

Cap stones

Mortar

4. Finish the top with as many flat, broad stones as possible. If you live in an area that experiences frost, mortar the cap as shown. Don't rake (indent) these joints; level them flush with a piece of scrap wood to prevent water from collecting.

Retaining walls

If your home sits on a sloping lot or a hillside, a retaining wall may be needed to hold back the earth and prevent erosion. Homeowners have a choice of three basic wall-building materials—wood, stone, or concrete—and now a number of new modular masonry systems have been developed with the owner-builder in mind (see below). These proprietary systems come with complete instructions for installation.

Simple wood or masonry retaining walls, less than 3 feet high and on a gentle slope with stable soil, can be built by a do-it-yourselfer, but it's a good idea to consult your local building department for even a low retaining wall. Most communities require a building permit for any retaining wall and may require a soil analysis in any area suspected of being unstable.

In general, it's best to site your retaining wall so it results in the least possible disruption of the natural slope, but even so, extensive cutting and filling may be needed. The hill can be held back with a single wall or a series of low retaining walls that form terraces. Though terracing is less risky, both methods disturb the hill and should be designed by an engineer. If space permits, the safest approach is not to disturb the slope at all, but to build the wall on the level ground near the foot of the slope and fill in behind it.

In any case, the retaining wall should rest on cut or undisturbed ground, never on fill. Planning for drainage is also essential. Usually, you'll need a gravel backfill to collect water that dams up behind the wall. Water in the gravel bed can be drained off through weep holes in the base of the wall or through a drain pipe that channels the water into a storm sewer or other disposal area.

Slope is cut away and excess earth is moved downhill. Retaining wall now holds back long, level terrace.

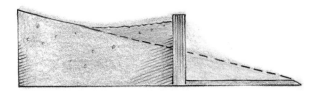

Earth is cut away and moved behind tall retaining wall. Result is level ground below, high, level slope behind.

Total wall height is divided between two terraces, resulting in a series of level beds.

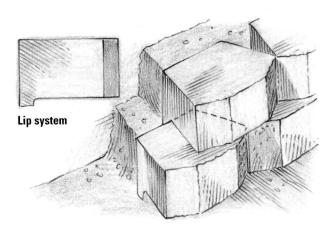

Lip system

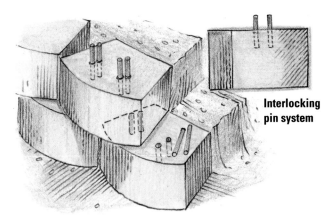

Interlocking pin system

For low retaining walls or small raised planters, modular masonry systems are available in various styles and weights. Most use cast "lips" (left) or interlocking pins to establish the setback and resist outward pushing forces. Fiberglass or steel pins drop through holes in upper blocks and stop in grooves on units below, joining each to two beneath (right).

STEP-BUILDING BASICS

Laying out low, single, back-garden steps does not involve as much time and effort as planning runs of well-designed formal steps; the latter require an understanding of proper proportions.

The flat part of a step is called the tread; the vertical element is the riser. Ideally, the depth of the tread plus twice the riser height should equal 25 to 27 inches. Based on an average length of stride, the ideal outdoor step should have a 6-inch-high riser and a 15-inch-deep tread, but riser and tread dimensions can vary. Risers should be no lower than 5 inches and no higher than 8 inches; tread depth should never be less than 11 inches. The overall riser-tread relationship should remain the same. All the risers and treads in any one flight of steps should be uniform in size.

To fit steps evenly, you must calculate the degree of slope. Using the drawing as a guide, first calculate the distance from A to B; this is the rise, or change in level, of the

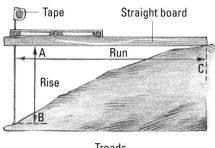

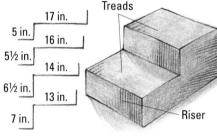

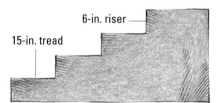

Ideal tread-riser relationship

slope. The horizontal distance from A to C is called the run.

To determine the number of steps you will need, divide the desired riser height into the total rise of the slope (in inches). If the answer ends in a fraction (and it probably will), drop the fraction and divide that number into the rise; this time, the resulting figure will give you the exact measurement for each of the risers. Then check the chart (left) to see if the corresponding minimum tread will fit the slope's total run.

Plan on a minimum width of 2 feet for utility steps and 4 feet for most others. If you want two people to be able to walk abreast, allow 5 feet.

Rarely do steps fit exactly into a slope. More than likely, you will have to cut and fill the slope to accommodate the steps. If your slope is too steep for even 8-inch risers, remember that steps need not run straight up and down. Curves and switchbacks make the distance longer but the climb gentler.

Timbers or ties

Both railroad ties and 6-by-6 pressure-treated timbers make simple but rugged steps. To begin, excavate the site and tamp the soil in the tread area firmly. Lay the ties or timbers on the soil, then drill a hole near both ends of each tie or timber. With a sledge, drive either ½-inch galvanized steel pipes or ¾-inch reinforcing bars through the holes into the ground.

Or, for extra support, pour small concrete footings and set anchor bolts in the slightly stiffened concrete. When the concrete has set (after about two days), secure the ties to the footings with the bolts.

Once the tie or timber risers are in place, fill the tread spaces behind them with concrete, brick-in-sand paving, gravel, grass, or another material.

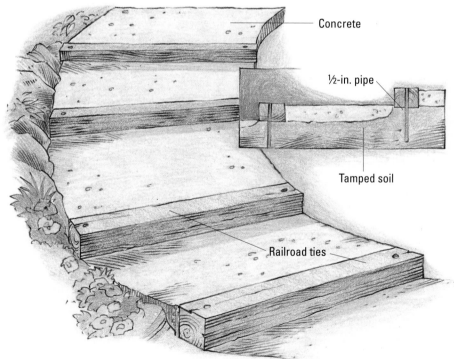

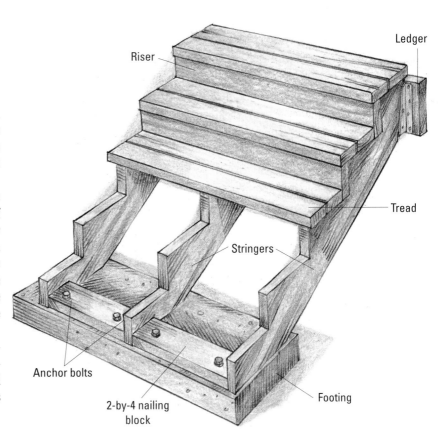

Riser

Ledger

Tread

Stringers

Anchor bolts

2-by-4 nailing
block

Footing

Wooden stairs

Formal wooden steps are best for a low-level deck or for easy access to a doorway. Make stringers from 2 by 10s or 2 by 12s. If the steps are more than 4 feet wide, a third stringer will be needed in the middle.

Use galvanized bolts or metal joist hangers to secure stringers to a deck beam or joist; if you're running stringers off stucco siding or another masonry surface, hang them on a ledger, as shown. Note that when bolts are used, the first tread is below the surface of the interior floor or deck; when joist hangers are the fasteners, however, the first tread must be level with the floor.

Attach the stringers at the bottom to wooden nailing blocks anchored in a concrete footing. Build risers and treads from 2-by material cut to width; treads should overlap the risers below and may hang over slightly.

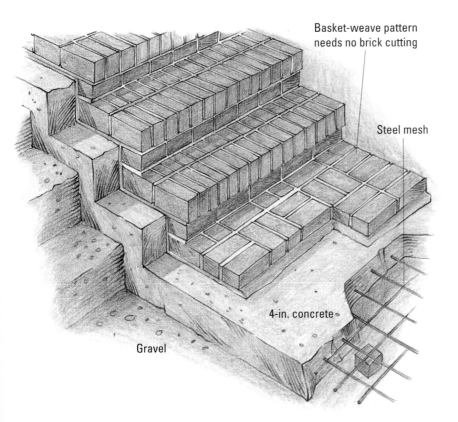

Basket-weave pattern
needs no brick cutting

Steel mesh

4-in. concrete

Gravel

Masonry steps

Steps can be built entirely of concrete or, for a finished look, the concrete can be used as a base for mortared masonry units.

First, form rough steps in the earth. Allow space for at least a 6-inch gravel setting bed and a 4-inch thickness of concrete on both treads and risers. (In cold climates you will need 6 to 8 inches of concrete, plus a footing that is sunk below the frost line.) Add the thickness of any masonry units to tread-and-riser dimensions. Tamp filled areas thoroughly.

With 2-inch-thick lumber, build forms like those shown on pages 392–393. Lay the gravel bed, keeping it 4 inches back from the front of the steps; you will pour the concrete thicker at that potentially weak point. Reinforce with 6-inch-square welded wire mesh.

Pour and screed the concrete as for a poured concrete footing. To make treads more weather safe, broom the wet concrete to roughen it's surface, then cure as for a concrete footing (see page 393).

INSTALLING A GARDEN POND

With either a flexible plastic or rubber pond liner and a bit of elbow grease, even a beginner can fashion an average-size garden pond in a single weekend, though plantings and borders will take somewhat longer to establish.

Even a pond with an unusual shape should not present a problem. A liner can take almost any shape, accommodating curves and undulations. It's also possible to weld two pieces of liner together with solvent cement, or have the supplier do it for you.

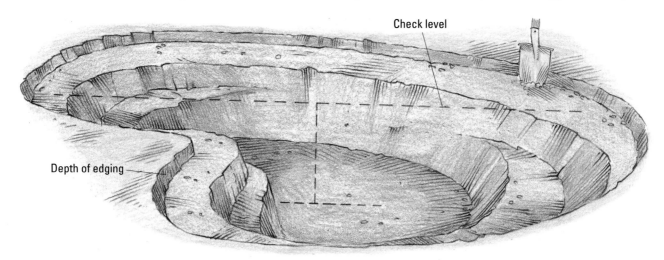

Check level

Depth of edging

1. Mark the pond's outline with a hose or a length of rope. Dig all around the outline with a sharp spade; remove any sod and keep it in a shady spot for later patching. Excavate the hole to the desired depth and width, plus 2 inches all around for a layer of sand. Dig down to the thickness of any edging material. Check level carefully, using a straight board to bridge the rim.

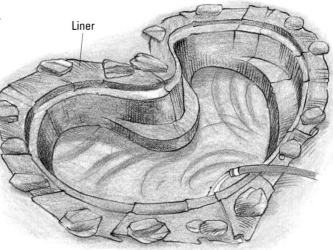

Liner

3. Open up the liner and let it soften in the sun. Then spread it over the hole, evening up the overlap all around. Place heavy stones or bricks around the perimeter to weigh it down, then slowly begin to fill the pond with water.

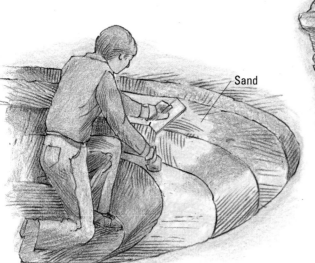

Sand

2. Next, remove all protruding roots and rocks and fill any holes with soil. Pack a 2-inch layer of clean, damp sand into the excavation. Smooth the sand with a board or a concrete float.

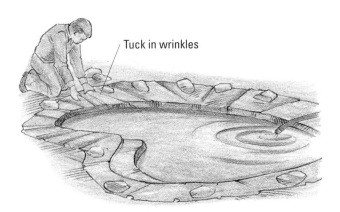

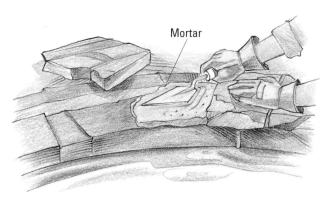

4. Continue filling, tucking in wrinkles all around; as required, fold pleats at hard corners (they won't be visible when the pool is filled). You can wade into the pool to tuck in the lining, but the water's weight will make it fit the contours of the hole.

5. When the pond is full, add overhanging edging. Lay flagstones or brick in a thin bed of mortar. Bring the liner up behind the edging, then trim the liner. Drain the pool and refill it with fresh water.

Fountains and Falls

Water in motion, whether gently spilling, gurgling, or energetically tumbling, is always enchanting. Both fountains and waterfalls help bring the sparkle and the musical sounds of falling water into the garden.

Surprisingly, fountains can be simple to create. A wooden planter box, a metal basin, or a large pot, for example, can easily be converted into a small fountain. Just coat the inside of a wooden container or an unglazed pot with asphalt emulsion or epoxy paint, or use a flexible liner. Then drop in a submersible pump with a riser pipe and add water (in shallow water, a few rocks can conceal the pump).

For larger holding pools, many designers prefer precast rigid fiberglass or reinforced concrete. A wall fountain's raised holding pool is often concrete or concrete block, covered with plaster or faced with brick, tile, or stone above the water line. A submersible pump and water pipes can be combined to add a fountain to an existing wall. An electrical switch, perhaps

located indoors, controls the pump-driven flow; a ball or 3-way valve allows alteration of the flow, depending on your taste. To automatically replace water lost through evaporation, hook up a float valve to the water supply line. A drain is also handy.

Waterfalls pose some unique design considerations. The major technical concern is waterproofing. Before plunging into construction, determine which pump, pipes, and other plumbing hardware you'll need to provide the desired flow. For a waterproof channel, use either a flexible liner, free-form concrete, a fiberglass shell or series of splash pans, or a combination of the above.

If you opt for a liner, position waterfall rocks carefully, making sure not to damage or displace the liner. Once the basic structure is complete, secure secondary stones and add loose rocks or pebbles to provide visual accents or to form a ripple pattern. Only creative experimentation will reveal the most pleasing sights and sounds.

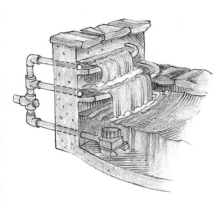

A formal wall fountain combines a raised holding pool, masonry wall, and decorative spill shelves. Water tumbles from pipe outlets to spill shelves to a holding pool; a submersible pump sends it back around again.

Waterfall design calls for a watertight channel, natural-looking stones, and adequate camouflage for plumbing parts. Flexible liner is the simplest channel option; stone placement conceals liner.

INSTALLING IRRIGATION SYSTEMS

The benefits of a permanent irrigation system are well known—water and time savings, healthier plants, and reduced maintenance. The information given on pages 328–329 can help you choose the best system for your garden. Shown here are installation procedures for the two main types of irrigation systems—sprinkler and drip.

Most systems can be attached to an existing water supply pipe (1-inch diameter or larger is best). Because drip systems require only low water volume and pressure, you may be able to connect a drip system to a convenient outdoor faucet; the manufacturer's literature will help you determine whether this is best for your situation. You will want to pick out some possible locations to place your valves. Consider how they might be concealed (they can be unsightly) and, if your system will be automated, where you'll put the timer and how far it is from an electrical connection.

No matter how you connect your system to the water supply, you will need proper filter, pressure regulator, and backflow devices. Filters ensure that emitters don't clog. Pressure regulators prevent too much water pressure from building up in the system and possibly forcing the emitter heads off the supply lines. Backflow devices, which are usually required by law, prevent irrigation water from backing into the home water supply.

Whether or not your irrigation system is automated, check it frequently for broken or clogged sprinklers or drip emitters.

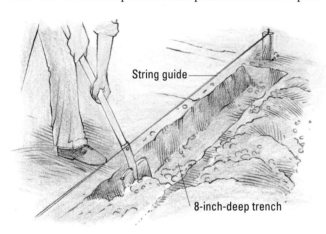

1. Sprinkler system must be laid underground. First, dig 8-inch-deep trenches for pipes. To keep trench lines straight, run string between two stakes.

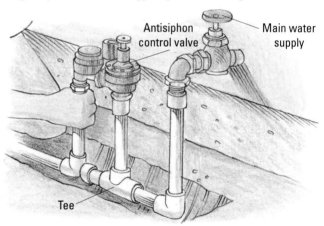

2. Connect pipes to the water supply pipe, then attach control valve (with built-in antisiphon valve) at least 6 inches above ground. Use thick-walled, ¾-inch PVC pipe.

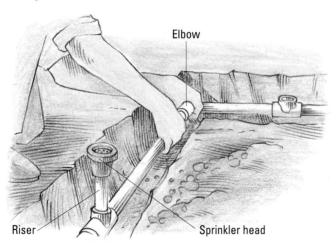

3. Assemble pipes from the control valve outward, fitting risers and sprinkler heads to elbows, tees, and side outlets. Joints may screw together or require PVC solvent cement.

4. Flush out pipes with heads removed. Then fill in trenches, mounding loose soil along center of trench. Tamp the soil firmly with a hand tamper. Avoid striking the sprinkler heads.

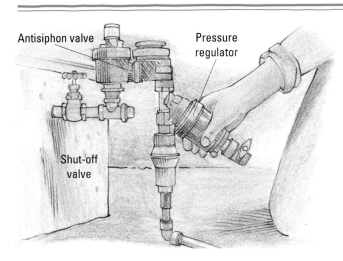

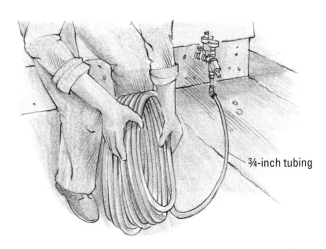

1. Drip irrigation system assembly starts with connecting the control valve, filter, and pressure regulator to the water supply line (for hose-end system, use a hose bib).

2. Connect ¾-inch flexible polyvinyl tubing and lay out main lines on the surface of the soil or in shallow trenches. For a more sturdy system, use buried PVC pipe for main lines.

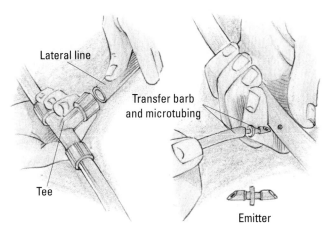

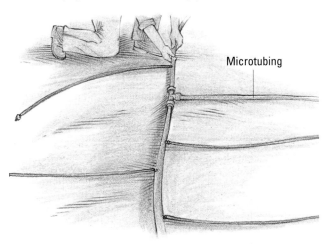

3. Lay out and attach lateral lines using tee connectors (left). Many kinds hold tubing without cement. Attach end caps, then insert emitters or transfer barbs for microtubing (right).

4. Flush system to ensure that all emitters work properly. Cover the lines with a thin layer of mulch, if desired, but leave the emitters and microtubing above ground.

Switching to Drip

If you have an existing sprinkler system with an underground distribution line of PVC pipe, you can simplify the installation of a drip system by retrofitting it. But if you have a galvanized pipe system retrofitting it is less practical than replacing it because over time pieces of flaking metal can clog the drip emitters.

Commercial products make switching to drip easy. At right are two retrofit kits for sprinkler systems. The system you choose depends on the layout of your garden and the number of sprinklers you plan to change.

Multioutlet bubbler heads

Capped riser

Generally, it's best to change the entire line on one valve to drip than to mix sprinklers and drip along it (if you have lawns and borders on the same line, for example). Because of different output from sprinklers and drip fittings, trying to adjust watering times on a mixed system is difficult. But in some cases you will have no choice.

The system shown at top delivers water through ¼-inch tubing and multioutlet bubbler heads. The simple retrofit shown at bottom uses only one riser; other risers are capped, as at right.

BUILDING A RAISED BED

Raising your garden above the ground can solve some of the most frustrating problems gardeners face. An easy-to-build bed makes it possible for plants to thrive where soil is poor, wildlife is hungry, or the growing season is short. And if you need easy access to your plants—due to a disability or simply to eliminate back-bending labor—you can sit on the edge of the bed and garden in comfort.

Fill the bed with the best soil you can. Good soil means that plants can be placed closer together, making a small area more productive. Line the bottom of the bed with wire screening to keep out pests, or fit it with a PVC framework for bird netting.

A raised bed can be any size, but if it is more than 4 feet wide it will be difficult to reach the middle from either side. If the sides will double as benches, build the frame 18 to 24 inches high.

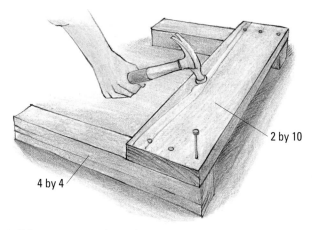

1. Orient a rectangular bed from north to south. For a 4-by-10-foot bed, first nail short sides of 2 by 10s to 3-foot-high 4-by-4 corner posts. Use rot-resistant lumber and galvanized nails.

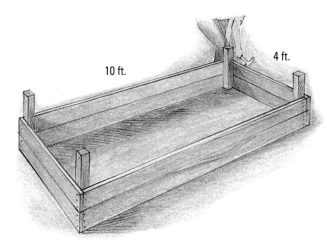

2. Flip over structure and nail 10-foot lengths to corner posts. For added strength, install wooden bracing or metal L-straps. Work on level ground so that bed is as square as possible.

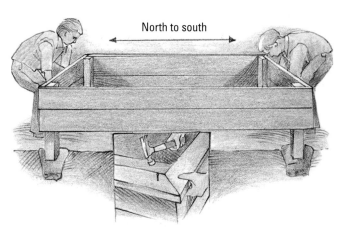

3. Set bed right side up and insert corner posts into predug foot-deep holes. Level if necessary. Cap the top with surfaced redwood 2 by 6s, with ends cut at a 45-degree angle (inset).

4. Place 3 to 4 inches of new soil in the bottom of the bed and mix it into the ground to aid drainage. This 20-inch-deep bed holds about 2½ cubic yards of soil.

RAISED-BED STYLES

Brick

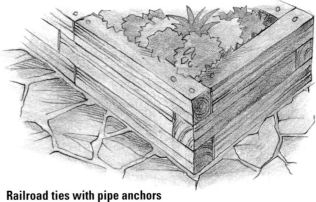

Railroad ties with pipe anchors

Staked logs

Vertical timbers

Easy-access Gardening

It isn't easy to garden from a wheelchair, but it's not impossible. It takes thoughtful planning to give maximum access to planting areas. Here are some features that make a garden accessible.

Raised beds can accommodate both flowers and edible plants. To put gardening chores within easy reach of a wheelchair, the beds should be about 16 inches tall and no more than 4 feet wide; they can be long or U-shaped, with the opening in the U just wide enough for a chair.

Paved paths, about 4 feet wide, can allow a chair to turn, maneuver, and glide easily. Ideally, the paths should be extensions of a paved patio at the rear of the house and a porch or terrace at the front. If the house is at a higher level than the garden, a wide, gently sloping ramp can angle off a back deck.

Hinged trellises can be lowered to tend or gather crops such as peas and tomatoes.

An automatic irrigation system eliminates the need for routine watering. See pages 328–329 for options.

Railings for walks and ramps should be sunk in concrete footings for extra support.

Special tools are available with extra-long handles to reach into beds from a chair.

Mulch—with fabric or loose materials—reduces the need for frequent weeding, which can be a chore.

Plant for low maintenance. Choose trees that don't shed a lot of litter, opt for a reduced lawn—or no lawn at all—and choose plants that don't require frequent maintenance or pest and disease control.

WORKING SAFELY

Although the garden is not generally a hazardous place, any time you pick up a tool, climb a ladder, or start moving heavy materials, you can injure yourself—or someone else. If you are planning to carry out any of the landscape construction shown in the previous pages, follow the guidelines given here.

Safety accessories and clothing

Many masonry projects call for safety precautions. To protect yourself from flying particles of dust or rock when cutting stone or brick, wear safety goggles or a full face mask. Look for comfortably fitting, fog-free types made of scratch-resistant, shatterproof plastic. Dry portland cement is irritating to the eyes, nose, and mouth, so wear a dust mask

when mixing concrete. Wet concrete and mortar are caustic to the skin, so wear heavy rubber gloves and tuck your sleeves into them. Also wear rubber boots if you must walk in the concrete to finish it off. Wash your skin thoroughly with water if wet mortar or concrete contacts it.

When using lumber products, protect your hands from wood splinters with all-leather or leather-reinforced cotton work gloves. If you are sanding wood, wear a disposable painter's mask. For work with solvents, finishes, or adhesives, wear disposable rubber or plastic gloves.

Working safely with power tools

Portable power tools can cause injuries in an instant. Handle these tools with respect, and follow some basic safety precautions.

Read the owner's manual before using any tool.

When you operate a power tool, try to do so without interruption or distraction. If possible, block off the work area to keep all visitors away—especially children and pets.

Never wear loose-fitting clothing or jewelry that could catch in a tool's mechanism. If you have long hair, tie it back.

Never use a power tool if you are tired or under the influence of alcohol or drugs.

Before you plug in a tool, check that safety devices such as guards are in good working order. Also tighten any clamping mechanisms on the tool, ensure that the blade or bit is securely installed, and set up any necessary supports or clamps for securing the work.

Ensure that your hands and body—and power cord—are well away from a tool's blade or bit.

Never stand on a wet surface when using a power tool that is plugged into an electrical outlet unless the outlet is GFCI protected (see opposite page).

Never cut wet wood, and if you can't avoid cutting warped boards or must cut through a knot, be on your guard for kickback—when the tool lurches back out of the wood.

Make sure there are no fasteners in any lumber that you are sawing or drilling.

If a blade or bit jams in a piece of wood, turn off and unplug the tool before trying to extricate it. To keep your balance, don't reach too far with the tool; move closer to it and keep a stable footing.

Always allow the bit or blade to stop on its own before setting down the tool.

Unplug a tool before servicing or adjusting it, and after you have finished using it.

Follow the manufacturer's specifications to lubricate and clean power tools, and make sure all blades and bits are sharp and undamaged.

If you are using a rented concrete mixer, read the instructions carefully. Never reach into the rotating drum with your hands or tools. Keep well away from the moving parts, and do not look into the mixer while it is running.

Working safely with electricity

Tools powered by electricity are essential for most outdoor construction projects. But unless a drill, circular saw, or other power tool is double-insulated, it must be properly grounded or it can give a serious shock. Double-insulated tools should be clearly marked (the plug will have only two prongs). When you are working in a damp area or outdoors, a ground fault circuit interrupter (GFCI) is essential.

When working outside, you will probably need to use an extension cord for your tools. Use the shortest extension cord possible (long cords can overheat, causing a fire hazard), and make sure it's rated for outdoor use. The longer the cord, the less amperage it will deliver, which means less power for the tool's motor. Look for the nameplate on the tool that contains its amperage requirement. Avoid crimping the cord; don't run it through a door that will be continually opened and closed.

A main disconnect allows you to shut down your entire electrical system whenever you need to change a fuse or in case of an emergency. If you need to work on an outdoor switch, circuit, or outlet, you'll need to shut off power to a branch circuit. *Never* work on a live electrical circuit. Two typical disconnects are shown at right. Familiarize yourself with them before you start to work.

TWO DISCONNECTS

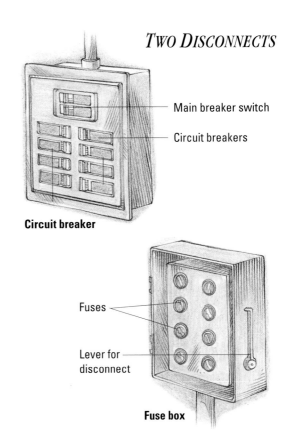

Main breaker switch

Circuit breakers

Circuit breaker

Fuses

Lever for disconnect

Fuse box

To lift heavy objects, spread your feet a comfortable width apart. Then bend your knees and, keeping your back straight, pick up the object—never bend at the waist or you could injure your back. If an object is very heavy, get help.

When working on a ladder, wear sturdy shoes with good traction. Overlap the sections of an extension ladder by three or four rungs and tie the top of the ladder to a stable object. Haul up your equipment using a rope and bucket, as shown.

SUBJECT INDEX

Italic page numbers refer to pages on which there are relevant photographs. **Boldface** page numbers indicate charts, lists, or plans.

PLANT INDEX

Italic page numbers refer to pages on which there are relevant
photographs or plant displays.

ACKNOWLEDGMENTS

Our thanks to the following for allowing us to show their merchandise in this book:

Gardeners Eden; Hadco®Outdoor Lighting; Nightscaping by Loran; Smith & Hawken.

Our thanks also to the following for their contributions to the book:

American Lung Association of California; Arterra, Inc.; Tom Bressan (The Urban Farmer Store); Cooperative Extension, Maricopa County; Brent Crane; Owen Dell (County Landscape and Supply); Fresno Rotary Club's Sneezeless Garden; Friends of the Urban Forest; Joyce Gagnon (King County Commission for Marketing Recyclable Materials); Bob Galbreath (Garden Technology); Dr. Ali Haravandi (UC Cooperative Extension, Alameda County); Alice and Chris Hoover; Iseli Nursery; Ted Kipping; Land & Place; Los Angeles State and County Arboretum; Richard Molinar (UC Cooperative Extension, Fresno County); MsK Rare Plant Nursery; John Munn (California Department of Forestry and Fire Protection); National Interagency Fire Center; Native Seeds/SEARCH; Pacific Gas and Electric; Plant Amnesty; Robert Raabe (Department of Plant Biology, UC Berkeley); Helie Robertson; Santa Barbara Fire Department; Richard Schell (California Department of Forestry and Fire Protection); Southern California Edison; Southland Sod; Sundance Spas; Britta and Lennart Swartz; David Sweet; George Taylor (Oregon State University); Sydney Thornton (State of California Air Resources Board); Tucson Botanical Gardens; Turfgrass Producers International; USDA Natural Resources Conservation Service; Van Dusen Gardens; West Coast Turf; Ethan Wilde; Joyce Yokomizo and Ron Russo (Yokomizo Associates).

PHOTOGRAPHY CREDITS

For pages with 4 or fewer photographs, each image has been identified by its position on the page: Left (L), center (C), or right (R); top (T), middle (M), or bottom (B). On other pages, photographs are identified by their position in the grid (shown right). Photographs on the back cover are designated as "back".

L	LC	RC	R
1	1	1	1
2			
3			
4			

Air Resources Board: 315 B. **Larry Albee, Longwood Gardens:** 42 T. **Teena Albert:** 164; 165 B. **Scott Anger:** 296. **AP Wide World Photos:** 298 T. **Scott Atkinson:** 169; 368 R. **David Belda:** 249 R2; 257 C2; 279 L1, LC; 289 RM. **Derek Berwin, The Image Bank:** 102 T. **Jacek Bogucki:** 145 M. **T. Boyden:** 321 T. **Ernest Braun, California Redwood Association:** 142 T; 143 B; 145 T. **Marion Brenner:** 14 B; 15 T; 33 B; 34 T, B; 35 LT, LB; 157 T; 220 LB; 221 LB; 222 B, 224 T; 245 L; 269 RT; 337 RT; 389 B. **Kathleen Brenzel:** 210; 249 L3, C1; 310 LT. **Barbara Butler:** 165 T. **Ed Carey:** 256 LB; 257 R3. **Marissa Carlisle:** 136; 384 T. **Luis Castaneda, The Image Bank:** 292. **David Cavagnaro:** 230 M. **Jared Chandler:** 177. **Jennifer Chandler:** 157 B. **Chelsea ExCentrics:** 263 LB. **Glenn Christiansen:** 284 LT, RT; 285 RT, RB. **Peter Christiansen:** back RC; 84; 85 M; 86; 87; 104 T; 105; 106; 107; 174; 213 B; 267 R2; 268 RB; 376 B; 381 RB. **Ed Cooper:** 50; 51; 52 T. **Glen Cormier:** 150; 151 RB. **Crandall & Crandall:** 318 L; 395. **Grey Crawford:** 156. **Claire Curran:** 32 B; 182 T; 209 RC; 220 CB; 221 CB, RB; 241 B; 245 LC, RC; 302 LB, RB; 319 L, RC; 320 R3; 337 LC, RC. **Dalton Pavilion, Inc.:** 155 T. **Hank deLespinasse, The Image Bank:** 326 T. **William Dewey:** 220 M; 249 C3. **Laura Dickson:** 2; 120 T, B; 121 T. **Ken Druse:** 14 T; 149 R2; 198 T. **Macduff Everton:** 94. **Derek Fell:** 175 B; 186 T; 202; 240 T. **Cheryl Fenton, GE:** 265 L1, C1, R1. **Cheryl Fenton:** 264 RC1. **Gateways:** 269 RM. **Hadco Lighting:** 276 L1, L2, LC2, RC2, R2; 277 L3, L4, LC4. **Jeff Haggin:** 250 R2. **Al Hamdan, The Image Bank:** 322 T. **David Hamilton, The Image Bank:** 4. **Philip Harvey:** 10; 22; 28; 42; 43; 44; 45; 68 LT; 206 M, B; 226; 227 L2, L4; 241 RT; 248 B; 249 C2; 250 L2; 254 B; 255 RB; 256 RB; 257 R1; 263 LM; 264 RC2; 266 T; 267 R1; 268 LB; 269 RB; 272 B; 273 B; 279 R1, R3; 282 B; 288 L; 316 T; 364; 366; 367; 368; 373; 376 T; 380; 381 LT; 382 L4; 383 LB; 389 T; 406. **Archie Held:** 291 LB. **Erik Holdeman:** 46; 47. **Saxon Holt:** back RT; 25 LT, LM; 30 L; 31 LM; 32 T; 35 RT; 78; 79; 80; 81; 139 B; 140 T, B; 142 B; 146 LB, RB; 149 L4, C4; 152; 155 T; 159 T, M; 161 T, B; 162 B; 167 B; 178 LT; 182 B; 184; 185; 192 T; 197 T; 198 M; 200; 201 L, RB; 205 M; 208 R; 212; 216 T, B; 218 T; 220 T; 224 M, B; 227 R2; 233 RC; 236 T; 243 L, RC; 246; 259 LT, RT; 262 LT; 275 LB; 281 T, B; 288 R; 290 RT; 306 T, LB; 308 L; 311 T. **James Housel:** 68 CB; 69. **Joseph Huettl:** 168 R. **Jardin Botanique du Montreal:** 314 M, B. **Jon Jensen:** 286 R2. **Deborah Jones:** 272 M; 289 LB. **Ted Kipping:** 190 T. **Kirsten Leitner, Friends of the Urban Forest photo file:** 191 T, B. **David Duncan Livingston:** 25 RB; 274. **Los Angeles Building Department:** 294 LT. **Ron Lutsko:** 27 B. **Renee Lynn:** 278 T; 385 T. **Allan Mandell:** back RB; 58 B; 62; 63; 236 LB, CB, RB; 237 B; 385 B. **Charles Mann:** 15 M; 24 T; 25 LB; 26 T; 27 T; 31 RT, LT, RB; 108; 110 B; 111; 112; 113; 114; 115; 116 T, RB; 117; 147; 149 R1; 153 T, B; 171 RT; 176 B; 179; 181 LB, RT; 201 RT; 203; 205 T; 208 L; 216 M; 218 M, B; 220 RB; 222 T; 227 R4; 230 T; 233 R; 234 M; 238 T, M, B; 240 LB; 245 R; 248 T; 263 RB; 267 L3; 268 LT; 290 RB; 318 R; 319 LC; 320 RC3. **Niki Mareschal, The Image Bank:** 314 T. **David McDonald:** back LC; 26 B; 35 RB; 52 B; 159 B; 192 B; 201 CB; 204; 209 L; 214 T, B; 232; 233 L, LC; 234 B; 240 RB; 337 LB. **Jack McDowell:** 382 L1, L2, L3, R1, R2, R3. **Charles McGrath:** 158; 294 RT. **Andrew McKinney:** 170. **Keeyla Meadows:** 148 LB; 163 B; 261 T, B; 270 L, R; 271 B. **Mellor/Crandall:** 336 L. **Terrance Moore:** 151 RT. **Nightscaping:** 275 LT; 277 L1, LC1. **Don Normark:** 25 RM; 64 LM; 142 M; 149 R3; 160; 167 LB; 171 RB; 180 B; 263 RM; 289 RT; 322 LB. **Normark/Westock:** 178 RT. **Victoria Pearson:** 286 R3. **Kathlene Persoff:** 1. **Karl Petzke:** 264 L1, R3; 279 RC2. **Chuck Place:** 298 B. **Norman A. Plate:** 15 B; 25 RT; 88 C; 89; 175 T; 194; 197 B; 209 R; 211 T, B; 250 L1, R1; 251 C1, C2, R3; 255 LT, RT; 256 T; 257 L1, L3; 258 T, B; 259 B; 260 LT, LB, RB; 265 C2, C3, C4; 266 B, 267 C2; 269 LB; 273 M; 280 LT; 287 C2; 291 RT; 307 B; 310 B; 328 LT; 329; 403. **Rob Proctor:** 27 M; 122; 123; 124 T, RB; 125; 126; 127 T; 128; 129 B; 132; 133 B; 134 RT, RB; 135. **Jeffrey Reed:** 263 LT. **Richard Rethemeyer:** 265 L2, L3. **Marc Romanelli, The Image Bank:** 102 B; 103 M. **Susan Roth:** 192 M; 244 LT. **Royal Design Studio:** 282 T; 283 R1, C1, C2, R4. **Rex Rystedt:** 70. **Jim Sadlon:** 264 R1; 272 T; 279 L3; 287 L3, C1. **Bill Sanders:** 145 B. **Phil Schofield:** 316 B; **Paul Serra:** 109. **Chad Slattery:** back, LT; 31 LB; 82; 83; 90 T; 91; 92; 93; 96; 97; 162 T; 163 T; 168 L; 178 LB; 198 B; 252 T, B; 253;

263 RT; 267 R3; 291 LT. **Lauren Springer:** 130 L; 131. **W.D.A. Stephens:** 338. **Strybing Arboretum:** 332 T. **Sean Sullivan:** 141 B; 251 L3, C3; 267 C1; 278 B; 287 L1; 289 LT. **Michael Thompson:** back LB; 30 R; 33 T; 53 T; 54; 55; 58 R; 59 M; 60; 61; 64 LT, R; 65; 66; 67; 71; 72; 73; 146 T; 149 R4; 153 M; 167 RB; 196; 222 M; 227 R1, R3; 234 T; 243 LC, R; 254 T; 262 RT; 302 T. **Trex, Inc.:** 384 RB. **Larry Ulrich:** 74; 76; 77; 101; 102; 118; 119. **Ulf Wallin, The Image Bank:** 48. **Darrow Watt:** 244 RT, RB; 302 MB; 328 CT, RT; 378 B; 379 B. **Jonelle Weaver:** 166; 257 L2; 264 LC1; 279 LC3, R2. **Peter O. Whiteley:** 311 B; 98; 99; 138; 139 T, M; 141 T; 148 RB; 161 M; 168 C; 172 B; 178 RB; 180 T; 181 LT; 205 B; 214 M; 249 L2; 268 RT; 273 T; 280 RT, B; 289 LM; 290 LT; 310 RT; 377 RB. **Nick Williams:** 332 B. **Doug Wilson:** 209 LC; 384 LB, CB. **Suzanne Woodard:** 276 LC1, R1. **Tom Woodward:** 3; 5; 6; 9; 56 T; 85 T; 88 T; 90 B; 110 T; 116 LB; 124 LB; 134 LT; 189; 221 T; 253 TR; 299; 308 R; 309; 315 LT, RT; 319 R; 320 L2, R1; 321 B; 336 R. **Tom Wyatt:** 21; 322 RB; 328 B; 330; 378 L; 379 T, M; 388. **Linda Younker:** 56 B; 57. **Yowler & Shepps:** 283 C3.

DESIGN CREDITS

Our thanks to the designers, artists, and companies who allowed us to show their work in this book:

Steve Adams: 150; 151 RB. **Ruth Bancroft Garden:** 240 B. **Jim Barbour:** 290 RT. **Michael Bates:** 215. **Julia Berman:** 208 L. **Marcus Bollinger:** 15 M. **Judie Bomberger:** 266 T. **Ned and Jean Brockenbrough:** 196. **Barbara Butler, Artist/Builder:** 164; 165 T, B. **Ceramic Tile Design:** 380. **Jack Chandler:** 170; 177. **Steve Chase:** 381 RB. **Chelsea Ex-Centrics of San Francisco:** 263 LB. **Thomas Church:** 35 RT. **Bob Clark:** 25 LB; 216 M; 224 T; 389 B. **Gary Clinkscales:** 287 C2. **Gary Cushenberry:** 142 T; 145 T. **Dalton Pavilions, Inc.:** 155 T. **Topher Delaney:** 255 LT; 267 R2; 268 RB; 274; 284; 285. **Delaney & Cochran:** 25 RB. **Owen Dell:** 174. **Design Toscano:** 266 T. **Marcia Donahue:** 266 T; 269 RB. **Phil Edinger:** 193; 199. **Enchanting Plantings:** 34 T. **Filoli Gardens:** 31 RB; 184; 185. **Fine Homebuilding:** 145 M. **William Fortington:** 266 B. **Galleria Tile:** 380. **Sonny Garcia:** 275 B. **Garden Jazz:** 236 RB; 250 L2; 276 LC1, LC2. **Gazebo Nostalgia:** 154. **Lisa Gimmy:** 31 LB. **Glass Block Design:** 381. **Michael Glassman & Associates:** 168 C; 310 RT; 311 B. **Scott Goldstein:** 291 LT. **George Gonzales:** 181 LT. **Lisa and Tim Goodman:** 34 B. **Becky Gray (Gateways):** 248 B; 269 RM. **Jackie Gray:** 223. **Isabelle Green:** 182 B. **Gordon Bennett:** 266 T; 268 LB. **Sarah Hammond:** 31 RT. **Virginia Hayes (Santa Barbara Water Gardens):** 291 RT. **Archie Held:** 291 LB. **Linda Hoffman (Guided Imagery):** 280 RT. **Eric and Mary Holdeman:** 46; 47. **Joseph Huettl (Oak Creek Designs):** 157 T; 168 R. **Jersey Devil:** 145 B. **Christopher Klos:** 143. **Rick LaFrentz:** 235; 239; 240. **LMNO Arts:** 249 L2. **Ron Lutsko:** 27 B. **Lyngso Garden Materials, Inc.:** 254 B; 376 T. **Virginia Macedo (Sol à Sol):** 273 T. **Jean Manocchio (Belli Fiori):** 258 T, B; 259 B; 260 LT, LB, RB. **Sally Marr and Peter Dudar:** 256 T; 257 L3. **Steve Martino:** 24; 181 RT. **Sandy and Mike Martuscello:** 141 T. **Keeyla Meadows:** 148 L; 163 B; 222 B; 261 T; 270 L, R; 271. **Joleen and Tony Morales (Redwood Landscape):** 139 M. **Pat Morgan:** 254 T. **Andy Neumann and Scott Rowland:** 162 T. **New Leaf Gallery:** 266 T; 268 RT. **Sharon Osmond:** 35 LT; 269 RT. **Gary Patterson:** 231. **Jonathan Plant:** 14 T. **Suzanne Porter:** 15 T. **Joni Prittie:** 219. **Roger Raiche:** 306 T, LB; 385 B. **Jeff Reed:** 136; 137; 263 LT; 384 T. **Royal Design Studio:** 282; 283 R1, C1, C2, R4. **Ann Sacks Tile & Stone:** 380. **Page Sanders:** 139 T. **Barry Sattals:** 32 B. **Seattle Arboretum:** 186. **Paul Serra:** 153 B. **Mike Shoup:** 147; 258 T. **Solutions:** 272 B. **Freeland Tanner:** 140 B; 152; 159 T; 203 M. **Christine Ten Eyck:** 27 T; 171 RT; 203 C; 230 B. **Jay Thayer:** 33 B. **Randy Theume:** 35 LB. **Tilecraft Ltd.:** 230. **Tom Torrens:** 249 C2. **Trex Company, LLC:** 284 RB. **Greg Trutza:** 149 R1. **Turner/Alvet Studios:** 280 BR. **David Turner (Rock Farm):** 266 T. **Bruce Wakefield:** 205 T. **Dale Waldo:** 156. **Walk Maker, Inc.:** 383 RT, RM, RB. **Terry Welch:** 146 T; 153 M; 262 RT. **Jerry Williams:** 163 T; 168 L. **Nick Williams & Associates:** 161 M; 172 B; 180 T; 310 LB. **Matt Wilson (Second Nature):** 255 RT; 269 LB. **Wind & Weather:** 266 T; 267 R1. **Richard William Wogisch:** 178 RB; 385 T. **Richard Wogisch and Abel Cruz:** 269 LM. **Agatha Youngblood:** 178 LB; 252 T, B; 253; 263 RT; 267 R3. **Yowler & Shepps Stencils:** 283 C3.